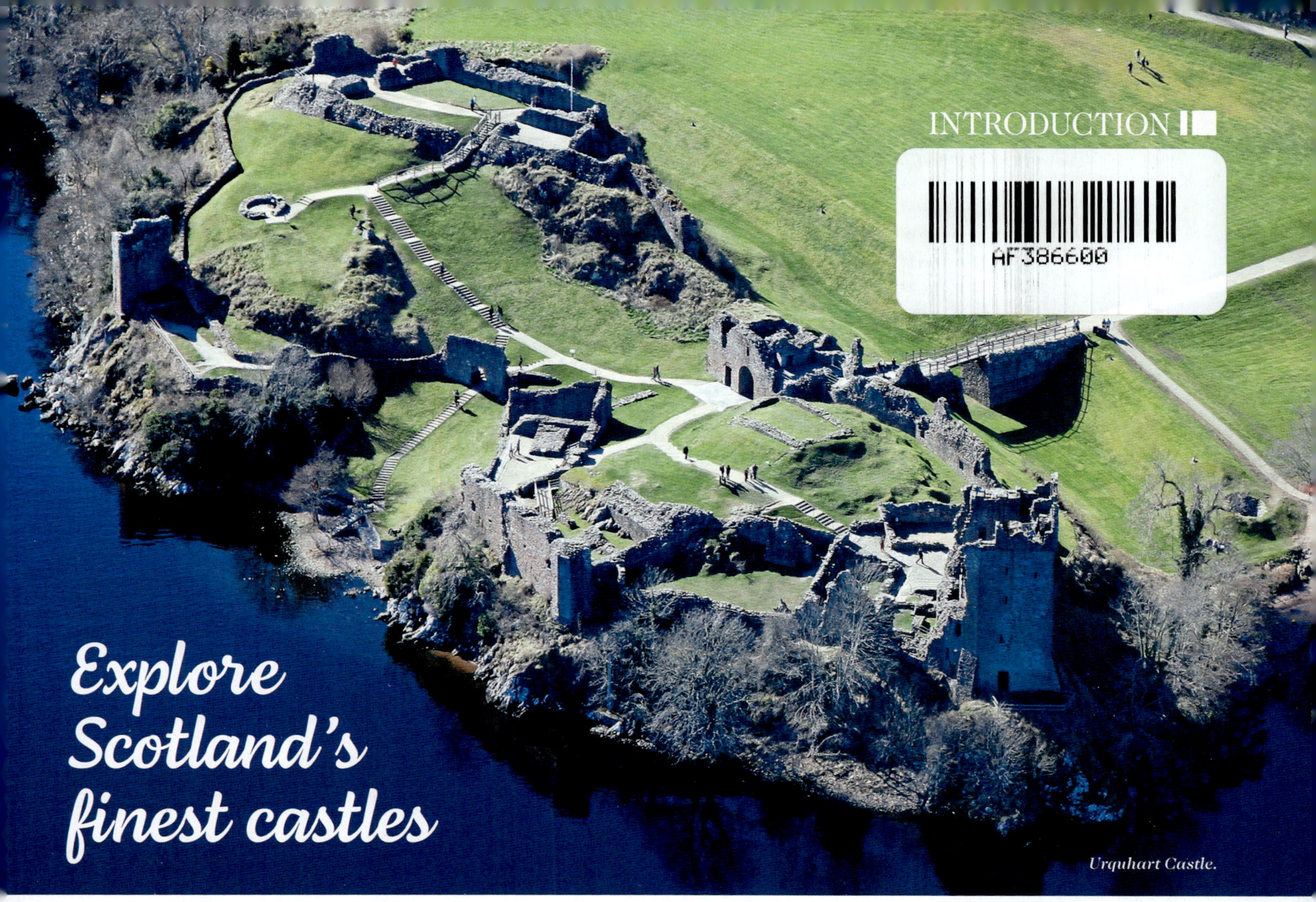

Explore Scotland's finest castles

Urquhart Castle.

I have been fortunate to view Scotland from the air and capture many images. Aside from the varied land and seascape, my attention was quickly drawn to castles on cliffs towering above the sea. Not only were they dramatic from above, each castle gradually revealed a tale which played a part in the rich tapestry of the story of Scotland. The twists and turns of fate, power struggles and battles form the expected part of the picture but there are surprises woven into the following pages. For example, the last court jester in Scotland who saved his clan as fire raged around him and the traitor rewarded with gold which was the death of him.

Scotland has more than 2,000 castles, which I consider as defendable homes or forts occupied in the past or present time by persons of high status. Around 500 of these have been listed as structures considered of special architectural and historical importance by Historic Environment Scotland. From my image library I have selected photographs of over 50 and added a short history with location and access information. The background to some of the many clans who occupied these castles has also been included. The invaluable help of Robbie Roberts as my pilot on castle flights is appreciated. Also a big thanks to Suzanne Sutherland for checking my typing.

SUMMARY

This publication gives details of more than 50 castles in Scotland, with location, access, websites and historical background. New aerial photography shows them clearly to help readers decide which to visit and encourage exploring beyond the well known.

Notes on clans connected with the castles detail their turbulent pastimes and current chiefs with websites highlighted.

A timeline of the history of Scotland is included to unravel the sequence of events.

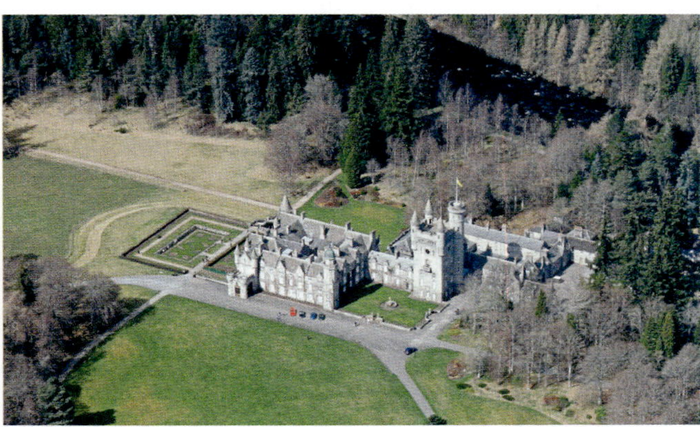

Balmoral Castle.

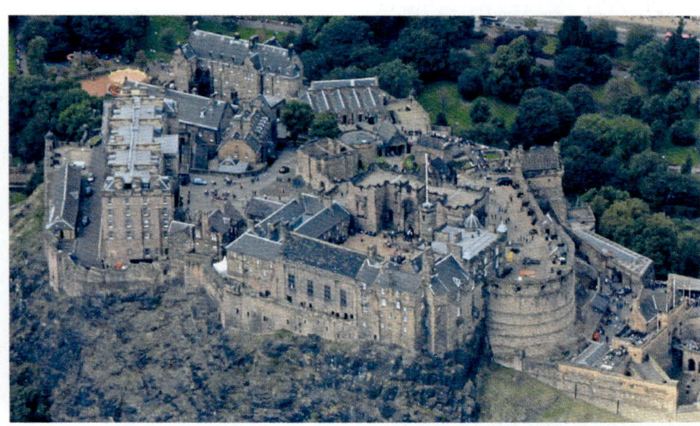

Edinburgh Castle.

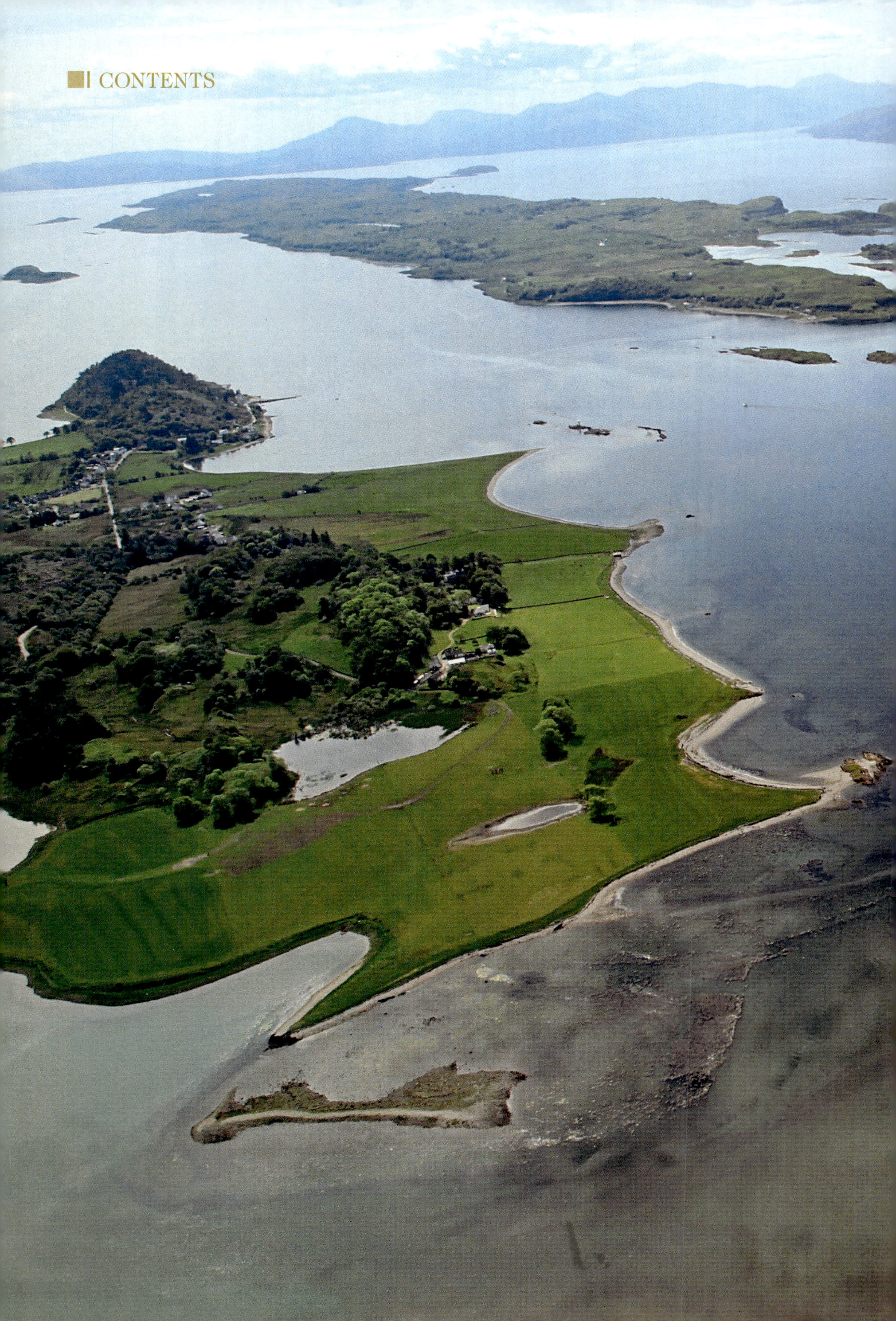

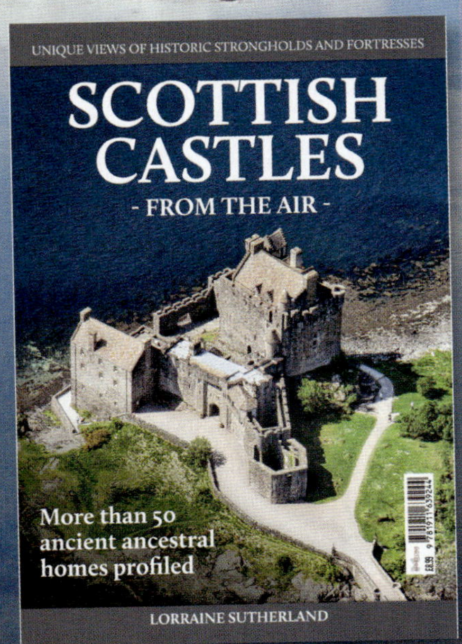

COVER PICTURE: Eilean Donan Castle.

▉▎ SCOTTISH CASTLES FROM THE AIR

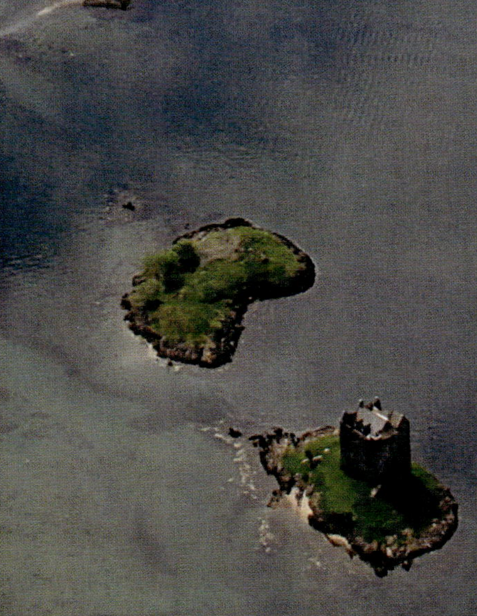

Author:
Lorraine Sutherland

Design and Reprographies:
Craig Lamb,
Kriele Ltd
design_lamb@btinternet.com

Publisher:
Steve O'Hara

ISBN:
978-1-91163-24-4

Published by:
Mortons Media Group Ltd,
Media Centre,
Morton Way,
Horncastle,
Lincolnshire,
LN9 6JR.
Tel: 01507 529529

Printed by:
William Gibbons and Sons,
Wolverhampton
Copyright:
©2021 Mortons Media Group
Ltd.
All rights reserved.

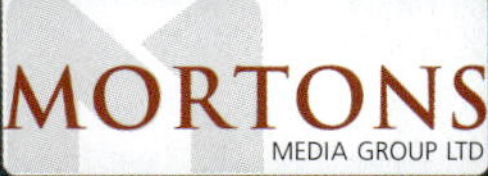

Scottish Timeline

250-1000 The Picts Celts and Scots create forts using natural features. For example hillforts. Some are later reused as the sites for castles such as Auchindoun.

1100-1150 Motte and Bailey castles appear built on earthworks and with timber stakes as defensive boundaries. The fort on top was also made of timber, for example Duffus castle in its first stage.

1150-1160 Unrest simmers, breaking into skirmishing between the established Gaelic clans and incoming Vikings and Normans.

1200-1290 Stone begins to replace timber as the best castle material. Curtain walls are added as an extra defence. They could be substantial as at Dunstaffnage or smaller such as the wall surrounding the island castle at Eilean Donan .

1263-1266 The Norse Vikings finally leave the Hebrides after defeats at Rothesay and Largs. The Treaty of Perth is signed in 1266, granting the Viking lands back to Scotland except the Orkneys which return around 250 years later.

1250-1330 Expansion of the basic stone castle to include gatehouses, inner keeps and corner towers. Examples included in this book are Kildrummy and Balvenie.

1295-6 Edward I of England invades, firstly destroying Berwick on Tweed and killing many civilians there. He takes and holds many castles in Scotland forcing more than 2,000 Scots nobles and high status clergymen to sign a document of submission, the Ragman Roll.

1297-1298 Andrew the Earl of Moray and William Wallace retake castles from the English and have a big victory at the Battle of Stirling bridge in 1297. Andrew dies of wounds shortly afterwards, depriving Wallace of his master military tactician. In 1298, Wallace loses a battle at Falkirk; his foot soldiers are overwhelmed by hails of arrows and betrayed by one of the Comyns who refuses to commit his force of horseback knights to battle. Wallace then resigns his position as Guardian of Scotland which is taken over by Robert the Bruce jointly with John Comyn, his enemy, but Bruce resigns in 1300. Bruce desires the Kingship instead.

1300-1305 Edward I the 'Hammer of the Scots' takes Scottish castles by force. He also has William Wallace tortured then executed in 1305 in a gruesome manner, with his quartered body sent to corners of the kingdom and publicly displayed. Unrest increases in Scotland.

1306-1308 Robert the Bruce murders Sir John Comyn in a Dumfries Kirk. At last Bruce is crowned King Robert at Scone in March 1306. Edward I reacts quickly; Bruce's wife, daughter and sisters are captured and imprisoned in England. Countess Isabella is locked in an iron cage at Berwick castle, one of Robert's sisters is caged at Roxburgh; both are treated poorly as outlaw's kin. Bruce's brothers are hanged, drawn and beheaded. Bruce goes into hiding, becoming 'The Outlaw King' and organising raids on his enemies including the slighting of many Comyns castles across the north east, and then attacks Urquhart and Inverlochy in the Great Glen. He has become an expert in taking castles which are considered well defended. It is likely he uses subterfuge, bribery and what we now call psychological warfare because he certainly did not have heavy siege machines. He leads the campaign south as far as Galloway, making castles useless for any future English armies. In May 1307 he wins his first battle against the English at Loudon Hill. His success encourages more nobles to support him. Edward I dies on the English side of the Solway firth in July 1307 after losing his long battle with an illness instead of leading his latest large army into battle to crush the Scots.

1309-1314 The Bruce campaigns successfully to win back many major castles with a huge triumph at the Battle of Bannockburn in 1314 leading to the surrender of nearby Stirling castle afterwards. A bonus is the capture of many English knights who are used to gain the release of his surviving family in exchanges.

1327-1329 In 1327 Edward II is deposed by his queen Isabella and dies in prison. Robert invades Northern England and threatens to annex these lands. The English King Edward III then makes peace with Scotland. Robert the Bruce can finally retire and dies at his mansion by Dumbarton in 1329.

1390 The Wolf of Badenoch raids across Moray from his Lochindorb base, destroying Elgin Cathedral but failing to take Spynie Palace nearby.

1400-1500 Regional noble landowners build stone castles to protect their families and possessions and to display their wealthy status such as at Cawdor. The advent of cannon prompts design changes, including artillery platforms and thicker walls as found at Broughty and Blackness castles. Stirling castle is also made a stronger fortress.

1603 The Scottish and English crowns unite.

1637 Charles I forces the use of the Book of Common Prayer on Scotland, riots break out and result in the Covenanters becoming a military force in opposition to the Royalists who support Charles.

1639-1652 The wars of the three kingdoms ravage Scotland with the plague endemic as well, creating the bloodiest times for Scotland. The Marquis of Montrose leads a Royalist army.

1652-1655 Oliver Cromwell sends General Monck and seasoned troops to Scotland to put down the uprisings. In 1652, Dunottar is the last Royalist castle stronghold to be taken by his forces, one of many taken and slighted.

1689 First Jacobite rising led by Viscount 'Bonnie' Dundee. Supporting the restoration of the Stewart dynasty. The Battle of Killiecrankie is won by his forces but he dies as a result and support ebbs away.

1698-1700 Huge financial losses across Scotland's banks and investors occur when the attempt to set up a trading company in Darien (Panama) fails. For example Forbes of Tolquhon castle lost his fortune and home.

1707 Acts of Union of parliaments. England pays off some of Scotland's debts incurred by the Darien fiasco as part of the deal.

1715 The second Jacobite rising is led by the Earl of Mar. He captures Aberdeen, Dundee and Inverness, after the Battle of Sheriffmuir... a draw, he loses at Preston and the rising fades away. In the aftermath 250 miles of new roads and bridges are built linking forts, military barracks and towns. This expensive project is designed to enable government troops to subdue unrest quickly. The Jacobites later find them useful as well.

1719 Spanish troops land in West Scotland at Eilean Donan castle and are later brought to battle in Glen Shiel where the Spanish and Jacobite troops are defeated by government forces.

1745 Bonnie Prince Charlie lands then gathers support for another Jacobite rising. Many of the Highland clans provide men and even the North East produces supporters. Edinburgh castle is taken, the battle of Prestonpans is won, and the advance reaches Derby causing panic in London. However the French fail to send soldiers. The Prince wants to continue but his war council votes to retreat, based partly on false reports of enemy numbers from a spy. A wintery retreat is planned despite many desiring to fight. So they marched back to the relative safety of North Scotland only just ahead of their pursuers. At Falkirk they win another victory against government forces fighting a confusing series of skirmishes during a winter storm into the night.

1746 The Jacobite army faces a disaster on Culloden Moor near Inverness. The Jacobite musket lines are broken by cavalry charges. British army forces gain the victory. Surviving Jacobites are rounded up and imprisoned or executed. Estates are forfeited, the clan system is dismantled and weaponry, plaid and pipes are outlawed. Bad news for the highlanders, but the lowland Scots celebrate. Ironically the Highlands later became a great source of soldiers for the Crown and other armies across Europe. Scotland has a population at this time which matches England in numbers.

1750-1850 Castles are restyled and newly built in Scots Baronial and Gothic designs. Examples include Blair and Dunrobin. At Balmoral Queen Victoria and Prince Albert ensure that their rebuild meets all their fantasy ideals.

1911-1915 The last new castle in Scotland is created at Carbisdale.

No short summary of the history of Scotland could convey the story of shifting support between clans, nobles and royal families. For example during the Jacobite uprisings, Clan chiefs would sometimes place sons on opposite sides to ensure they had a winning result. In one lifetime a noble could be found supporting Royalists and later the Covenanters.

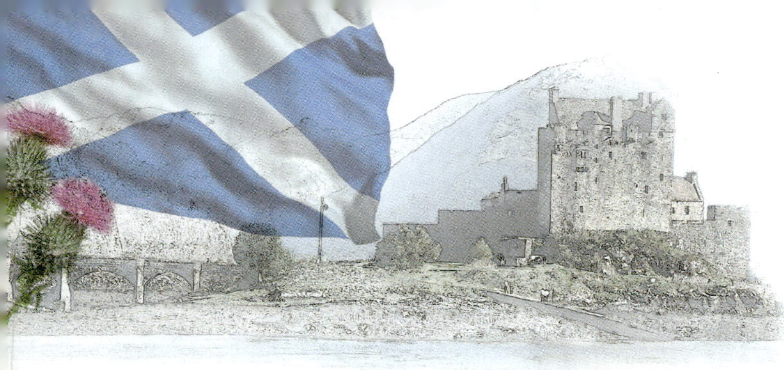

Ackergill Tower

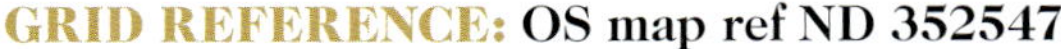

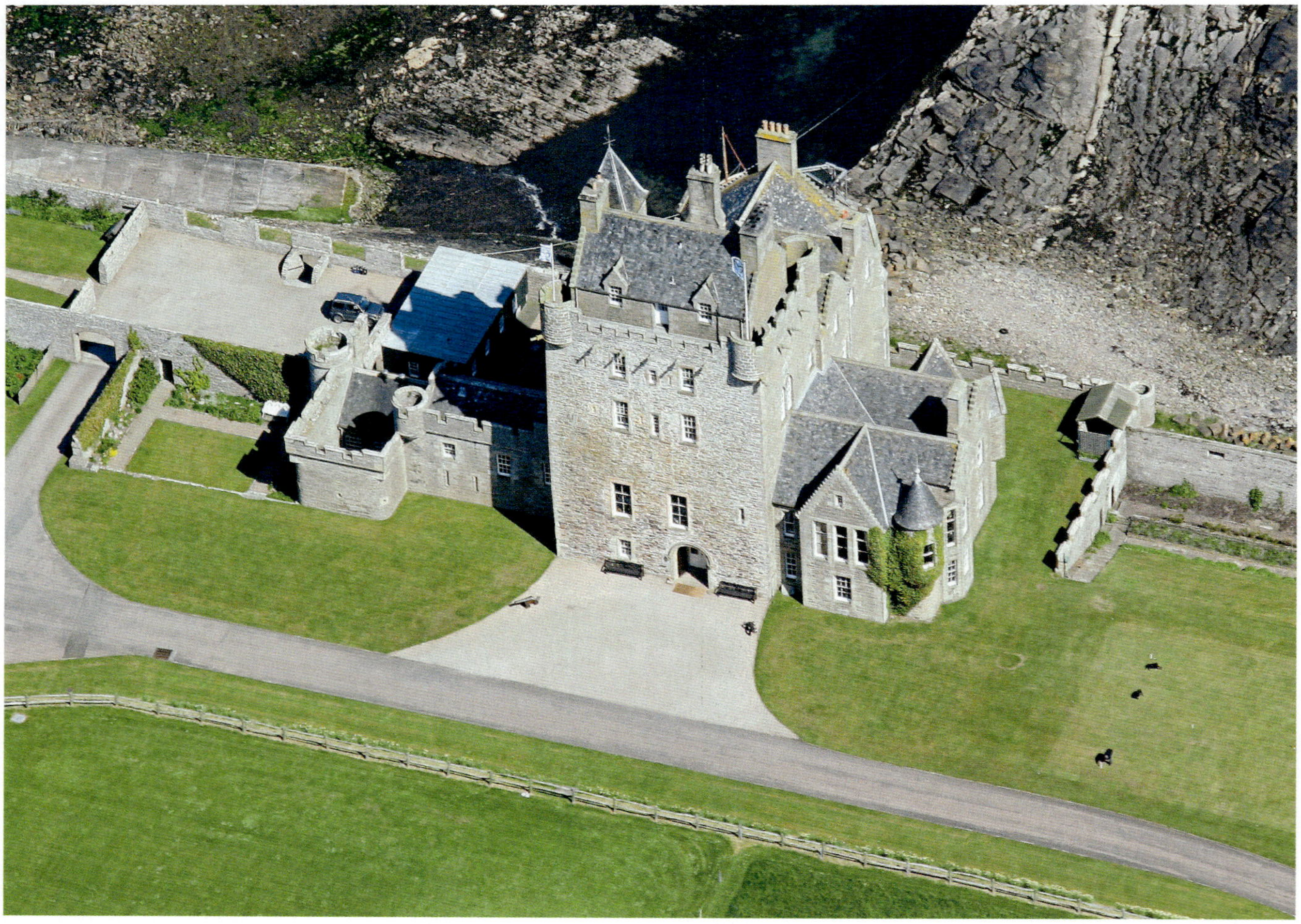

Here can be seen the spot where Helen Gunn fell to her death onto the slate-strewn seaside from the high tower. She was one of the many victims of the long dispute between the Keith and Gunn clans. A daring night raid is detailed below as part of the feuding. After the clans came custodians, renovations, hotel guests and currently a private owner.

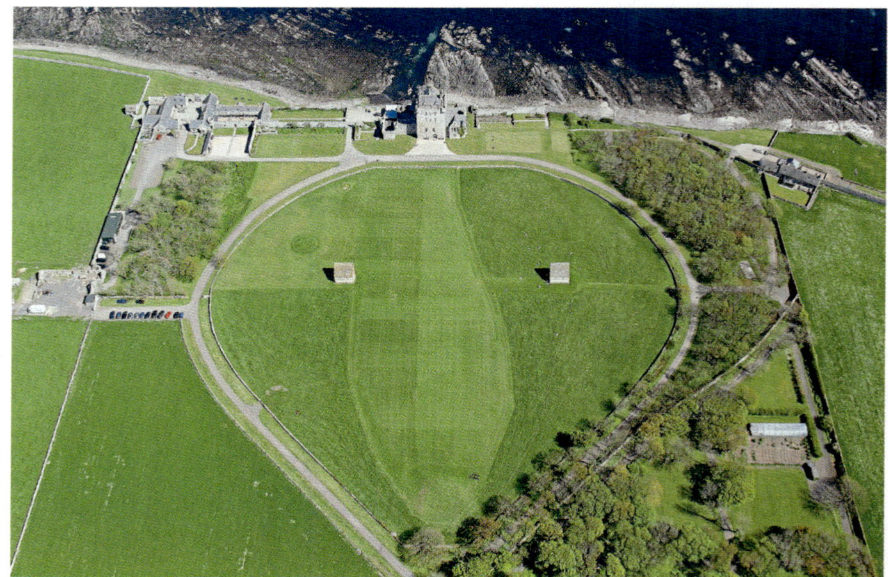

Visitor Details

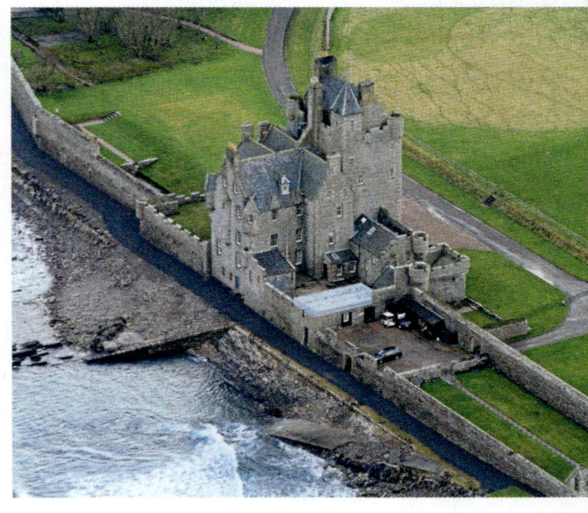

Ackergill Tower is a private residence and not open to the public.

The tower became a private property in 2019 after a time as a hotel. Some websites are still showing accommodation as available which is incorrect.

Location: Ackergill Tower is two miles north of Wick on the edge of Sinclair's Bay, Caithness and Sutherland. It can be seen from the small village of Ackergillshore. To get there, turn north from the A99 onto the short road passing the street side houses of Ackergill until you arrive at a small harbour. In good weather and at low tide you can walk along the coast to view the tower from outside.

The Cheyne Clan was an Anglo-Norman family with lands in what is now Aberdeenshire and Caithness. Ackergill Tower has a first written mention in 1538, occupied by John Keith of Inverugie. John was the second son of one of the most powerful men in Scotland, Edward Keith the Marischal. He married Mary, one of the two daughters of Reginald Cheyne, in 1354. This enabled his inheritance of the lands around Ackergill. The tower house was gradually surrounded by a courtyard wall (Barmkin) enclosing domestic buildings such as a brew house (safe water), stables (reliable transport) and dovecots (convenient food supply). A haunting story linked to the tower describes happenings in the early 15th century. Helen Gunn was known locally as the Beauty of Braemore and was about to be married to her cousin, Alexander Gunn, a childhood sweetheart. This detail did not stop Dugald Keith from kidnapping her, hoping she would yield to him while imprisoned in the tower. He led the raid on the pre-wedding feast, slaughtering Alexander and others present. After these horrors took place it is not surprising that the stifling seclusion inside the small tower drove Helen to despair. She convinced her guards that she needed to gaze across the landscape from the tower top. Suddenly she ran, and then jumped, falling fatally onto the shore below. A marked stone is today said to show where she landed. At her home in Braemore, a Rowan tree grows that is known as 'Fair Ellen's Tree'. Her ghost, 'the Green Lady' has been seen around Ackergill. A terrible tale indeed, this fuelled the hatred of the Gunn Clan for their neighbours the Keiths. After several costly clashes, it was decided around 1478 to hold a meeting of both clans at the Chapel of St Tayre near Girnigoe to make a peace deal with the agreement to only send 12 horses each.

The chieftain of Clan Gunn and 11 of his men were inside the chapel but were attacked by 24 of the Keith's; they had arrived with 12 horses but two men on each! Many perished that day and the dried blood was still on the chapel walls almost 200 years later. At the urging of their clan members, the Chief of Clan Keith, Sir James Ian Keith, Earl of Kintore, and the Commander of Clan Gunn, Ian Alexander Gunn of Banniskirk, signed a 'Bond and Covenant of Friendship' on July 28, 1978, at the site of St Tayres on the 500th anniversary of the battle there.

Meanwhile, a long time ago in 1547, the Sinclairs of Castle Girnigoe, led by George Earl of Caithness, suddenly attacked Ackergill tower, seizing Alexander Keith and his servant, making them both hostages at Girnigoe. After an appeal, the Regent of Scotland, Queen Mary, granted remission and the tower was passed to a caretaker who went by the name Lord Oliphant in 1549. Not one to give up a grudge, the Earl of Caithness,

a Sinclair, took over Ackergill after a siege in 1556, depriving William Keith Earl of Marischal of his home. Again remission was given: the Sinclair Earl was forgiven by the crown and the Keith Clan Earl Marischal was back in his tower. His next problem was in that year when his brother Robert Keith took the tower by force, also intending to keep hold of the surrounding estate land. Robert was declared a rebel by the crown and vacated the tower. One dark night in 1598, the clansmen of John Keith used stealth and scaling ladders to climb walls and the tower. This daring raid was without any deaths but the servants were roughed up by the attackers. Night fighting was very uncommon in those times in Scotland. The Earl seems not to have been home because later he complained to the Privy Council that "his place of Ackergill" was taken and John would not give it back. Council power prevailed and the tower was returned to the Earl.

A property sale in 1612 did enable the Sinclairs, Earls of Caithness, to become legal owners of the tower. Having gained possession, the Sinclairs took little interest in maintaining the buildings so they were later reported as being in poor condition. When besieged in 1623 by Sir Robert Gordon, the castle surrendered quickly. He did not keep hold of the property because records show that in 1676 it was transferred to John Campbell, Earl of Breadalbane to repay debts owed by the Sinclairs. Renovating old castles has always been an expensive challenge.

The next owner, Sir William Dunbar, began the new century of 1700 by adding a large lean-to extension onto the tower, forming better accommodation. The tower in 1726 was still in need of repair though. His family continued making changes to it into the mid 19th century, including larger windows, raised bartizans, an extended roof and cap house.

As the estate shrunk from 100,000 acres to less than 4,000, by 1986 the income raised could not keep pace with repairs so again the tower was sold. The new owners John and Arlette Banister organised and financed a 2 year plan of careful restoration saving it from ruin. They sold up in 2009 however the tower was in for a treat because a luxury hotel company spent £2 million on upgrading the property gaining a five star rating.

The five-floor tower has 32 bedrooms and sits in 30 acres of ground with a lease for shooting and fishing in the surrounding 3,000 acres. Valued at £3.9 million, the latest sale in 2018 has returned the tower to its origin as a private home.

The latest owner, Episcopalian minister Dr Betsee Parker from Virginia, has a long interest in Scotland's history. She has also carried out philanthropic work in Senegal, Kenya, and Sierra Leone. A fine custodian for this tower which has such a varied history.

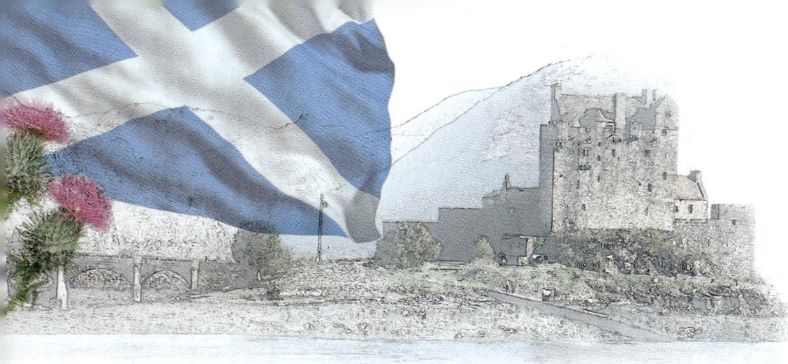

Auchindoun Castle

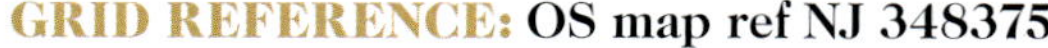

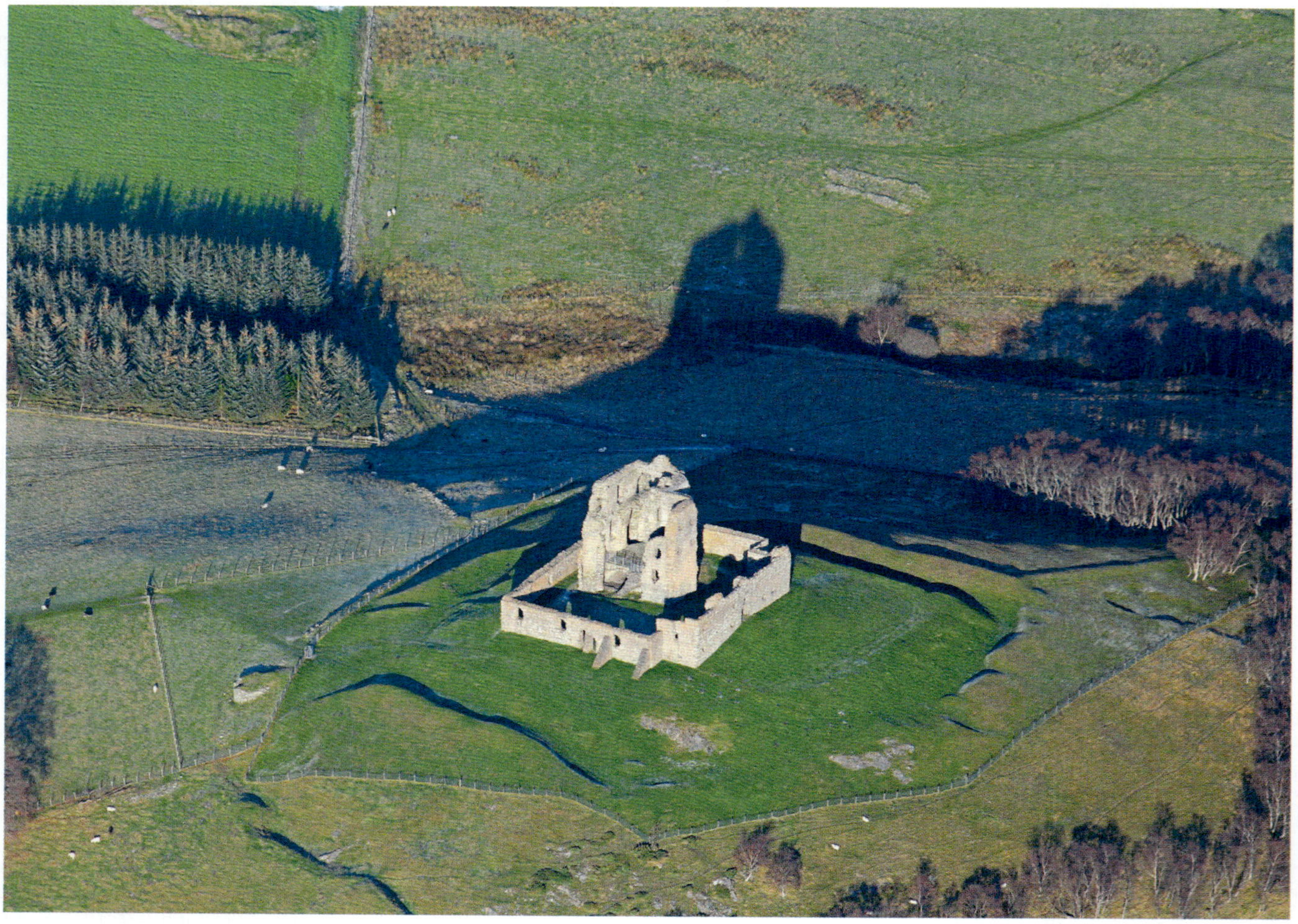

Once a mighty stone stronghold sat astride an already ancient fortification. An old folk ballad, The burning of Auchindoun, tells of the fiery attack by Clan Mackintosh. "As A cam in by Fiddichside, on a May mornin A spied Willie MacIntosh an oor before the dawnin Tarn again, tarn again, tarn again, A'se bid ye If ye barn Auchindoun, Huntly he will heid ye…" The aftermath was also a tragic story retold here.

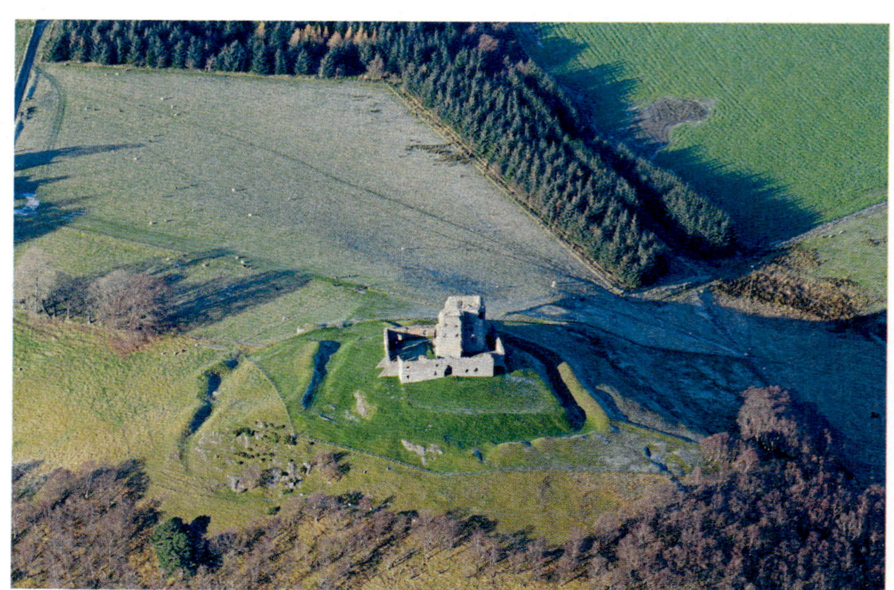

Visitor Details

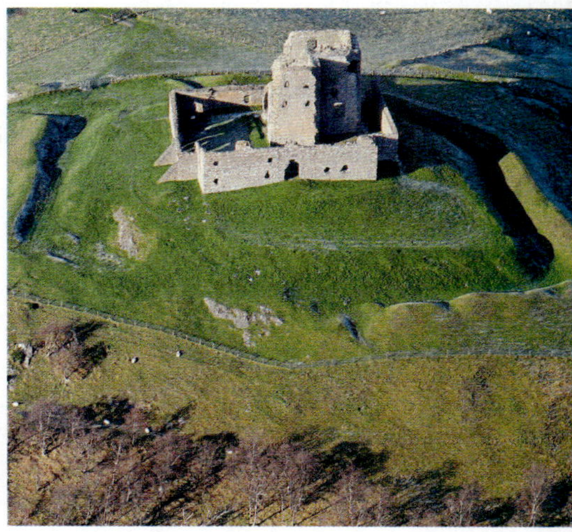

- No website.
- No telephone.
- The castle site is open all year.
- No facilities.
- Nearby Dufftown has several restaurants.
- A well-rendered illustration on a display panel by the castle depicts the tower house as it used to be: three storeys high also with a vaulted cellar and a wine store. The surrounding buildings included stables, a kitchen and the essential brew house.

Location: Auchindoun Castle is two miles south of Dufftown on the A941, Morayshire. The path to the castle can be accessed from the Dufftown to Rhynie main road by following a track to a small car park. Access is on foot only from here. The steep path is slippery when wet. Treat this as a short half-mile hill walk and take all your own food and drinks. On the route, you will pass a large stone structure housing a spring and also a ruined farmhouse.

The aerial views show the surrounding ditches that are the remains of an Iron or Bronze Age fort although, as with many of those structures, dating evidence has not been found. Agriculture and quarrying has disturbed much of the ground, adding to the difficulty of interpretation. The castle's hilltop location provides excellent views of the main route between Strathspey and Aberdeenshire (when it is not raining or snowing). Horsemen from the castle could quickly check passing wagons and groups on foot, keeping control of trade.

The earliest mentions of this castle site note that John the Earl of Mar was the occupier. He met his end when visiting Craigmillar Castle, where his brother King James III murdered him. After that the King gifted Auchindoun to his friend, master mason Robert Cochrane, with a suggestion that he use his skills to fix it up. He was later killed by being hung from Lauder Bridge in 1482 after falling out with nobles who were led by the Earl of Angus. By 1489, Clan Ogilvy were the residents but only for a generation because the Gordons took over some time between 1535 and 1567. Sir Adam Gordon of Auchindoun Castle favoured the imprisoned Mary Queen of Scots to take on the crown of Scotland. However, others wanted the infant James VI as the next king. This conflict erupted locally when the Forbes Clan, just 20 miles south at Corgarff Castle, championed the cause of young James. A clash was inevitable. However, the manner of attacking the Forbes family at Corgarff sent shockwaves of horror across medieval Scotland in the winter of 1571. With no Forbes clansmen at Corgarff, the siege should have been short. However, the wife of John Forbes injured a Gordon clansman with a pistol shot to his knee. In a fury, Adam Gordon ringed the small Corgarff Castle with brushwood and set the fire in such a way that none of the 28 women and children trapped inside survived.

Clan Mackintosh surrounded Auchindoun in 1591 and the ensuing siege badly damaged the buildings. The setting of fires below castles often destroyed the timber supports inside towers, causing floors to collapse. The clan sought revenge for the murder of an ally, the Bonny Earl of Moray, at Donibristle by Sir Patrick Gordon. He only had the castle for two more years because the king declared him to be a rebel and the estate was forfeited to Sir George Home. He was a diplomat and used funds from his influential position in the Royal household to fund a lavish manor house in Berwick. It is doubtful he ever visited the windswept remains at Auchindoun.

The Ogilvys came back into ownership in 1594. When Charles II returned to the throne he awarded the castle to the Marquis of Huntly in 1660. The upkeep and repair costs had risen so much that the decline back to ruin was inevitable. By 1725, stones were being robbed for other buildings in the region, such as Balvenie Castle. Enough remained to provide shelter for Jacobite troopers in the first rising in 1689.

Until fairly recently, the masonry was unsafe but after consolidation by Historic Scotland the castle reopened to visitors. During these works, a large deeply cut mysterious chamber in the bedrock was rediscovered inside the castle which remains on view to the public.

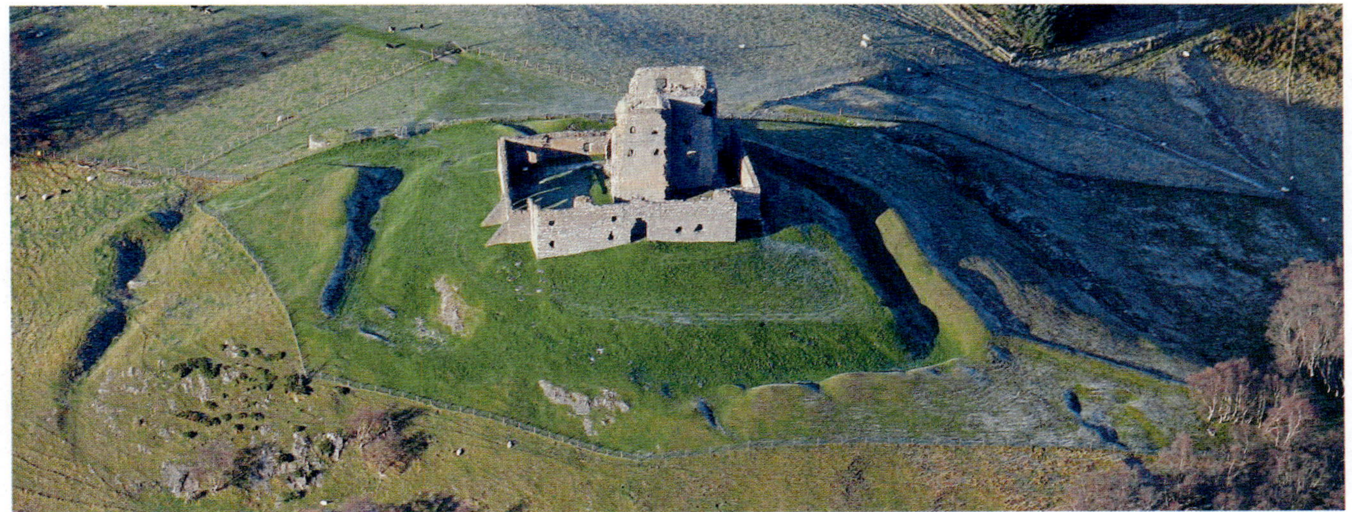

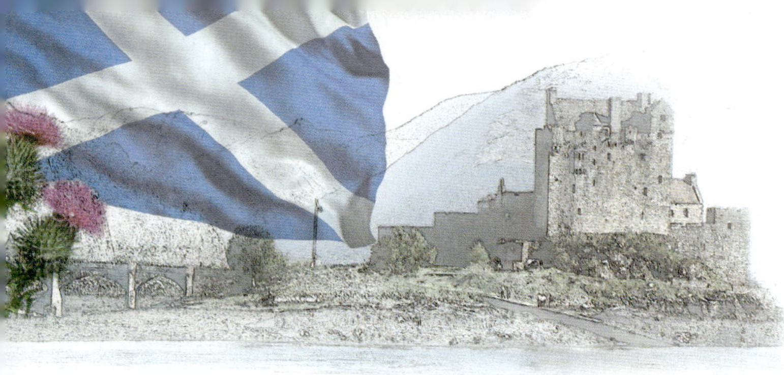

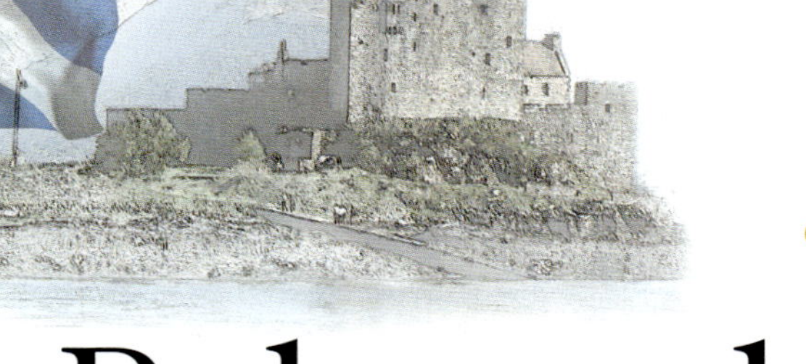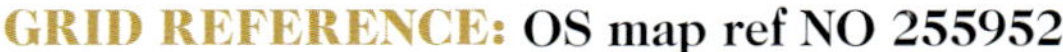

Balmoral Castle

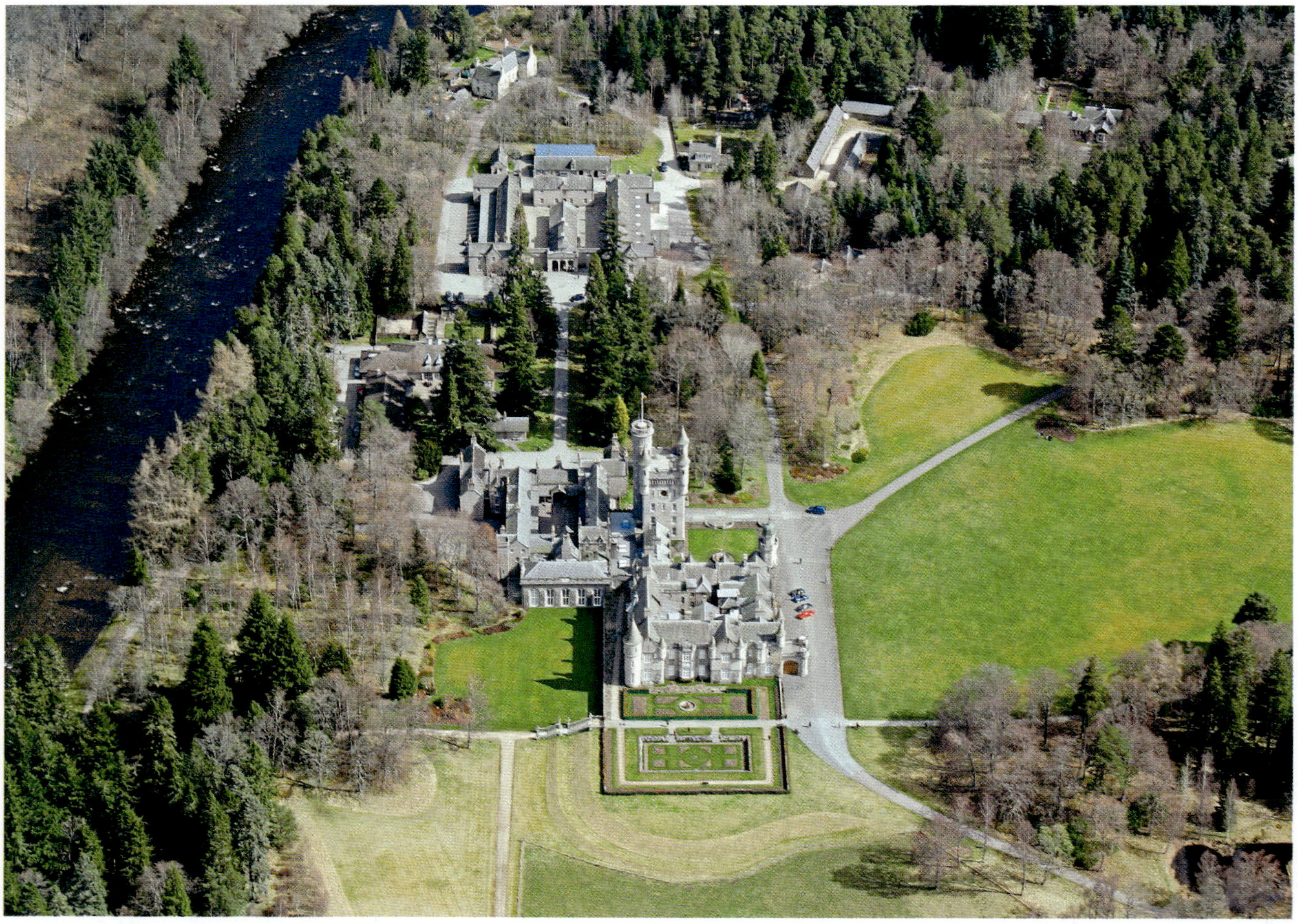

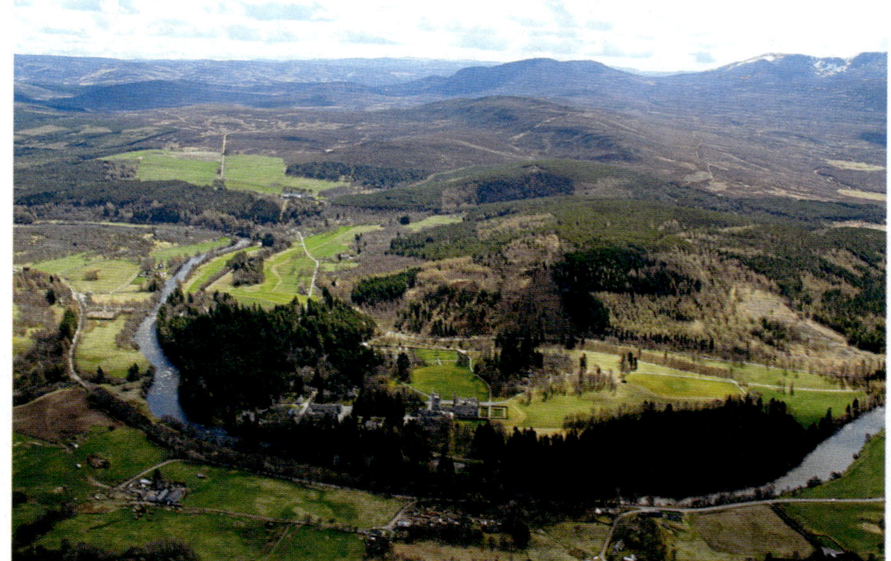

This well known Royal house in Scotland was not always a well kept residence but was lovingly transformed into a grand Highland retreat for Queen Victoria and her consort. The effect was to transform the region into what is now called Royal Deeside. Today this magnificent castle remains a Royal residence that is owned, maintained and sometimes occupied by Queen Elizabeth II.

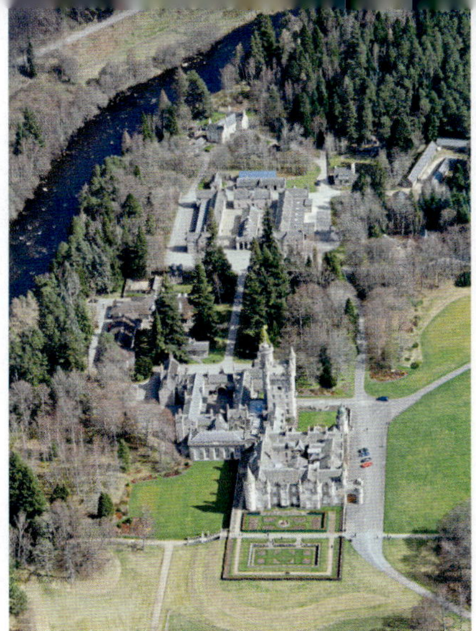

www.balmoralcastle.com

01339 742534

The extensive gardens are open to the public daily between April and the end of July. Guided tours are available in addition to those months, see website for current timings.

There is access for the disabled to the gardens, WC, shops, exhibition and cafe.

A cafe and shops are on site.

The ballroom is the only room in the castle that may be viewed by visitors. Inside are displayed artworks including paintings and some royal carriages.

Location: Balmoral Castle is in Kincardine and Deeside between Braemar and Ballater off the A93, seven miles west of Ballater. There is coach and car parking on site.

King Robert II of Scotland had a hunting lodge in this area. A house at Balmoral was built by Sir William Drummond in 1390. The estate was recorded in 1451 as Bouchmorale then occupied by Alexander Gordon, second son of the first Earl of Huntly. A tower house was built on the estate by the Gordons. This had bartizans at three of the corners and the usual walled courtyard with outbuildings.

By the time of the Jacobite uprisings, the Farquharson Clan of Inverey were in control of the house and estate. They supported the losing side so after 1745 the property was forfeited to another branch of the clan who supported the Hanoverians. Debts forced a change of lease to Sir Robert Gordon and he had local architect John Smith add extensions after 1830.

Queen Victoria and Prince Albert started making tours of Scotland in 1842. At this time, London had become the most populated city on the planet. With this rapid growth came pollution and disease. Scotland became an attractive alternative for part of the year and they searched for a suitable holiday home. Locations visited included Blair Castle and Ardverikie house by Loch Laggan. Here they encountered huge swarms of midges and heavy rain, therefore the Queen's doctor, Sir James Clark, suggested Deeside as being a healthier climate. Prince Albert took the lease of Balmoral in 1848.

The original Balmoral Castle was considered too small so new buildings were commissioned in the Scottish baronial style to John Smith and his son William. Prince Albert also changed some design details to suit his taste. This was planned as a family-owned home with room for important guests. Albert enjoyed the surrounding mountain views and the walks reminded him of his homeland in Germany. When the new country manor house was ready, the old castle was demolished in 1856.

Keeping with tradition, the Royal Family still makes annual visits to Balmoral, often attending the nearby Braemar Gathering in September. The estate is owned and funded by Her Majesty The Queen personally rather than as Sovereign. The total annual expenditure of the estate is over £3 million, which is all spent locally. The objectives of this include providing employment and housing and generating economic activity in the local area, as well as the conservation and regeneration of the surrounding natural environment.

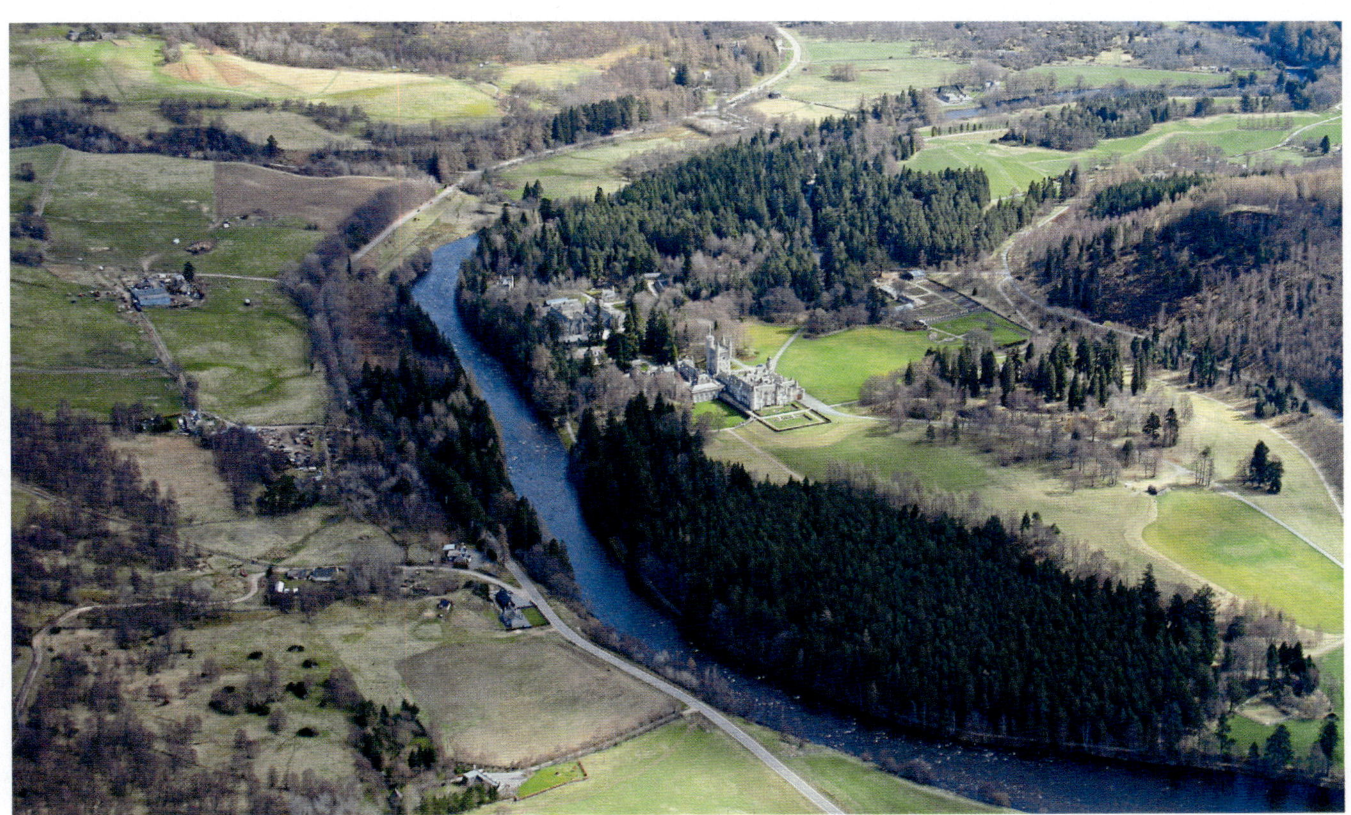

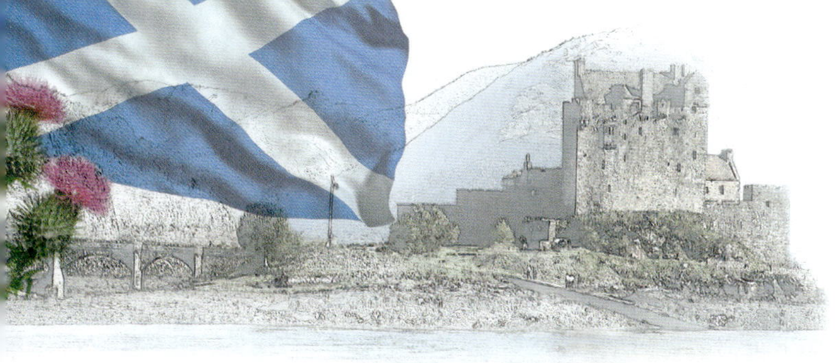

Blackness Castle

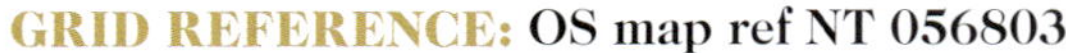

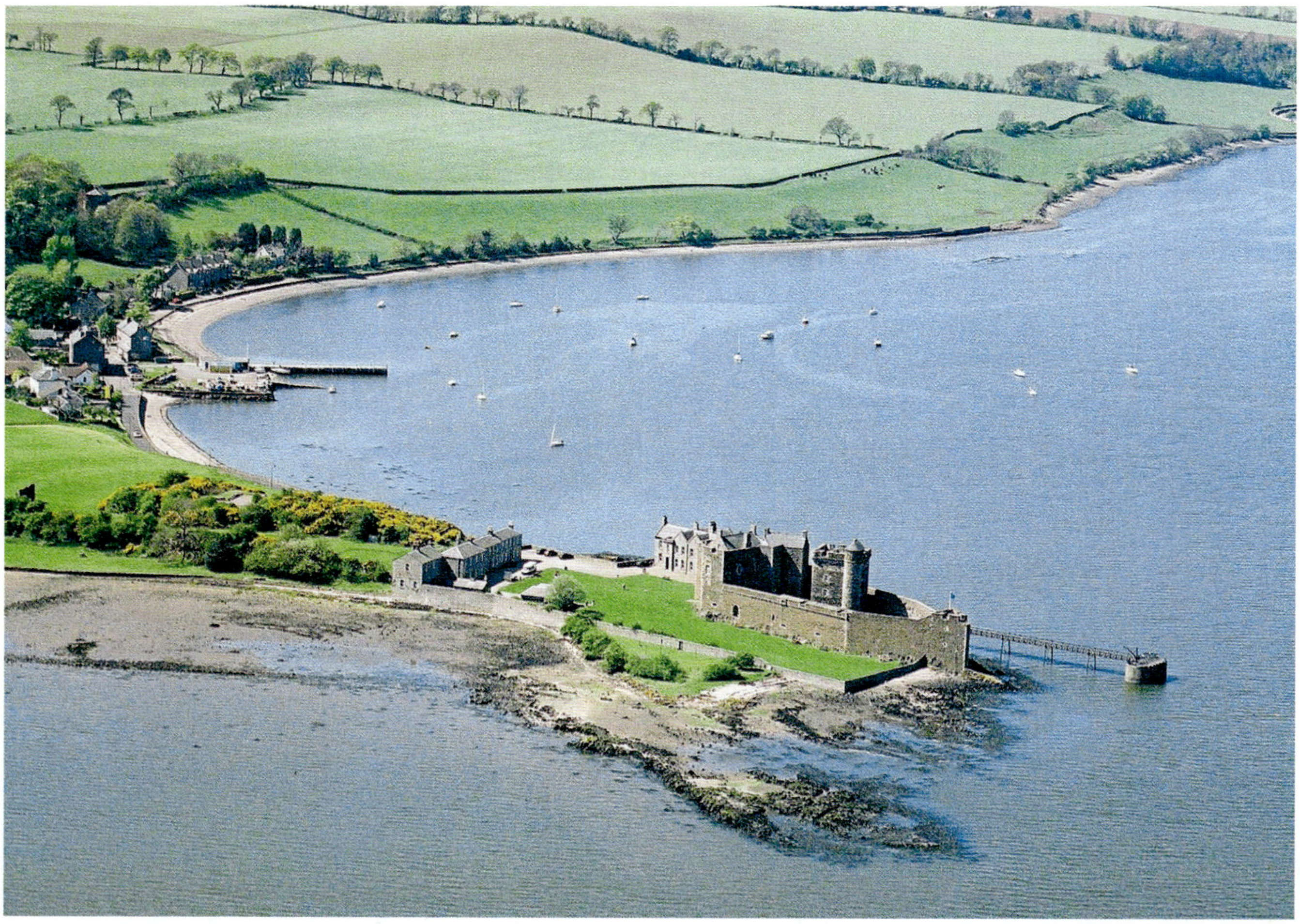

Blackness is the stone ship that never sailed, jutting out into the River Forth anchored by the spirits of its many former prisoners. Its current shape arose from the need to make it resistant to cannon fire from attacking fleets. Inside it remains remarkably grim, meaning that it has been easily able to stand in as a jail in the Outlander film series, as well as making appearances in other films.

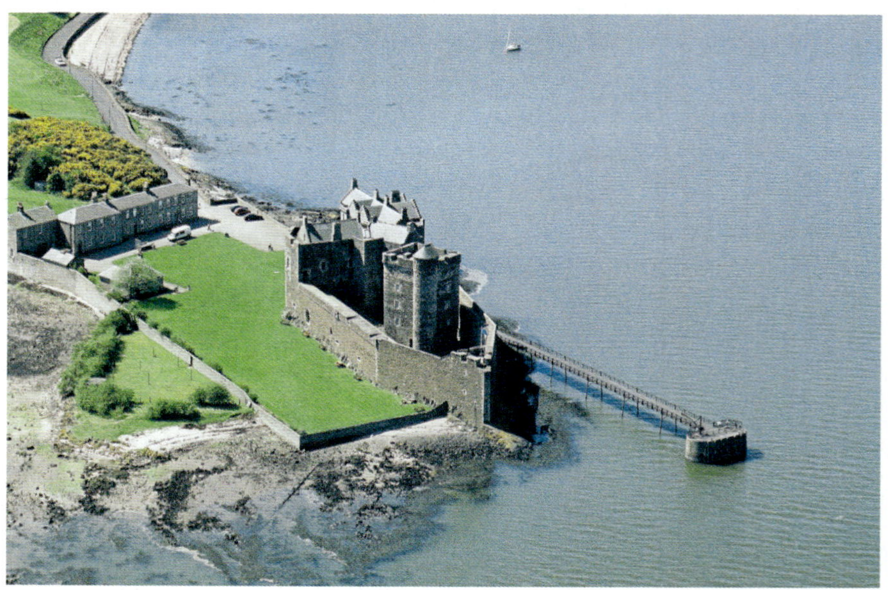

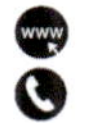
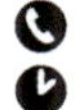

Visitor Details

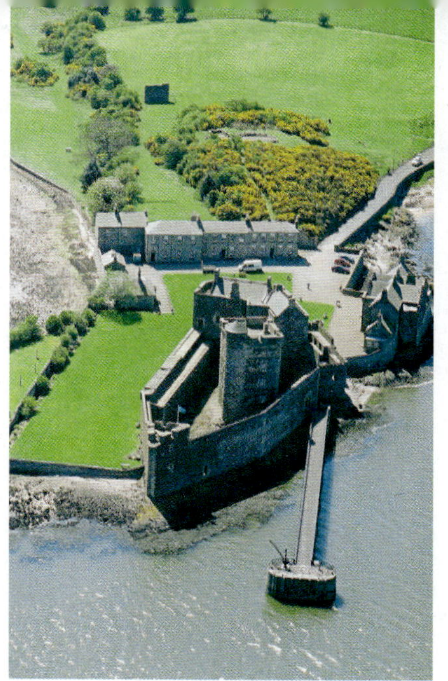

www.historicenvironment.scot/visit-a-place/places/blackness-castle

01546 834507

All visits to Blackness Castle must be booked in advance via the website. To guarantee entry, choose a time slot. Parking on site is limited to 90 minutes due to capacity restrictions. Unfortunately, visitors are unable to remain parked on site after their allocated timeslot expires.

Disabled access limited due to rock outcrops.

Gift shop and refreshments on site.

Blackness has a village pub, The Lobster Pot, with fine ales and fresh food. Book ahead for a table or to arrange a takeaway: 01506 830086. Also it has a small shop adjoining: https://www.facebook.com/TheLobsterPotBlackness/

Location: Blackness Castle is four miles east of Bo'Ness, or five miles west of the Forth Bridges, on the south side of the Firth of Forth. It is close to Junction 2 on the M9. Follow the A904 and then the B903 to Blackness village and Castle.

Blackness Castle is beside the Firth of Forth, close by the small port that served the royal burgh of Linlithgow in medieval times. Constructed inside a high thick curtain masonry wall, the first substantial building on site was a four-storey keep. This rose from a solid rocky outcrop and remains unchanged today. For a relatively short time it was a residence for the Viponts then came the powerful Crichtons; Sir George Crichton was the brother of the chancellor of Scotland.

By 1449 it was also in use as a prison, especially for nobles who had fallen foul of the King. The most famous was Cardinal David Beaton, Archbishop of St Andrews, in 1543. However, fallen nobles did get the benefit of their own fireplace and latrine. The son of George Crichton, James, tried to inherit the castle in 1453 but his father opposed him. After James took the castle by force, he took his father prisoner until the King forced a surrender.

Being a seaside castle made it vulnerable and in 1481 an English fleet burned it substantially. This weakness was overcome when an artillery fort was completed in 1542. This gave it the shape when seen from the sea side of a huge stone ship, albeit one that never sailed, with three towers and holes for the many cannon. For a while it held off several sieges. The bombardment by massed artillery of Cromwell's troops in 1650 was, however, a devastating attack which left the castle wrecked until the prison was restored in 1660.

During the civil wars of the 1670s and 80s, King Charles II and later King James VII had many covenanters kept in gaol here. Later world conflicts led to prisoners from Spain, France and the USA also suffering here. A tower in the sea also concealed a pit prison which opened to the sea at high water, a terrible torture. The jetty was added in the 19th century to enable the supply of ammunition to ships. As a result, the central courtyard was covered over to form stores for powder and shot as the main munitions depot for Scotland.

By 1919, the historical aspect was considered more important. Military use ceased at last and a programme of restoration was started in 1926 lasting nine years.

The castle's current appearance has been attractive to film makers seeking a historical but bleak back drop. Films include Hamlet and Ivanhoe and standing in for Fort William in the series Outlander.

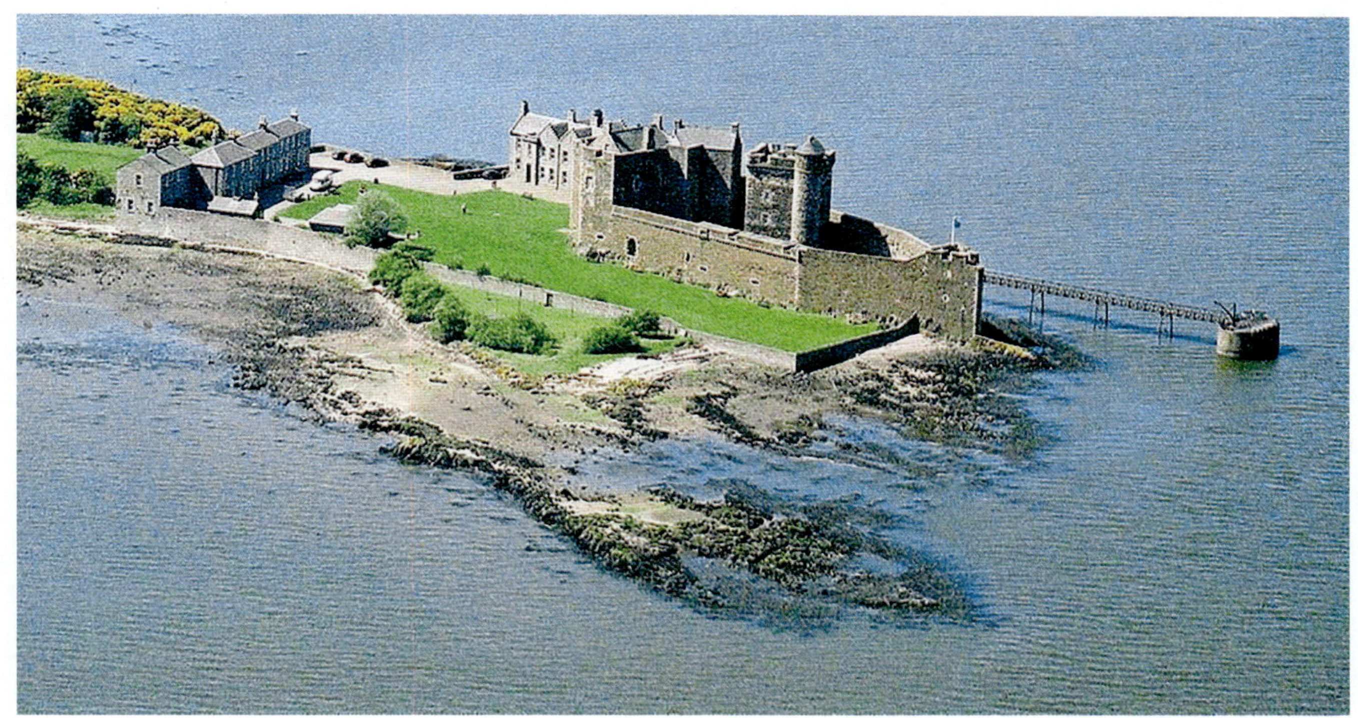

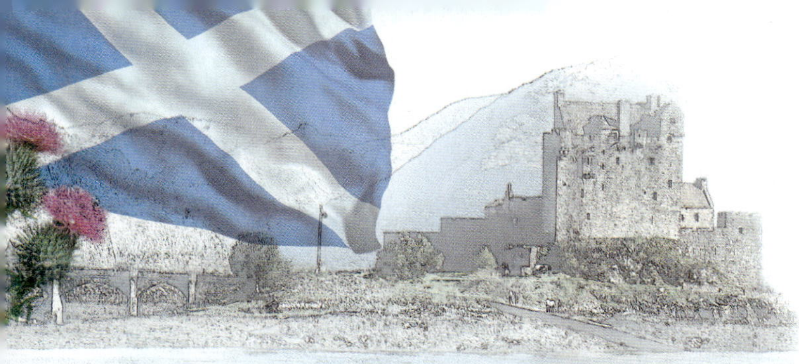

Blair Castle

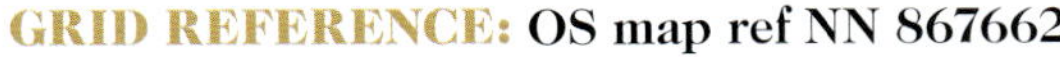

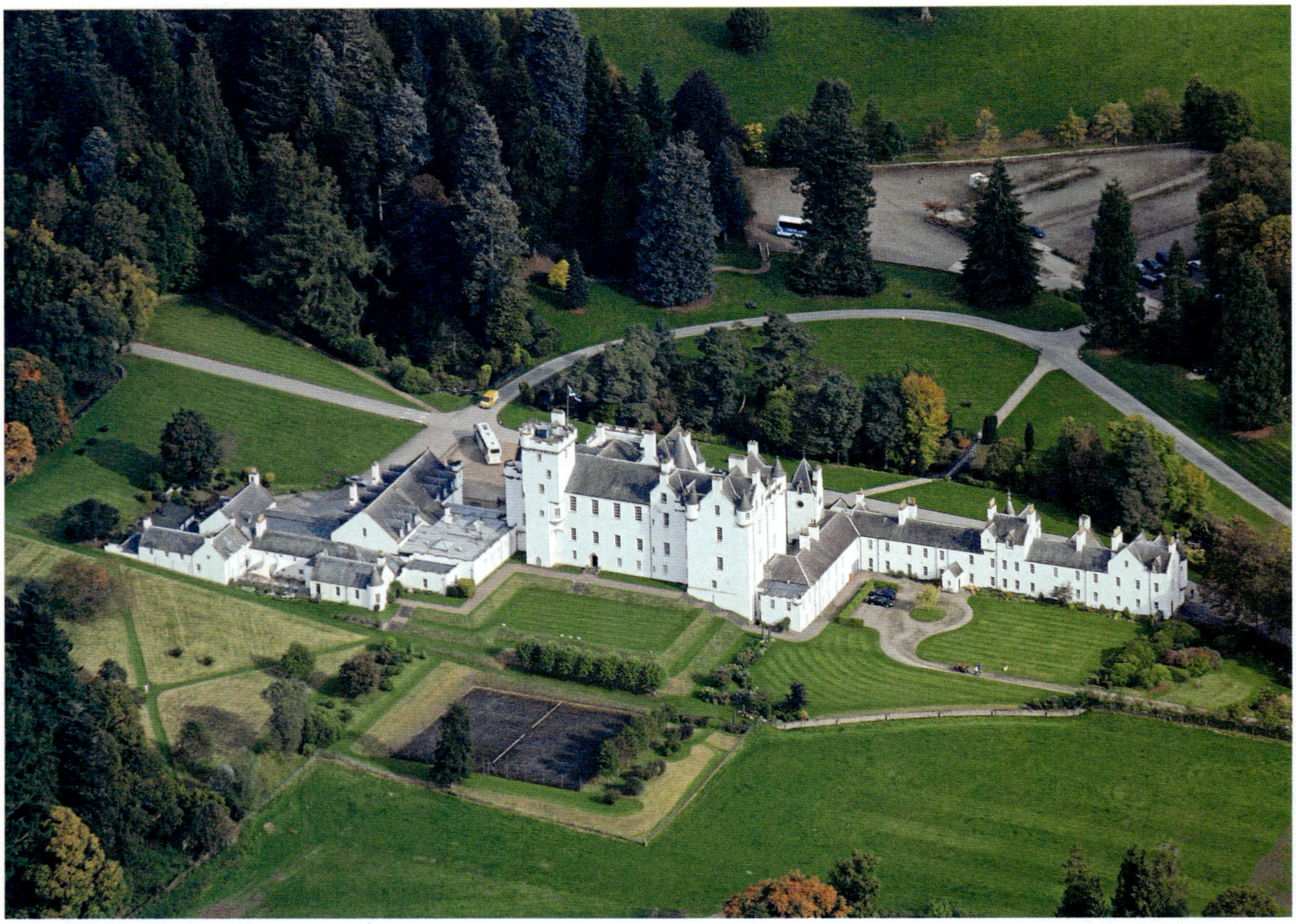

Built without the landowner's permission while he was away on crusade in the Middle East this strategically placed castle became a focus for much fighting and a very long siege, the last siege of a castle anywhere in Britain. Today it is more mansion house than castle and has modern facilities. It also encompasses a recently added exhibition space.

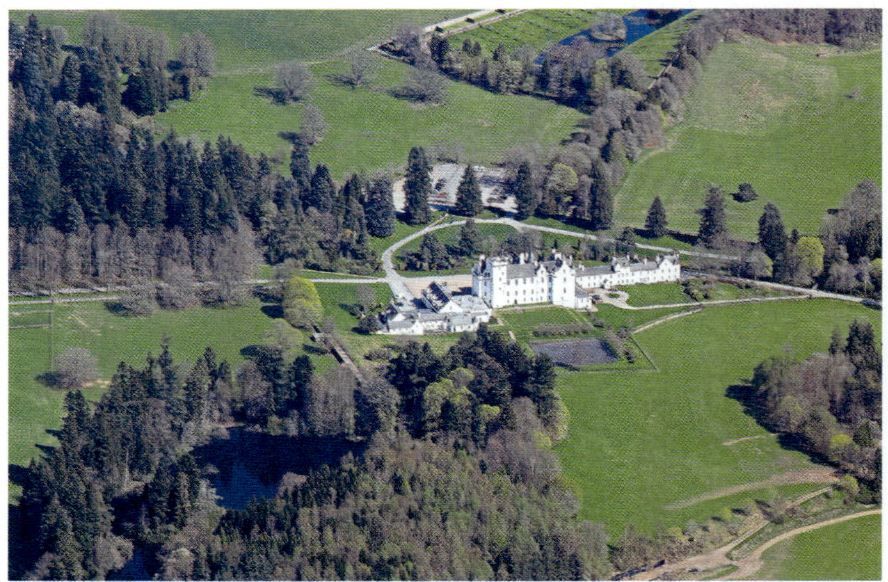

Visitor Details

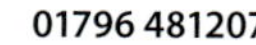
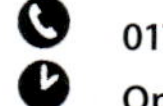

www.blair-castle.co.uk

01796 481207

Open April to the end of October. The gardens and grounds opening hours are 10am to 5.30pm with last admission at 4pm, seven days a week. Always check by phone or website for updates before travelling to the location.

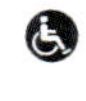

Disabled visitors should get guidance and help from reception staff on arrival at the ticket office who will direct them, if appropriate, to park close to the castle. Accompanying carers will not be charged entry to Blair Castle. In addition, the castle welcomes guide dogs, caring dogs and other recognised assistance dogs.

Restaurant with good reviews and gift shop.

There is much to view inside the 30 rooms: Jacobite relics, walls decorated with weapons of many eras, tapestries, paintings and costumes. The gardens are extensive with a play area. The castle is now the most visited family trust run location in Scotland.

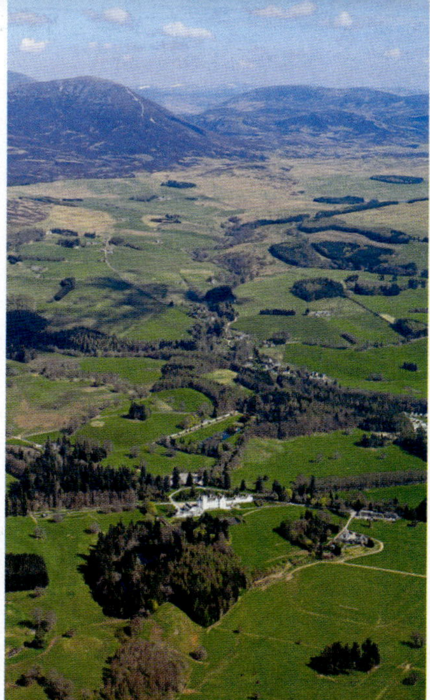

Location: Blair Castle is seven miles north of Pitlochry. Turn off the B8079 a mile north-west of the town of Blair Atholl. Follow signposts for the castle.

The Earl of Atholl, aka David the First of Strathbogie, went off to join the crusade against the Sultan of Babylon and the Saracen armies. Seen as a form of penitence, the partaking of crusading entitled the Earl to forgiveness of his sins. This campaign was an expensive failure for the crusaders however. On his return in 1270, unwell from maladies caught in the Middle East, he was shocked to discover that John Comyn, Lord of Badenoch, had built a fortified tower house on his estate without his permission. The Earl made a complaint to the youthful King Alexander the Third which promptly ensured that his land was returned with the bonus of a new tower house at the location. Additions were then made to the tower house which was regarded as a defensive building rather than the main residence.

King Alexander died in 1286 aged just 44 after he fell from a cliff top in Kinghorn Fife when his horse stumbled on a stormy night nearing his home. His fairly stable reign was replaced with feuding to find his replacement. This prompted the Scottish Wars of Independence which enabled the rise of Robert the Bruce and William Wallace.

In 1308, the second Earl of Atholl opposed King Robert the Bruce and as a result lost his titles and estate when the King declared the Earl a rebel. Niall Mac Calein was then granted the estate, becoming the first of several owners courtesy of the King's wishes until John Murray, Master of Tullibardine became the Earl of Atholl in 1629 by way of marriage to an heiress. The Murray clan are the current family involved in the estate and castle, although it is now a charitable trust established by the 10th Duke, Iain Murray, in the 1960s before his death.

The Murrays supported the Royalist cause and the resulting siege of the castle by Cromwell's troops in 1653 led to its capture by Colonel Daniel. The attack also caused some damage to the structure of the castle. Later, when Charles II regained the throne, he awarded the title Marquess of Atholl to John Murray, the second Earl.

At the time of the first Jacobite rising started by Viscount 'Bonnie' Dundee in April 1689, the Marquess chose the government side but two of his sons fought for the Jacobites, a not uncommon choice in both risings for several clans to ensure a family place on the winner's side. Claiming illness, the Marquess stayed away in London while the castle was held by a Jacobite garrison under the orders of Patrick Stewart, a trusted family retainer. Then one of his sons, Lord John Murray, laid siege to his own clan castle. He was defeated when Jacobite reinforcements arrived led by Bonnie Dundee. Staying at the castle on the night of the 26th of July, they then held a council of war and planned a battle to take place at a narrow pass nearby Killiecrankie. Victory would enable the Jacobites to keep occupying Blair Castle. They did win the battle, but Bonnie Dundee was killed in action.

Unrest simmered in the Highlands and Islands after the first rising failed to gain an overall change and by September 1745, a Jacobite army stayed again at Blair with Prince Charles Edward Stuart in attendance. But they never made the castle a permanent garrison, not appreciating the strategic importance of Blair Castle. A lowland Clan, the Agnews, took it with government support in early 1746. A bitter siege ensued, the last siege ever for a castle in Britain, and starvation was only averted when the Jacobites withdrew to support the ill-fated forces massing at Culloden.

Gradually, the upper sections of the Comyns Tower were removed and the buildings turned into a Georgian mansion in the 18th century. Queen Victoria and her consort Prince Albert stayed at the castle mansion and were so impressed that she gave permission for the raising of the Atholl Highlanders, a Scottish ceremonial infantry regiment. They are the only remaining private army in Europe, and act as the personal bodyguard to the Duke of Atholl, Chieftain of the Clan Murray. During the Great War the castle became a hospital and the family lived in private apartments.

The last major change to the appearance of the castle was in 1872 when the renowned architect David Bryce cast his Gothic Scots Baronial magic design wand over the buildings creating the attractive castle of today. Works were also planned by architect David Burne. Modern services such as telephone, bathrooms and gas were installed.

In our current times a new exhibition space the Banvie Hall was added and the 1908 hydro electric scheme was overhauled and now provides the castle's power.

Special arrangements for visits inside were introduced during the Covid pandemic:

"We have developed a guide-led tour which will be restricted to pre-booked groups of 12 or less visitors with a pre-start introduction outside to welcome and advise on behaviour within the venue. Visitors to our guide-led tours will be asked to wear face masks while inside the venue so please do arrive prepared."

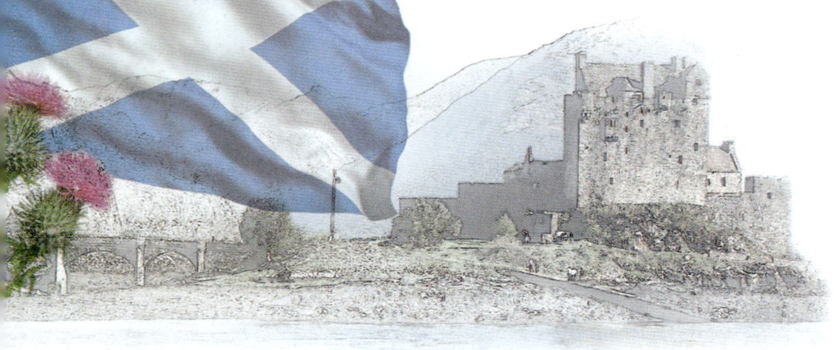

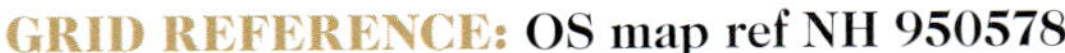

Brodie Castle

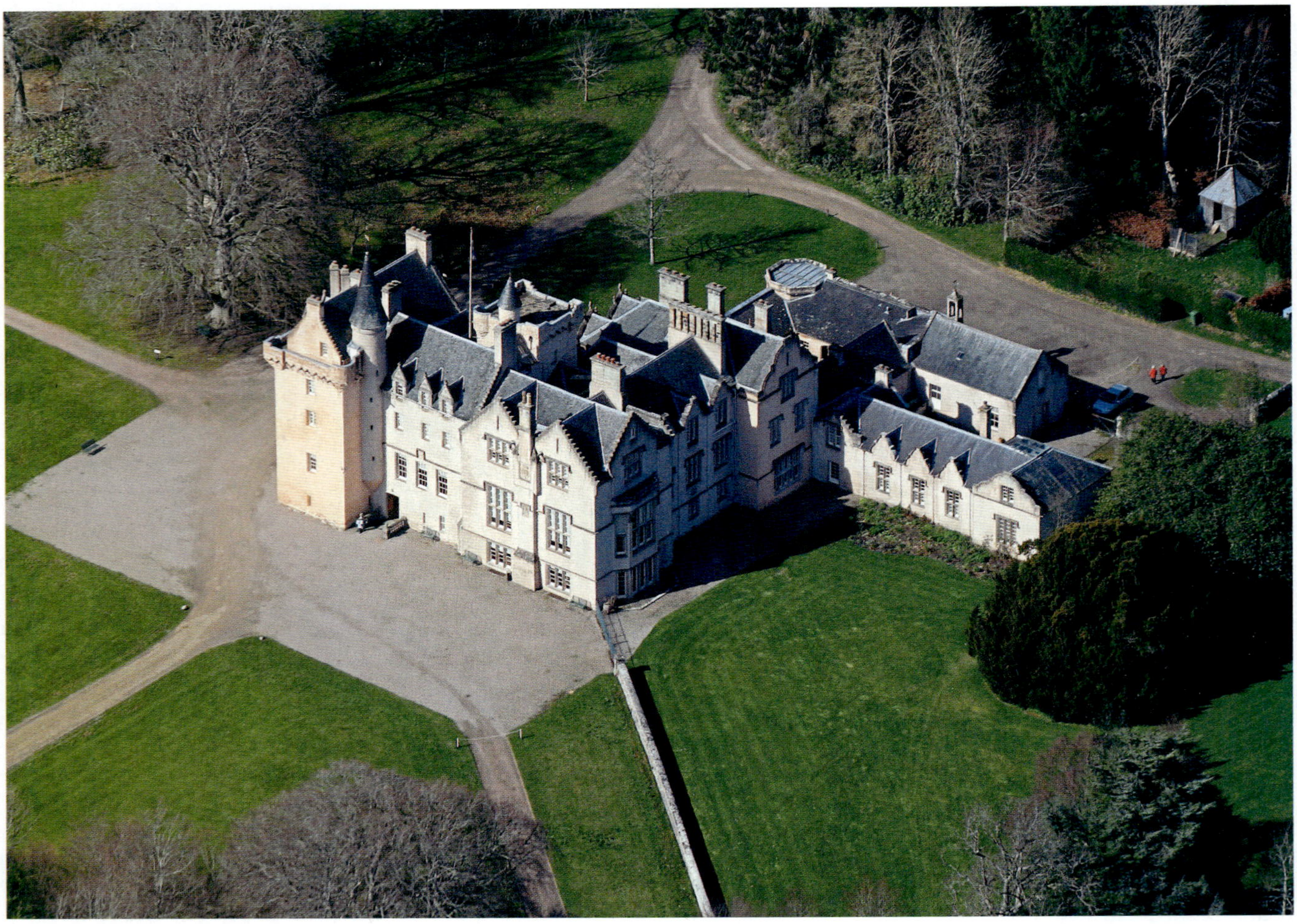

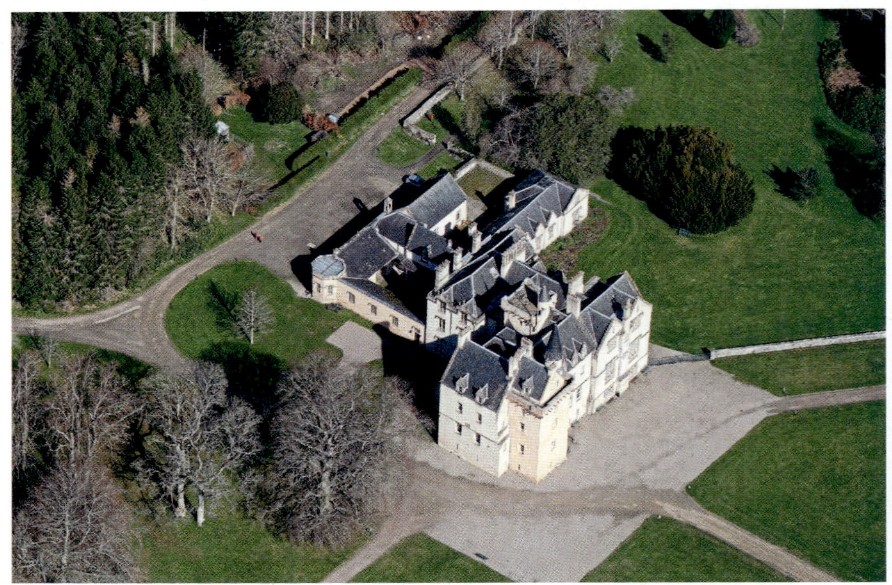

Constructed on the fertile coastal plain by the Moray Firth, Brodie survived as the home of the clan who had supported Robert the Bruce. The last member of the family died in 2003 and the castle retains a lived-in feel even today. Now surrounded by mature trees and a collection of many different daffodil species, it is a challenge to imagine this beautiful building resisting a siege.

Visitor Details

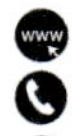 www.nts.org.uk/visit/places/brodie-castle

 01309 641371

The beautiful gardens are open all year and include a huge variety of daffodils. The castle is open from April to September. See the website for opening times.

Disabled access to grounds with accessible parking and toilets.

There is an excellent tea room in the impressive old kitchen on the ground floor.

There is no fee to visit the grounds but you should pay for car parking. An adventure playground is also on site.

The charge is reasonable for viewing inside the castle while National Trust for Scotland members can view for free. Many paintings are displayed in antique furnished rooms from when the castle was a family home. The nursery is charming and the library extensive. The castle still has a lived-in feeling rather than just being a museum collection. Guided tours can be booked.

Location: Brodie Castle is in the county of Moray, four miles west of Forres and just north of the A96 (Aberdeen to Inverness road). Turn off at Brodie then cross the rail line. There is a minor road but go slowly because the left turn into the castle grounds appears suddenly. On the wooded castle approach road, look out for the carved Pictish Rodney's stone under its own small shelter. The stone was found buried in a nearby burial graveyard at Dyke.

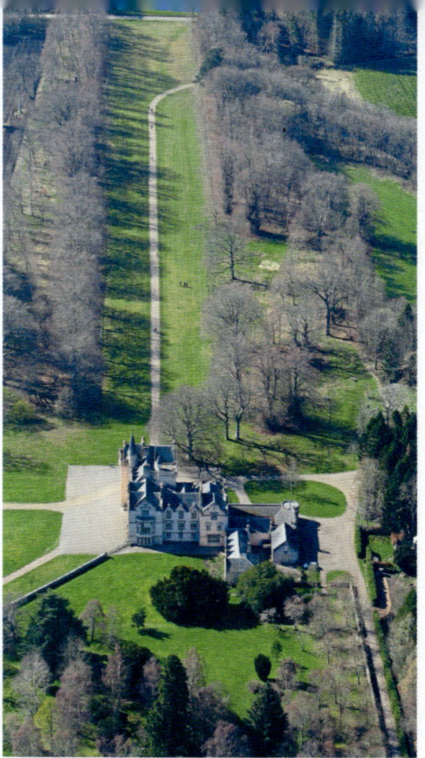

The first building here was a Z-plan tower house built in the late 16th century by Clan Brodie. It was attacked by Lord Lewis Gordon and his clansmen in 1645 because the Brodies supported the Covenanters. Fire caused some damage and again in 1786. The need for modern comforts resulted in a rebuild. The original keep still forms an impressive corner of the mansion and it might have a structure within from the 12th century.

Three ghostly apparitions have been recorded in the castle: a uniformed soldier in the blue sitting room, a small dog near the children's nursery and in the Best Bedchamber it is said the restless spirit of Lady Margaret Duff wanders. She perished in 1786 when she fell asleep in front of the fire, her clothes burning, and the blaze then consumed all in the room.

The National Trust for Scotland took over the castle and grounds in 1980. However, Ninian Brodie of Brodie (The Brodie of Brodie), the castle's last resident member of the family, had an agreement to continue to live in his castle's apartments. He was a friendly host who would sometimes guide visitors himself and supported local arts including the theatre.

When he died in 2003, his demise ended the Clan Brodie link going back to around 1160 when King Malcolm IV granted land to the family.

■ ABOUT THE CLAN Clan Brodie

The heartlands of Clan Brodie are in Moray, its clan castle built in 1567, is five miles west of Forres. This area was also a stronghold of the Picts with a headland fort at Burghead and they erected a unique large carved stone on what is now the North East edge of Forres town. A bloody battle is depicted on Sueno's Stone. The name Brodie may have evolved from a Pictish royal family named Brude. Malcolm Thane of Brodie is said to have descended from this family. Robert the Bruce granted land in Moray to the thane's son based on this lineage rather than services rendered.

The Clan Brodie has had a long friendship with Clan Mackenzie. This is due to support given in 1466 at the Battle of the Park (Blar Na Pairce) near Strathpeffer. Johne of Brode the 7th chief brought his clan to jointly defeat Clan Donald. They forced many of the Clan Donald islanders into the River Conan where they drowned. In 1550 Chief Alexander Brodie and 100 others were denounced as rebels for attacking the Clan Cumming of Altyre.

The "blasted heath" where Macbeth is said to have met the three witches was located on the lands of Brodie at a place still called Macbeth's Hillock. The event was featured in Shakespeare's play Macbeth in 1606. A strong Covenanters belief in Presbyterian values led Alexander Brodie the 15th clan chief in 1640 to destroy carvings and paintings depicting the crucifixion and last judgement displayed at Elgin cathedral. This action brought him favourable recognition as he later progressed to become a member of parliament for Elgin. He also obtained confessions by trickery and condemned to death two witches. Fear and loathing for witches was not confined to the theatre.

In 1645 the clan was part of a covenanters force which lost at the Battle of Auldearn close by. Afterwards Clan Gordon attacked then sacked Brodie castle. This destroyed many of the historical clan documents. Oliver Cromwell had Brodie attend a meeting with him in London to discuss the Scottish Union in 1651. After Cromwell's death in 1658, Brodie became a judge which enhanced his diplomatic reputation. The castle and clan had a narrow escape from destruction in the 1715 uprising. Lord Huntley threatened the 18th chief James with a siege of Brodie castle but had to withdraw due to lack of enough artillery and supplies.

A well paid appointment for Brodie in 1727 was as the King of Arms. Not a military role as the name suggests. Instead, he was in charge of all matters of Heraldry in Scotland and the job title was Lord Lyon.

During the uprisings his clan supported the government but avoided any direct military involvement, passing on information from informants instead .Later he saved several Jacobite members of his office from prosecution and hanging. Although diplomacy was his main tactic he ensured that when violent methods were employed by his opposition, Lord Lovat, in a local by-election Brodie organised an equally forceful response.

The last Clan member to live at the castle, Brodie of Brodie, died in 2003. Now maintained and owned by the National Trust Scotland it is one of the few to contain contents originally collected by the clan. The current chief is the 27th Alexander Tristan Duff Brodie of Brodie.

Motto: Unite

The most active website regarding Clan Brodie is to be found here http://clanbrodie.us/index.shtml It includes a listing of Brodies of note.

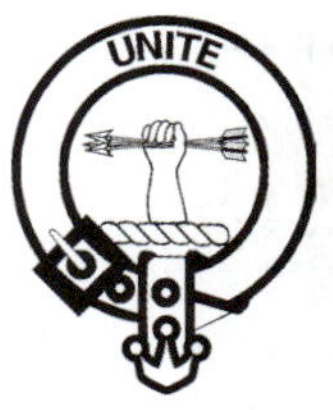

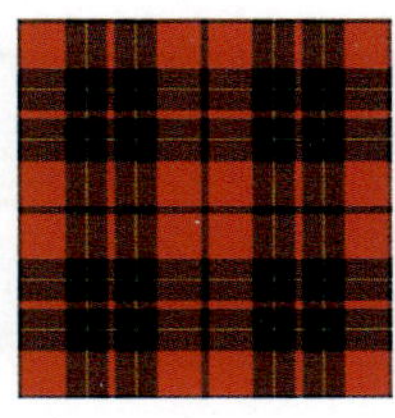

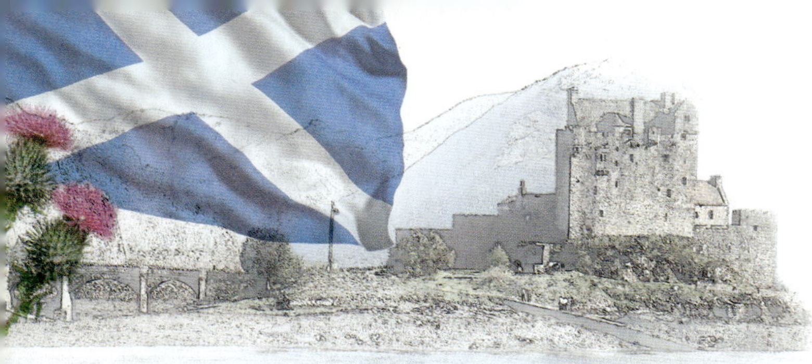

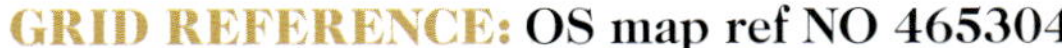

Broughty Castle

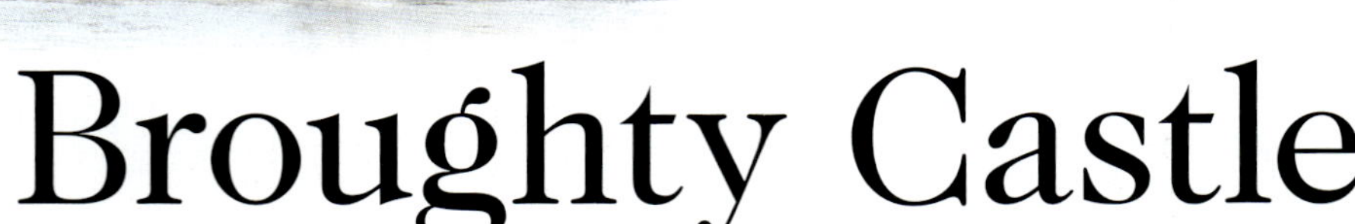

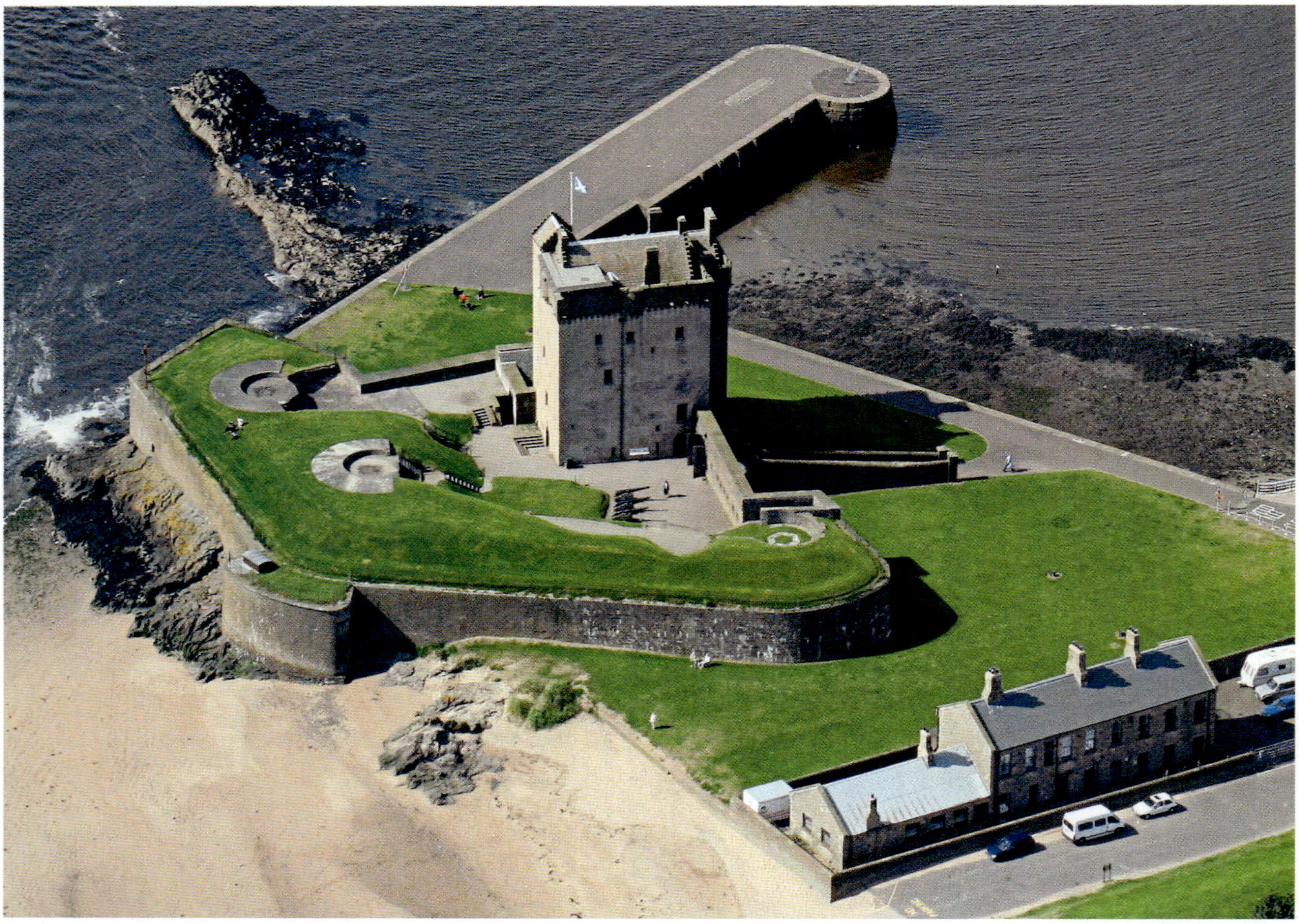

Still dominating the narrow mouth of the Firth of Tay, this substantial tower house saw many wars and was still serving a military function in the 1940s when it was needed as a lookout position and gun platform. Today this highly distinctive and prominently appointed building provides a useful navigation marker for shipping and aircraft heading towards Dundee.

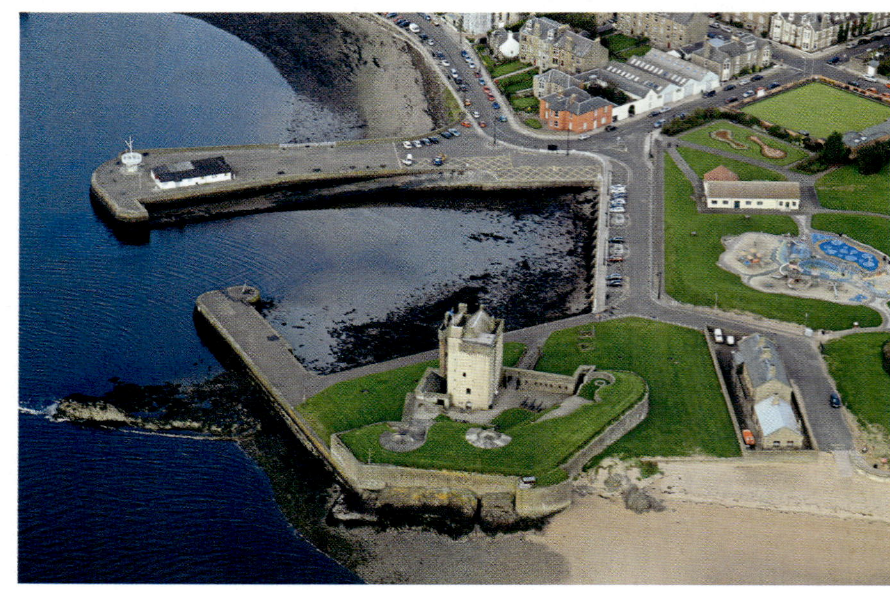

Visitor Details

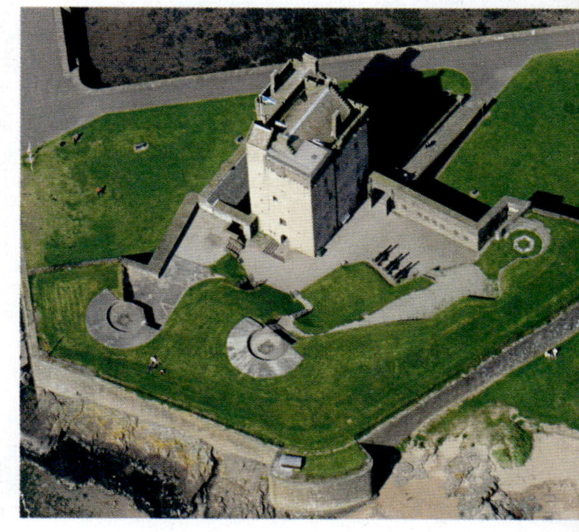

www.leisureandculturedundee.com/culture/broughty-castle

01382 436916

The castle is open all year. Detailed timings can be found on the website or by phone.

No wheelchair access.

Facilities include a WC, refreshments and a small shop.

Admission to the castle and museum is free. The museum has changing displays in addition to featuring local wildlife and history. Details of events are found on the website. This building is in the care of Historic Scotland.

Location: Broughty Castle is in the county of Angus and Dundee on the south shore of Broughty Ferry which is on the north side of the Firth of Tay. It is three miles east of Dundee, just south of the A930. There is car parking nearby which is also handy for the play park, beach and gardens. Buses to Broughty Ferry town have stops within walking distance of the castle and the rail station is about 10 minutes walk away.

The Clan Douglas were the first to reinforce the promontory in 1454. George, the 4th Earl of Angus took possession and his son inherited the site although he was forced to hand control to the crown. The four-floor tower house still standing today was finished by Andrew, the 2nd Lord Gray in 1495 after five years of construction. In 1547, the invading English army took the surrender of the castle from Patrick the 4th Lord Gray without any fighting. This was done by bribing him and some of his senior officers. In December 1548, Patrick was summoned to account for his treasons against the Government of Scotland, and although the French commanders argued for his execution, he was eventually pardoned at Regent Arran's command. With significant French help in 1550, the castle was back in Scottish hands but the storming meant that damage was severe. The siege took six weeks for the French Scots forces to succeed. It was not possible to bombard the castle from concentrated ships' cannon fire due to strong currents in the river mouth and the presence of several Royal Navy ships. In 1651 Cromwell's army rampaged across Scotland led by General Monck and reached the castle. This time threats from surrounding land artillery were enough and the Royalists gave up the castle quickly. After the castle was sold by the Gray family in 1666 it fell into ruin, being noted as roofless in 1821.

Before the building of the Forth and Tay Railway Bridges, another solution to crossing the two wide Forths on the east coast of Scotland was in use. This was the introduction of the first ever roll on- roll-off railway ferries. In 1846, the Edinburgh and Northern Railway Company purchased the castle ruin and the surrounding land to build a harbour and rail goods yard. Special rail-equipped ferries shuttled goods wagons from this harbour across to Tayport. Passengers used a separate ferry.

This harbour was now a strategic asset and the War Office decided the castle could be renovated as a strongpoint to defend the small port. So in 1855, they took ownership and by 1860, approved plans which added the wing and courtyard. Embrasures for nine large guns were constructed. By the time of the First World War, two 4.7in guns were added. An accommodation block was built in 1887 for navy personnel who would be sent on mine laying duties in the Tay estuary when needed. Around this time, a storage magazine was added for explosive devices such as shells and mines.

The top of the castle tower had look out posts added during the Second World War. Military use finished in 1949. In 1969, the council opened a museum in the tower.

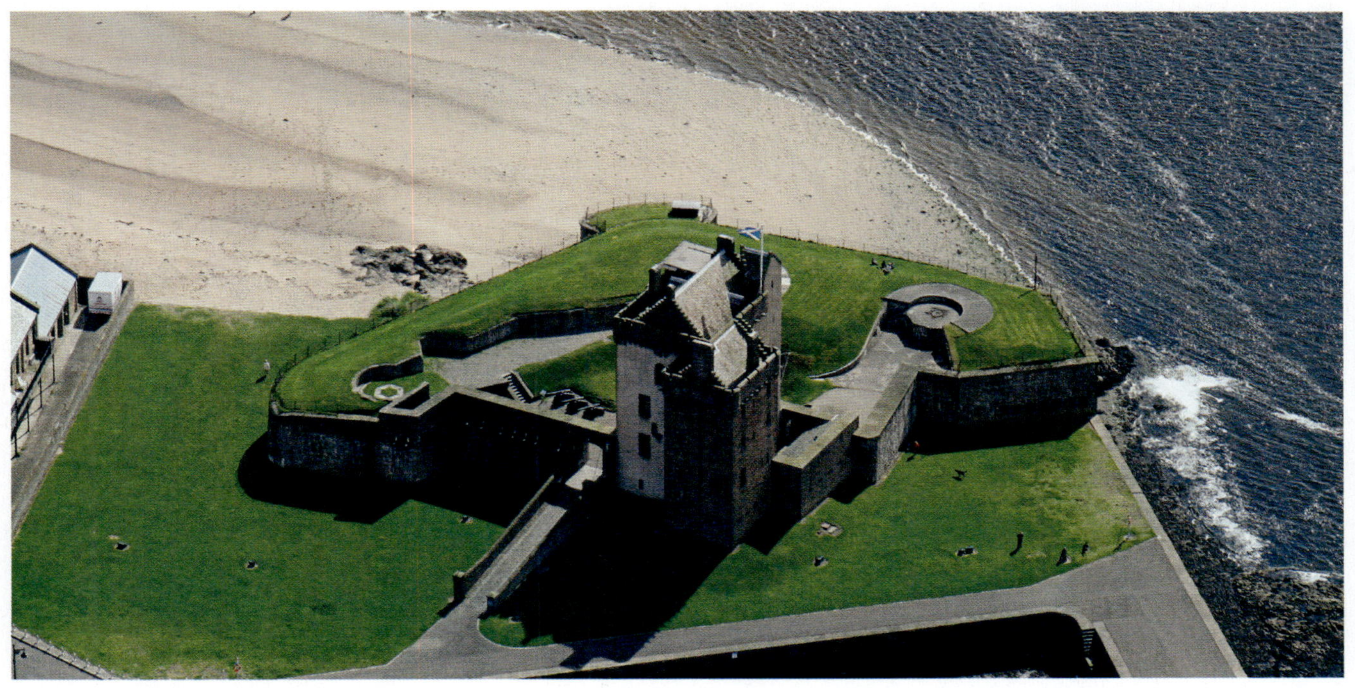

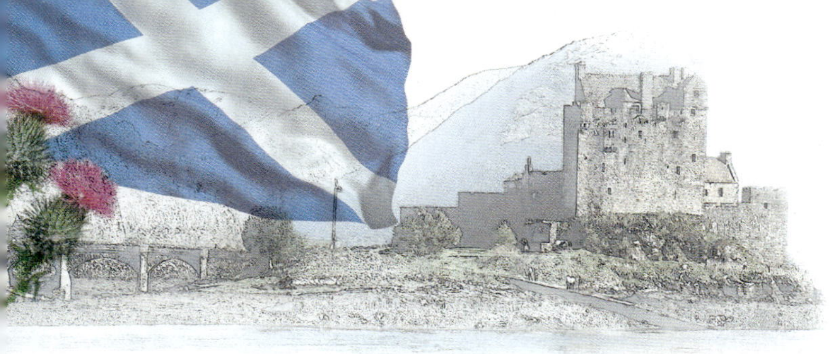

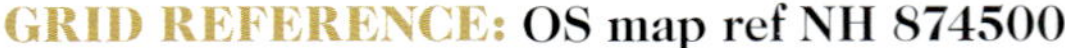

Cawdor Castle

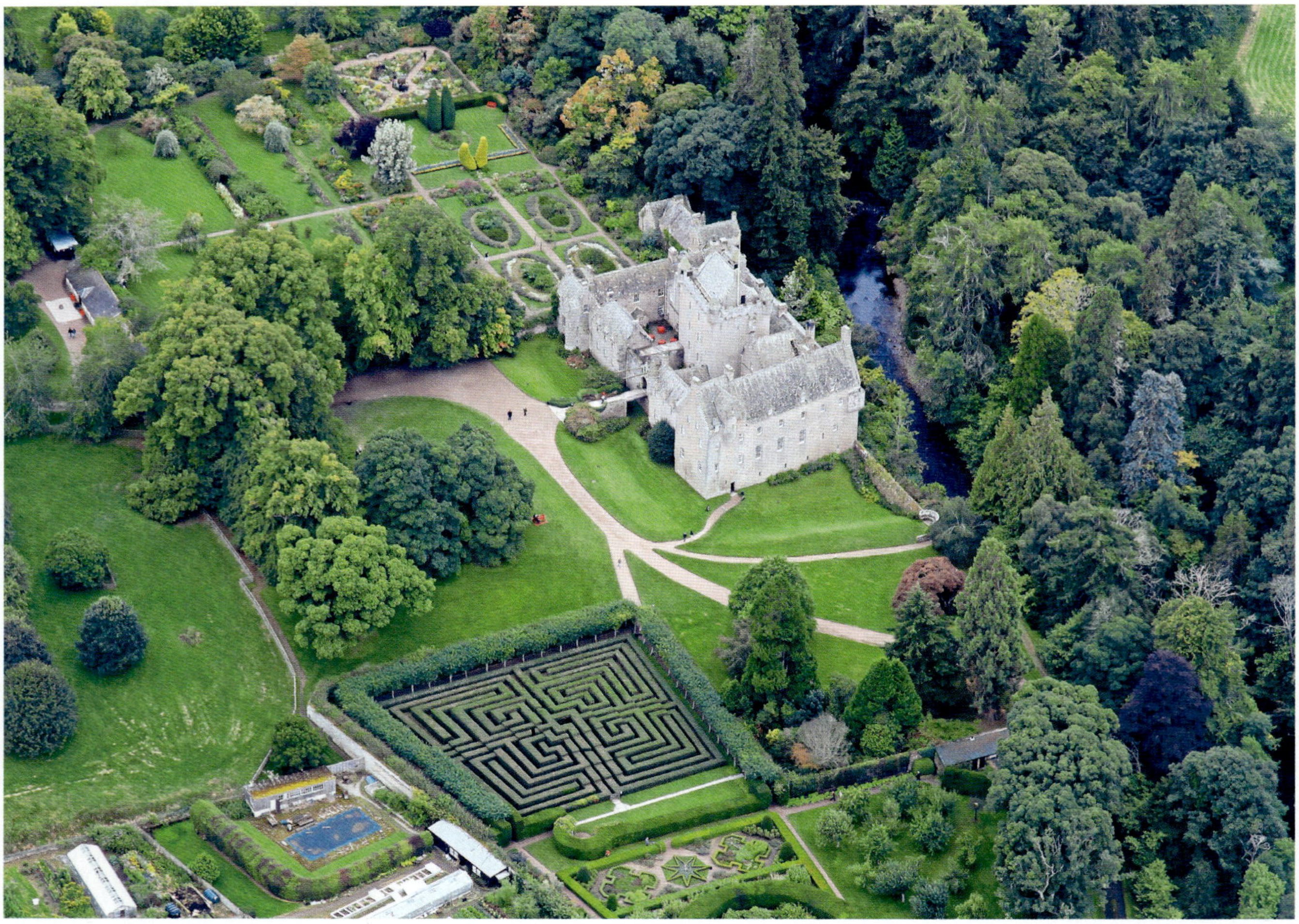

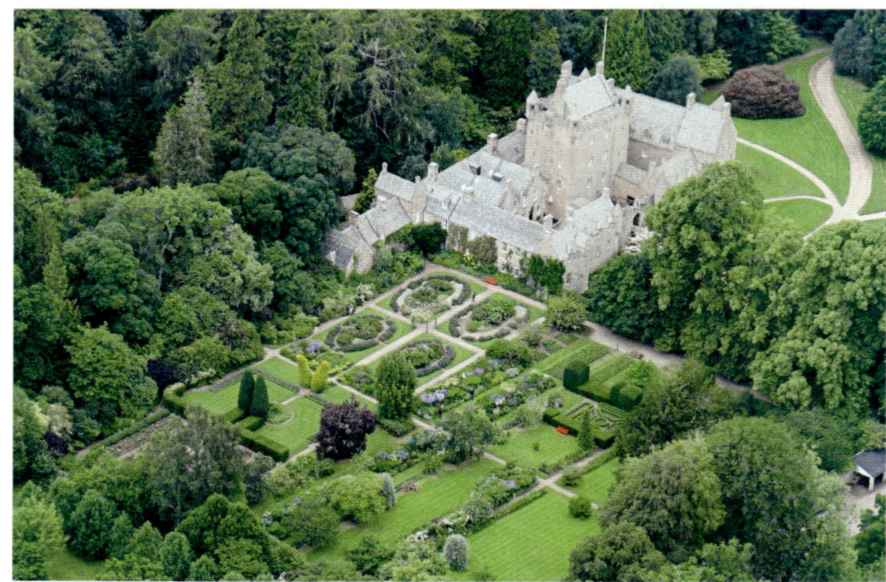

Cawdor may be well known thanks to its inclusion in the famous 'Scottish play' by William Shakespeare, but the real history is more interesting and, if anything, more shocking and bloody than the Bard's fiction. Easy to visit, this stunning castle is packed with historic features and boasts a grand garden featuring artistic sculptures that is surrounded by picturesque mature forests.

Visitor Details

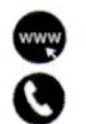

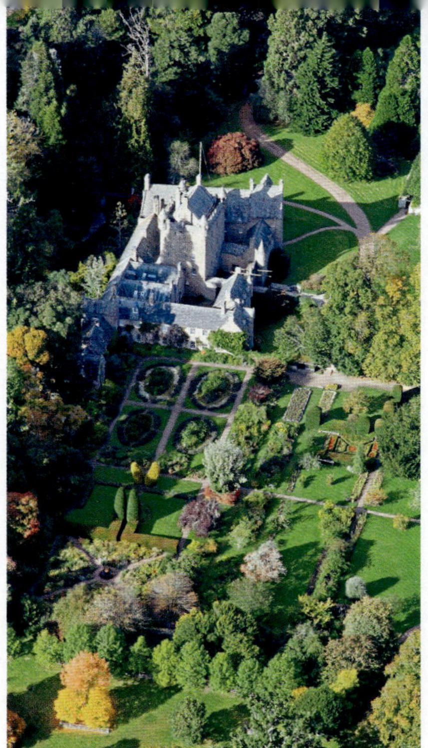

www.cawdorcastle.com

01667 404401

This 15th century tower house is usually open from May to September. The three gardens are open daily from 10am to 5pm with an admission charge. Updates on the castle interior opening can be found on the website or by phone.

Some disabled access to the castle and grounds is possible; again check before visiting.

The Courtyard Cafe is open for refreshments and has an adjacent shop and toilets.

This is probably the best-preserved stone keep in Scotland with ditch, drawbridge and later decorative additions. The grounds also have several magnificent gardens as a bonus. The inside of the castle is packed with displays, portraits, tapestries and antique furniture including a four poster bed from 1661. Clearly it is still a living home with many stories to be discovered if you visit. Auchindoune House on the estate (two miles from the castle) is the location for a special collection of plants and trees from Tibet. Within the Big Wood are several nature trails, the longest being five miles. Wildlife and plants flourish and the clean air promotes the growth of over 130 types of lichen.

Location: Cawdor Castle is nine miles north east of Inverness. Leave the A96 at Gollanfield crossroads and then follow the minor road south east for four miles. For other travel routes, see the detailed map and directions on the website.

A dungeon pit can still be seen in the basement of this tower and adjacent to it are the remains of a holly tree from the time when the castle was founded in 1380. Legend says the Thane of Cawdor dreamed of a wise oracle who instructed him to load a chest of gold onto the back of a donkey. The place where the animal rested would be a safe haven to build a castle for his family. The spot where it lay down next to this tree became the place where the tower build started around the then-living tree. Several other trees across Britain have castles built around them, for example Skipton. Perhaps this was for good luck. Certainly for centuries cutting down a holly tree was considered to bring ill fortune. The Cawdor family have encouraged good luck by planting 1,200 holly trees to create The Maze.

William Calder, the 6th Thane of Cawdor, was granted a licence to build the castle fortress in 1454. From studies of the stonework styles, historians believe the tower build was started around 1380. Could this be the earliest example in Scotland of retrospective planning permission? This early work was directed by Donald the 5th Thane.

Despite the references in the 'Scottish Play', Duncan was not murdered here as claimed by William Shakespeare, because this castle is not old enough. Actors do not refer to the tragic drama Macbeth by that name as they fear it will curse the performance and players. The real King Duncan was killed in battle near Elgin in 1040. Macbeth then ruled Scotland wisely from Dunsinane near Perth for 17 years. Among the annual events in front of the castle are open air performances and these sometimes feature the 'Scottish play'.

The threshold of the castle interior is protected by a huge wrought iron yett (gate). This was salvaged from the island castle at nearby LochIndorb when William Calder, under orders from the King, wrecked the castle there to deprive the notorious 'Wolf of Badenoch' of his stronghold in 1455.

Clan Campbell kidnapped the heiress Muriel Calder at the age of 11. This was at great personal cost to Campbell of Inverliver Lochawe when all six of his sons were killed during the pursuit from Kilravock Castle near Cawdor to the Campbells' castle at Inverary in Argyll.

Shortly afterwards in 1511, they arranged to marry her to the Earl of Argyll's son, Sir John Campbell. That brought the ownership of Cawdor to the Campbells. After they moved into the castle, they were placed under siege by four of Muriel's uncles who were not willing to give into the Campbells' claim on the property. The castle was not an easy target especially as it was assured of plentiful fresh water from a spring in bedrock under the kitchen. The Campbells would not surrender and the death of two of the attacking Calder uncles ended the siege, enhancing the Clan Campbell's reputation for fierce fighting skills.

A ghost wearing a blue velvet dress has been sighted in the castle and legend declares this is the spirit of Muriel Calder. Her marriage was a happy one though; she had many children and lived to the age of 77.

John Campbell, the 3rd earl of Cawdor, added a garden in 1635. After the Restoration of the monarchy in 1660, the west and north ranges were added using the skills of local stonemasons, the Nicolsons of Nairn.

Other changes included adding the entrance gateway, drawbridge, the parapet walk, and corner turrets on the keep. Careful design ensured that the imposing keep remained as the central imposing building with later additions around it being smaller in scale.

After 1680, the son of Sir Hugh Campbell married a wealthy heiress in Pembrokeshire and they stayed on her family estate in South West Wales. Meanwhile, his younger brothers managed the Cawdor estate, adding the walled flower garden in 1720 and developing the woodlands that continue to flourish today around the castle grounds.

The Jacobite Risings did not leave the castle untouched by upheavals. In 1746, the family hid 'The Fox' Simon Fraser, Lord Lovat, in a secret room inside a roof space concealed from government troops. His reputation was indeed wily, hence his fox nickname, switching sides often to suit his personal gain. He unwisely decided to leave the sanctuary of Cawdor and was captured, found guilty of many crimes including treason and beheaded in London.

The castle buildings have not been altered much in recent years. A big project was the renovation of the roof of the keep and repairs to masonry. The gardens change with the seasons and sculptured artworks continue to be added enhancing the views. The family have sold their Welsh estate and now live in the castle or in other estate properties such as Achindoune House when visitors tour the castle.

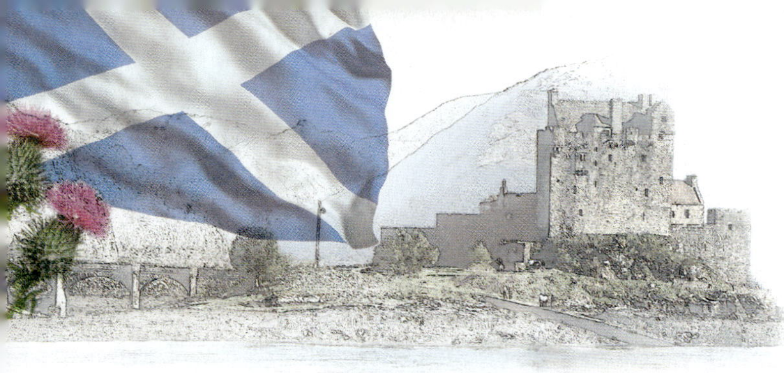

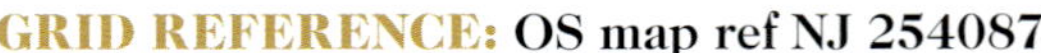
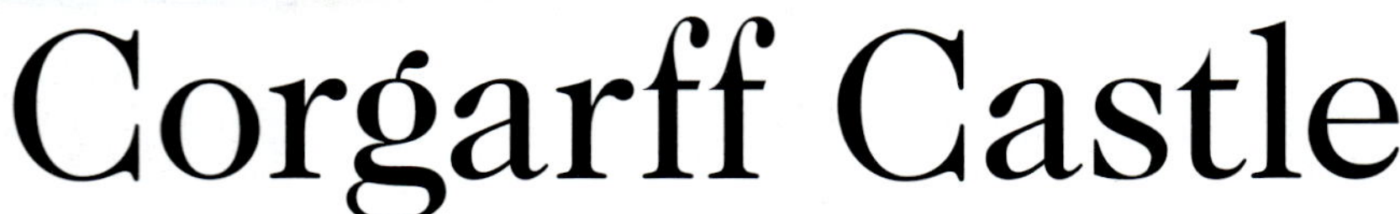

Corgarff Castle

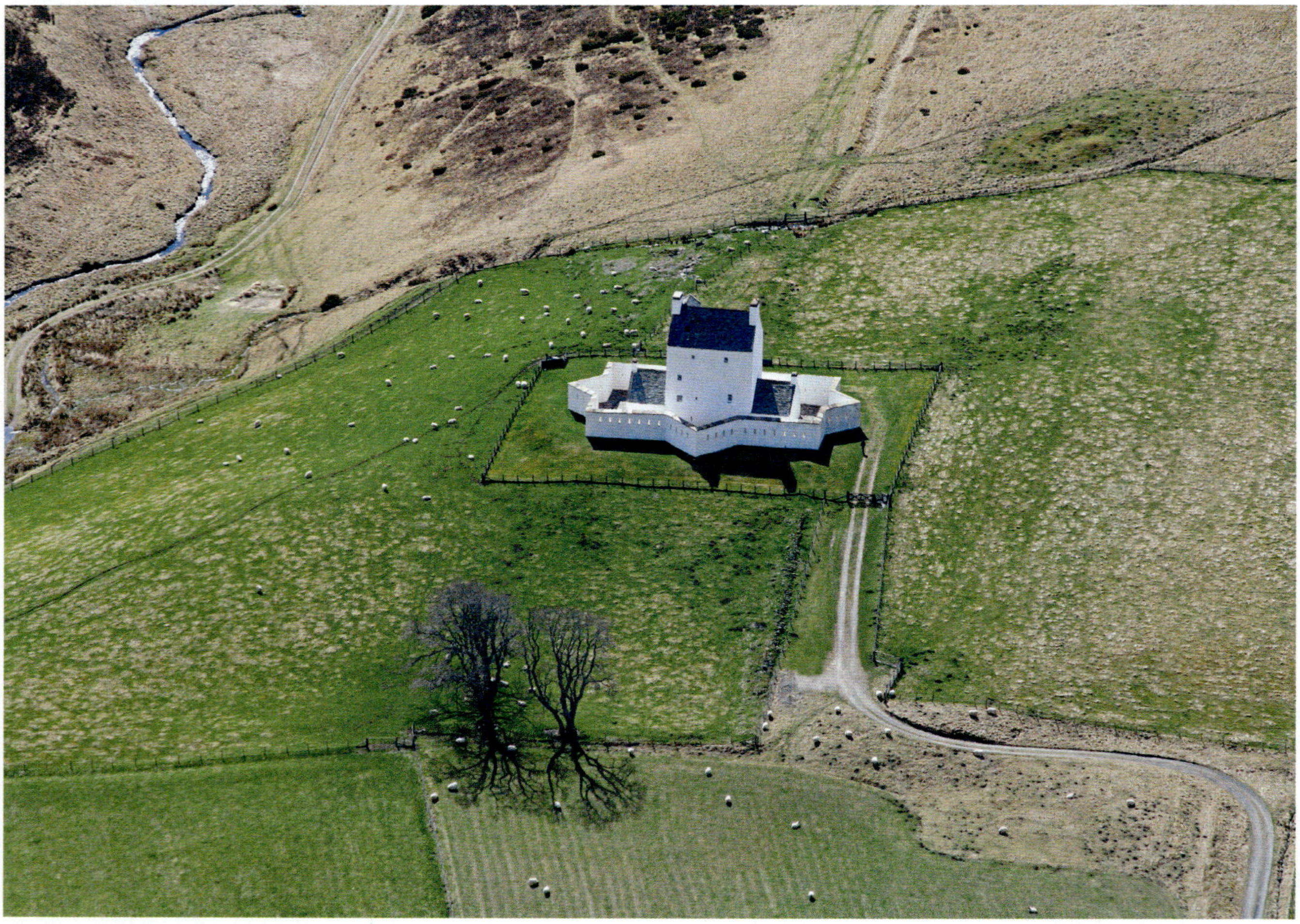

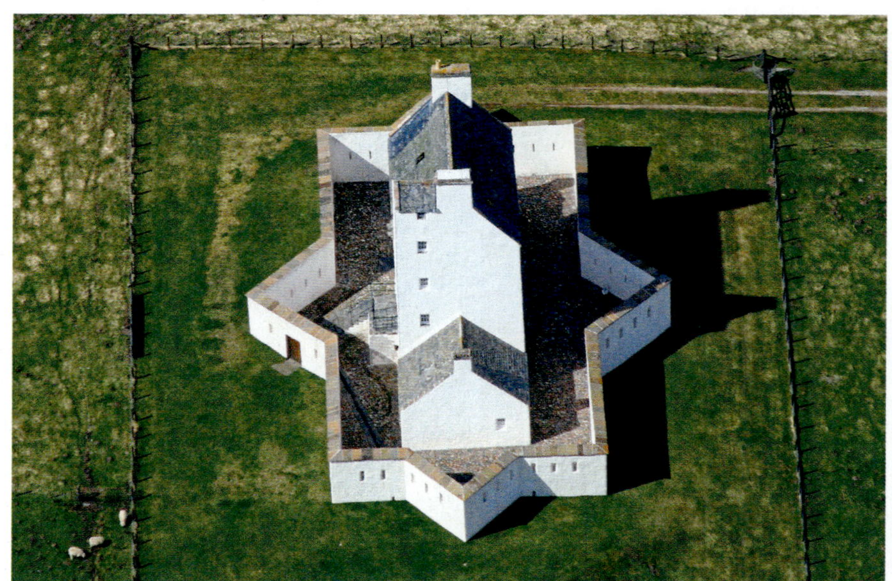

Rising from remote moorland, this outpost with its unusual star-shaped outer wall was the scene of a dreadful atrocity, the knowledge of which must surely have given sleepless nights to the military garrisons which came later. Only the brave would desire to spend a night there nowadays, though it certainly makes for an interesting picnic spot on the wind-blasted hills.

Visitor Details

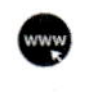 www.historicenvironment.scot/visit-a-place/places/corgarff-castle
Owner Historic Environment Scotland (HES)

 No telephone.

 Open April to September from 9.30am to 5pm, closed for an hour at lunch. Due to its exposed location it may be closed during adverse weather. Check the HES closure list online before travelling.

 Not suitable for wheelchairs due to steep gravel access path and internal steps.

No cafe due to small size of building. Picnics can be had, sheltered behind the star walls, however. Admission fee £6 with concession for children and senior citizens.

Location: As the Hooded Crow flies, 40 miles West of Aberdeen. By road, close to the A939 Ballater to Tomintoul road guarding the high mountain pass; car park below castle with a short inclined track to climb to the entrance. If time is short, a view can be had from the small layby on the A939 next to the standing stone sculptures.

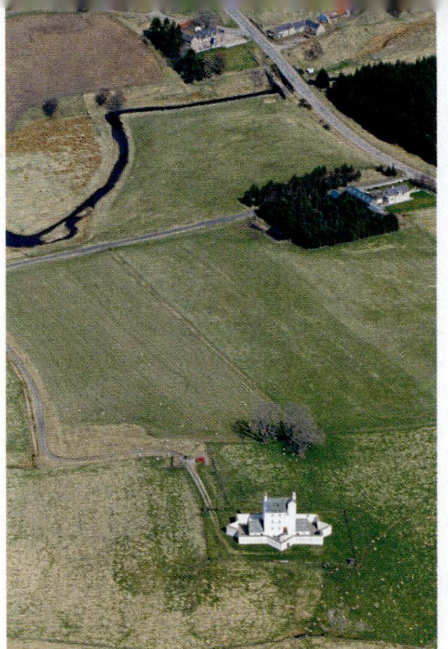

In the 16th century a four-storey tower house was constructed for use as a hunting lodge. The first residents were the Earls of Mar, who later granted the property to the Forbes clan. They were in a long running bloody feud with the Gordons of Auchindoun some 25 miles north across the wild mountains. Raids were common and a terrible fate befell the 28 women and children sheltering inside the castle in November 1571. Taking advantage of the absence of the clansmen, marauding Gordons set the floors ablaze, trapping the hapless occupants when they refused to surrender. No one escaped from the hell inside, including the wife of the Forbes clan chief. Perhaps this is the source of the haunting eerie noises reported by some visitors? Afterwards the tower was still used as a base by assorted outlaw gangs who preyed on travellers using the nearby high road. Eventually the Erskines, Earls of Mar, secured the castle and it was a muster point for the Marquis of Montrose in 1645 before his campaign. Two more destructive burnings occurred, in 1689 by Jacobites and in 1716 by Hanoverians after which the Forbes regained title. During the rising of 1745, the Jacobites stored arms and ammunition inside, however local informants passed word to the government forces. Using a blizzard as cover, a force of 400 Redcoats marched from Aberdeen and caught the Jacobites by surprise. After the final defeat of the Jacobites at Culloden, the government purchased Corgarff. The insides were rebuilt to house a small garrison. Outside, the star walls were added. For the next 85 years the army must have regarded Corgarff as a very rough posting. They searched surrounding hills for illegal whisky stills, Jacobite sympathisers and doubtless shivered a lot; perhaps not all the whisky was destroyed. For a short time in the 1820s, a legal distillery was in use on this site.

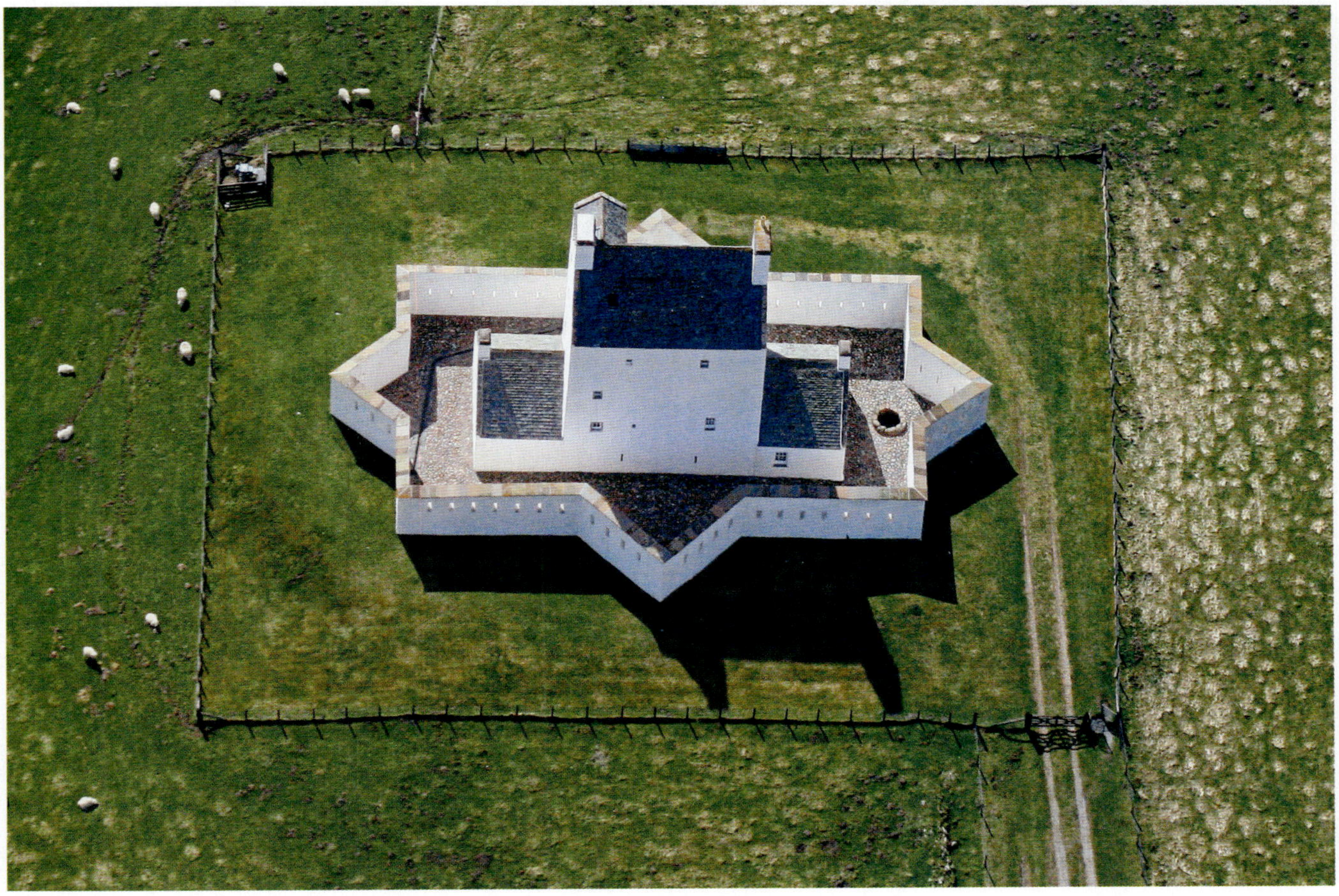

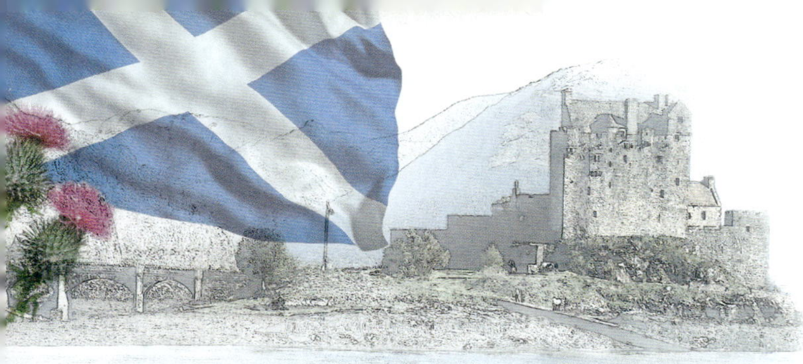

Craigievar Castle

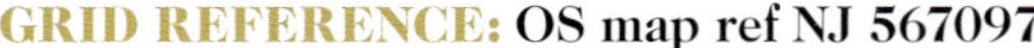

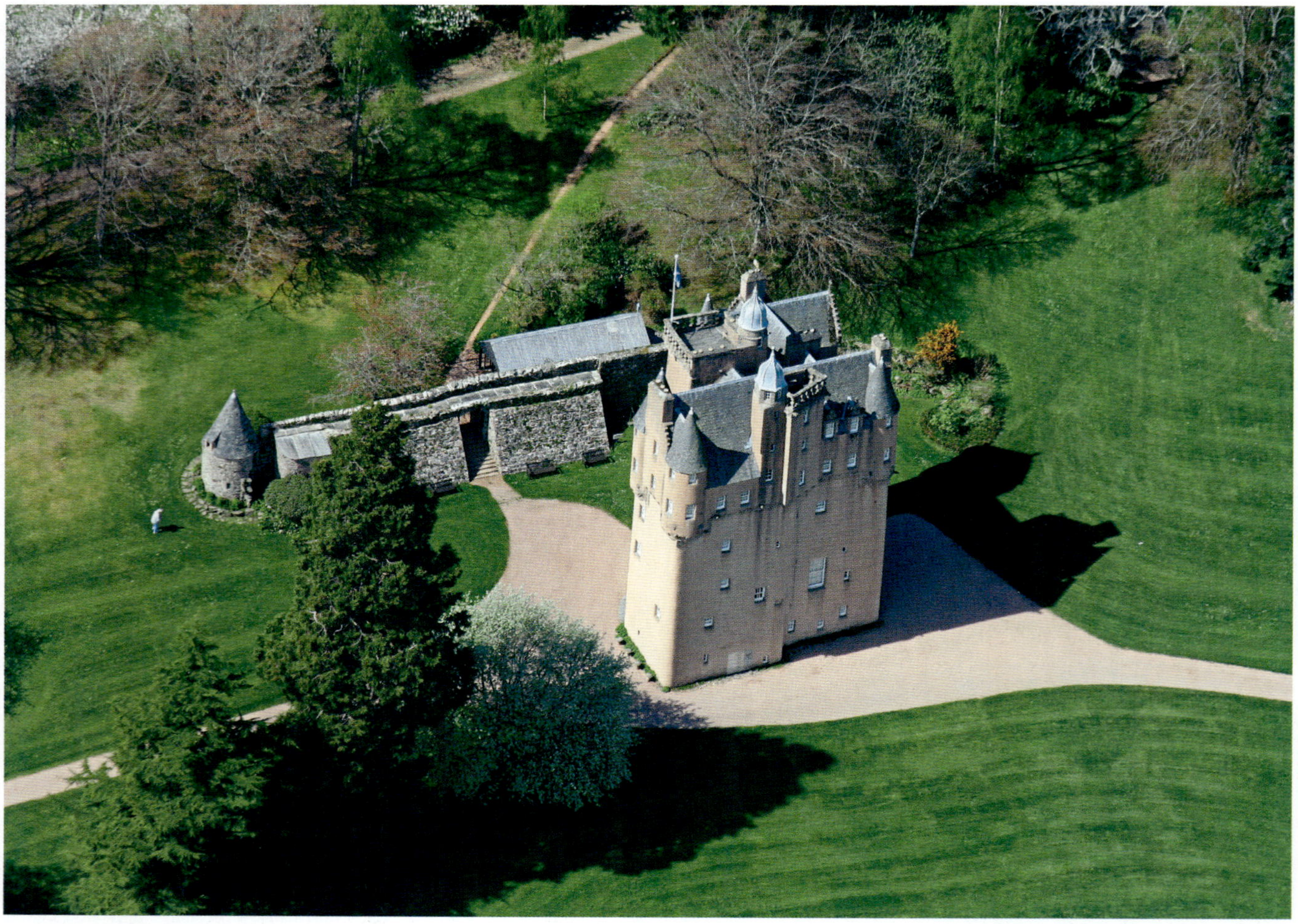

Having made his fortune in trade with the Baltic ports, William Forbes was able to create this masterpiece of castle design. Today, with most of its original defensive wall gone, it has an appearance more akin to that of a fairytale palace than a military stronghold. Its fantastic looks are said to have later inspired the creative Disney film and theme park builders.

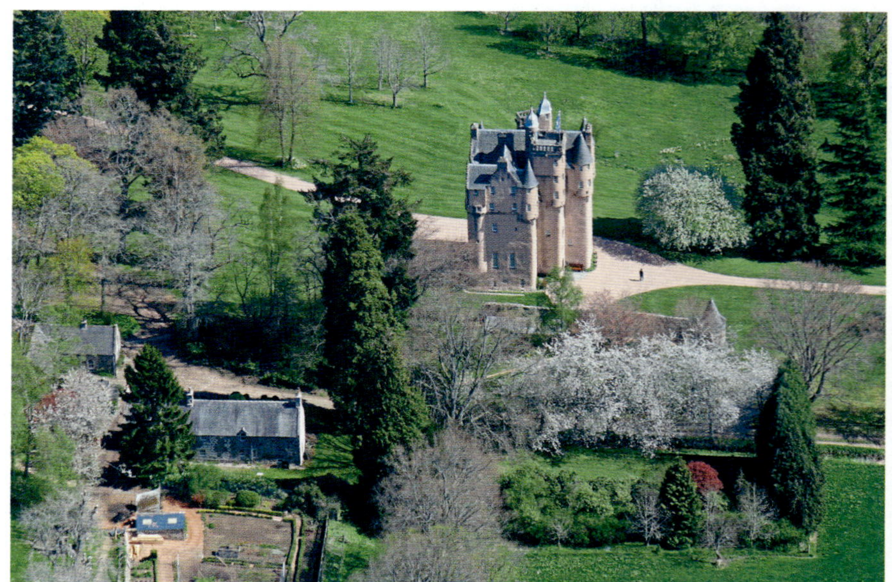

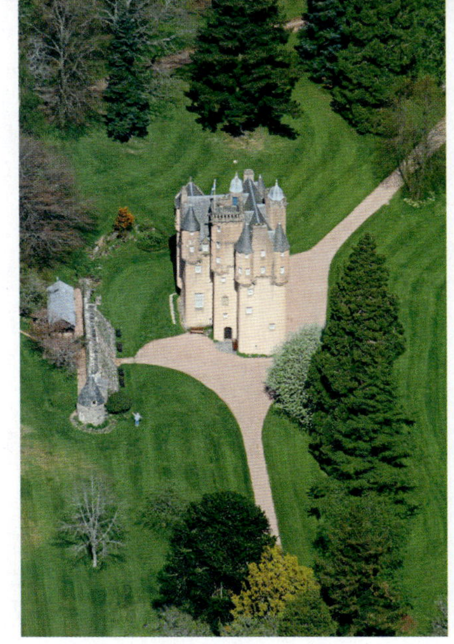

www.nts.org.uk/visit/places/craigievar

01339 883635

Pre-booking for castle interior guided tours is a must. All tours are guided and there is no individual entry. An entry fee is charged to non trust members. Tour numbers are limited to 24. Opening is seasonal too, so check before visiting.

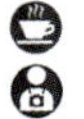

Access to the castle may be difficult for people with limited mobility as there are stone steps leading into the castle and shop; the upper floors are reached by a steep stone spiral staircase. The woodland trails are on unsurfaced paths; these too are very steep in sections and can be slippery in wet weather.

Toilets and small shop are on site. The nearest town, Alford, has cafes, hotel and a bistro.

The grounds are open all year, there is a charge for using the car park.

Location: Aberdeen and Gordon district. Off the A980, six miles south of Alford and 26 miles west of Aberdeen.

The first castle on this site was started by the Mortimers around 1455. However, rising costs forced a sale before completion. In 1610 the Forbes of Menie bought the project and spent another 16 years overseeing it to completion. The finance came from William Forbes, a merchant trader based at the thriving nearby Aberdeen port. He made his fortune concentrating on the Baltic area earning the nickname Danzig Willy. The design of the large seven-storey tower house was based on the L-plan and it was originally surrounded by a defensive walled courtyard with round guard towers, one survives intact. In the 1600s William organised the hunting, capture and hanging of Gilderoy and his gang of robbers. Folklore regards him as a North East Scottish Robin Hood but the unvarnished truth is that he caused misery and mayhem without any redeeming qualities. In addition to helping to keep the peace as Sherriff of Aberdeen, William campaigned for the Covenanters. At least two Jacobites were safely hidden in his castle's secret compartment to avoid capture.

The inside of the castle retains its lavish decor with fine plaster ceilings. This is due to the diligence of Sir John Forbes, who decided to have the roof rebuilt around 1820. At the same time as the ceilings were saved other castle repairs were made. Credit is due also to Aberdeen city architect John Smith who strongly advised against demolition of the castle and encouraged the restoration of this fine rare building. The proportions and pink lime based harling are said to have inspired the design of the Disney castles in film and at its theme parks.

The National Trust for Scotland became the owners in 1963. The castle interior includes a great hall that has the Stuart arms over the fireplace, a musicians' gallery, a secret staircase connecting the high tower to the great hall, Queen's bedroom and servants' quarters. Portraits adorn the walls; rooms feature antique furniture which captures the atmosphere of bygone times. Perhaps the resident ghost of a fiddler appreciates the presentations?

ABOUT THE CLAN

Clan Forbes

A long time ago many large bears roamed Scotland, raiding from the forests and mountain wilds to take livestock and sometimes people. It is said that Ochoncar Forbhasach, a descendant of the Pictish chiefs, organised the hunting down of these roaring raiders around 775AD. His reward was good lands around the River Don to be settled by his clan, which became known in this region as the Forbes.

In 1271, Alexander III granted a Lordship and lands to Duncan Forbes. This charter still exists in the Forbes family charter chest. The next written record in 1296 shows Duncan de Forboys giving homage to John Balliol and in the same year John Forbes signed the Ragman Roll.

By the 14th century, the Forbes were in places of power. Sir John de Forbes was a Justicar in Aberdeenshire. The medieval Justicar, a Royal judge, took its name from the justices who originally travelled around Scotland hearing cases on circuit or 'ayre'. He had four sons who added further branches to the family tree. Alistair of Brux established Skellater and Inverernan branches, William gave the Pitsligo branch, John gained Tolquhon. His eldest son excelled in combat, taking on Donald Lord of the Isles at the battle of Harlaw in 1411. This impressed

the Earl of Mar, who helped to promote him to become Lord Forbes around 1445. Later expansion included Forbes ownership of estates at Corsindale, Monymusk and Craigievar, making them very powerful with half of Mar owned and able to call on many men at arms.

Conflict with the other large clans was inevitable. The biggest clashes were with the Gordons aided by the Leslies. Two bloody battles ensued and a massacre of women and children at Corgarff castle took place. The parliament of Scotland could not allow such extreme activity to continue. The highlands were not without laws but in this case two new laws were passed by parliament naming the specific clans and binding them to make peace.

The Forbes gave support to the Jacobites in the 1745 rising. A detailed account called The Lyon in Mourning was published in the aftermath by Robert Forbes, the bishop of Ross and Caithness. At one stage he was imprisoned, accused of aiding Jacobites but he avoided a death sentence. Many of the Forbes lost land and property as a forfeit for choosing the losing side.

Castle Forbes still exists near Alford by the River Don. It started as a tower house but as threats decreased and comfort became

a priority it was demolished in 1815. In its place rose a mansion of castellated style. This was built by James Ochoncar the 17th Lord Forbes. Details of how to visit can be found here https://www.castle-forbes.com/ Castles with Forbes occupation featured in this book are Corgarff, Craigievar and Tolquhon. A website can be viewed at https://www.clan-forbes.org/ with further properties shown.

Motto: "Grace me guide."

The current clan chief is Malcolm Forbes the 23rd Lord Forbes Premier Lord of Scotland and he resides at the clan seat Castle Forbes near Alford. The estate website gives details of activities such as fishing and how a visit to the castle can be arranged for clan members. https://www.castle-forbes.com/

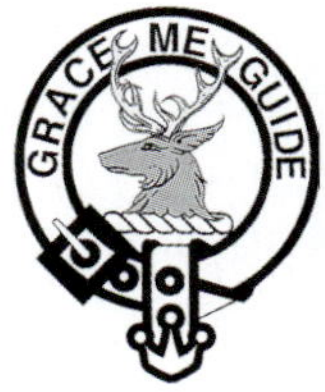

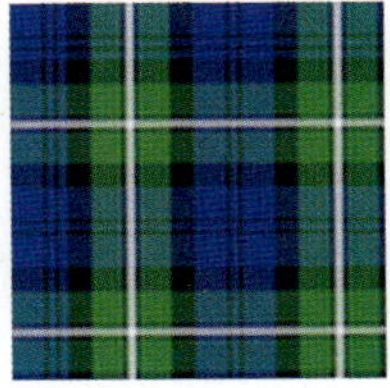

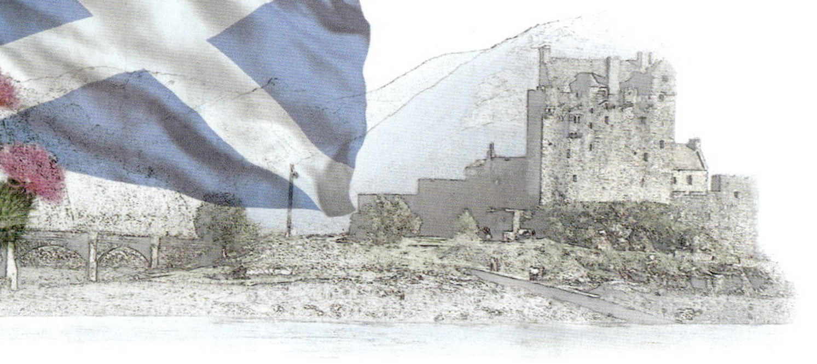

Craigston Castle

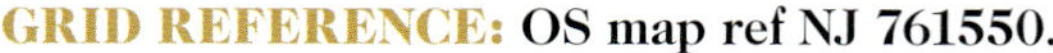

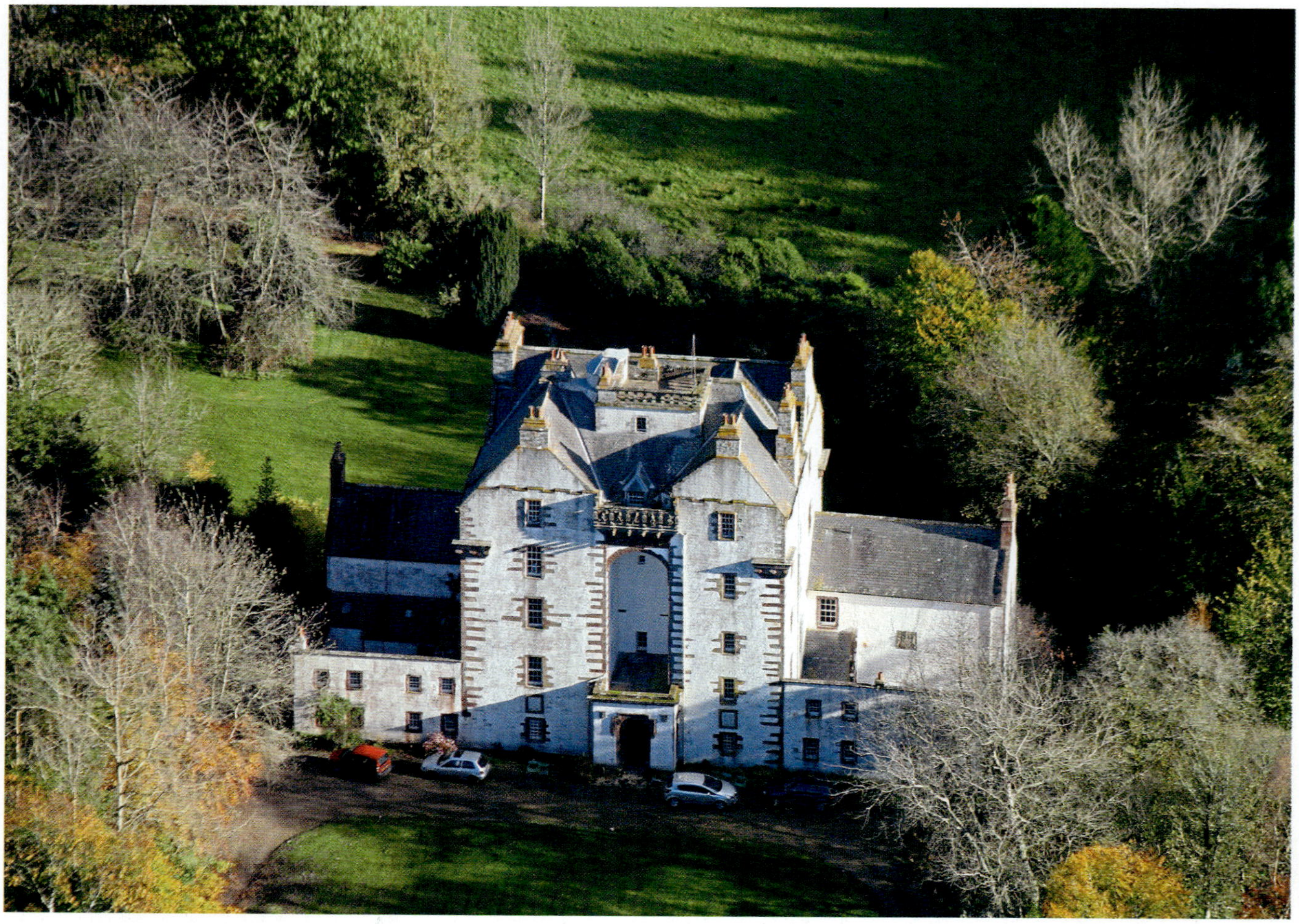

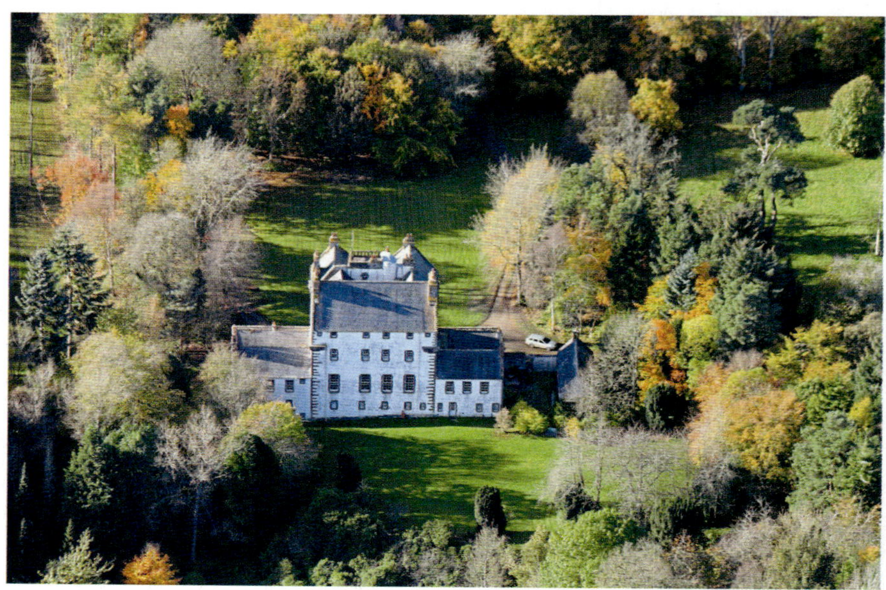

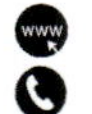
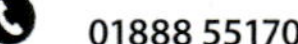
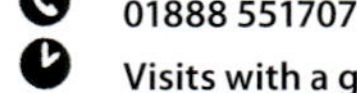

Visitor Details

www.craigston-castle.co.uk

01888 551707

Visits with a guided tour can be arranged by prior appointment throughout the year. Accommodation is available year round; check for availability.

Limited access due to stairs and the usual castle interiors.

Refreshments available in nearby Turriff town.

The following quote from their website hints at a wonderfully eccentric family history:

"The Urquhart family is one of the oldest in Scotland and can be traced back to Adam Urquhart the sheriff of Cromarty in 1357. However, according to the great Sir Thomas Urquhart (1611-1660), translator of Rabelais, the family can even be traced back to Adam and Eve through remarkable ancestors including Esormon Ourochartos (Prince of Achaia who married Narfesid, Sovereign of the Amazons) and Bithiah, the Pharaoh's daughter who found Moses in the bulrushes. These fantastic claims are symptomatic of the family's fondness for the romantic and the strange."

William Urquhart and his wife, Catrina, moved back to live at Craigston in 2007 and have two young sons who were born there. Gradually they have renovated a room at a time, added modern comforts and kept up with maintaining the contents of this unique home.

Location: Craigston Castle can be found in Banff and Buchan county, four miles north east of Turriff on a minor road east of the B9105, a half mile north east of Fintry by Craigston.

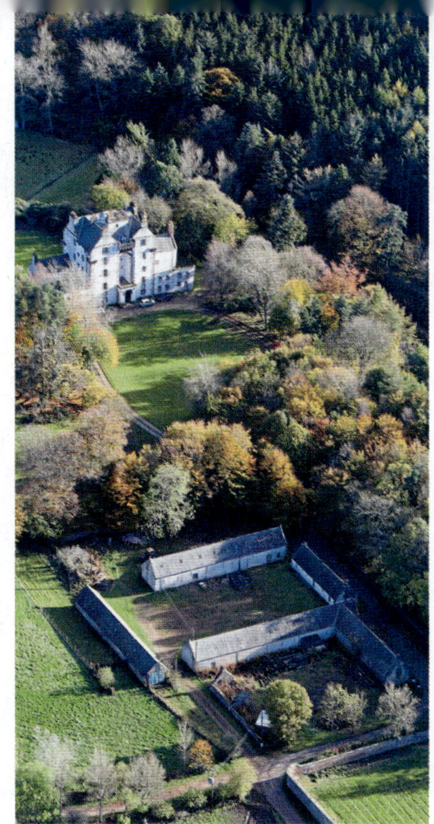

Craigston was built around 1605 by John Urquhart of Craigfintry, commonly called 'the Tutor of Cromarty', son of Alexander Urquhart, Sheriff of Cromarty. He was a man remarkable for his prudence. He died on November 8, 1631, and was buried in Banff. The masons of the Bell family designed the original castle.

It was sold by the Urquharts in 1657. However, the great grandson of the builder had by 1739 made a personal fortune in an unlikely manner. Captain John Urquhart obtained a licence to sail as a privateer for the Spanish Navy. This life as a legalised pirate clearly suited him; he was able to retire and became the Laird of Craigston, buying the property in 1739 at the age of 42. His closest brush with death in service was at the age of 19 when fighting for the Jacobites at the battle of Sherrifmuir. Perhaps he went to sea to escape being punished for his Jacobite treasons.

John Urquhart added the unusual flanking castle wings which are connected by an elevated arch and above that a lavishly embellished parapet.

With some design advice from William Adam, gardens were added in 1734. The unchanged exterior of the castle is unique in Scotland and Grade 1 listed. Inside the building, the original kitchen area is still in use on the ground floor with a vaulted ceiling (but the cooking methods have improved over 400 years). The drawing room has wood carvings from the 17th century depicting bible scenes, Scottish kings and heroes. Keeping with the international collecting trend are also gilded mirrors from the Palace of Versailles and heraldic emblems.

Local treasures include oak panels from the Great Hall at Cromarty Castle.

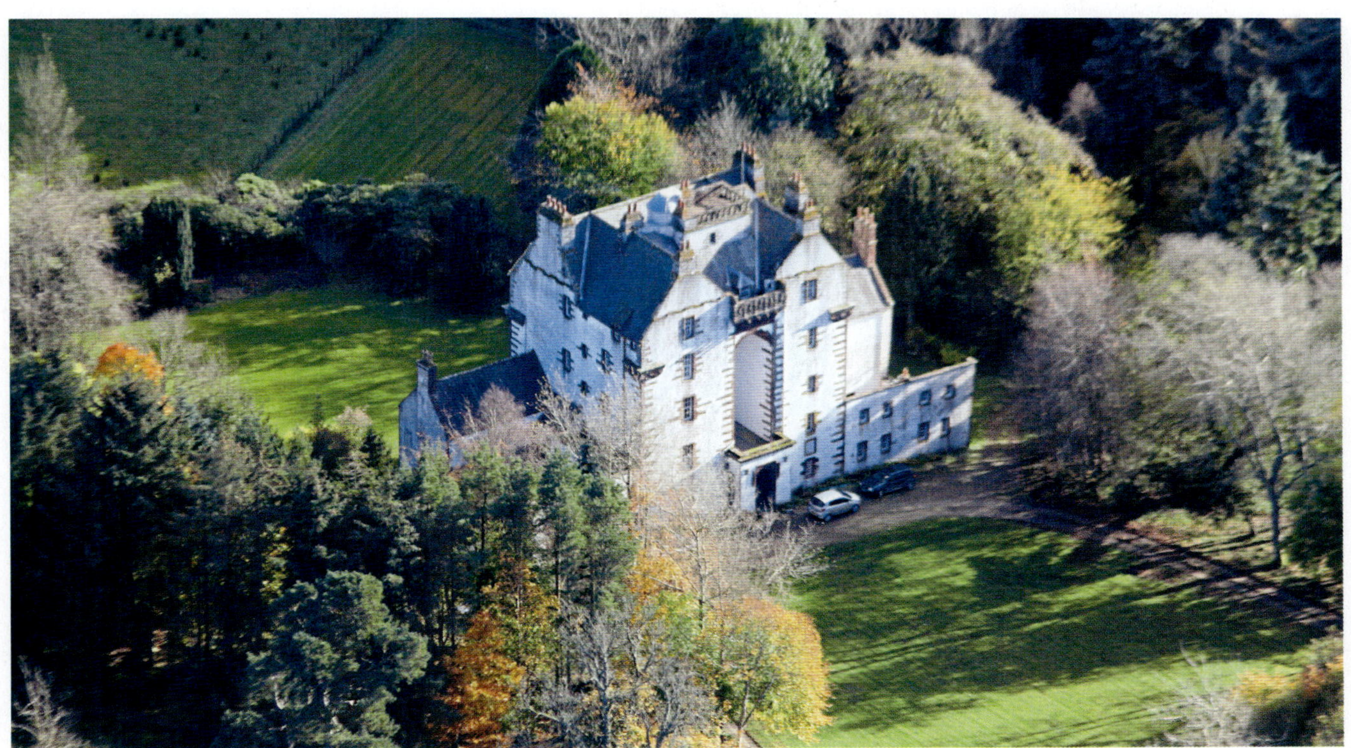

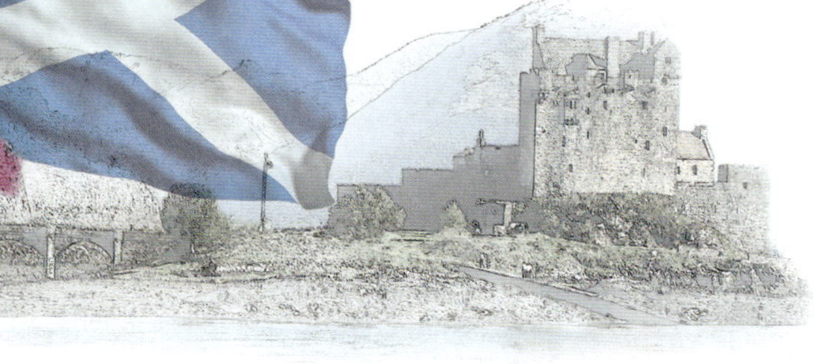

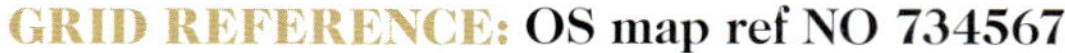

Crathes Castle

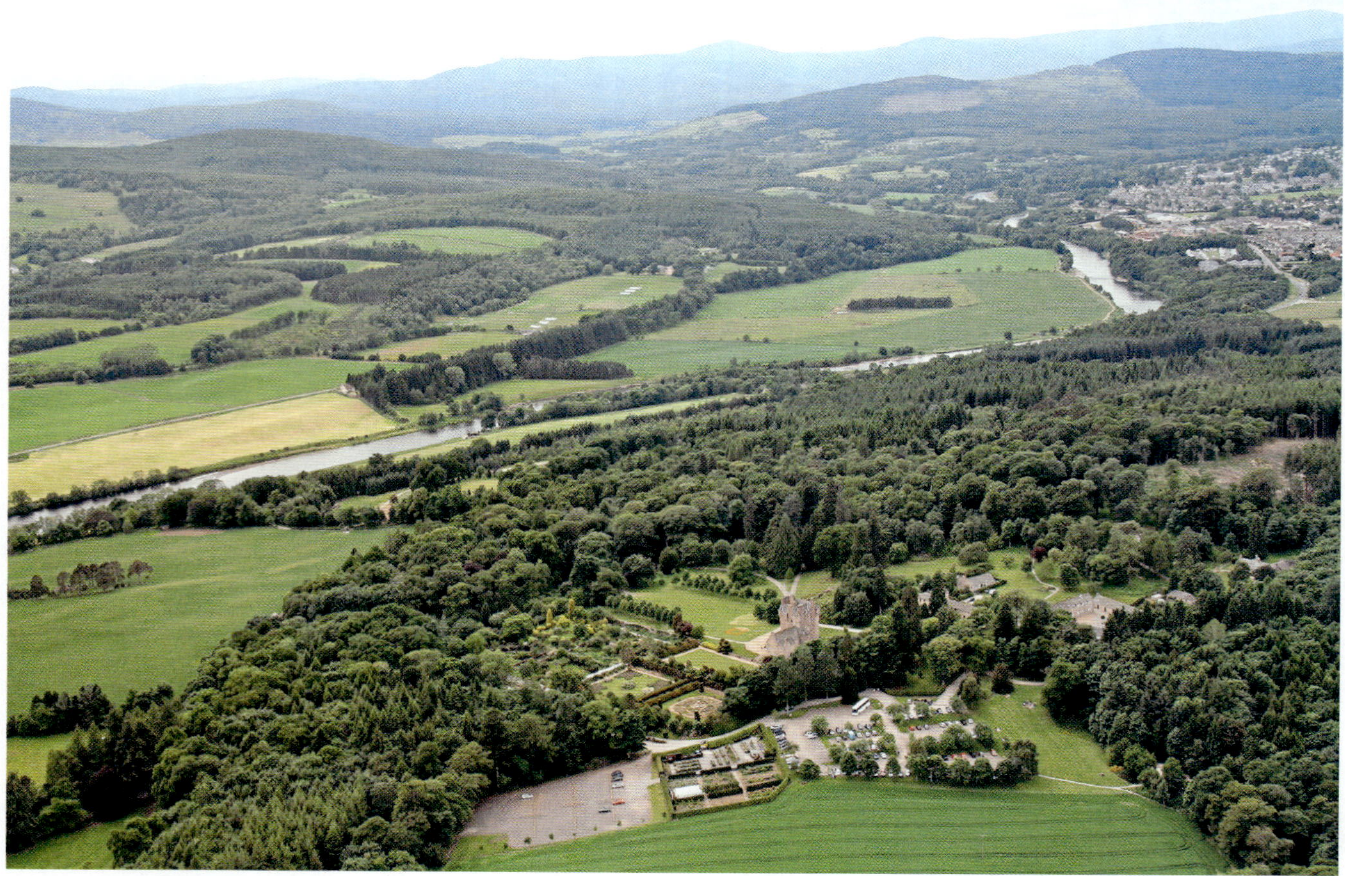

This magnificent tower house is a monument to the skills of the Burnett Clan. They wisely chose to support Robert the Bruce with skilled fighters. In return, he granted land and a jewelled ivory hunting horn which is proudly displayed here among other antiques. Never besieged, Crathes today retains many of its original features, including stunning ceilings painted with Renaissance art.

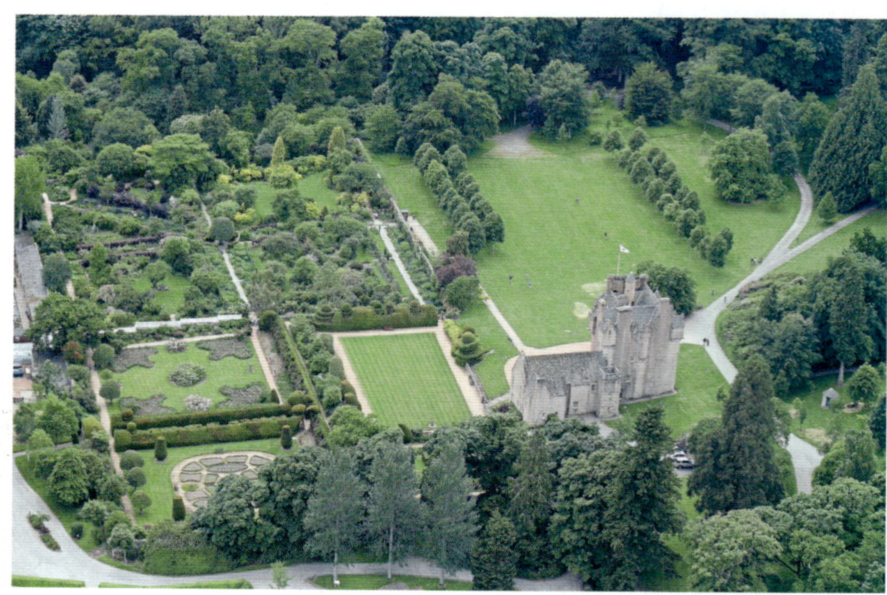

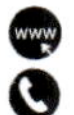

Visitor Details

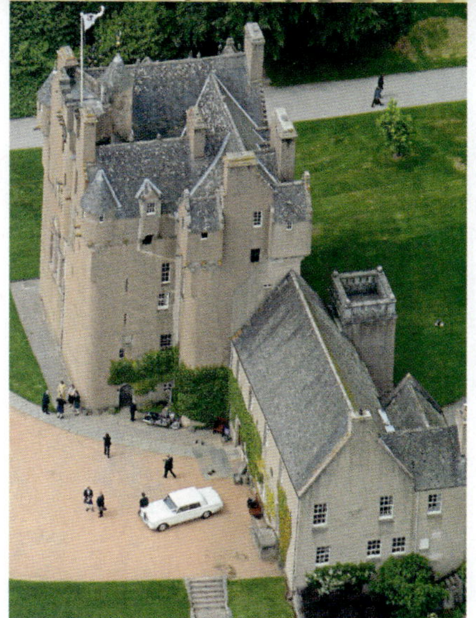

- www.nts.org.uk/visit/places/crathes-castle
- 01330 84452
- Crathes and its grounds are open to tourists throughout the year. Check the website for timings.
- Disabled access is possible on the ground floors and garden paths.
- The tea room and courtyard terrace provide traditional refreshments. A visitor centre provides information about the castle and its surroundings. As shown in the aerial views, weddings are catered for.

Location: Crathes Castle is situated in Deeside, three miles east of Banchory, just north of the A93. If you travel by bus, it is a one mile walk from the driveway entrance to the ticket office, cafe and gift shop.

The massive tower house seen today replaced a timber fortress built on an island in boggy land. This land, the Forest of Drum, was awarded to the Burnett of Leys Clan by King Robert the Bruce in 1323. In those days, a forest was a large tract of ground, not necessarily wooded, and commonly bare. It was reserved for the hunting of deer and, as such, belonging to the Crown. The clan had provided military support for the King's campaigns including the triumph at Bannockburn in 1314. In addition to the land he bestowed, a valuable jewel-studded hunting horn of ivory which has for centuries been proudly displayed above the fireplace in the castle's high hall can be seen. This land transfer firmly placed Deeside on the royal map long before Victoria and Albert resided at nearby Balmoral.

Alexander Burnett of Leys completed the building of the tower house in 1596 after a 43 year struggle with politics had slowed its progress. Usually a tower house would take about ten years to complete. An added challenge was the draining of the Loch of Leys during which he lost his son in an accident at the Loch. The Burnett Clan Chief, Sir James Burnett the 13th Baronet, gifted the castle and grounds to the National Trust for Scotland in 1951 ending 350 years of Burnett occupation. In those turbulent times, it was a tribute to the family's skills at diplomacy that no sieges took place. However, disaster struck in 1966 when a fire destroyed an 18th century wing. It has since been replaced by the two-storey range.

Unusual painted ceilings decorate some of the 13 castle rooms and these are treasured as being rare examples of Scottish Renaissance Art.

Many portraits of the family continue the theme of showing the wealth and power of the Burnetts to those guests who were lucky enough to be accommodated here. In the Green Lady's room, the ghost of a young woman crosses the room and vanishes at the fireplace carrying a babe in her arms. Small bones have been found behind the fireplace. This apparition is one of several seen in the castle and was witnessed by Queen Victoria. The grounds surrounding the castle cover 530 acres with a mix of formal walled garden, woodland, ponds and fields. There are marked woodland trails . Alongside the gravel paths many plants are named. The shaped topiary hedges of Irish yew date back to 1702 and divide the gardens into eight themed areas. An adventure playground for children is on site plus a car and coach park.

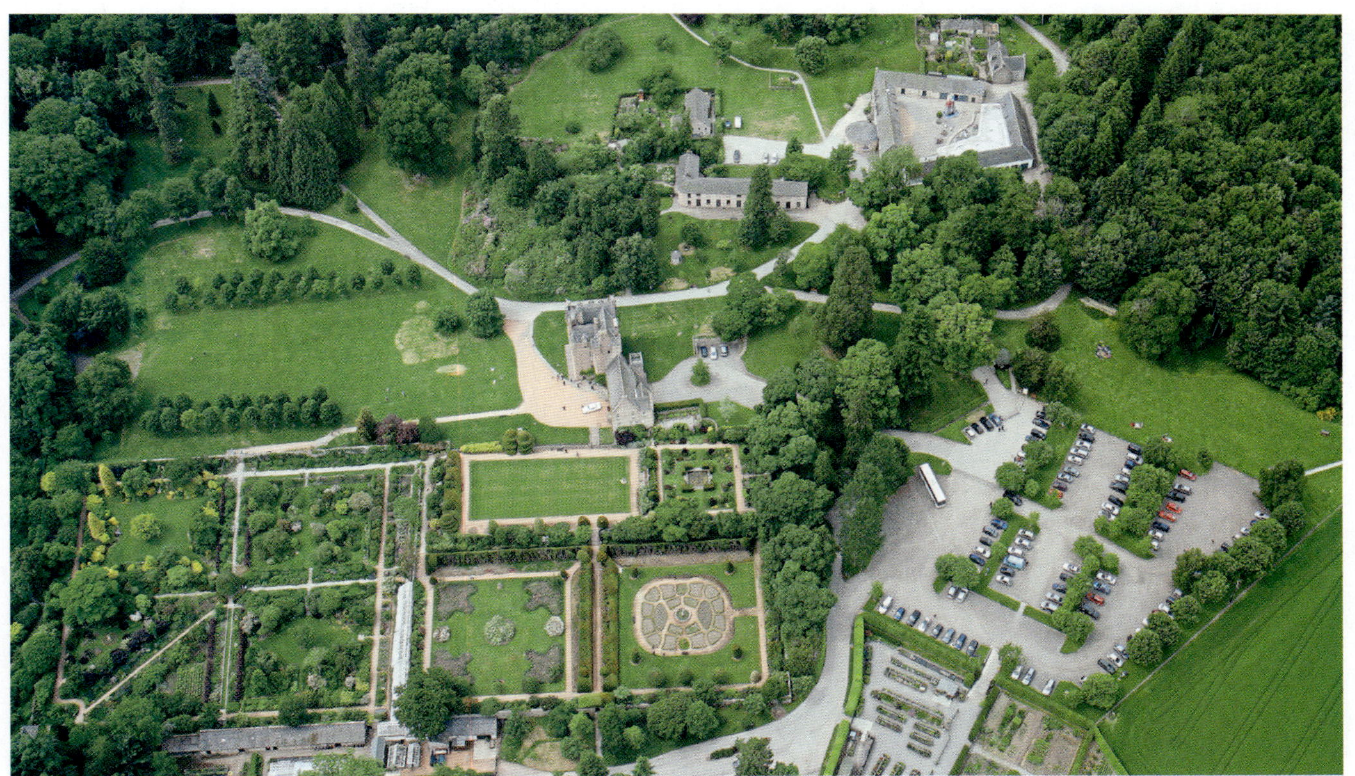

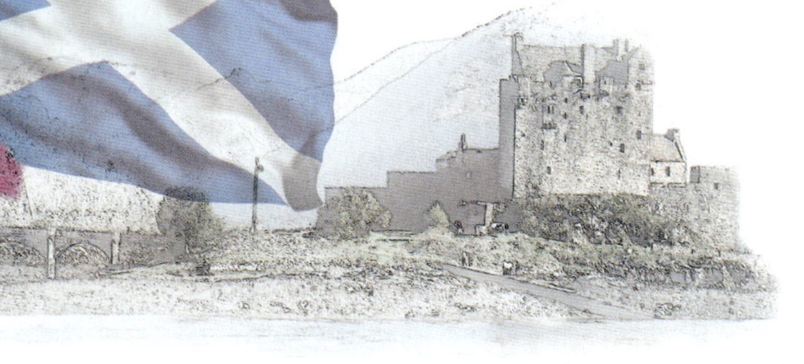

Crichton Castle

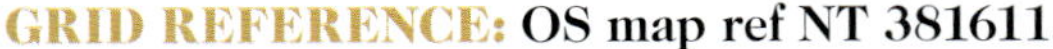

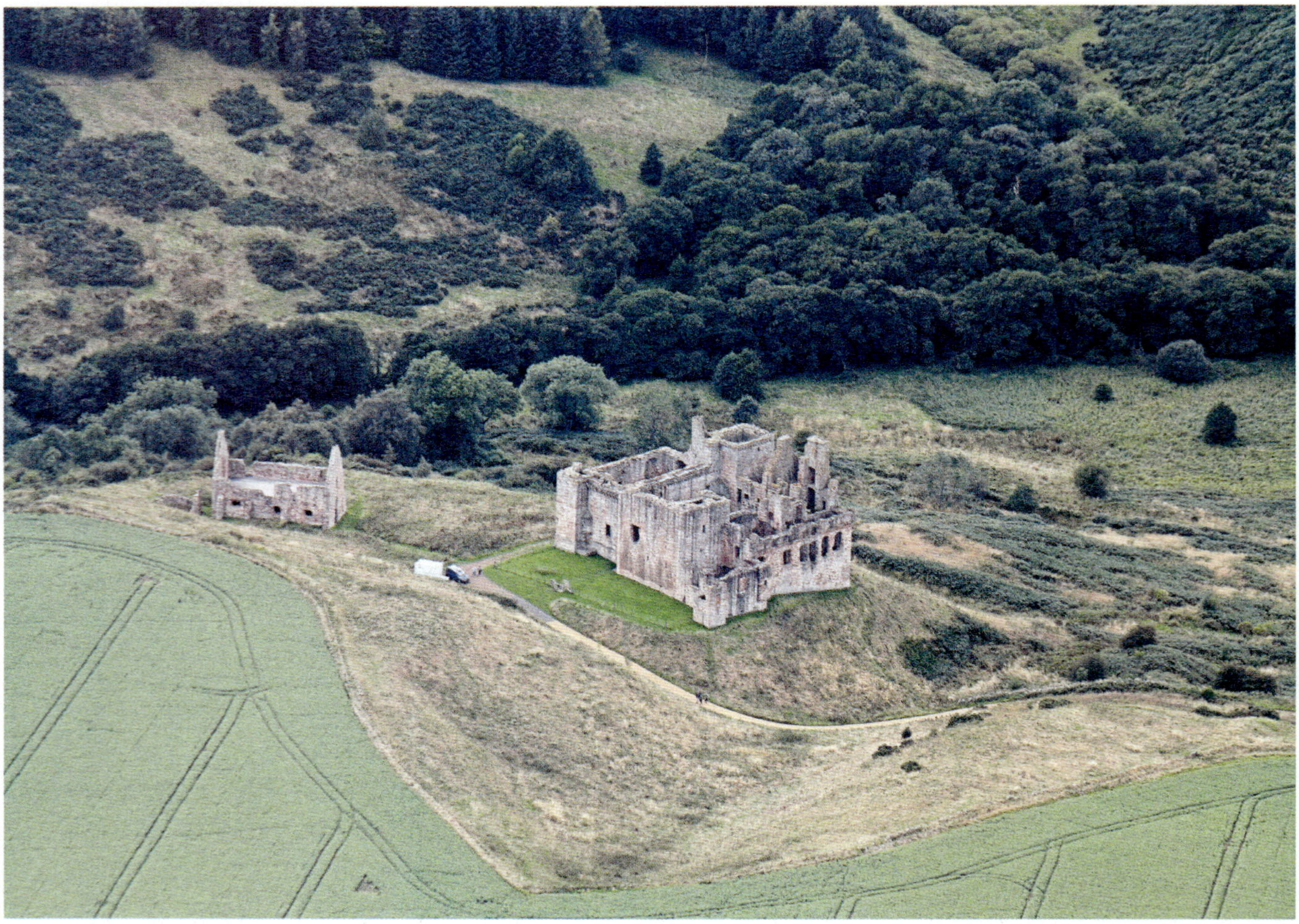

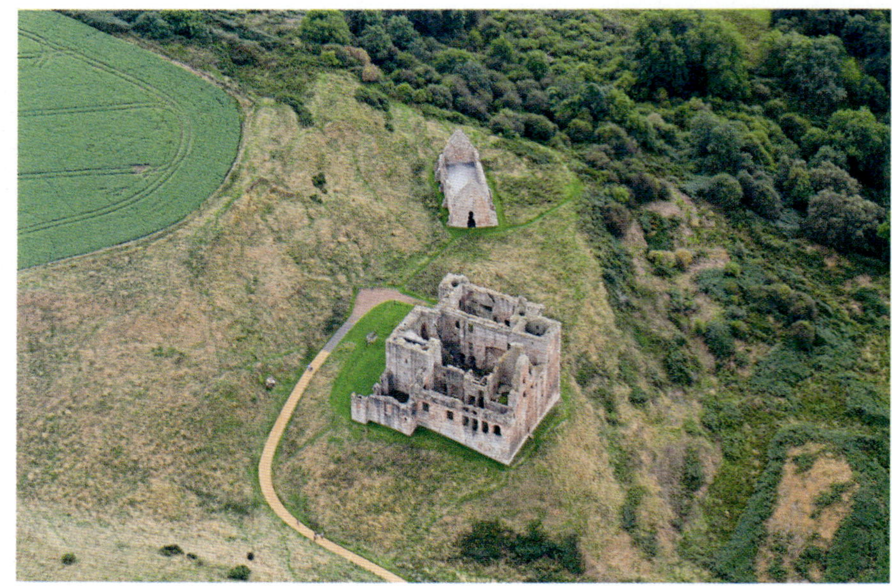

Weaving a path across the centuries, the Crichtons had a ruthless role in the turbulent history of Scotland. The castle bears the scars as well as evidence of the lavish lifestyle they aspired to. After changing hands numerous times, the castle fell into ruin during the 1600s and today stands as a monument to the ambitions of its long dead former owners.

Visitor Details

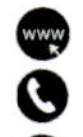 www.historicenvironment.scot/visit-a-place/places/crichton-castle

 01875 320017

The interior was closed for a time but was due to be reopened. Check the website for current details.

 There is access only to the ground floor but no toilet facilities.

Bring your own food and drink.

 A small shop on site for entry tickets.

Location: Crichton Castle can be found in the Moorefoot Hills 15 miles south east of Edinburgh. Leave the A68 at Pathead, follow the B road for two miles to Crichton village then follow the signposts to a car park just past the medieval church. The castle can be seen from here overlooking the River Tyne. Walk along the track for a half mile to reach the ruin. The large nearby roofless stone building is the former stable block.

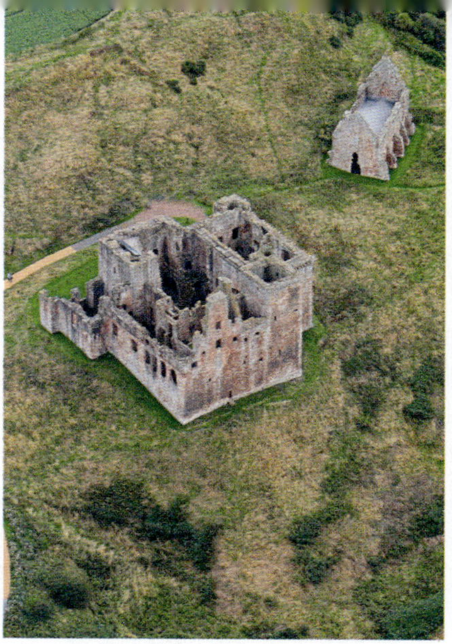

A strong three-storey keep was the first structure built on the site in the late 14th century. It included a pit prison and vaulted basement. This castle was to become the family home of the wealthy John De Crichton. His son, William, held the powerful position of Chancellor of Scotland and became a lord around 1443. In 1440, he eliminated his political opponents by having them attend a feast at Edinburgh Castle and then arranged the murder of the 6th Earl of Douglas, his brother and Sir Malcolm Fleming of Cumbernauld as they dined.

Perhaps William later had misgivings about ordering these three killings. He financed the building of the collegiate church in Crichton village and his restless ghost has been reported riding his horse through the castle's original entrance which is now walled off. A revenge attack on the castle happened as a direct result of the murders. In 1445, the chief of Clan Forrester called John of Corstorphine slighted the buildings with his raiding men. This resulted in some walls being pulled down and the keep damaged. This did not make William abandon his power base however. Instead, he rebuilt the tower house and walls. Then he added a three-storey gatehouse, ranges to enclose the small courtyard and built the nearby church. His funding also paid for a provost, eight canons, two choir boys and a sacrist to pray for the souls of the Crichton family at the church.

In 1482, Alexander Stewart, the Duke of Albany, led an invasion of Scotland by the army of King Edward IV. This failed when many Scottish lords opposed him. However, the third Lord Crichton supported his takeover bid and as a result his castle and lands were declared forfeit in 1483.

The new owners of the castle were the Ramsay Clan but they only lasted for five years in residence. Then in 1489, James IV granted Crichton to Patrick Hepburn who later became the Earl of Bothwell.

James Hepburn, the fourth Earl of Bothwell, remained loyal to the Catholic Mary of Guise despite a number of Protestant lords planning her overthrow. In 1559, he ambushed a convoy carrying 4000 crowns from Elizabeth I to support the Protestant lords' coup attempt. This was a significant robbery worth £137,000 today which could buy 121 horses in 1559. Soon afterwards, the Earl of Arran's troops besieged the castle and then gained entry, just missing the capture of James Hepburn. When he was told of the recent death of Mary, he fled to Norway expecting support from the Danish royal family. Found guilty of treason in Scotland while abroad, he lost his estate and castle. Matters worsened for him when he was imprisoned in Dragsholm Castle in Denmark where he spent his final 11 years suffering in severe conditions. Ironically that castle is now a luxury hotel.

After Bothwell's forfeiture, Crichton Castle was granted to Francis Stewart. In the 1580s, he made changes to the castle including adding the distinctive courtyard wall diamond-pattern stone carvings inspired by his travels to Italy in his younger years. Unfortunately, his openly hostile attitude to England's supporters incited him to murder a courtier. His attempt to raise support for an invasion of England led to him spending some time imprisoned in Edinburgh Castle. By 1591, rumours spread that he was using witchcraft to harm the king and a conviction for treason followed in 1595. Francis fled to Italy where he lived out his final days in Naples. His son tried to keep the castle and estate but debts forced a sale to the Hepburns of Humbie. They in turn sold the crumbling pile as a source of building stones. Sir Walter Scott highlighted the castle in his novel Marmion, Turner painted the ruin and the ghost still roams on horseback. In 1956, the owner gave the ruin to the state and this is how Historic Environment Scotland became custodians. Films such as Rob Roy have featured the castle. If walls could talk you would be astounded to hear the details of what they witnessed at this turbulent wild redoubt.

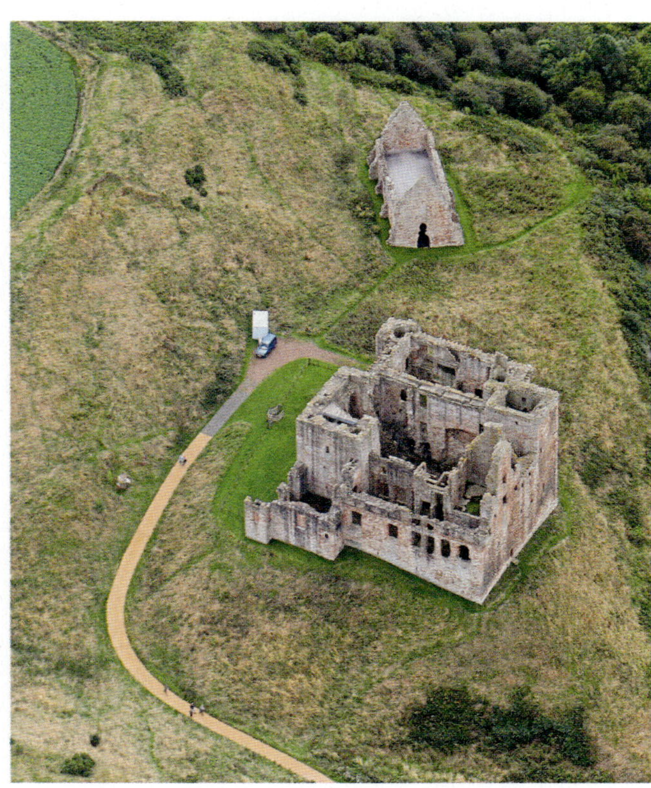

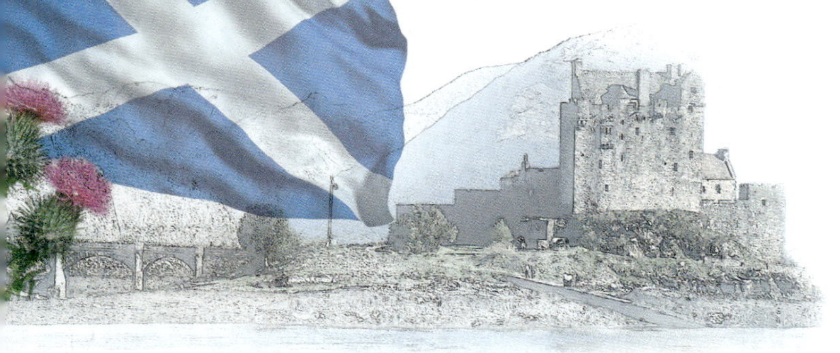

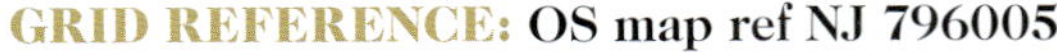

Drum Castle

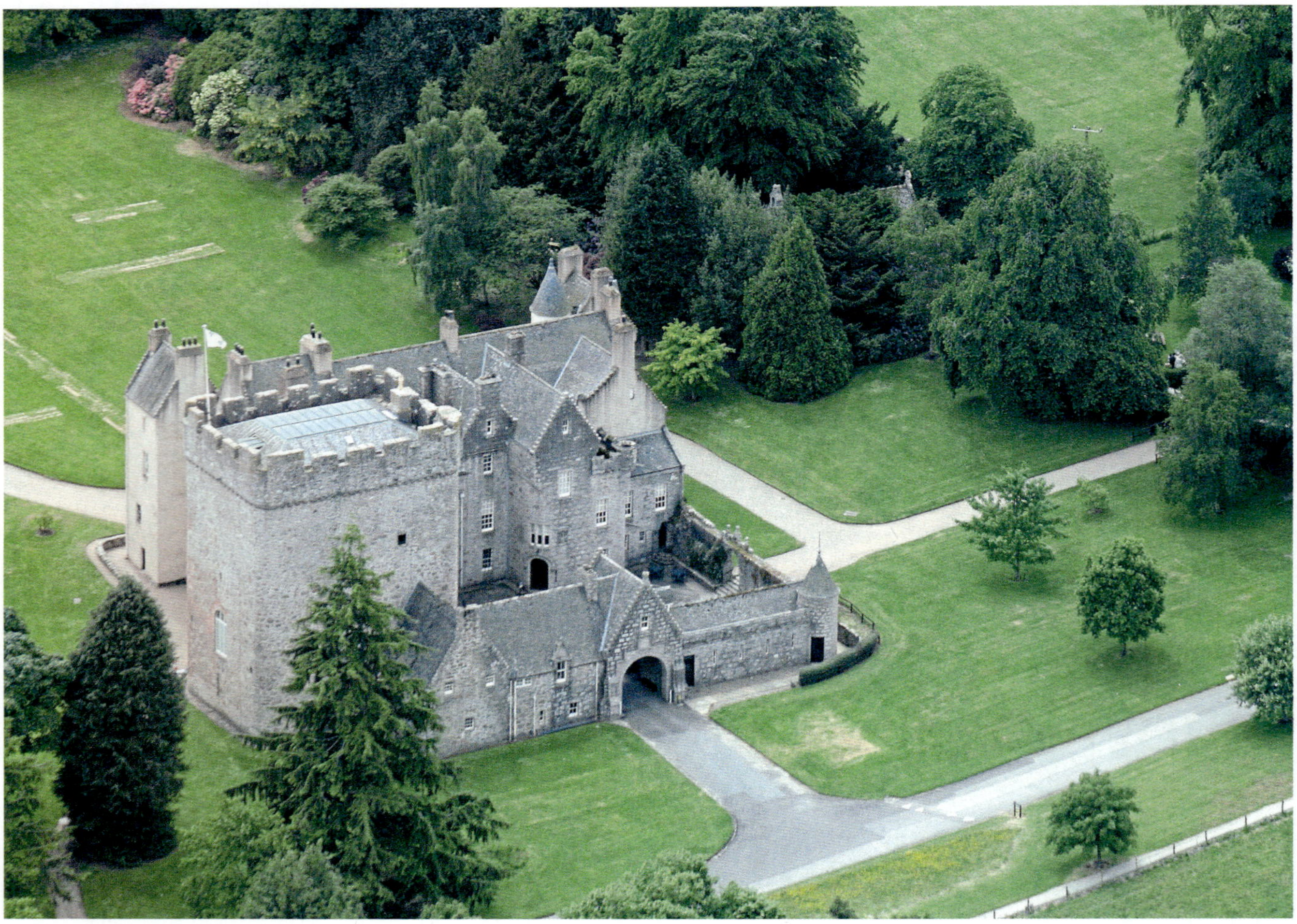

One of Scotland's oldest tower houses, Drum had been in the possession of the Irvine clan for an incredible 24 generations before it was finally taken on by the National Trust for Scotland in the 1970s. Surrounded by ancient oak woodland and accompanied by the beautiful Garden of Historic Roses, this grand building has sprawling extensions to explore too.

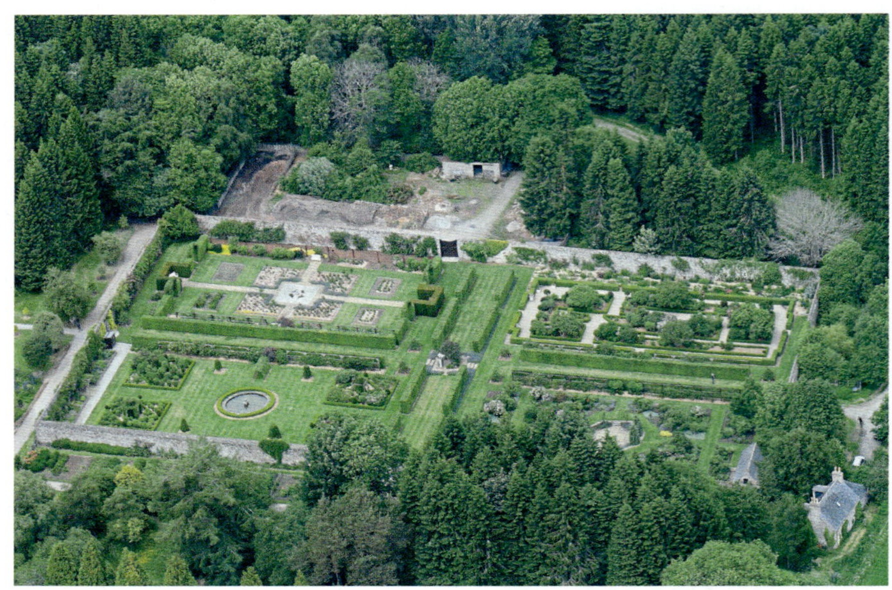

Visitor Details

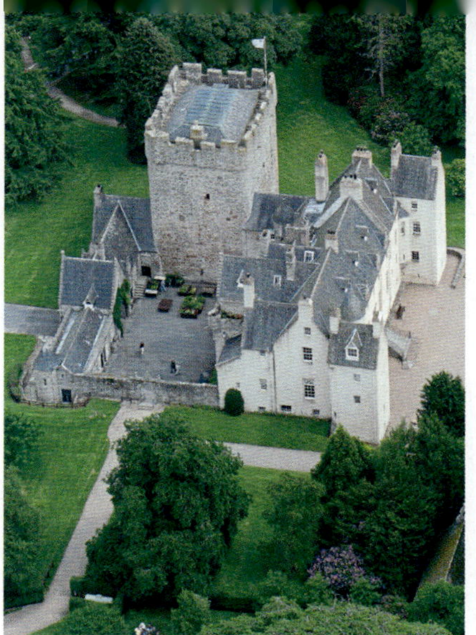

 www.nts.org.uk/visit/places/drum-castle

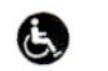 01330 700334

Normal opening times for the castle are from early April to September daily from 10am to 6pm.

Accessible car park and toilets.

Tearoom on site.

The grounds are open all year. Check the website or phone for updates.

Location: Drum Castle can be found in Kincardine and Deeside County. It is only a half mile from the A93. Travelling west from Aberdeen, pass through Peterculter. After three miles, turn right towards Drum Castle. Heading east from Banchory, journey eight miles and then turn left, progressing to Drum Castle.

King Robert the Bruce handed over the lands around what became Drum Castle to William de Irwyn in 1325. William was a close friend and held several official positions with the King: secretary, armour bearer and standard bearer (hopefully not all at the same time). Then followed 24 generations of the Clan Irvine occupying the castle spanning 650 years, a fantastic record. So little has been changed in the tower house that it was subject to an archaeological excavation in the 1990s.

It is likely that the tower house was built between 1280 and 1300 by Richard Cementarius, an architect of Aberdeen.

The mansion and Jacobean house that surround the tower were added by Alexander, the ninth Laird, in 1619.

Despite it being held by one family, the castle and clan had their share of local skirmishes and attacks. They were very good at recovering afterwards, but not so good at choosing the winning side. Here are some of the events:

* Supported the Royalist cause of Charles I, suffering two castle sieges and sackings in 1644 and 1645 by Argyle's government army.

* Supported the Jacobite cause in 1715 when the 14th Lord Alexander died from injuries inflicted during the battle of Sherrifmuir. In 1746, the 17th Earl took the field to fight at

Culloden. He then escaped capture by hiding in a secret part of the castle before he left for exile in France for a few years. Somehow he also avoided having the family property seized by the state in his absence.

In addition, a longer series of feuds continued with the local clans, the Forbes and the Keiths.

Alexander Forbes Irvine inherited the estate and castle in 1861, on the death of his father. In 1876, he had the courtyard restored and added an arched entrance and angle tower. The chapel was also improved. In 1878, Forbes was elected a Fellow of the Royal Society of Edinburgh for his work as an advocate, philosopher and amateur astronomer.

The castle and grounds became the property of the National Trust for Scotland in 1975. They have gradually improved the well-loved but worn buildings. After 1987, the trust also took on the big task of restoring the neglected gardens which were reported as derelict in that year.

The beautiful Garden of Historic Roses is divided into quadrants that show how roses have been cultivated from the 17th to the 20th century. The ancient oak forest adjoining the castle provides an insight into how forests used to look before commercial plantations spread.

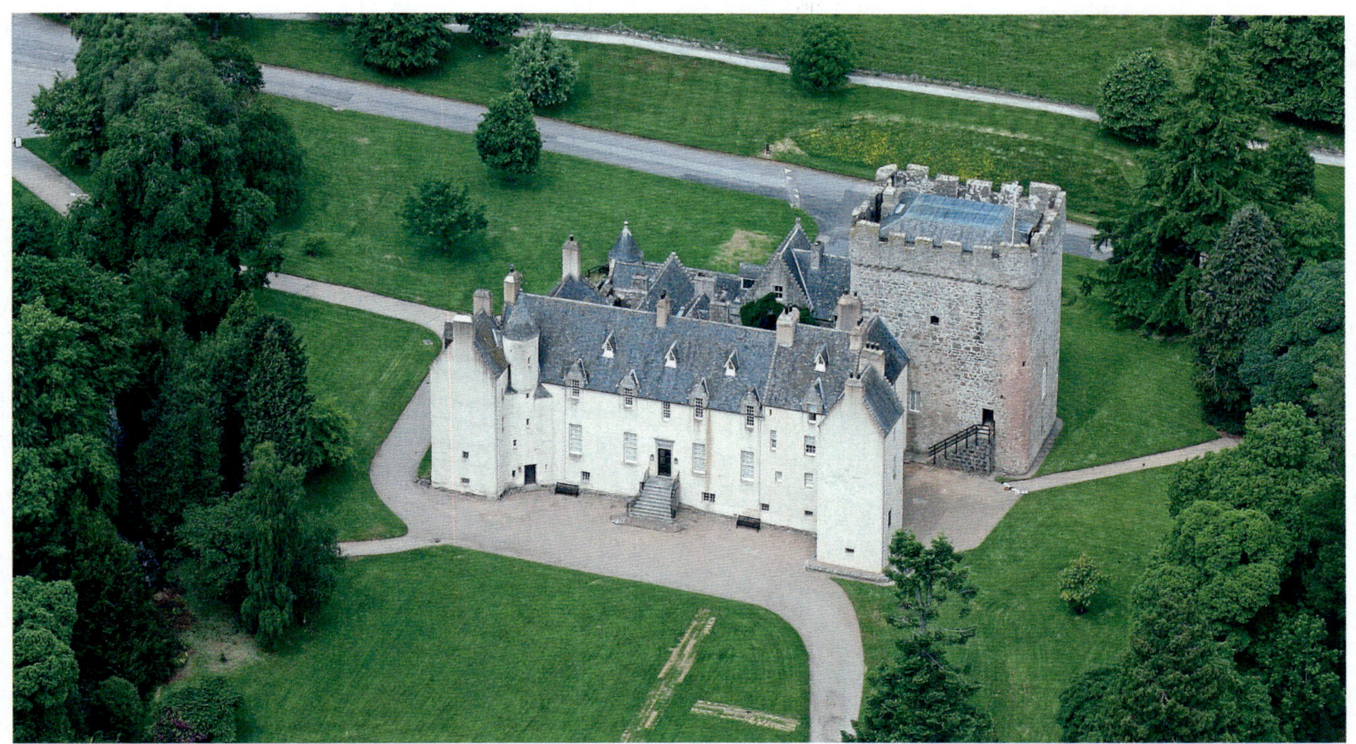

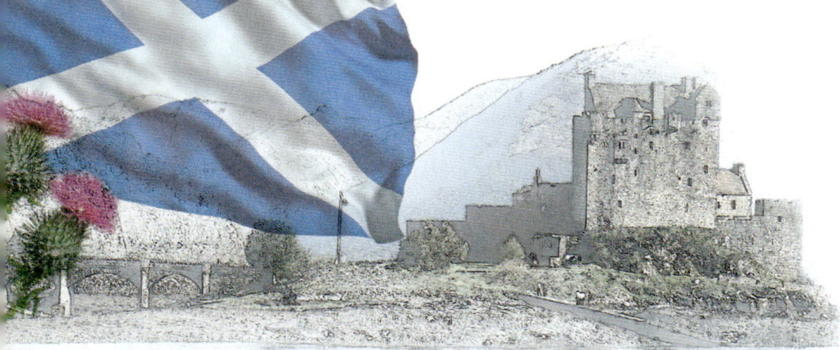

GRID REFERENCE: OS map ref NM 749355.

Duart Castle

Modern travellers may consider the location as out of the way, however, in earlier times the sea, firths and navigable rivers formed highways on the Atlantic fringe. From the castle battlements it is easy to view the three sea channels where Loch Linnhe, the Sound of Mull and the Firth of Lorne meet. Trade between the west of Scotland and what is now Ireland could be observed and controlled if needed. The rocky outcrop on Dubh Ard was a fort location held by Clan MacDougall in the 13th century before the first stone keep was built after 1360 by the new occupier, Lachlan Lubanach Maclean, the 5th Chief. He added the keep to the outside of the curtain wall and courtyard in the 14th century, making sure he had easy access to the well inside his keep. We know how Lachlan Maclean gained residence because records exist showing the castle was a wedding gift from the Lord of the Isles when Maclean was betrothed to Lady Elizabeth, the Lord's daughter in 1360. However, another Lachlan, the 11th chief Lachlan Cattanach, sowed the seeds of his own demise in the 1520s. He stranded his wife, Margaret Campbell, in chains on wave ravaged rocks in the firth expecting her to drown in the rising tide. Luckily for her, a passing fisherman rescued her in time. Her father, Campbell Earl of Argyll, became her protector afterwards and Lachlan Cattanach was put on the Clan Campbell hit list. The contract killing was fulfilled by Sir John Campbell of Cawdor

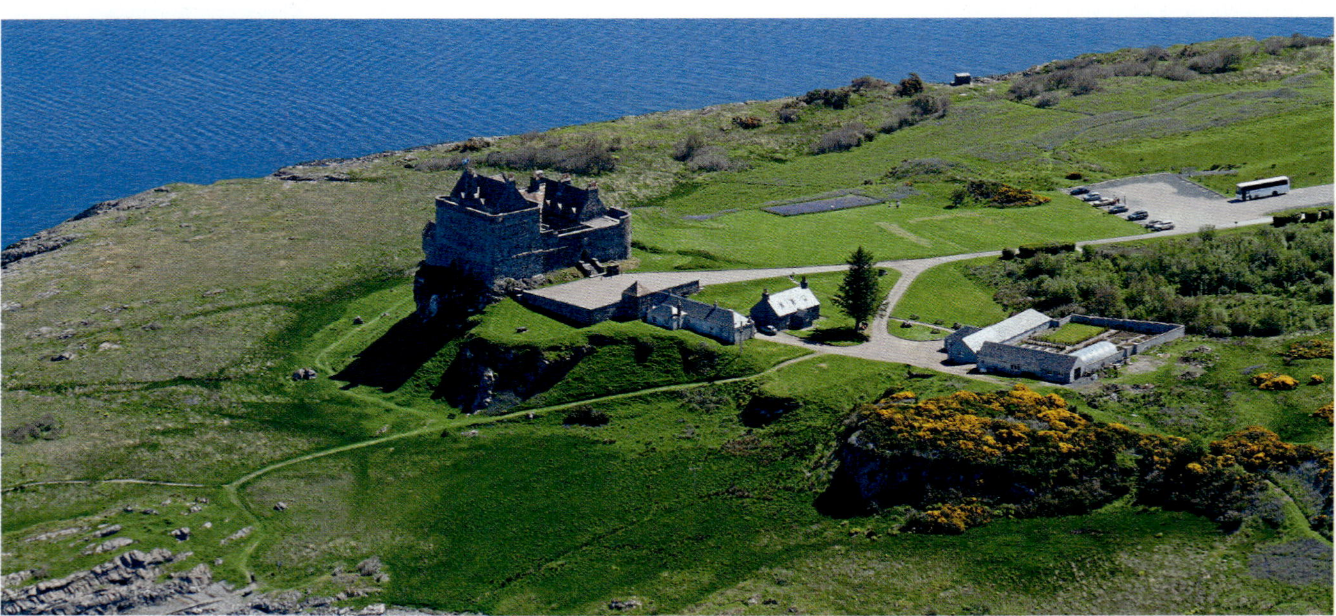

ABOUT THE CLAN

The clan's first chief was Gillean na Tuaighe, Gillean of the Battle Axe, a noble warrior who fought at the Battle of Largs in 1263 when the Vikings were beaten. His great great grandson settled in Mull. On these lands, granted in 1390 by Donald Lord of the Isles, two clan branches were established by MacLaine of Lochbuie and Maclean of Duart. These Macleans later expanded settlements into Tiree , Islay, Jura, Knapdale, Morvern and Lochaber.

The third chief Malcolm Mac Giliosa married the daughter of the Earl of Carrick. This placed the clan in a good position with the House of Bruce. Malcolm commanded the trade by sea in their region. This was a way to also increase the clans influence with the rulers of Scotland, their

Clan Maclean

Birlinns (galleys) were also troop ferries. Clan Maclean fought in support of Robert the Bruce at the Battle of Bannockburn in 1314. The 6th chief, Red Hector Maclean of Duart fought at the Battle of Harlaw in 1411. His epic single combat fight with the chief of Clan Irvine resulted in them both dying by wounds and resulting loss of blood. Lachlan Maclean of Duart was killed at the Battle of Flodden in 1513 when 56,000 fought in Northumberland and of those 14,000 died. It was a decisive English victory and remains the largest battle between the nations. Scotland's King James IV and many other Scots nobles perished in the battle. In 1560 the Irish King Shane O Neill paid for the military mercenaries of the Gallowglas

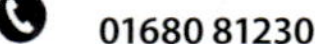

Visitor Details

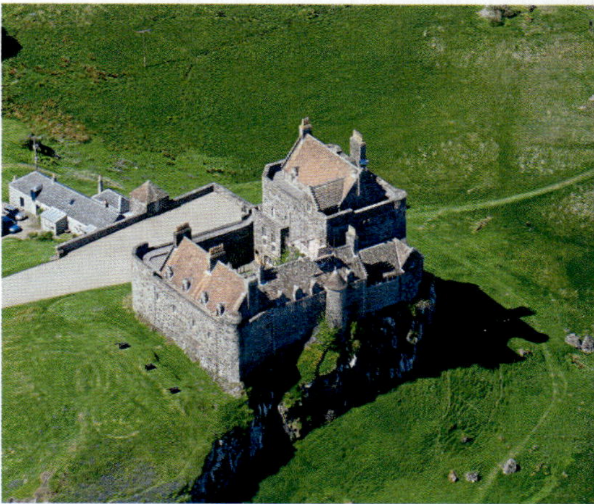

www.duartcastle.com

01680 812309

Duart Castle is also usually closed during the winter months from November to March. For admission prices, see website.

Disabled access to the castle interior is difficult due to the many steps which cannot be changed. There is access to the gift shop and tea room.

A tea room and gift shop are on site.

The castle sits astride a rock knoll above the promontory of Black Point, Dubh Ard.

Location: Duart Castle is semi-remote due to its location on the Island of Mull which is linked to the mainland by regular large ferries from Oban. The voyage takes around 45 minutes. The ferry terminal is at Craignure just three miles from the castle on the A839, the main island road.

when he murdered Lachlan in his bed in Edinburgh in 1527. The walls on the landward side of the castle are 3m thick. This proved useful in 1647 when Clan Campbell failed in a siege to overcome the castle's defences.

In 1604, Maclean of Duart and many other clan chiefs were kidnapped when they unwisely accepted an invitation to dinner and drinks on a Royal Navy ship in the Sound of Mull. The cost of his freedom was to surrender his war galleys and pledge allegiance to King James VI.

Being a Royalist led to many troubles ahead for the Duart Macleans. In 1647, the castle was taken by the forces of General Leslie. Several sieges followed and many men and much money were lost in supporting the Jacobites with the Battle of Inverkeithing in 1651 being the worst loss of clan followers. Cromwell despatched a flotilla of six ships to bombard the castle in 1653 but Maclean and his family had departed ahead of them. It was hard to sneak up when the castle lookouts had such a wide viewpoint! The ships anchored nearby but they were caught in a storm. It was September and even to this day that month can produce great gales in the region. Three ships were sunk just below the cliffs.

More recently, a team from Saint Andrews University have excavated the seabed recovering cannons and other artefacts some of which are displayed at the castle.

The Campbells still continued their vendetta. In 1678, the 9th Earl of Argyll, Archibald Campbell, took lands on Mull from the Clan Maclean also forcing Sir John Maclean to depart hastily from Duart and be given sanctuary by the Earl of Seaforth in Kintail. Later while the Clan Maclean were fighting at Killiecrankie

in 1689, the Campbells brought cannon-equipped ships to bombard the castle again. It was no longer safe as a family home. The final surrender of the castle took place in 1691 to the 1st Duke of Argyll, a Campbell of course. He also held much of the former Maclean lands as payments against debts. Gradually the Campbells reduced the castle stone works, some being used for local buildings. Government Hanoverian soldiers used the castle for a short time making certain to fire the buildings as part of the post-1745 punishment of royalist supporters. By 1751, the castle was roofless and the timber floor supports burned out.

Just after a century had passed, the ruined castle had left the clutches of the Campbells and in 1865, AC Guthrie held the Torosay estate including the ruins. Sir Fitzroy Donald Maclean, the 26th Clan Chief, purchased the derelict castle site in 1911 and started a 25 year restoration. This epic task returned the castle to what you can see today.

It is one of the very few castles occupied by members of the original clan who also recognise the clan society and host clan gatherings from around the world. The castle and its contents are a place of pilgrimage for many Macleans. Visitors have rated highly the knowledge of the guides and their friendly manner. The keep, dungeons, great hall and other suitably furnished rooms are open to view. Assorted weapons, portraits, trophies and clan memorabilia all clamour for attention.

The castle is owned by the Macleans of Duart and Morvern and is still a family home. The upkeep of such an old structure can no longer be met entirely by the family. Recently, an appeal to fund the £1.2 million cost of repairs was launched of which half has already been raised.

to increase his army's impact. He hired Clans MacKay, Macleod and Maclean as part of this task force. Sir Lachlan Maclean was made a Baronet of Nova Scotia in 1631. Later he brought his clan to support the Royalists in the Scottish Civil Wars. The clan supported the Jacobite cause in 1715. In 1716 Sir Hector was given a Jacobite peerage for his clans support. At the Battle of Culloden the clan was led by Maclean of Drimmin, he sadly did not survive. Although the Jacobites failed this did not deter the Macleans from serving with distinction in the British army later, for example all the chiefs that followed were soldiers of the crown. Duart castle on the Isle of Mull is the historic seat of the chiefs of the Clan Maclean and is

detailed elsewhere in this book. Sir Lachlan Hector Charles Maclean of Duart and Morven, 12th Baronet, CVO, DL is the 28th chief of the clan and resides at the castle.

Castle Spioradain, west of Inverness near the current Bona lighthouse, was the location of a castle guarding a ford of the River Ness held by the Macleans of Dochgarroch in around 1420. The name means castle of spirits and a legend says that during a skirmish between the Macleans and the Camerons several Camerons were executed and their bodies were hung from the walls. The apparitions of the dead are said to have terrorised the castle ruin and the area. The site was destroyed by flooding when the Caledonian Canal was built and human

bones were found. The writer Alistair MacLean is known for his novels, some becoming films such as The Guns of Navaronne. He wrote the screenplay for When Eight Bells Toll and this was filmed at Duart Castle.

Motto: "Virtue mine honour".

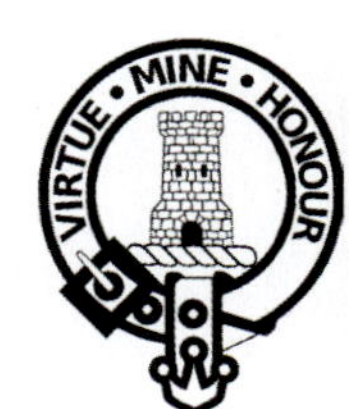
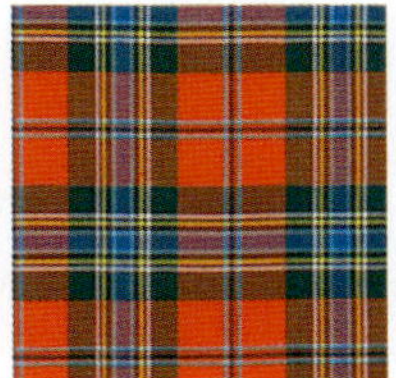

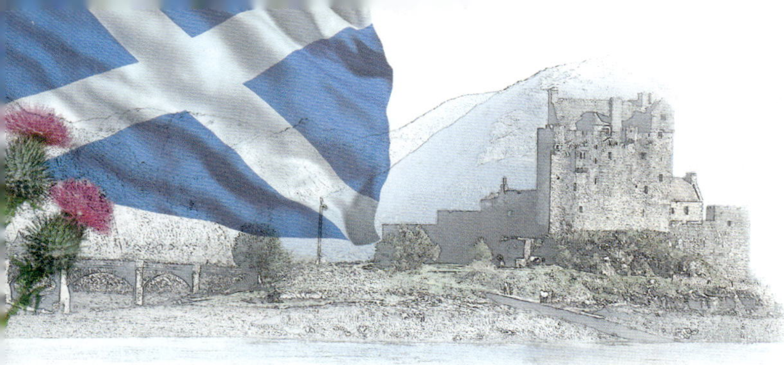

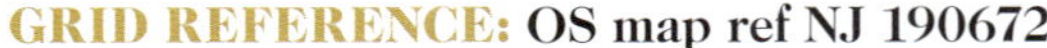

Duffus Castle

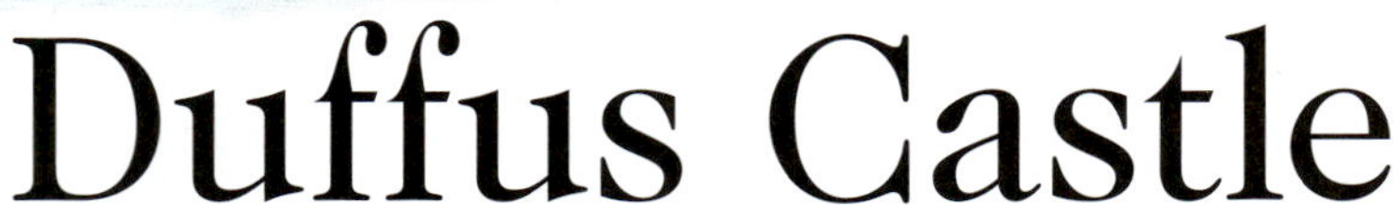

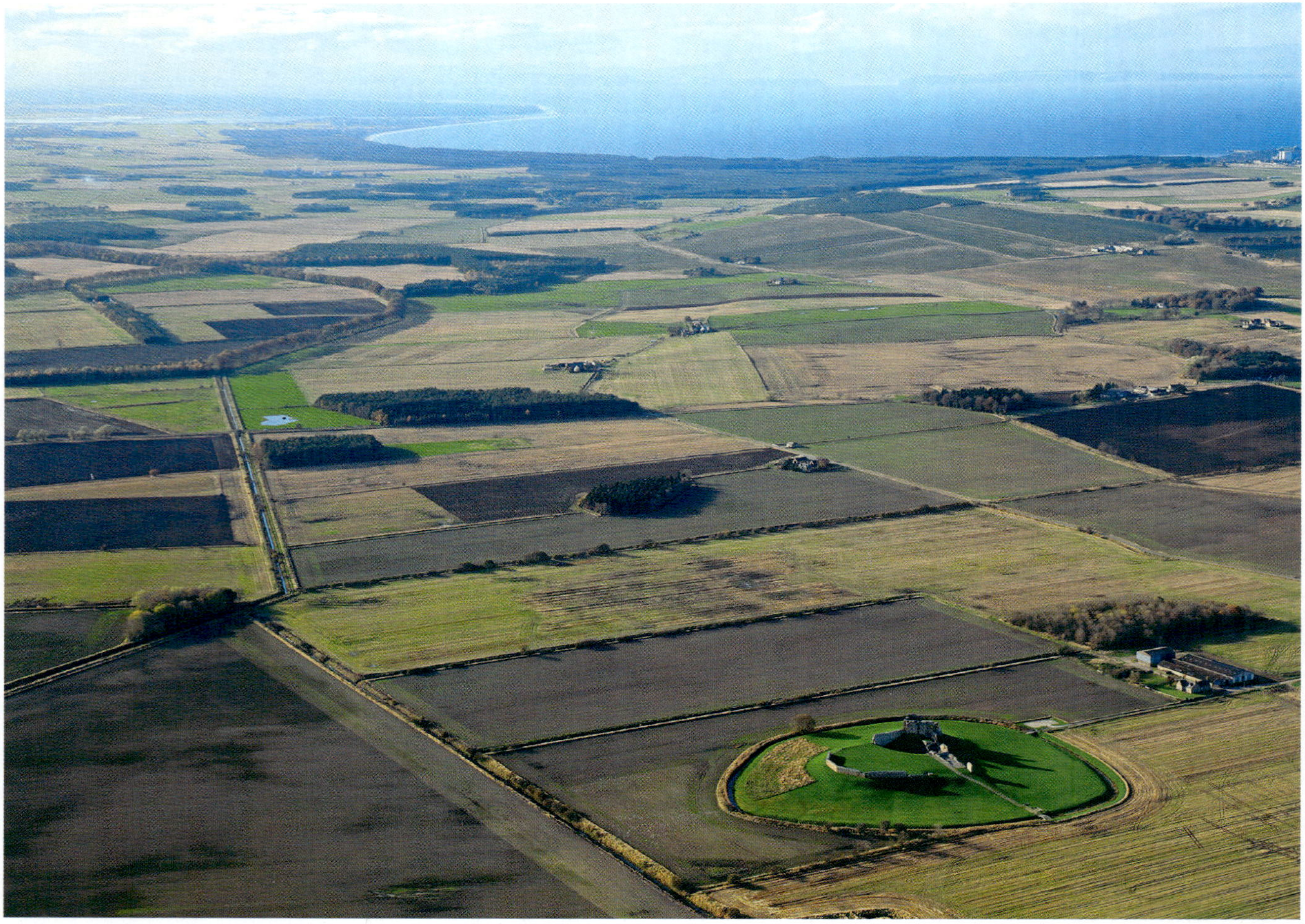

Norman lords built this motte and bailey fortress as a means of imposing their power and authority over the local people and its ruins still stand guard over the surrounding landscape. While those ancient displays of military might have long since been consigned to the history books, visitors today can experience a relatively new form of military power, as RAF jets can frequently be seen flying overhead.

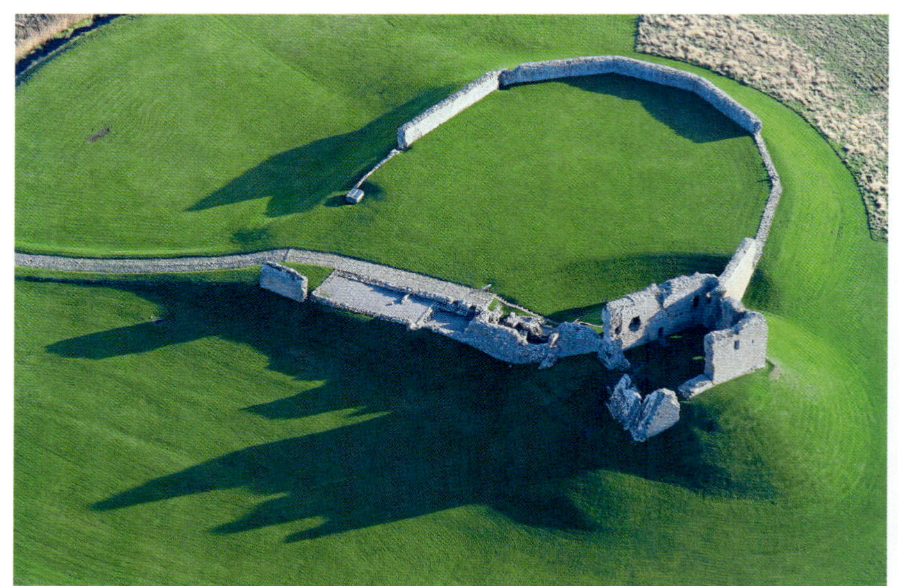

Visitor Details

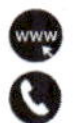 www.historicenvironment.scot/visit-a-place/places/duffus-castle

 No telephone.

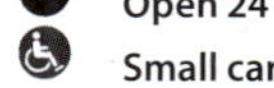 Open 24 hours.

 Small car park. Exploring the ruins involves climbing grassy banks and stout footwear is needed.

No facilities on site.

Lossiemouth town a few miles north east has cafes along the river side and harbour.

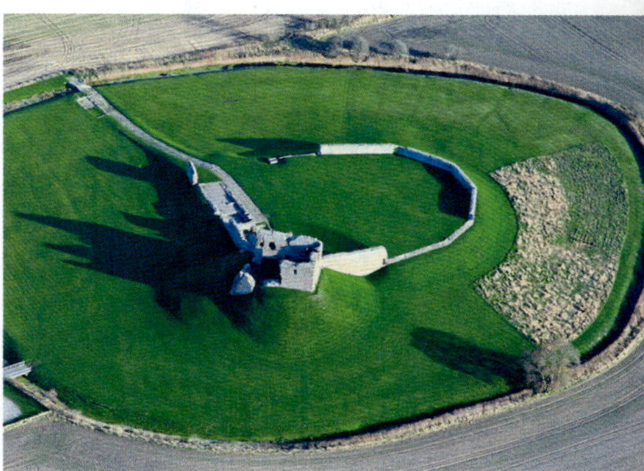

Location: Between Elgin and Lossiemouth in the county of Morayshire. Turn west off the B9135 passing the south edge of RAF Lossiemouth airfield for two miles, car park and castle visible on a mound from this minor road.

Originally this castle rose as a timber fort on its man-made mound above a wild area of marshland known as the Laich of Moray. The builders of this style of fortification, motte and bailey, were the Normans. They never conquered Scotland but sought to extend power from scattered castle bases . The local men of Moray indeed challenged the keeper of the castle, Freskin, a Flanders knight, in 1116 and 1130. He maintained his influence though, later becoming known as Freskin De Moravia. His family line later became defenders of Scotland.

By the 14th century a stone keep was added to the mound, the timber buildings having suffered in raids by the Scots. The master was then Sir Reginald de Chen who turn paid homage to Edward I of England.

By marriage the owner later became Sutherland Lord Duffus in 1350, also regaining the line of House of Freskin. Some time after the last recorded attack on the castle by Montrose royalists in 1645 they witnessed the final days of the keep which during terrible storms and heavy rains cracked open leaving the ruin seen today.

The family moved to a new nearby mansion called Duffus House which is said to include some castle stonework.

In 1934 this location formed the starting point of the internationally famed Gordonstoun School, keeping Moray well connected to the wider world.

Duffus castle as a memorial to the Normans remains impressive and is the largest of its type in Scotland. While viewing the stabilised ruin, keep watch for the modern defenders of the area, the Typhoon and Poseidon jets of the Royal Air Force.

ABOUT THE CLAN

Scotland and the Normans

The Normans originated as Scandanavian settlers in the 10th century around the Rouen Seine area of what is now called Normandy in France. Ironically the first Viking leader Rollo (baptised later as Robert) living in the area did so at the invitation of a Frankish King in exchange for protection against more Viking raiders who had been pillaging rich monasteries in the region. Hence the first Duchy of Normandy was created and grew with local conquests. The seafaring prowess of these North Men and trade with small Viking settlements in Kent gave them an insight into the politics and potential land prospects across the channel in England. The Dukes of Normandy paid homage to the King of France but they raised their own taxes, struck coinage, dispensed justice without courts and kept their lords loyal with fiefdoms, also gifting valuable lands to abbeys.

William the Conqueror was a descendent of Rollo. He decided after growing up in violent times that he was entitled to become King of England as promised to him by his distant relative Edward the Confessor. Instead, Edward chose Earl Harold Godwinson. The solution William chose was to plan a violent takeover which culminated in an invasion fleet leading to a clash with Harold's Anglo-Saxon army at Battle, near Hastings, in 1066. Unusually the site of the epic clash is certain because William had an abbey built there in gratitude to his Christian god. The Normans had arrived and never left.

Norman nobleman Odo of Bayeux, half-brother of William the Conqueror, is the most likely patron which enabled the creation of a huge embroidery artwork now called the Bayeux tapestry. This almost 1,000 year old 68m long wall hanging tells the story of the events before and during the battle. The arrow in Harold's eye was added in the 18th century to match the story. For many years the tapestry was only displayed on special occasions which has helped it to stay so vibrant.

Having taken the crown William was keen to take control of England and Wales despite opposition. Most of the land belonged to the Crown now and his civil servants criss crossed England recorded everything worth taxing in a massive manuscript, The Domesday Book, completed in 1085.

Tax exempt status was granted to the City of London and some church held lands. Also absent from the records are details of Scotland which remained independent after a failed invasion in 1072. So valuable was this survey that the manuscripts have survived. As recently as the 1960s, it was still referred to in court cases regarding ancient land and property rights.

Aside from listing land, records of livestock were also made. Another revelation is that at the time ten percent of the population were held as slaves (often taken as prisoners during raids from other regions). This was not approved of by the Normans and the concept of servants was introduced with better conditions as a result.

The takeover of Scotland was partially achieved by giving Norman nobles land in Scotland as a reward for services in battle, a castle was then built in the area to ensure the Normans stayed in control. This was not welcomed by many of the local population resulting in roving bands of 'Silvatici', The Wildmen, marking the start of harassment by outlaws. Also influence was gained by marriages the most prominent being the betrothal of William the Conqueror's young son Henry to the daughter of Malcolm Canmore, King of Scotland. He became King Henry I in 1100. Queen Maud's younger brother, David, was raised in the court of Henry. He spoke French and had many Norman friends, later marrying the widow of a Norman lord. She brought as her dowry large areas of land in England. In 1124 he became King David I of Scotland.

The sounds of the Normans can be heard in our speech. Poc (pork) and Boeuf (beef) were expensive meats of the nobles while the farmers looked after pigs, sheep and cows. Until 2004, a land or house purchase in Scotland included payment of a Feu duty which started with the Normans who introduced Feudal Tenure. We still have Sheriff courts to dispense justice. For 300 years after their arrival, the language of the landowners and courts was based on French while the commoners spoke middle English and in parts of Scotland Gaelic and Scots. Notably the great leaders had multilingual abilities such as Robert the Bruce (Robert De Brix, a Normandy area) who spoke Anglo-Norman, Gaelic, Latin, Scots and Middle English.

Other clans have origins in Norman families for example Comyn, Fraser and Grant.

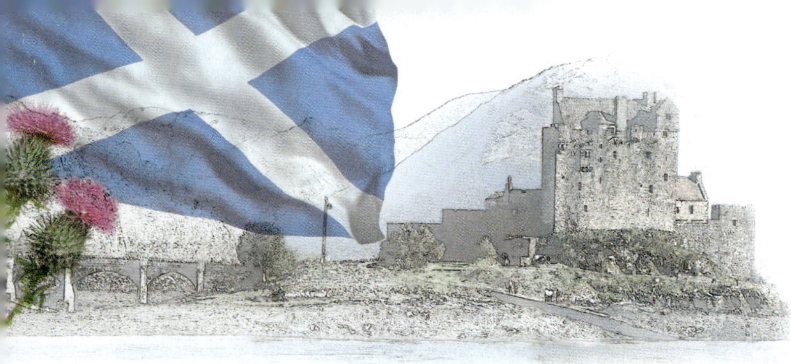

Dunbeath Castle

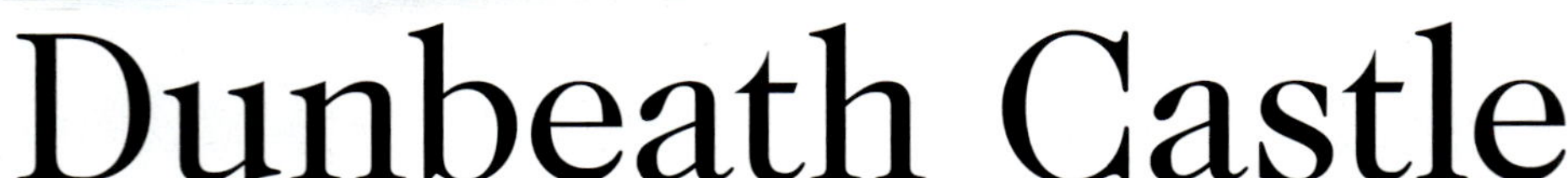

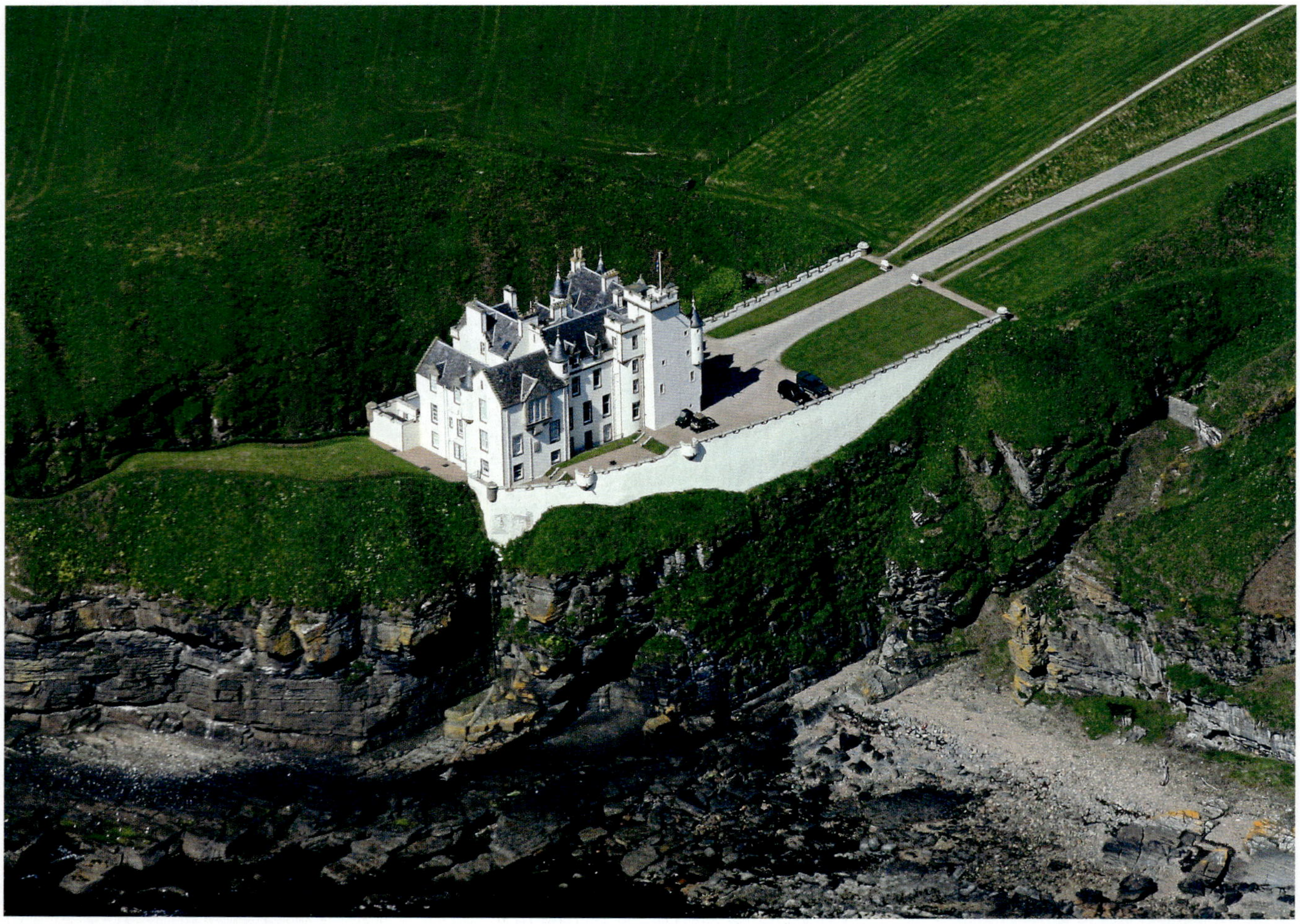

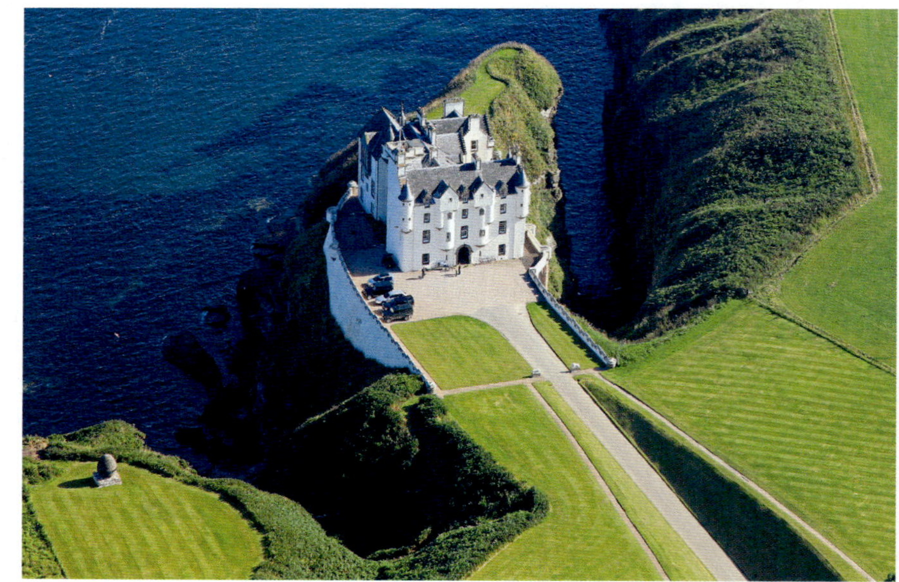

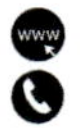

Visitor Details

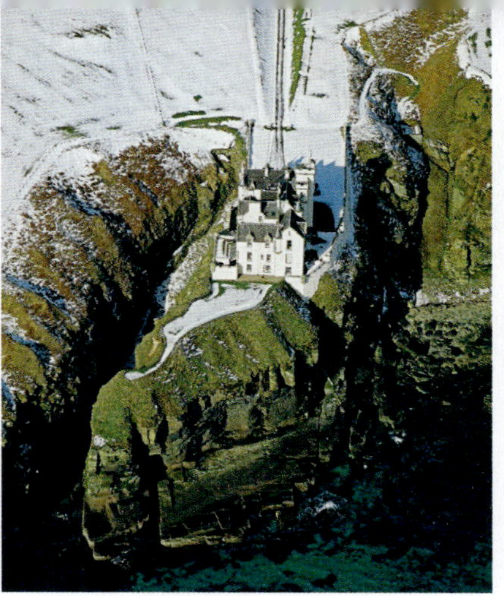

www.dunbeathgardens.co.uk

01593 731308

Dunbeath Castle is a private residence and not open to the public.

Garden paths accessible.

Tearoom for garden visitors.

The gardens are open by appointment all year round.

Location: One mile south of Dunbeath in the county of Caithness and Sutherland, perched on top of cliffs. Visible from Dunbeath. Detailed directions by road to visit the gardens are available on the website.

The first record of a castle on this clifftop included a map which depicted it on a small island. This is likely because the landward defence included a steep ditch across the peninsula. In 1452, the occupiers were the Crichtons. In 1507, the Innes Clan became residents. By marriage, the ownership passed in 1529 to the Sinclair Clan of Geanies. They added a four-storey E plan tower house in 1620. A siege in 1650 by the forces of the Royalist Marquis of Montrose took the castle but their garrison only occupied the castle for two months. The Marquis also tried and failed to capture Dunrobin Castle.

After the defeat of the royalist forces at the Battle of Carbisdale, Dunbeath Castle was retaken by the Sinclair Clan and supporters. They continued to improve the castle with gun loops and shot holes. The basement is vaulted and includes the kitchen with fine sea and coastline views, a large fireplace, wine cellar and stairs.

However, the biggest visible changes occurred in 1853 and 1881 when architect David Bryce was commissioned to add his typical Scottish baronial style embellishments such as bartizans, gables and carved doorways. He created garden designs which included the dramatic castle approach view along the wide cutting he had carved into the local bedrock with walled gardens on both sides. The southern garden was created as a pleasure garden and has remained in good shape over the years. In 1999 it was remodelled by Xa Tollemache, a Chelsea Garden Gold Award winner.

The Sinclair Family ceased to own the castle after 325 years in 1945. When the current owner, Stuart Wyndham Murray-Threipland, purchased the castle and estate in 1997, he brought back a family with strong Jacobite connections. His ancestor had been a personal physician to Bonnie Prince Charlie.

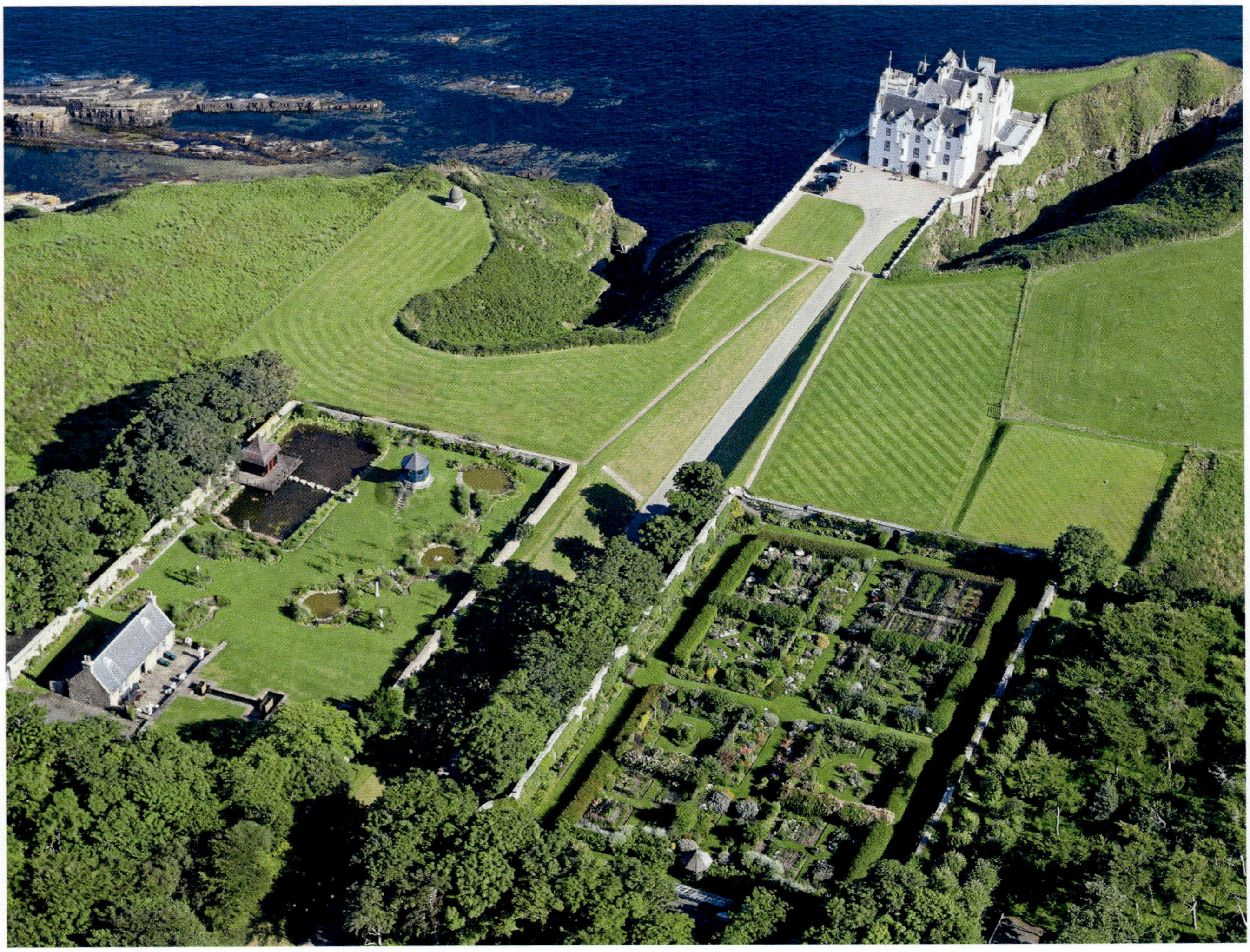

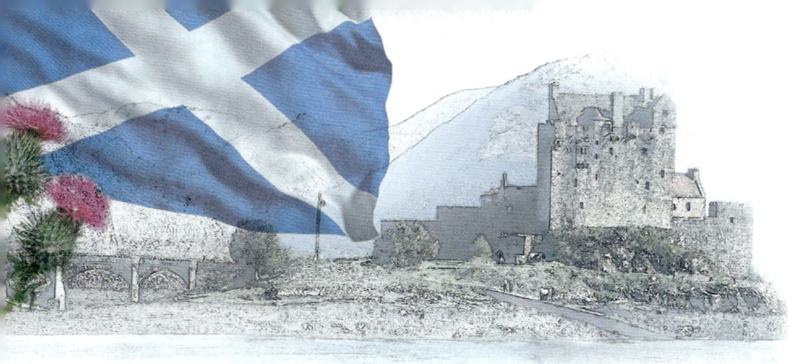

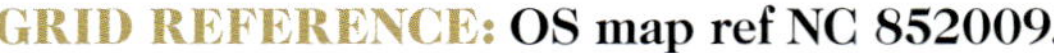

Dunrobin Castle

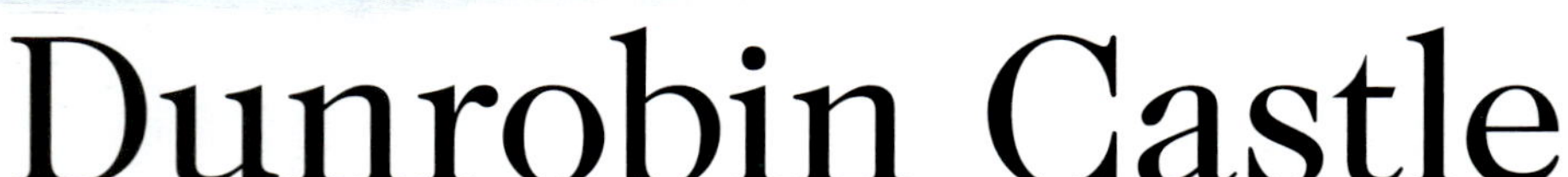

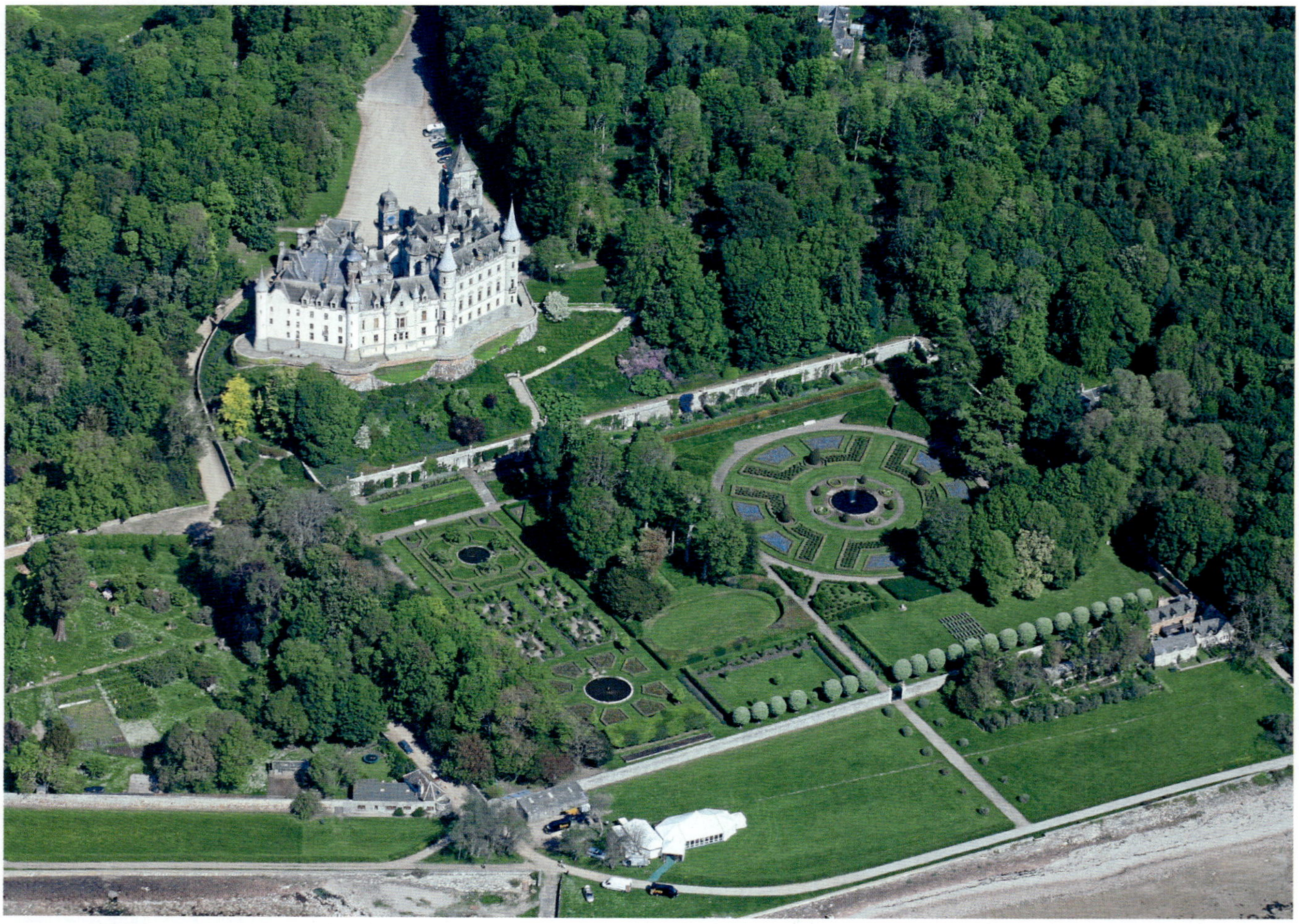

◼ ABOUT THE CLAN

The Norse seafarers also known as Vikings settled Orkney and Caithness and called the rest of the mainland Sudrland, meaning Lands to the South, hence the English name Sutherland. Later a Flemish Knight, Freskin, was given land in Moray by King David I. Following the traditional method of gaining influence and allies, his sons married into the House of Moray becoming known as 'de Moravia'. Freskins grandson, Hugh de Moravia became Lord de Sudrland taking hold of lands in Sutherland as Viking power faded. His eldest son William became the 1st Earl of Sutherland in 1235. This left another relative to establish the line of the Murray clan from Duffus castle.

By 1314 the clan chief William de Moravia was taking part with clansmen in the Battle of Bannockburn defeating the English army. The next Earl Kenneth Sutherland fought at Halidon Hill in 1333 but lost his life. Another Earl, the

Clan Sutherland

5th, William Sutherland, led the clan on a siege of Cupar castle in Fife. His wife Margaret was the daughter of Robert the Bruce.

In 1346 William, Earl of Sutherland and 10,000 troops accompanied King David II of Scotland into England, supported by French supplied weapons and a small French detachment. Both the King, Earl and many more Scottish nobles were captured at the Battle of Nevilles Cross in Durham. This English victory crippled the ability of the Scots to make border raids for the next 20 years .The Earl and King remained in prison for over ten years before being released on payment of huge ransoms.

Setting aside the fights south of the border the local clan feuding continued. Ranged against them were Clans Sinclair, Mackay and Macleod. Nicholas Sutherland of the Duffus branch murdered the chief of the MacKays and his heir at Dingwall castle under the expectation of a

Visitor Details

www.dunrobincastle.co.uk

01408 633177

Open between April 1 and October 31. Tickets between £7.50 and £12.50.

As is usual for a historic building, there are a number of areas where access is not possible for visitors using a wheelchair or those with limited mobility. Contact the castle staff to discuss any access issues when planning your visit. Wheelchair access to the gardens can be arranged on request.

A tea room and gift shop are on site.

The castle admission fee includes the excellent twice daily falconry displays, museum with Pictish stones and extensive gardens.

Location: Overlooking the northern shore of the Moray firth in the county region of Caithness and Sutherland, a half mile north of Golspie signposted from the A9 road. Unusually it has its own railway station on the far north line which links Inverness to Wick and Thurso.

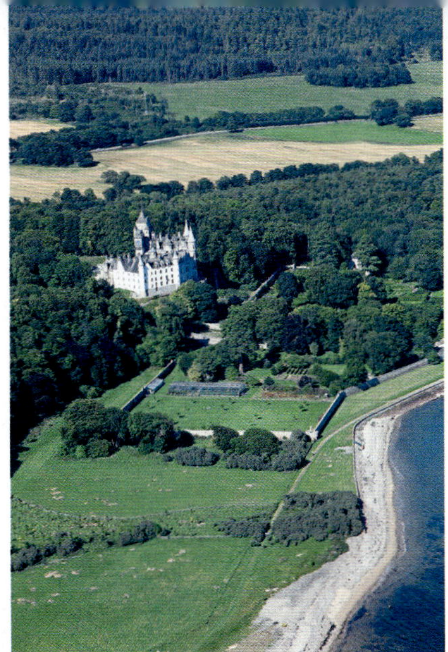

At the heart of the current castle is a keep from the 15th century. It still has its vaulted levels and a cast iron Yett (gate) Much of the earliest structure is hidden behind later Gothic styled improvements, later occupants having decided that home comforts were of greater value than stark stone defences. The early residents included Freskin de Moravia, a Norman baron who helped William the Lion conquer the lands first seen by their sea faring Viking ancestors. In his time the castle was of the motte and bailey type, a ruined example of this type of fortification can still be seen on the opposite coast at Duffus near Elgin. The Norman occupation also heralded the spread of feudal society into Scotland.

Later, in 1235, a Freskin grandson inherited the Earldom of Sutherland; thus began the association of the castle with the Clan Sutherland. The sixth Earl named Robin or Robert built the first castle keep on site and thereafter the name Dunrobin came into use. The current Earl Alastair Sutherland is the 25th of the title.

During the second Jacobite war the 16th earl, John Sutherland, was supporting the Hanoverians from his Dunrobin castle home. In April 1746 incredible news reached the Jacobite 3rd Earl of Cromartie that the forces of Bonnie Prince Charlie had triumphed on the Culloden Moor. He took his men and captured Dunrobin castle for the Jacobite cause. Sadly he had been misled. After being surrounded by local troops he was captured in the castle.

Later sentenced to death for high treason he was pardoned in 1748 but had to give up his estates and title. The place of his capture in the castle is named The Cromartie Room in his memory. In the 1830s the estate passed to the wealthy Marquess of Stafford on marriage to Elizabeth Gordon, the Countess of Sutherland. They were keen on improving the estate bringing new roads, a railway, harbours and thousands of sheep. However, the harsh way in which some of their employees treated the mostly Gaelic speaking tenants has never been forgotten. The clearances of tenants from land and homes were sometimes done in a cruel manner with reports in the press eventually resulting in the factor Patrick Sellar being tried for murder and fire raising. He was acquitted, aided by his legal skills, later becoming a respected local sheep farmer.

Between 1845-1851 the architect Charles Barry remodelled the castle interiors after fire damage and designed the beautiful garden layout evident today. His decorative flourishes also grace the Palace of Westminster, London. Another advocate of Scots Baronial and gothic revival styling, Sir Robert Lorimer, continued to add to the lavish layouts between 1915 and 1921. Also around this time some of the castle's many rooms saw use as a Royal Navy hospital supporting the Great War fleet at nearby Invergordon. This strong link with the navy is maintained with regular visits by the crew of HMS *Sutherland*. A public school also used the castle between 1963 and 1972.

truce to discuss a peace deal. In revenge, the MacKays ravaged Dornoch town, setting the cathedral on fire and hanging many Sutherland clansmen. In 1370 they also killed the 5th Earl of Sutherland which ensured the hatred lasted another 400 years between those clans. The 6th Earl Robert started building the first Dunrobin castle in 1401; its history is described separately.

In 1715, the Clan Sutherland protected Inverness castle against the Jacobites under the command of Earl John Gordon. Clansmen also fought for the crown at the Battle of Glenshiel in 1719 helping to defeat the Jacobites and Spanish troops in a narrow mountain pass. At the end of the last uprising in 1746 the Earl had to go to London to appear at the parliament where he had been summoned to prove he had stayed loyal to the government.

A dispute with the Gordon clan broke out in the 18th century over the Sutherland earldom. This was settled after these prolonged arguments were considered in the House of Lords. The Countess of Sutherland was awarded the right to the title on 1771. After she married the Marquis of Stafford he became the 1st Duke of Sutherland in 1833.

The current clan chief is Alastair Charles St Clair Sutherland, 25th Earl of Sutherland.

Motto: "Sans peur" French for "Without fear". The clan also has a slogan "Ceann na Drochaide Bige!" or "The Head of the Little Bridge!"

Some castles of the Sutherlands: Skibo from 1872 to 1895 sold to Andrew Carnegie and extensively altered. Dunrobin featured in this book. Dornoch castle which has been converted to a hotel in the town centre incorporating some original features. Do

not miss this small town when in the area it is lovely. The Clan Sutherland Society of Scotland has a website here... https://www.clansutherland.org.uk/

The home of the Clan Grant Society Worldwide is the old Church at Duthil, close to Grantown-on-Spey, and now known as the Clan Grant Centre. https://clangrantvisitors.org/listings/duthil-church/

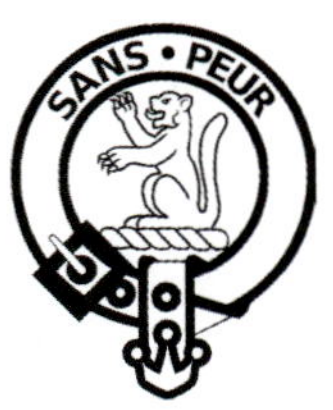

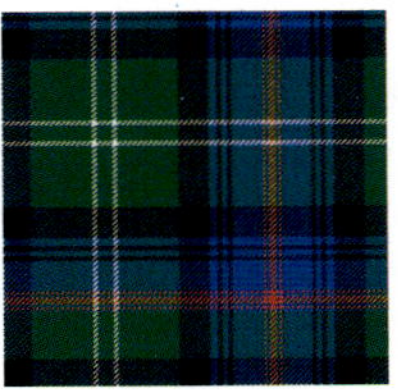

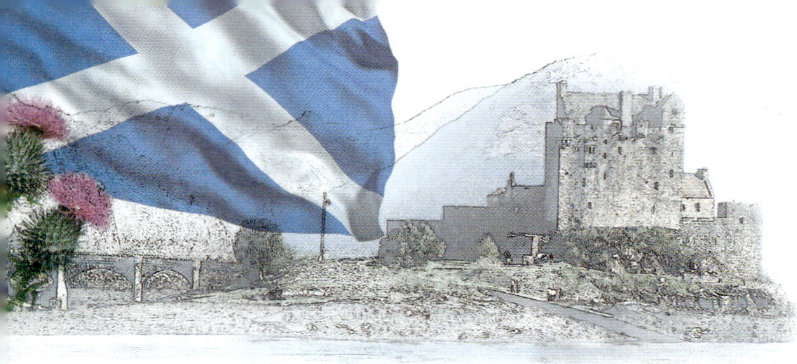

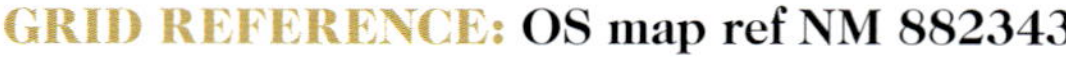

Dunstaffnage Castle

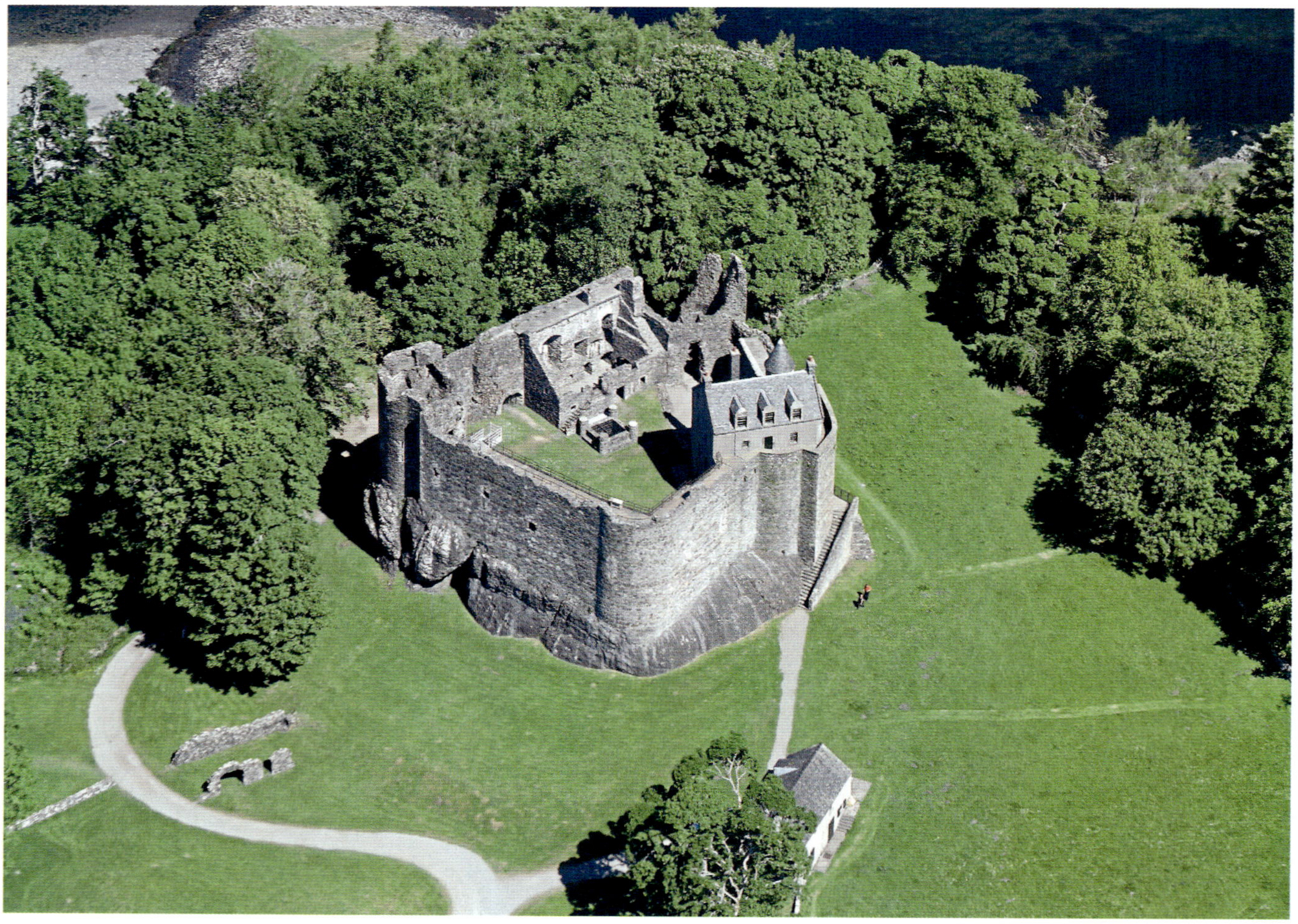

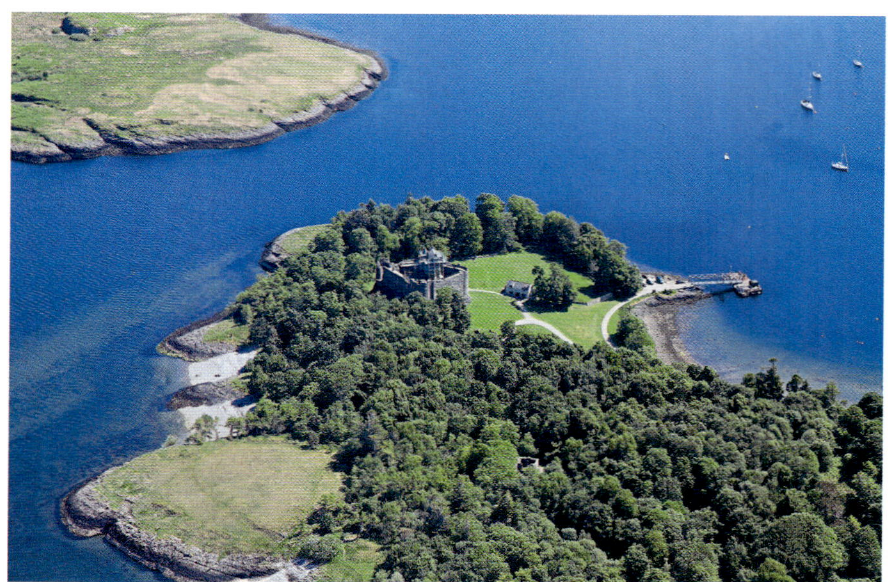

Grasping a rocky outcrop near the sea lanes this castle was used for around 600 years. Its austere stone walls, defensive turrets and raised position are more than enough to indicate its primary purpose as a military stronghold, rather than as a comfortable clan residence. Although partially ruined today, it offers spectacular views of the surrounding scenery.

Visitor Details

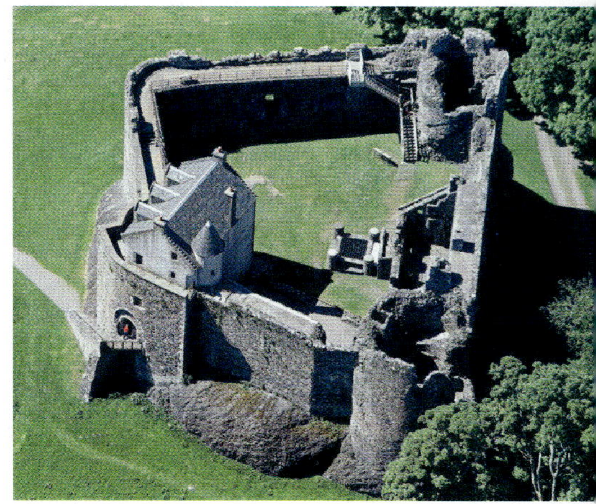

- www.historicenvironment.scot/visit-a-place/places/dunstaffnage-castle-and-chapel
- 01631 562465
- Dunstaffnage Castle is usually open during the day all year round though advance booking is required.
- The castle, shop and toilet, including one for the disabled, are all accessible.
- Gift shop on site, refreshments at nearby venues such as Science Park and village.
- Due to Covid precautions, there have been some changes to access on parts of the site. Check for more details.

Location: This castle is in Argyll and Dunbartonshire County three miles north east of Oban. From the A85 at Dunbeg, follow the minor road north just past the modern SAMS campus and the European Marine Science Park. The main car park is 200m from the castle. There is a small parking area 50m behind the castle.

About 60 million years ago, the Atlantic was being stretched as America and Europe drifted further apart, and a line of volcanoes emerged along the western seaboard of Scotland. One such volcano produced the now solid plug of basalt rock which the castle seems to grow out of. Two other ancient volcanoes are now the sites of Stirling and Edinburgh Castles.

This peninsula pointing into the Firth of Lorne attracted Celtic settlers as part of the Dalriada Kingdom in the seventh century. They realised it could be defended easily, with the sea on most sides, and therefore added a stone-built fortified settlement known as a Dun. Evidence of the Dun Monaidh occupation was found when hut circles were excavated during the building of the Science Park.

Around 1220, Argyll and the Western Isles were the scene of skirmishes between the Scots and Vikings. The Lord of Lorne, Duncan MacDougall, built the castle here to control activity around Loch Etive. But in 1308, the Clan chose to support the English in the Wars of Scottish Independence. It was the wrong choice which cost them the castle and lands when Robert the Bruce triumphed. The castle remained as a royal property until 1470 when James III granted it to Colin Campbell, Earl of Argyll. In 1644, James Graham, the Earl of Montrose, tried and failed to take the castle in the Civil War when it was held by anti-royalists.

The 9th Earl of Argyll burned the castle in 1685 during a siege by Royalist troops. During both risings of Jacobites, in 1715 and 1745, the government garrison held the castle. Flora MacDonald was briefly imprisoned here after she aided the escape of Bonnie Prince Charlie. She later admitted she wanted him gone as his presence was a threat to her family.

Fierce fire returned in 1810, however, this time by accident. It gutted the castle, which then became a ruin. The state took over custody in 1958 and gradually made it safe to visit.

The last improvements came in 2014 when the two-storey hereditary keeper's house was restored. The views from the castle walls over the bay were mentioned as "a most splendid prospect" by Walter Scott in 1814.

You might hear heavy footsteps and hammering around the castle but see no one working. That will be the oft-reported ghost of handicrafts hanging around. Another ghost seen sometimes is the Ell Maid in a green dress. She is a gruagach, a spirit who can foretell events ahead for the castle's owners. A short walk through the nearby woods leads to the roofless 13th century chapel with a burial area for the Campbells of Dunstaffnage. In spring you can enjoy the carpet of bluebells and the plentiful wildlife. Peace now pervades the peninsula after centuries of turmoil.

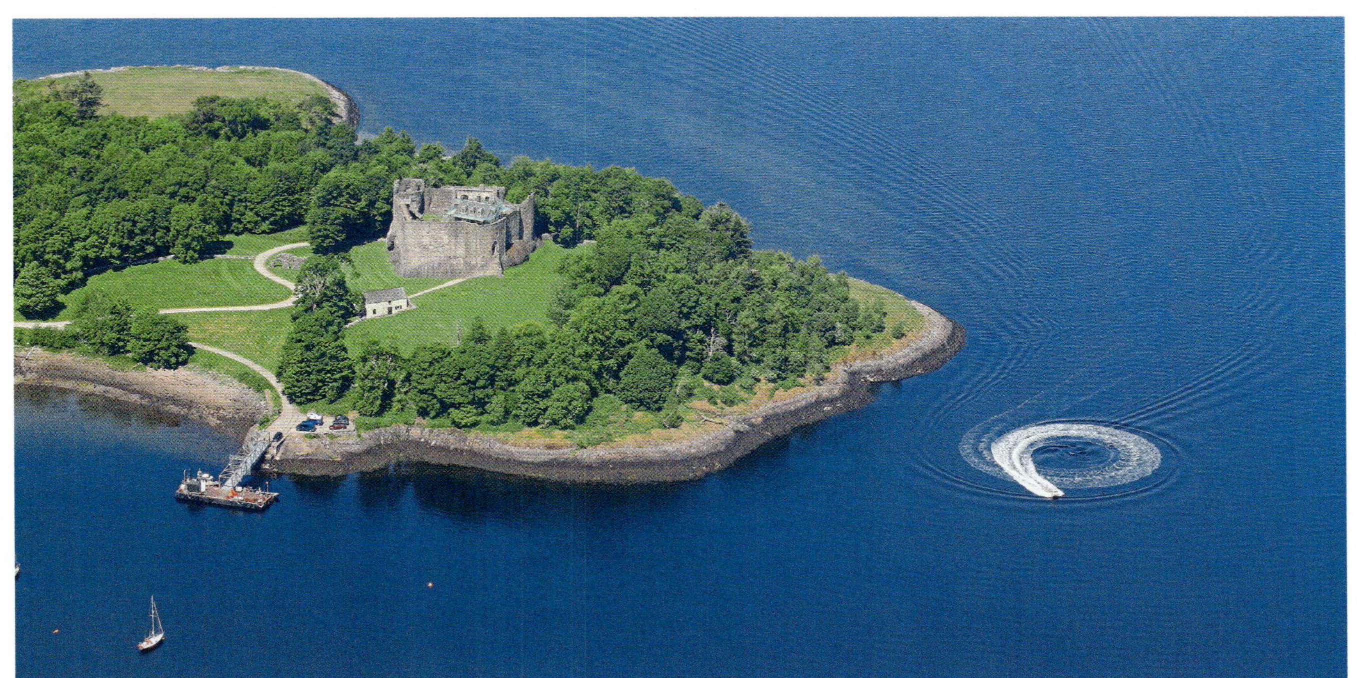

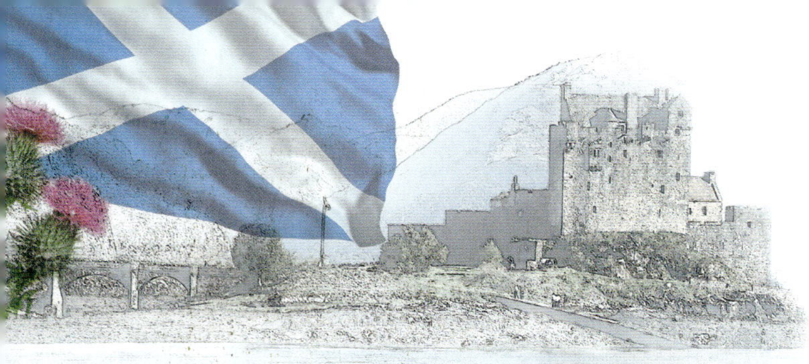

Dunvegan Castle

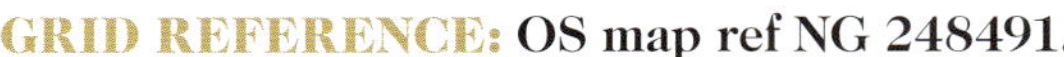

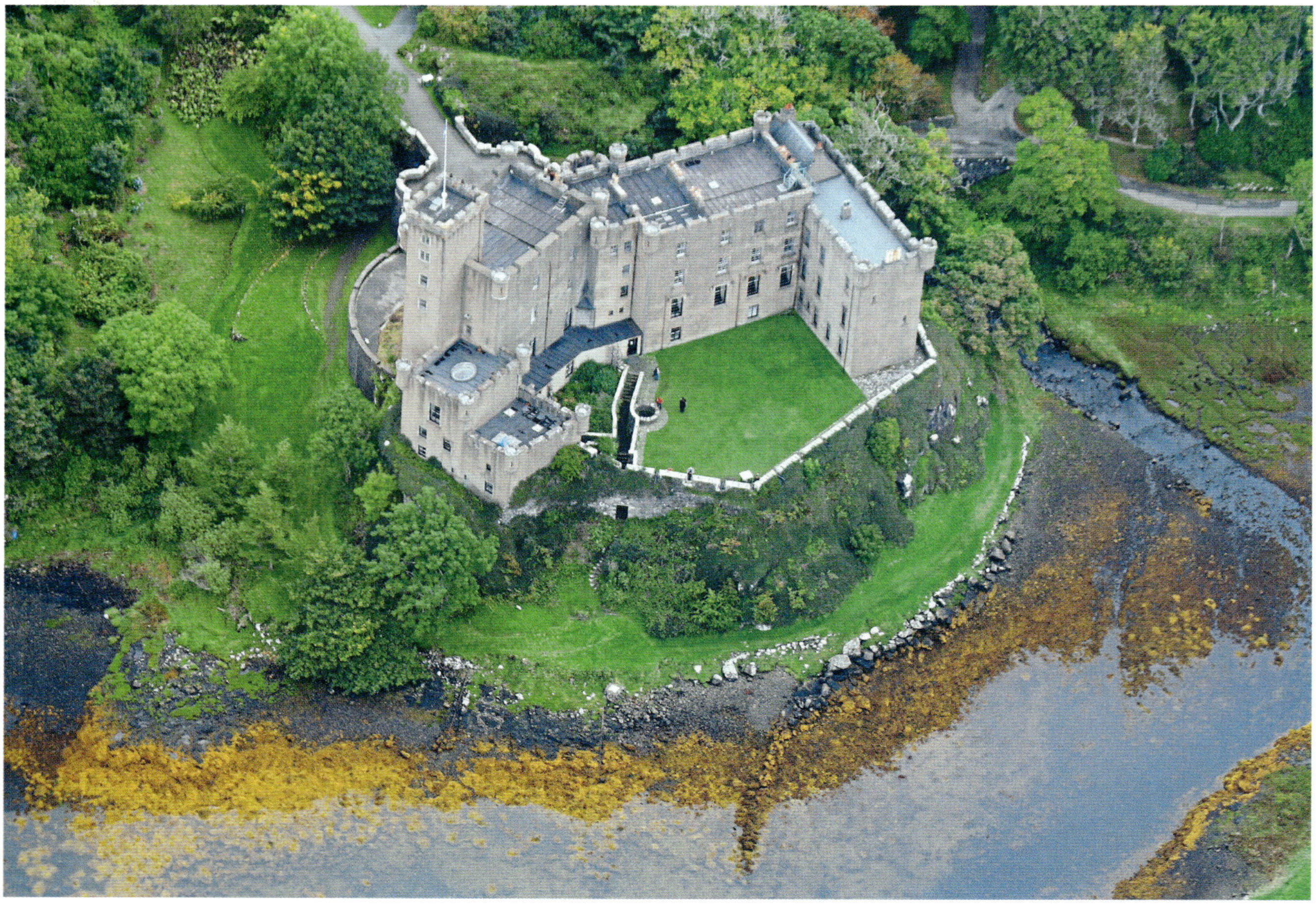

This large and impressive edifice is said to have its origins in the time of Viking raiders, when it served as an important guardian of sea routes around Skye. Occupied without a break by Clan Macleod, it has a huge collection of clan treasures such as the Fairy Flag and the Dunvegan Cup. Like Dunrobin, it hides the still-surviving fabric of its earlier incarnations beneath later building works.

◼ ABOUT THE CLAN

The clan descended from Norse Vikings who for many years regarded the Irish Sea, Hebrides and Orkneys as an outlying territory of Norway. The Norse King was called Godfrey and the nickname his followers gave the Western Islanders was Ljotr, spoken as Lodge in Gaelic which gradually evolved into Leod. A recent DNA study of some clan members has produced evidence of Viking ancestors. In the West the Macleods settled Lewis and Skye. On the east coast they prospered in Strathpeffer, however ownership of Castle Leod was eventually taken by the Mackenzies.

The Macleods were a seafaring clan with fine galleys and they supported Donald, Lord of the Isles. The king of Scotland did not approve of the clans who supported Donald, especially when they claimed Ross. In July 1411 Donald marched towards Aberdeen with around 2,000 clansmen including many Macleods. Their attempt to take the town was blocked

Clan Macleod

by a force of around 8,000 lead by the Royalist Earl of Mar near Inverurie. His force included many knights on horseback. So much blood was spilled that it became known as the battle of Red Harlaw and by nightfall no clear winners had been declared, but many knights and other noblemen perished. The Earl and his force slept on the battlefield, exhausted, and expected to resume the fight at dawn. At daybreak he was surprised to discover Donald's surviving clansmen had departed for home to the west. The King punished the clan Macleod by asking the chief to provide a charter showing ownership of Lewis which he could not manage; this enabled Mackenzie of Kintail to gain formal ownership of Lewis. By 1613 the clan was established in their castle at Dunvegan where Chief Rory Macleod was knighted. The chief supported the creation of a piper's college for the MacCrimmons at Dunvegan; they became the chief's hereditary pipers.

ABOUT THE CASTLE

Visitor Details

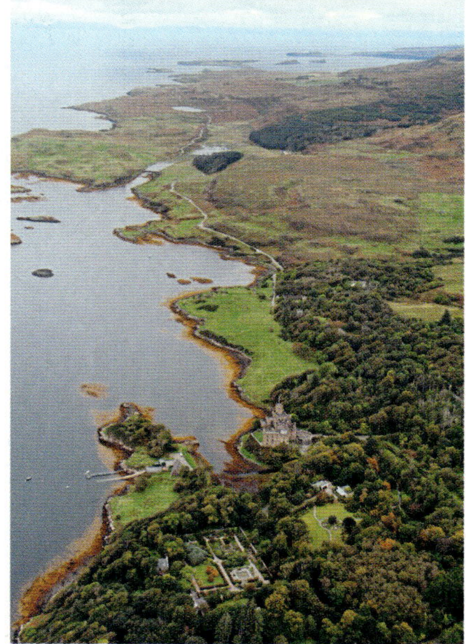

www.dunvegancastle.com

01470 521206

Normally stays open all year. Visit the website for timings and details of any Covid precautions in use.

Access for disabled has been provided where possible and facilities include toilets and entry for guide dogs.

The castle is remote and therefore has developed a gift shop with cafe and restaurant.

Aside from a castle interior packed with clan history, the surrounds include a walled garden, water gardens, woodland walks and fantastic viewpoints. Wildlife includes seals with boat trips to a nearby colony possible.

Location: The castle sits on a hidden rocky knoll above the promontory of Black Point, Dubh Ard, and one mile north of the village of Dunvegan on the Isle of Skye.

The first structure on this site was a basic fort on an island in Loch Dunvegan which usefully is a sea linked loch. By the 13th century a curtain wall surrounded what had become an easily defended promontory with slippery seaweed festooned rocks on three sides.

The marine location favoured the seafaring history of the occupiers Clan Macleod whose ancestors including Leod, son of Olaf the Black, the Viking King of the Isle of Man.

A large four-storey keep was added in the 14th century. Over the next three centuries more buildings were added, the largest being the Fairy Tower around 1500, which included a great hall for the frequent feasts to impress guests.

When James V was hosted in 1540 he was treated to a lavish open air banquet at Macleod's Tables, a nearby flat-topped hill. The Clan chief was confident that no one could top that royal gathering.

By 1840, the mixture of buildings were given a makeover in the ornamental baronial style of the times which included addition of turrets and battlements. The entrance was now from the East over a drawbridge. Extensive repairs took place between 1938 and 1940 after a fire.

It is now the family residence of Hugh Magnus MacLeod, the 30th chief of Clan Macleod. His inheritance in 2007 also included associated ancestral clan territories, which still extend to over 42,000 acres on the Isle of Skye. Preserved inside the fairly recent

outer castle walls are 750 years of clan Macleod history. These include artifacts such as the ancient Fairy Flag, a small fragile 18 inch square of silk, originally covered in small red elf dots on a yellow background. Perhaps it was a relic from Viking times or a remnant from a larger Crusader ensign? Powers of the Fairy flag include keeping the clan chief and spouse fertile, increasing the size of the clan's warrior host on the battleground, charming herrings to shoal near the castle ready for harvesting and curing cattle of ailments. Generations of Macleods have believed in the good fortune brought by the flag to the clan and some aircrew took photos of the flag with them on combat missions in the Second World War.

Among the host of treasures displayed proudly is also the Dunvegan Cup. A unique meather dating back to the 10th century, it was gifted by the O'Neils of Ulster as a token of thanks to one of the clan's most celebrated chiefs, Sir Rory Mor, for his support of their cause against the armies of Queen Elizabeth I of England in 1596. Originally it was solely for mead, made of wood and with silver ornamentation added at a later date. It has witnessed many feasts where shared use has made the silver very thin in most places.

Dunvegan castle and estate is a great example of historical preservation combined with modern estates management. It has earned a good reputation for hosting weddings, conferences and thousands of tourists annually.

In the 16th century Clan Macleod battled often with Clan Macdonald of Sleat. Perhaps this was the background to the opening sequence of the fictional film Highlander, where Connor Macleod leaves a castle with his clan for battle. That castle is Eilean Donan, which was never a Macleod stronghold. Have a look at the page about that castle in this book to see why film makers love its appearance. The Macleods raised a force to help the Jacobite cause in 1715, however by the time of the 1745 rising the Dunvegan clan chief decided to support the government by raising several independent companies between 500 and 1,000 men in strength. The Macleods' home at Dunvegan castle remained with the clan after the risings and is detailed elsewhere in this book.
 Meanwhile, another clan branch from Raasay fought at Culloden as part of the Glengarry regiment. This action really upset Norman Macleod chief at Dunvegan. With his 700

clansmen he destroyed and pillaged much of Raasay in 1746 becoming for ever after known as The Wicked Man. This highlighted the divisions within some clans and the fragility of clan loyalty. A direct result of the Jacobites losing at Culloden was the dismantling of much of the clan system. Setting aside the romantic aspects fuelled later by Sir Walter Scott's fictions, the near constant feuding and unlawful cruel attacks by clans had to be stopped but this took many years of government action. Outside Scotland it is also true that feuds between neighbouring large groups have resulted in violence and intimidation. In the 1300s the Coterels brought terror to Derbyshire and the Folvilles rampaged in Northamptonshire. As in Scotland, the government sometimes recruited from them for military service.

Unusually the clan chief in 1935 was a woman, Dame Flora Macleod. Clan gatherings are still

held at Dunvegan castle. This clan has ten societies across the world. More details are available here... https://clanmacleod.org/ This is the home page for the Associated Clan Macleod Societies. Branches of the clan are known as Septs and this list shows many surnames connected with the clan, https://clanmacleod.org/about/septs/

Motto: Hold fast
Plant badge: Juniper

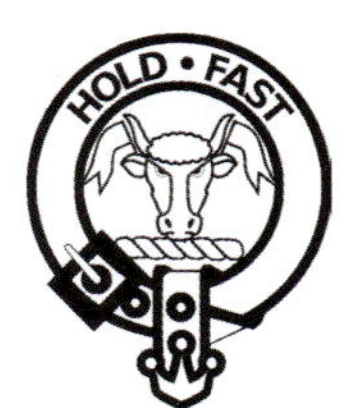
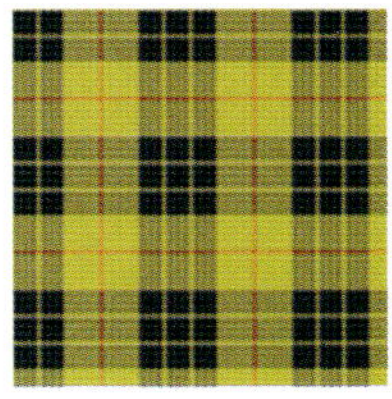

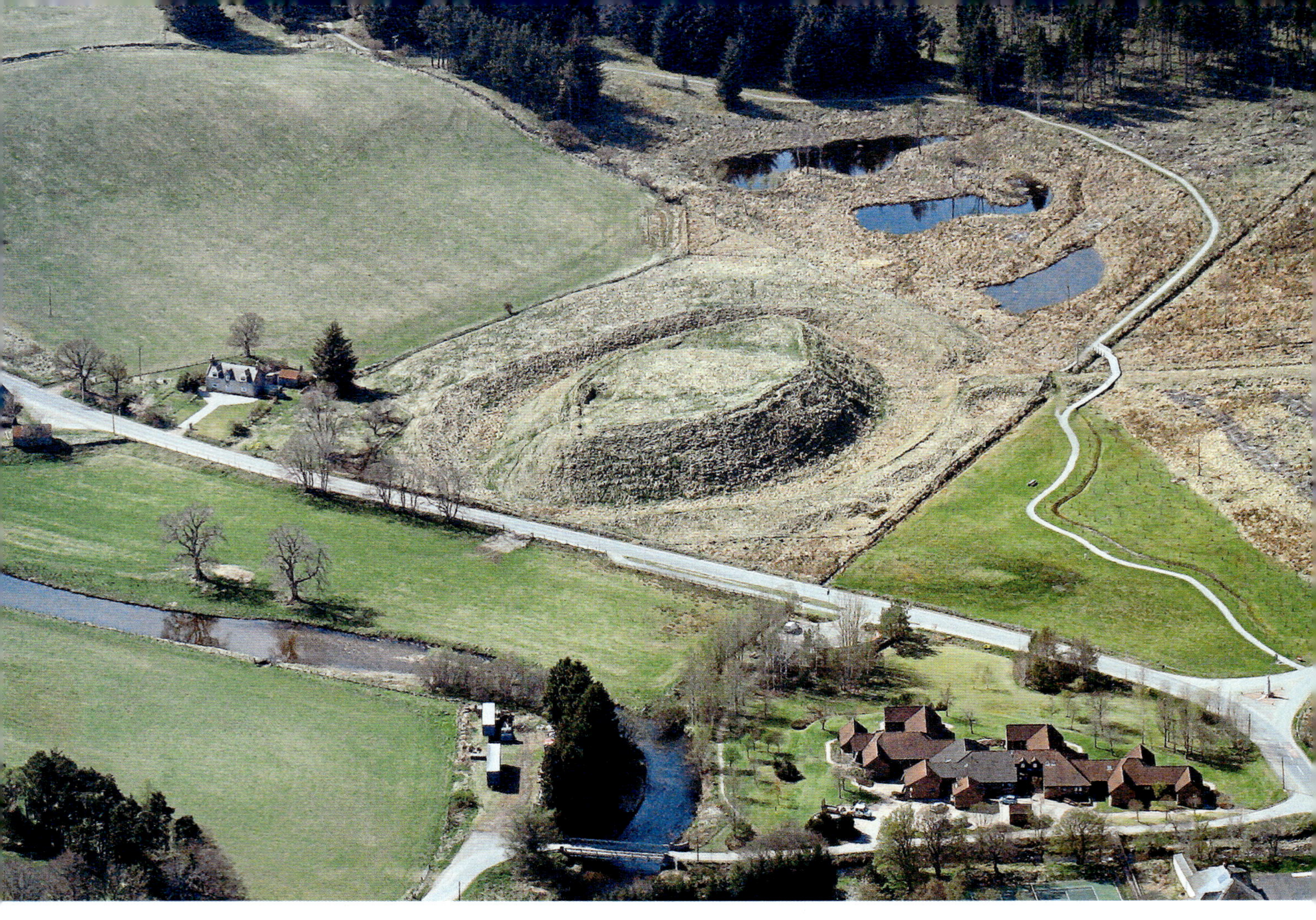

Types of castles and development

Scotland's castles evolved over time, from purely defensive military structures to comfortable family homes and finally to beautiful architectural showpieces.

The earliest fortifications took advantage of the varied geology found across Scotland. Coastal locations had many promontories where ditches dug across the narrow neck at the landward end made fairly secure bases. Some had room for timber huts and later were occupied by stone castles which covered earlier structures. Examples include Burghead, where the Pictish era fort has almost disappeared beneath the current town and Dunottar. Another type of defensive living area was created by placing huts on timber posts above stone platforms in shallow areas of lochs. This created a Crannog, the photo on the opposite page shows a replica displayed on Loch Tay. Higher ground enabled hill forts to be built and some, such as Bennachie near Aberdeen, had a large number of occupied circular huts adjacent.

The arrival of the feudal Norman lords in Scotland brought defined land ownership and taxes. They desired a secure building with space for entertaining and administration. The castles were also a base for the armies needed to enforce the rule of King David in return for the lands assigned to his Norman knights. Artificial mounds were created, surrounded by a ditch topped with an enclosure and timber fort. This is known as a motte and bailey. A surviving one can be seen at Duffus castle. The Doune of Invernochty is an example where just the mound remains. However timbers could be fired and subject to rotting in the damp climate.

The next change came with the building of substantial stone walls in a near circular pattern enclosing the living area. Inside this redoubt were the timber halls, kitchens, storage huts and barracks. Dunstaffnage castle illustrates this stage. After the year 1200, substantial stone keeps towered in the centres of some of these walls. To pacify the Lords of the Isles and beat off Viking raiders, huge expensive castles appeared such as at Rothesay. It was not at first impregnable but developed gradually into a solid stronghold with a water filled moat and corner towers to give all round protection. Some clans created strongholds by the water as at Dunvegan, Stalker and Eilean Donan.

Smaller castles sprung up so that clans could control waterways and cattle drove roads. These were three- and four-storey stone towers following an L or Z shaped foundation plan. Around these

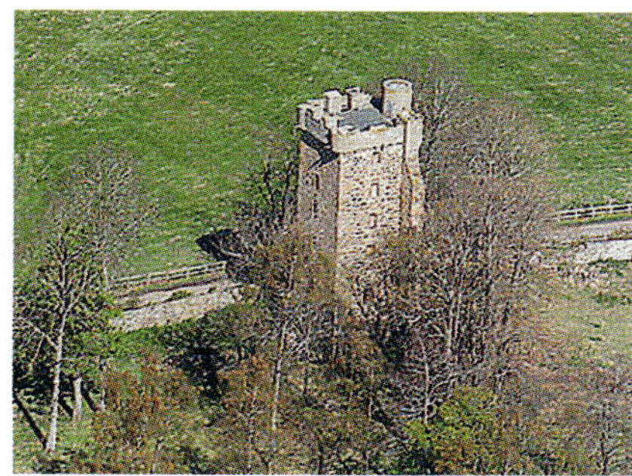

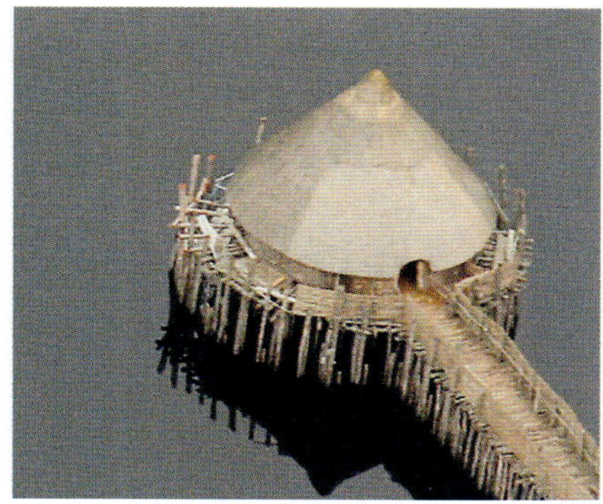

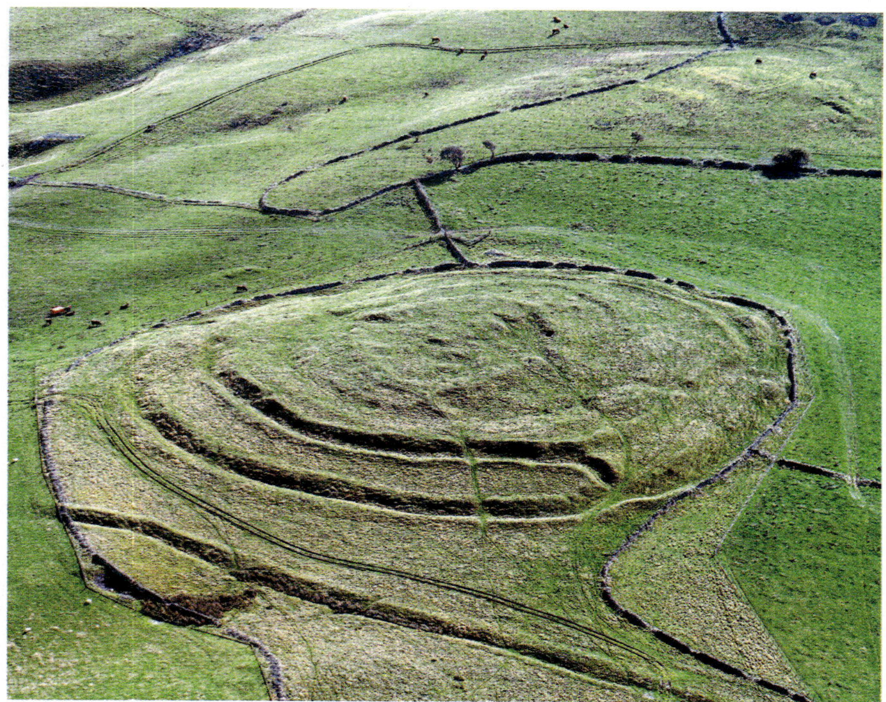

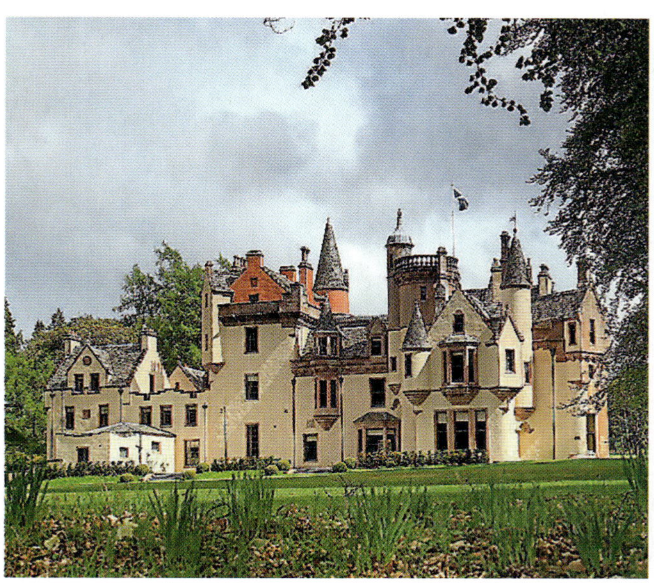

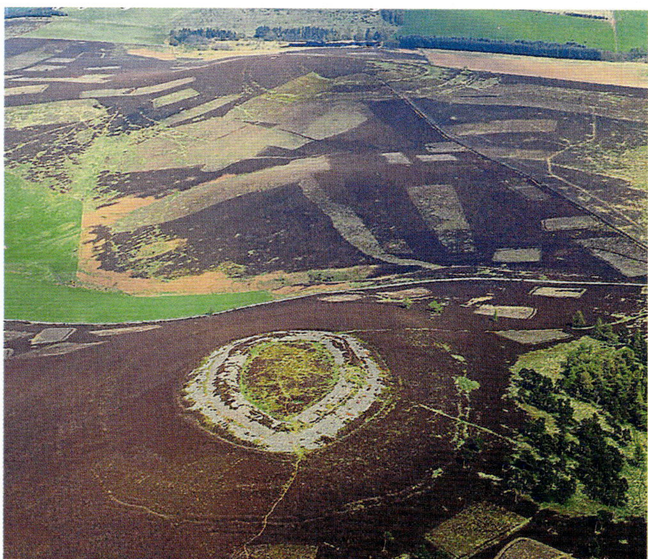

towers were lower but substantial stone walls to protect cattle and provide space for domestic buildings. A fine unchanged example is at Corgarff.

Gradually the need to have comforts in these stone dwellings led to extensions such as at Huntingtower where a new tower was built next to the earlier one and then joined together. Others went for striking designs and bright colours; Craigievar in a pink lime wash is a merchant's show home, towering above Strathdon. That region is well represented with examples such as Tolquhon, Drum, Crathes and Fraser showing the peak of lordly castle comforts. Due to civil uprisings and threats from sea borne invasions, the government imposed several artillery forts on the landscape; Fort George, Blackness and Broughty are detailed in this book.

The ultimate castle developments are actually pleasure palaces built or repurposed when Scotland was part of the union and defences were no longer an issue. The romantic ideals and baronial gothic elements produced attractive castles such as Dunrobin, Balmoral, Aldourie and Carbisdale.

OPPOSITE PAGE:

Doune of Invernochty, a 12th century castle of which only the base earthworks survive today.

THIS PAGE:

Top left: Bridge Tower House.

Mid-left: A crannog, effectively an artificial island, was one of the earliest forms of defensive structure.

Top right: Milkieston Rings, a prehistoric hill fort near the village of Eddleston, about three miles north of Peebles.

Lower left: The gothic baronial Aldourie Castle as viewed from the banks of Loch Ness.

Lower right: The Caterthun forts are Iron Age earthworks near Brechin.

FOLLOWING PAGES:

The picturesque remains of Dunnottar Castle, dating from the 15th to the 17th centuries, on the northeastern coast, south of Stonehaven.

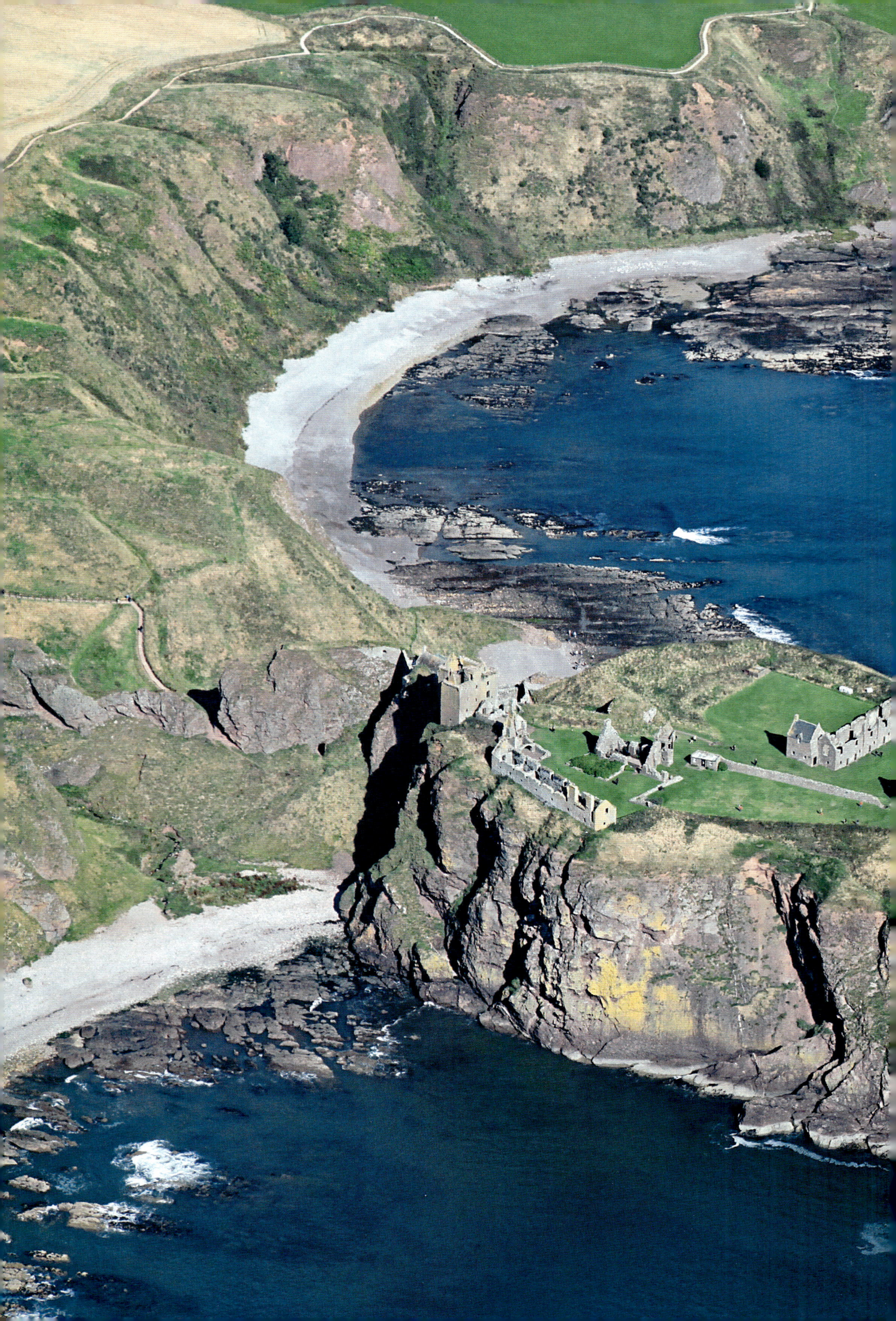

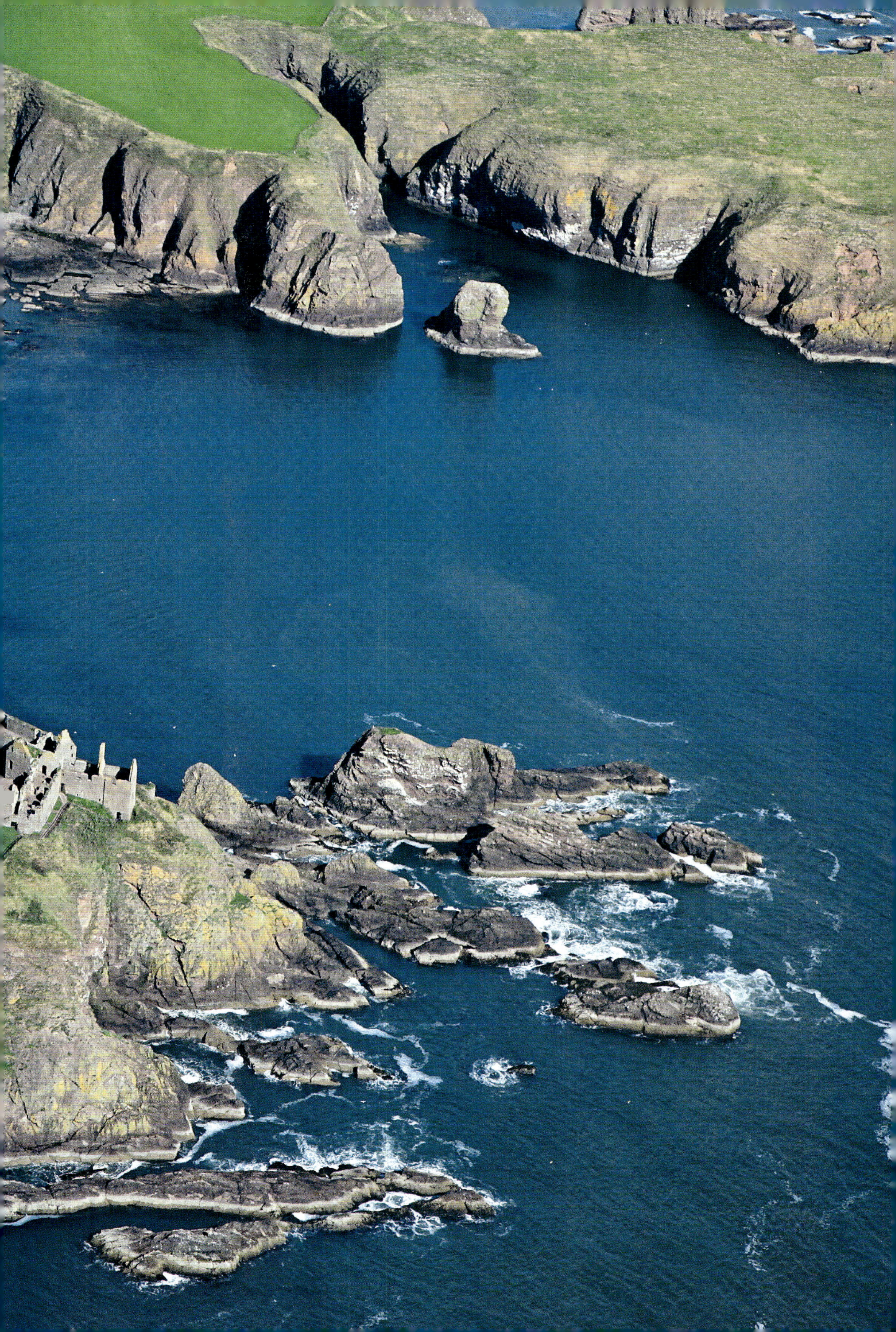

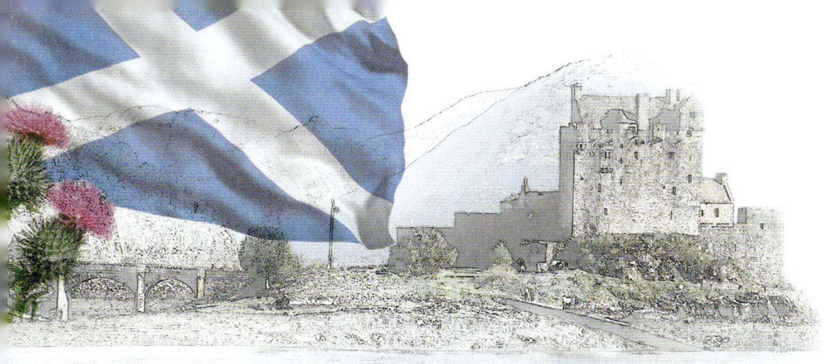

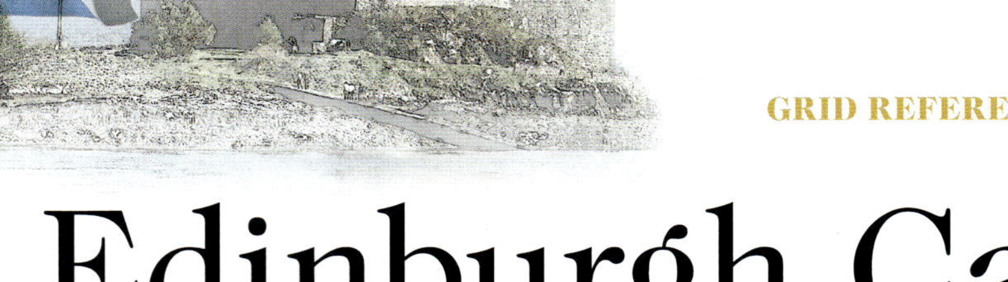

Edinburgh Castle

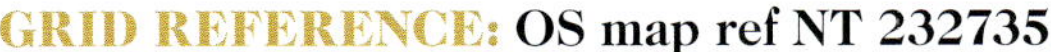

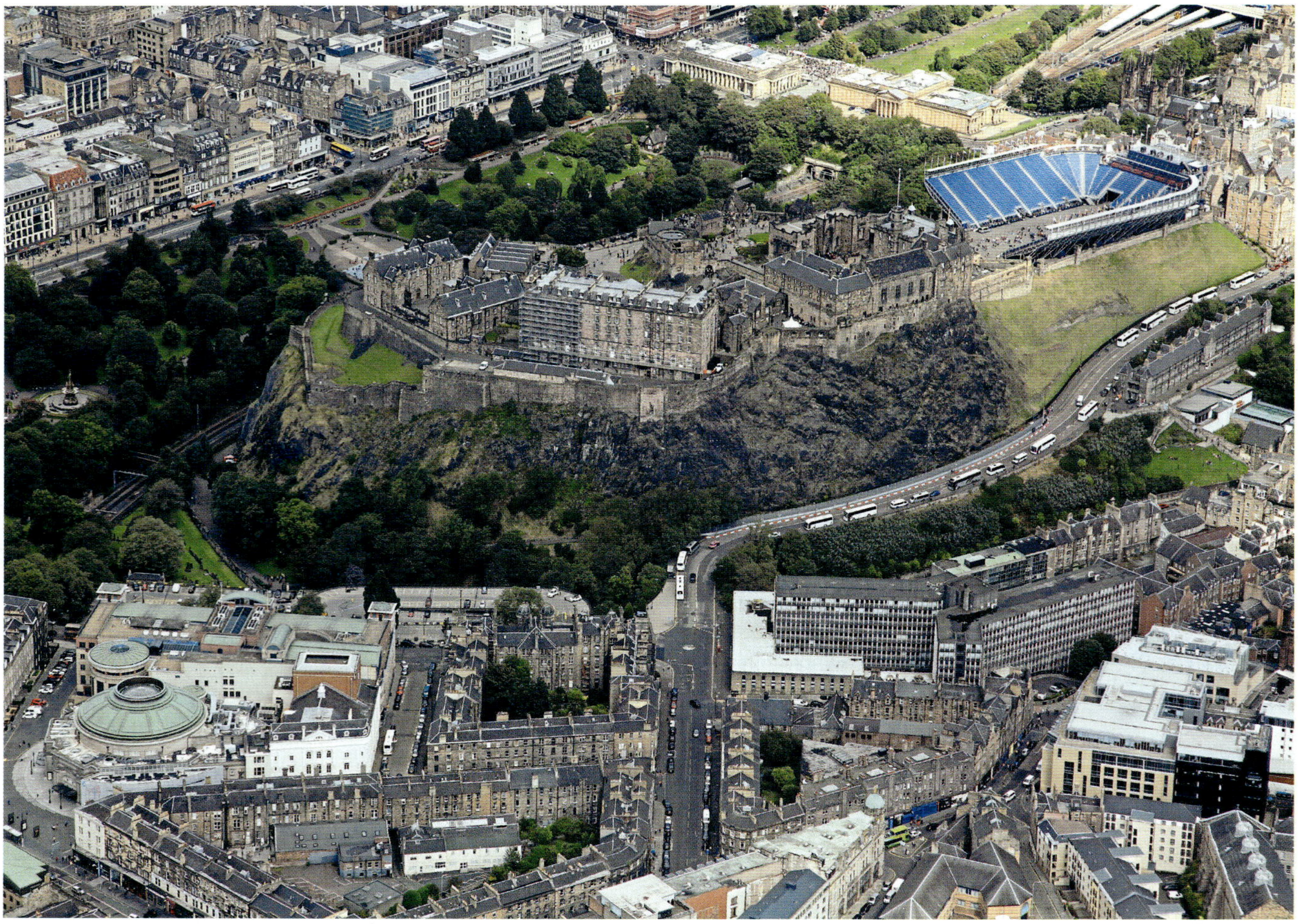

This impressive Royal castle has dominated the city skyline for centuries. If walls could talk, this castle would have never ending stories to tell. Far removed from the pretty Disney-style confection seen elsewhere, this sturdy and purposeful castle is the most visited in Scotland for good reasons.

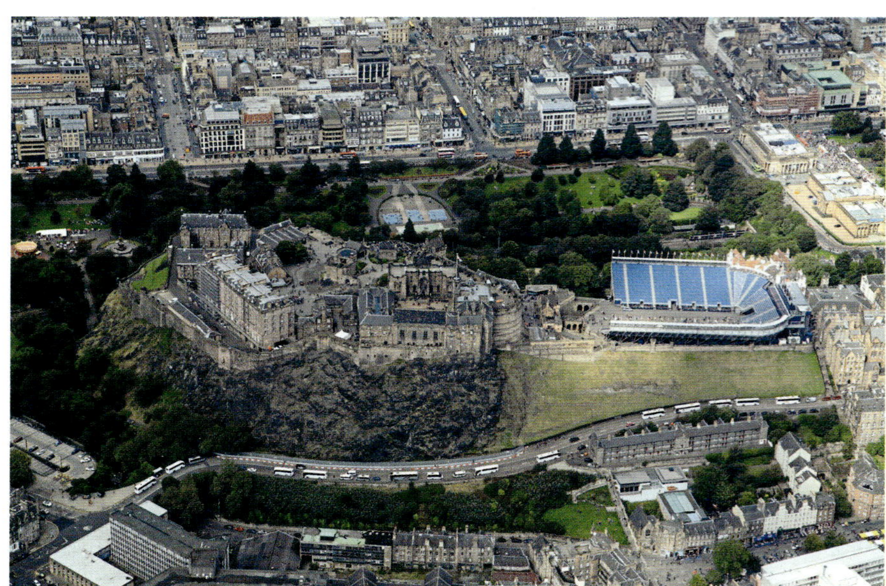

Visitor Details

 www.edinburghcastle.scot

 0131 225 9846

 The castle is usually open all year except Christmas Day and Boxing Day. Detailed timings can be found on the website or by phone.

 Good support for disabled visitors has been provided with a few special parking zones available when pre-booked. The access guide is published online.

 Facilities include ample toilets, restaurant, tea room and several shops.

The castle approaches along the royal mile have the highest concentration of gift shops, tea rooms and buskers in Scotland.

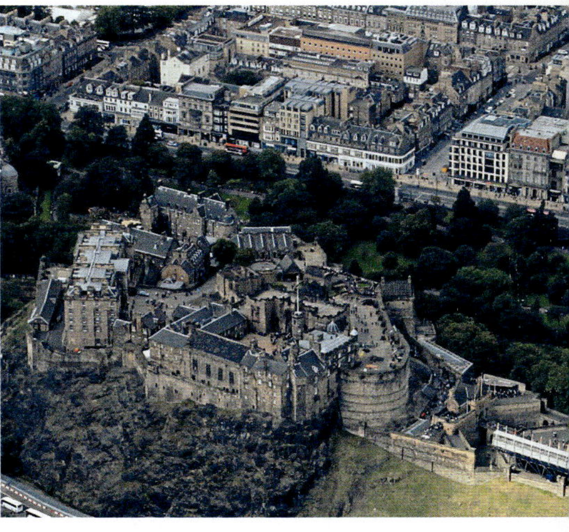

Location: Situated in the centre of Edinburgh at one end of the Royal Mile, Edinburgh Castle is about ten minutes' walk away from Edinburgh Waverly train station. Several large car parks are located close to the castle. The NCP car park at Castle Terrace offers a discounted rate for castle visitors.

A long time ago, volcanoes dominated the local area. The craggy basalt stump of an extinct one was later eroded by a glacier to form the high ground that was sought as a place to create a fortress. The cliffs are 80m (260ft) high. The tail of some ancient eroded material also forms the slope where the Royal Mile now stands.

Excavations of middens have revealed evidence that an Iron Age fort was the first structure on the site. An early medieval Welsh poem mentions Din Eidyn, the stronghold of Eiydn. This is possibly the Castle Rock site. Welsh warriors of King Gododin feasted for a year here before heading off south to defeat at Catreath. Another early name for the location is the Castle of the Maidens and some sources claim connections with Arthurian legends.

Most of what we can view today dates from the 15th century, but the oldest intact building is a small Norman chapel dedicated to St Margaret, wife of Malcom Canmore. After his death in 1093, a siege of the castle was made by his brother Donald Bane. This was the first of 26 sieges in the history of the fortress. Although it stands protected by high cliffs of basalt on three sides, the rock is not able to collect water. Once the deep storage well ran dry, the resulting drought made surrender inevitable unless a relief force arrived in time. For many centuries, a castle siege was the preferred method of seizing power. Battles were far less common, being difficult to arrange and costlier in lives lost and injuries.

The use of the castle as a seat of Scottish royal power came when King David I, between 1139 and 1150, held an assembly of earls and clergy at the castle.

After his defeat at the Battle of Alnwick in 1174, King William the Lyon was forced to surrender Edinburgh and three other Scottish castles to the English king. He regained ownership when, upon marriage to his English bride, he was granted the castle as dowry in 1186.

The First War of Scottish Independence resulted in the invading English army of Edward I pummelling the castle into submission with a three-day bombardment. A large English garrison was in occupation by 1300. The Earl of Moray attempted to seize the castle for Robert the Bruce in 1314.

Under the lead of William Francis, 30 of the Earl's best men made a daring night time climb of the north cliff face, then scrambled over the wall at a weaker point above the cliff. The garrison were caught off guard and surrendered. Following orders from Robert, the castle was slighted.

After another invasion from England, the forces of Edward III in 1333 reoccupied the castle and made repairs to it by 1335. In 1341, the garrison were tricked when a regular supply of food was delivered. A cart was jammed into the gate, enabling more men to rush inside. The traders were actually disguised Scottish men at arms who took possession, killing all the 100 defenders. Determined that the castle should remain in Scots hands, David II added a tower which still carries his name, an L-plan keep and sturdier curtain walls surrounding the edges of the crag. David's Tower is now concealed within later structures.

Another bloody episode at the castle in 1440 was the murder of 16-year-old Earl William Douglas and his younger brother after they had accepted the hospitality of the Chancellor William Crichton. He was determined to break the power of the Douglas clan but only incurred their everlasting wrath, resulting in a nine month siege and much destruction after capture by the Douglases. After restoration and the creation of the Great Hall in 1483, the castle was ready for use again as a palace. By 1500, the royal family were also using Holyrood House a mile away and they preferred the more comfortable homely lodgings there. But the castle still had many uses as a prison, armoury, safe storage for valuables and records, and an arsenal where small arms were made and beautifully finished deadly cannon were cast from 1498. The brooding prescence of the strong fortress did send a powerful message to all who saw and spoke of it.

A happy event in 1566 was the safe birth of the future King James VI within the castle. His mother, Mary Queen of Scots, had harder times ahead with a forced abdication and later imprisonment on an island in Loch Leven. Supporters of Mary held the castle and this resulted in the Lang Siege from around 1570 to 1573. This included artillery duels between the castle's cannon and those surrounding the castle which caused great destruction of property in the city as well as the eventual smashing of castle walls leading to surrender. In May 1573, over 3,000 cannon shots were fired at the castle in just 12 days.

Chaos swept the land in the 1640 when the Covenanters roved out making certain to take the castle after a short siege but giving it back to Charles after a local treaty a few months later. In 1641, they starved out the garrison, forcing surrender after a three-month blockade. By 1650, the Covenanters had decided to support Charles II with his Royalist cause. This gave Oliver Cromwell good reason to bring his army north to subdue the Scots. After beating the Covenanter army at Dunbar, he took three months to force the surrender of the castle causing significant damage. It is recorded that the castle governor, Colonel Dundas, changed sides and gave up earlier than some

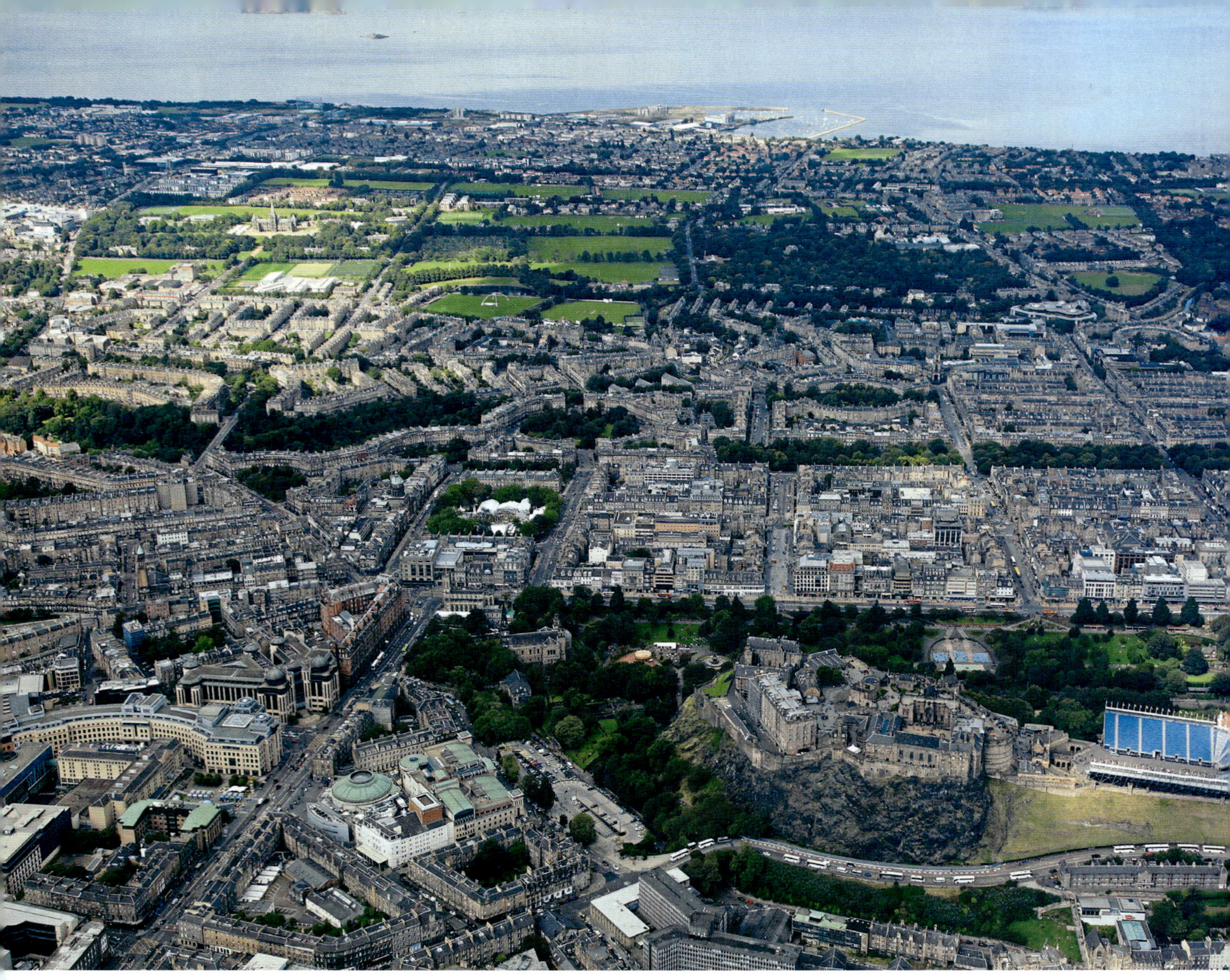

expected. Perhaps his critics had never endured constant artillery bombardment.

With Charles II in possession, the castle had major upgrades which included many of the buildings still visible today. Another change in 1660 was the decision to keep army units based at the castle occupying newly constructed barracks. This garrison was in place until 1923.

When the Jacobites tried to take the castle in 1715 they failed, even with insider help. Those inside misjudged the height of the walls. As dawn broke the Jacobites were still outside, unable to use the ladders dropped to them. They fled but the helpers inside were captured and flogged or hung. Later the renowned army surveyor, General Wade, inspected the castle defences during his residence there and as a result of his report, improvements were made. This included building artillery platforms covering more angles.

When the army of Bonnie Prince Charlie took the city of Edinburgh in 1745, the castle garrison held out and at times bombarded the town. He abandoned the blockade and moved on. This was the last assault attempted on the castle.

In 1811, 49 French prisoners ,taken during the Napoleonic Wars tunnelled out of the dungeon and escaped down the south wall and cliffs with great skill and luck. By 1814, the castle prisons were considered unsuitable for the purpose.

The historical aspects of the castle were becoming popular with visitors. This included paying a fee to view the Scottish Crown Jewels, which were rediscovered by Sir Walter Scott after being hidden in a sealed room for over 100 years. These are still on view alongside the Stone of Destiny on which many monarchs were crowned over hundreds of years.

Apart from the fine views and solid structures, the castle has many other historic items displayed. These include a huge siege cannon, Mons Meg, made in 1457 which after retirement to the castle was fired for ceremonies until it burst in 1681. Massive carved stone balls were fired and could travel as far as two miles but usually the intent was to bombard castle masonry at closer ranges. When visiting Edinburgh, be careful as 1pm approaches (except Sunday, Good Friday and Christmas Day). A modern artillery gun on top of the Mills Mount Battery is used to fire a blank round as a time check. This was originally for shipping at Leith.

The castle grounds include the Scottish National War Memorial inside a beautifully converted barrack block. Recorded inside are the names of all Scottish soldiers lost in wars since 1914. Monuments to all Scottish regiments are displayed. The Royal Scots also maintain a regimental museum at the castle. Many units used to parade on the esplanade approaching the castle gates. This is the area used every autumn for the Edinburgh Military Tattoo.

The aerial castle views presented here show the temporary seating in place for this event. Unusually, the army is still present at the castle with a garrison for ceremonial duty. Soldiers stand on armed guard at the gatehouse and also keep the Crown Jewels known also as the Honours of Scotland safe.

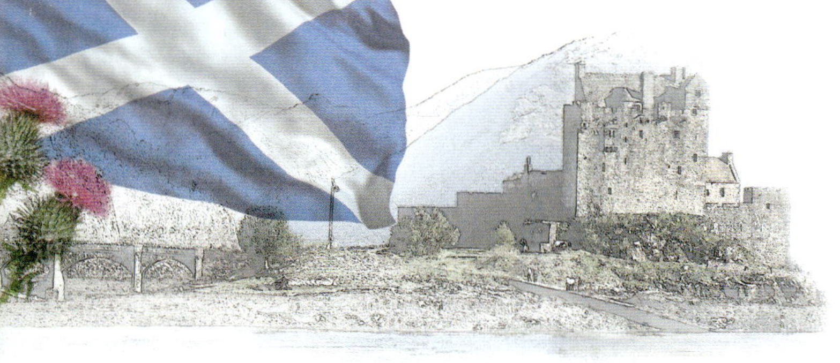

GRID REFERENCE: OS map ref NO 595694.

Edzell Castle

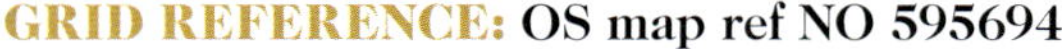

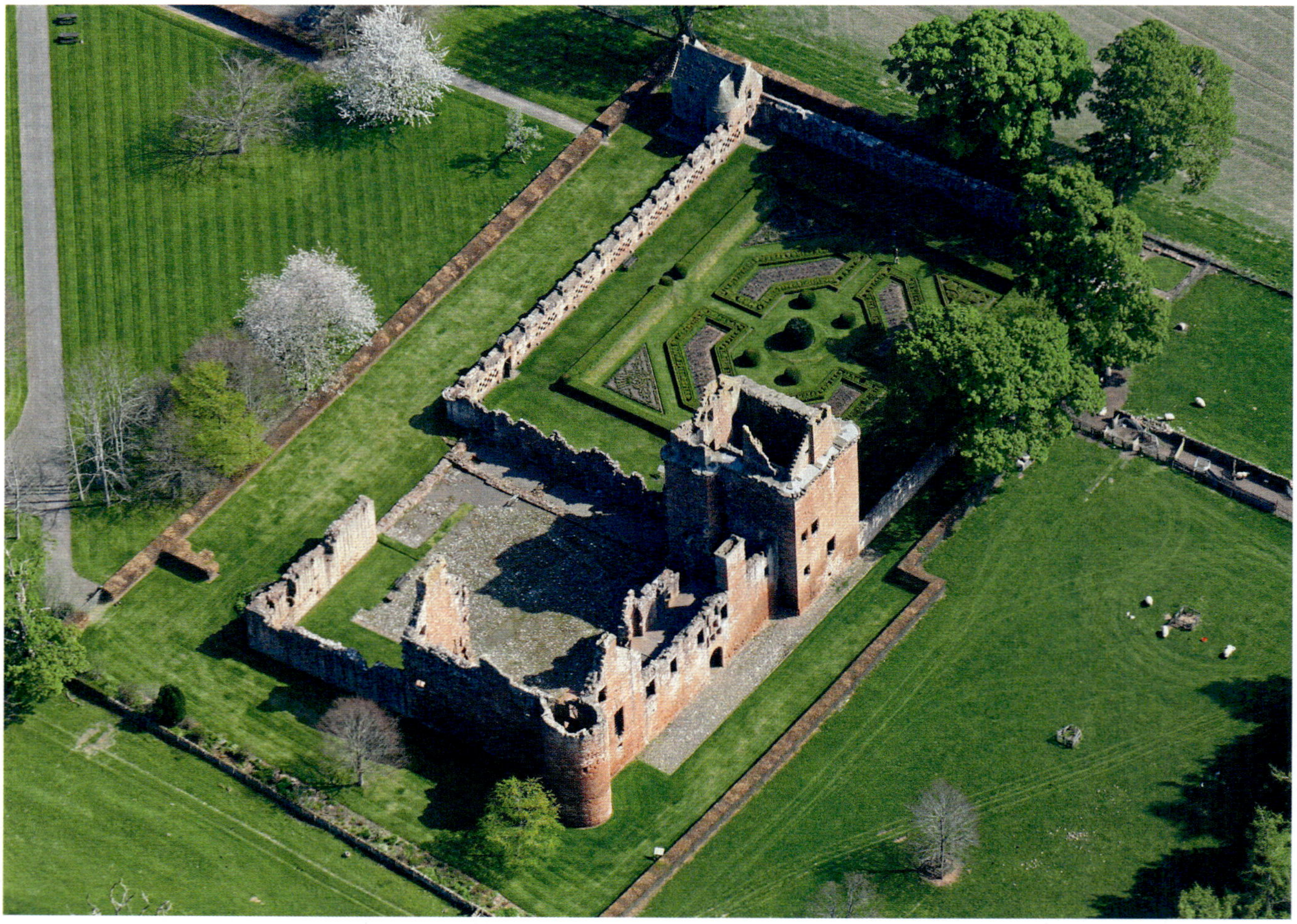

The Lindsay clan held this castle for many years and it became a fortified home with a Renaissance era garden. This has still visible educational carvings. Eventually debts forced the owners to sell the property and soldiers occupying it later caused ruination. Today it is said that a spectre known as the White Lady haunts the grounds of this still-beautiful shell.

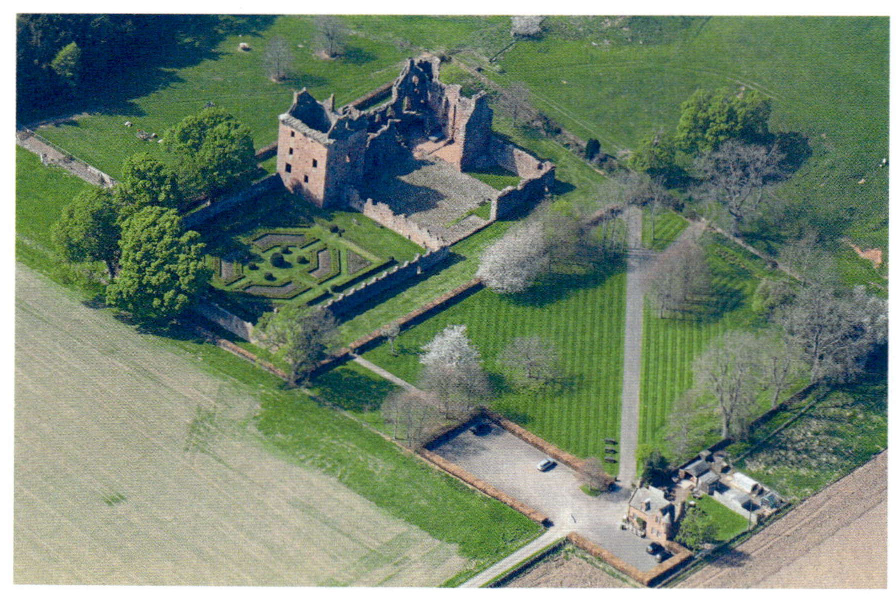

Visitor Details

 www.historicenvironment.scot/visit-a-place/places/edzell-castle-and-garden

 01356 648631

 Open all year, check website for times. Admission fee payable. The garden is best viewed in July when bedding plants rule supreme.

 There is parking and parking for the disabled by the visitor centre. Wheelchair users can access the ground levels of the castle and garden.

 There is a small shop selling gifts and refreshments but no cafe. Nearby Edzell has a cafe and restaurant. This building also houses a toilet and disabled facilities.

Steps enable a higher view of the garden.

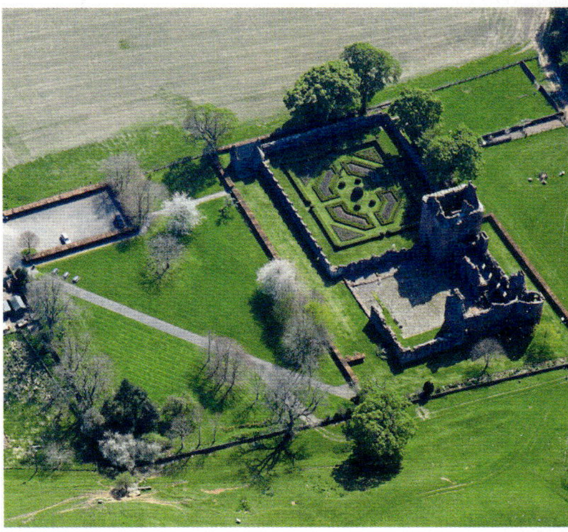

Location: Edzell Castle is located in the Angus district, five miles north of Brechin on minor roads west of the village of Edzell, just off the B966. When in the area, also have a look around Brechin Round Tower, built circa 1100AD, one of only two Irish-style round towers still standing in Scotland.

Edzell Castle consists of a ruined L-plan tower house of 16th century origin and later additions of outbuildings along the line of a walled garden. The now unique garden and carved surrounds date from Renaissance times and would have been known by the description of 'A Pleasance'. The intricate stone carvings along the walls depict scenes of philosophical mysteries indicating that the owners and guests shared interests of an esoteric nature. Combined with a lavish patterned garden layout you could rightly conclude that this castle was not a strategic redoubt but more of a manor house.

The proud first owners were the Lindsay Clan. David, the 9th Earl of Crawford, had the tower house commissioned to replace an earlier wooden motte nearby. His son, a knighted lord of the manor, oversaw the garden design around 1604. A notable welcome guest in 1562 was Mary Queen of Scots and her Privy Council. Cromwell's invading army took advantage of the accommodation in 1651 and two years later returned the favour by rescuing a kidnapped John Lindsay from Royalist forces. By 1715, debts had forced a sale of the castle and land to the Maule Earl of Panmure. The Maules supported the Jacobite cause in 1715 and again in '45 and the resulting forfeit led to a destructive occupation by soldiers. The York Building Company purchased the remains and removed items of use. Although the Maules regained the castle in 1764 the damage was beyond repair, leading to it being abandoned as a home.

A keeper was appointed by the family in 1879 to maintain the property and show visitors around. A keeper's house was built in 1901 and this now houses the visitor centre and shop. In the 1930s the ruins came into state care which led to the restoration of the garden and stabilisation of the ruins.

Some ethereal inhabitants have never left, including a White Lady said to be the spirit of Catherine Campbell who died in 1578. As her grave was being robbed in the nearby Kirk yard, the thief went to cut her rings off when she suddenly revived in pain and staggered back to the castle door leaving behind a terrified robber. No entry was given to her shrouded shape banging on the door as the occupants feared the wraith-like figure. Sadly she perished in the bitter cold overnight and was re-interred the following day. Sightings include being seen and photographed in a castle window and back at the Kirk yard.

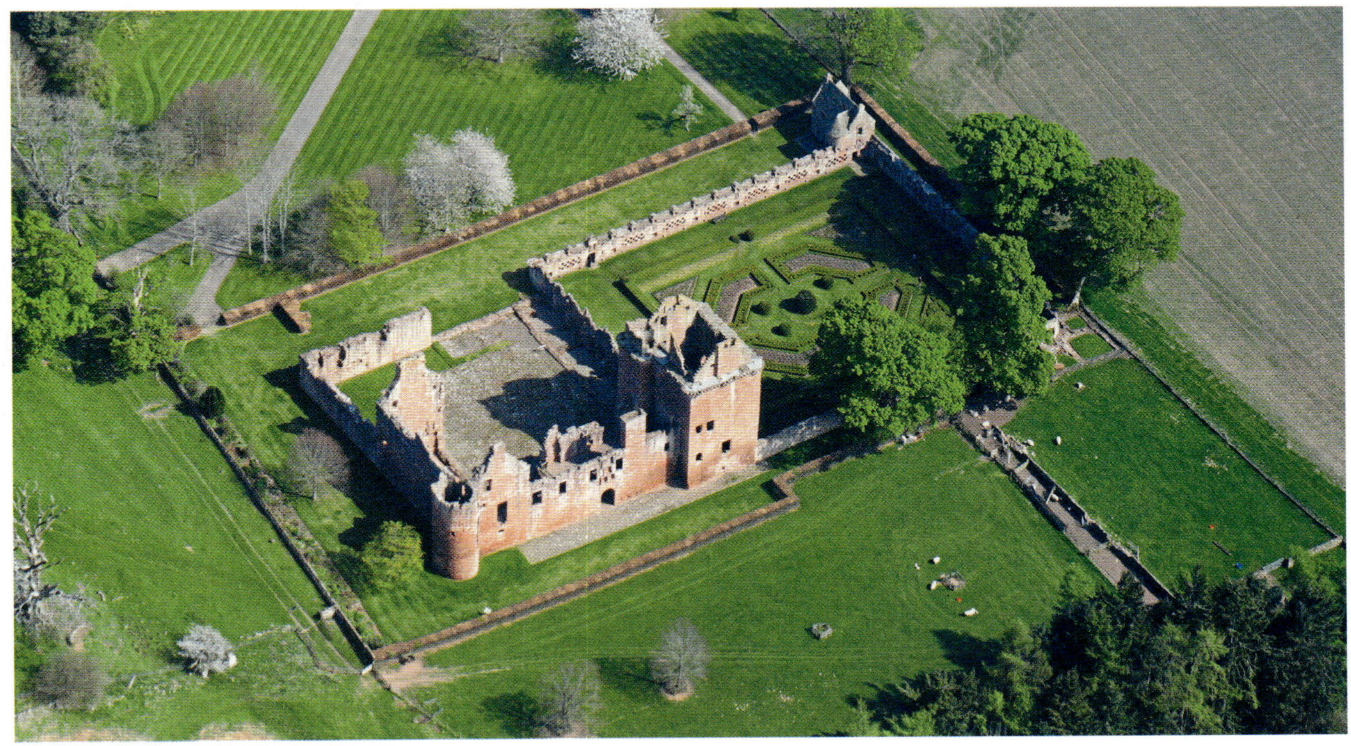

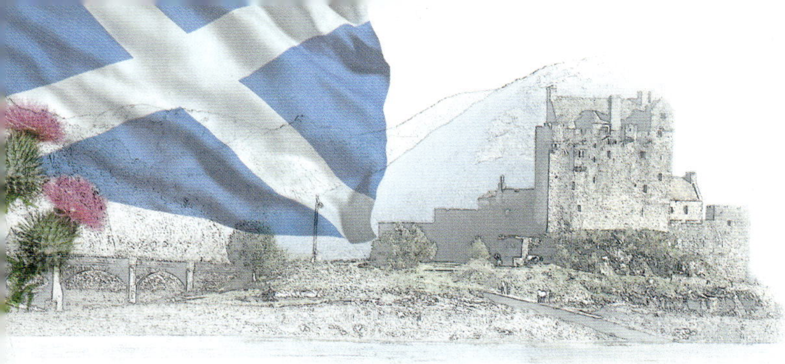

Eilean Donan Castle

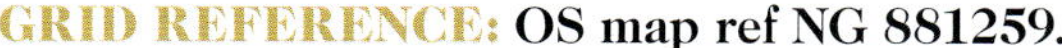

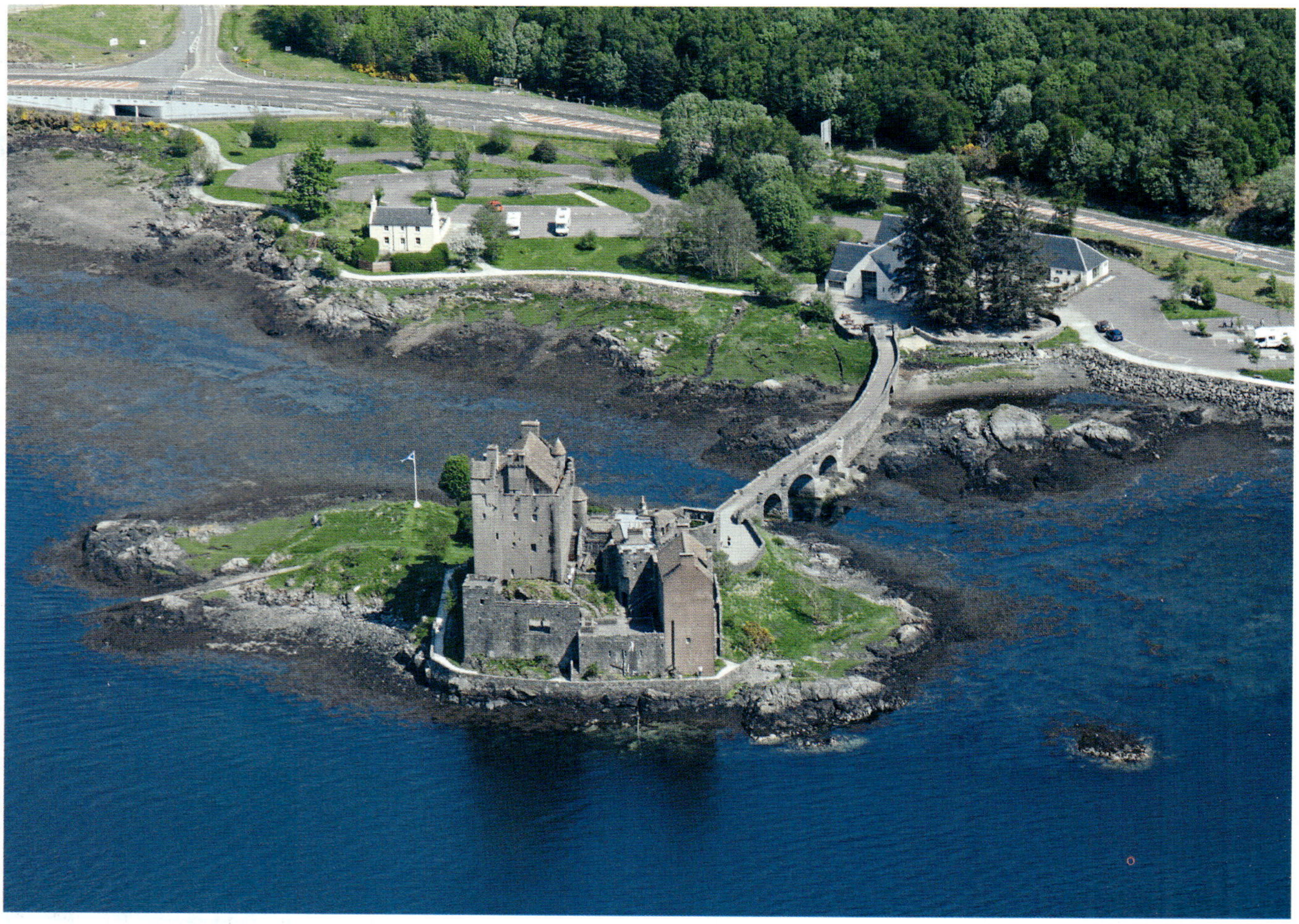

Now famous as a romantic image of Scotland's past, the events that unfolded explosively at Eilean Donan Castle were far from romantic in historical times. Fortunately the severed heads are long since gone and the peaceful location combined with extensive vistas serve to attract filmmakers, photographers and tourists from all over the world.

ABOUT THE CLAN

In the 13th century, the first members of Clann MacRath emigrated from Ireland to the area around Beauly on the estate of Lord Lovat. This branch of the clan later included notable members of the church with surnames such as MacReath, McCree and several variations of Macrae. Descendants became active in civic roles such as provosts and attornies around the Black Isle and Inverness. The three sons of the Macrae chief had a severe falling-out with the Frasers of Lovat which resulted in resettling in three new regions: one near Dingwall (later accounting for the Black Isle branch), another in Argyll and the last in Kintail. This latter region was where a lasting bond between the Mackenzies and Macraes was strengthened when one of the brothers married into the Macbeolan family who were local landowners before the Mackenzies.

Clan Macrae

The defence of Eilean Donan castle was for many years shared by Clan Macrae and Mankenzie. In 1488, Big Duncan of the Battleaxe beat the champion of Macdonald, Lord of the Isles, which ended an attempt to take the castle. In 1539, the Macdonalds came back in over 50 warships. During this siege, Duncan Macrae fatally wounded the Macdonald clan chief Donald Gorm by firing an arrow into his foot. This brought the long feud to an abrupt end.

During the Civil War in 1645, due to the shifting allegiances of the Earl of Seaforth, the clan fought for the state and lost at the Battle of Auldearn. Later they battled on the Royalist side. But worse was to come.

The first Jacobite uprising in 1715 led to great sadness after the Battle of Sheriffmuir was fought on heathland near Stirling. Due to the removal of protecting Jacobite

Visitor Details

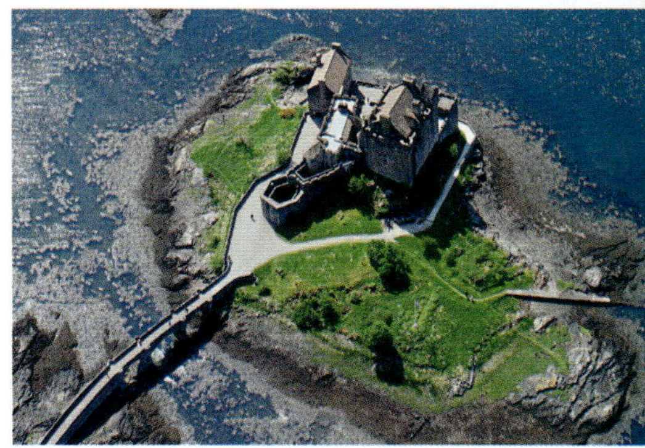

- www.eileandononcastle.com
- 01599 555202
- February to December (closed Christmas Eve, Christmas Day and Boxing Day.
- There is wheelchair access to the visitor centre but due to so many steps and levels, there is no access to the castle. Car park adjacent to the A87, tickets at the visitor centre.
- Coffee shop.
- Gift shop and tourist information.

Location: Just off the A87, south of the village of Dornie, seven miles east of the Kyle of Lochalsh, on the north side of Loch Duich.

The small island of Donan was first settled in the Iron Age. Evidence of a fort has been found. This timber and rock structure had been burned with the resulting very high temperatures converting parts into glass-like solids through a process called vitrification. After the defeat of King Haakon's Norse army at Largs in 1263, a grateful Alexander III granted Eilean Donan castle to Colin Mackenzie, leaders of the defenders at Largs. Around this time, a curtain wall enclosed most of the island with two sea gates for access to the beaches. Construction of a three-level keep was completed and an orchard established.

Later the Earl of Ross claimed ownership but after hosting Robert the Bruce in 1306, the Clan Mackenzie's loyalty resulted in David II granting a royal charter gifting the castle and important local estates to the clan. They retained Clan Macrae as constables to occupy and hold the castle. This confirmed the start of centuries of kinship between these two clans. Visitors to the castle in 1331 were witnesses to the gory sight of 50 severed heads on spikes outside the castle. This was the outcome of the execution of criminals ordered by the Earl of Moray ahead of his inspection. Feuding between the Macraes and Macdonalds continued to, at times, involve the castle. Eventually, the Macraes prevailed, holding the castle on behalf of the Mackenzies.

On May 17, 1719, a force of 300 Spanish marines occupied the castle which was by then in poor condition with no surrounding curtain walls. This was part of an early bid to re-establish the House of Stuart in Scotland. Three Royal Navy frigates anchored just off the castle and sent a boat towards the island under a flag of truce to request a surrender. The Spanish marines opened fire and the boat hastily returned to the ship. Shortly afterwards, the Navy commenced a sustained bombardment of the castle. The cannon were silent during the short Highland night. By dawn, the broadsides thundered again across Loch Duich to cover the landing of boats carrying a raiding party to attempt to take the castle. This was done with relative ease as only 44 of the 300 remained: the rest had headed inland to support Jacobite rebels who numbered around 1,000. This mixed force of Jacobites and Spanish marines were defeated by government forces at the Battle of Glen Shiel. Most of the Jacobites escaped and the marines, being regulars, were sent back to Spain.

Marking the 300th anniversary of the battle in 2019, an archaeological survey revealed ammunition from the coehorn mortars used against the Jacobite forces.

Gunpowder captured at the castle was used to demolish the walls. Two hundred years later, in 1919, local stone mason Farquhar Macrae was employed to make the site look like a tidy romantic ruin. He had a vision of how the castle used to look and made sketches, persuading his employer, Lt Colonel John Macrae-Gilstrap, to re-construct the ruin. He, in turn, commissioned architect George Mackie Watson to draw-up plans. The rebuild took 22 years and cost £250,000 paid for by Gilstrap's money from his maltings business and inheritance. Also included was a bridge which eased movement of building materials and for the first time linked the island to the mainland. Now Eilean Donan Castle is one of the most photographed castles in Scotland. It has featured in over 20 films including Bonnie Prince Charlie (1948), Highlander (1986), Rob Roy (1995), and Entrapment (1999). Open to visitors for most of the year, the castle is run by the Conchra Charitable Trust.

cavalry, the Macraes lost 58 men – almost a quarter of the total Jacobite casualties. These included Duncan Macrae who used his claymore to despatch at least seven of the government troops with only a musket ball felling him. His hefty claymore was displayed in the Tower of London for many years. By the time of the third Jacobite uprising of 1745, the clan, like many others, was divided over who to support. Some joined the 'Independent Companies' under Captain Colin Mackenzie formed to patrol the Highlands in support of the government. Others were recorded as being part of the 3rd Earl of Cromarty's Jacobite troop commanded by Earl George Mackenzie. In continuation of the warrior tradition, many members of the clan served in both World Wars. The granite monument to the fallen of the First World War is located at Clachan Duich which is the ancient burial ground land and church of the clan a few miles south of the castle. A memorial at Eilean Donan Castle names 423 members who died during the First World War. Clan Macrae has no present-day clan chief. The person responsible for the restoration of Eilean Donan Castle, Lieutenant Colonel John Macrae-Gilstrap, was recognised as a senior figure in the clan. However, during a court case involving a claim on the chieftainship he stated "all the Macrae families are more or less on an equality." His legacy has ensured that the castle is now in the care of the Conchra Charitable Trust founded in 1983. There are very active Clan Macrae societies worldwide including Scotland, North America, Canada, Australia, New Zealand and South Africa. This is an indication as to why the clan has been called the 'scattered children of Kintail'. The North American society has a DNA expert who, with the help of members, is discovering how the Macraes are related to each other.

Motto: Fortitudine (Latin for 'with fortitude')
Plant badge: A sprig of clubmoss (staghorn grass) on a bonnet or chest.
Slogan/war cry: Sgurr Uaran – so called after the highest peak of the mountain range known as the 'Five Sisters of Kintail', Sgurr Fhuaran.

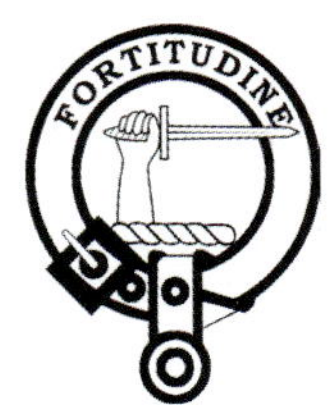

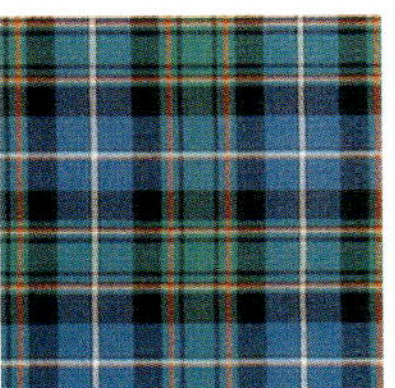

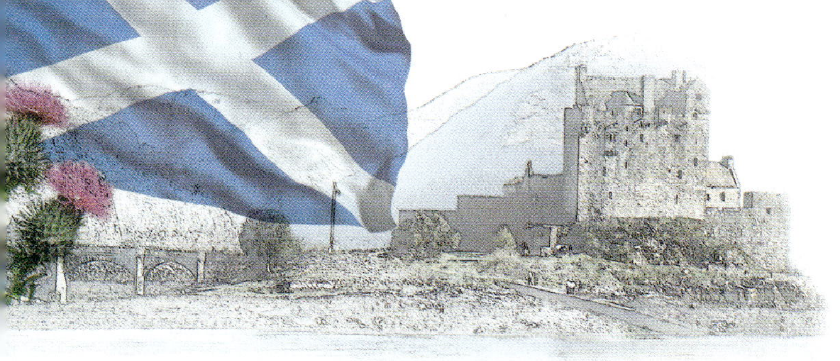

Fort George

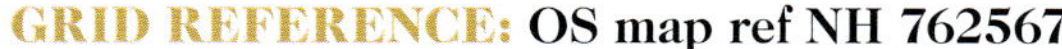

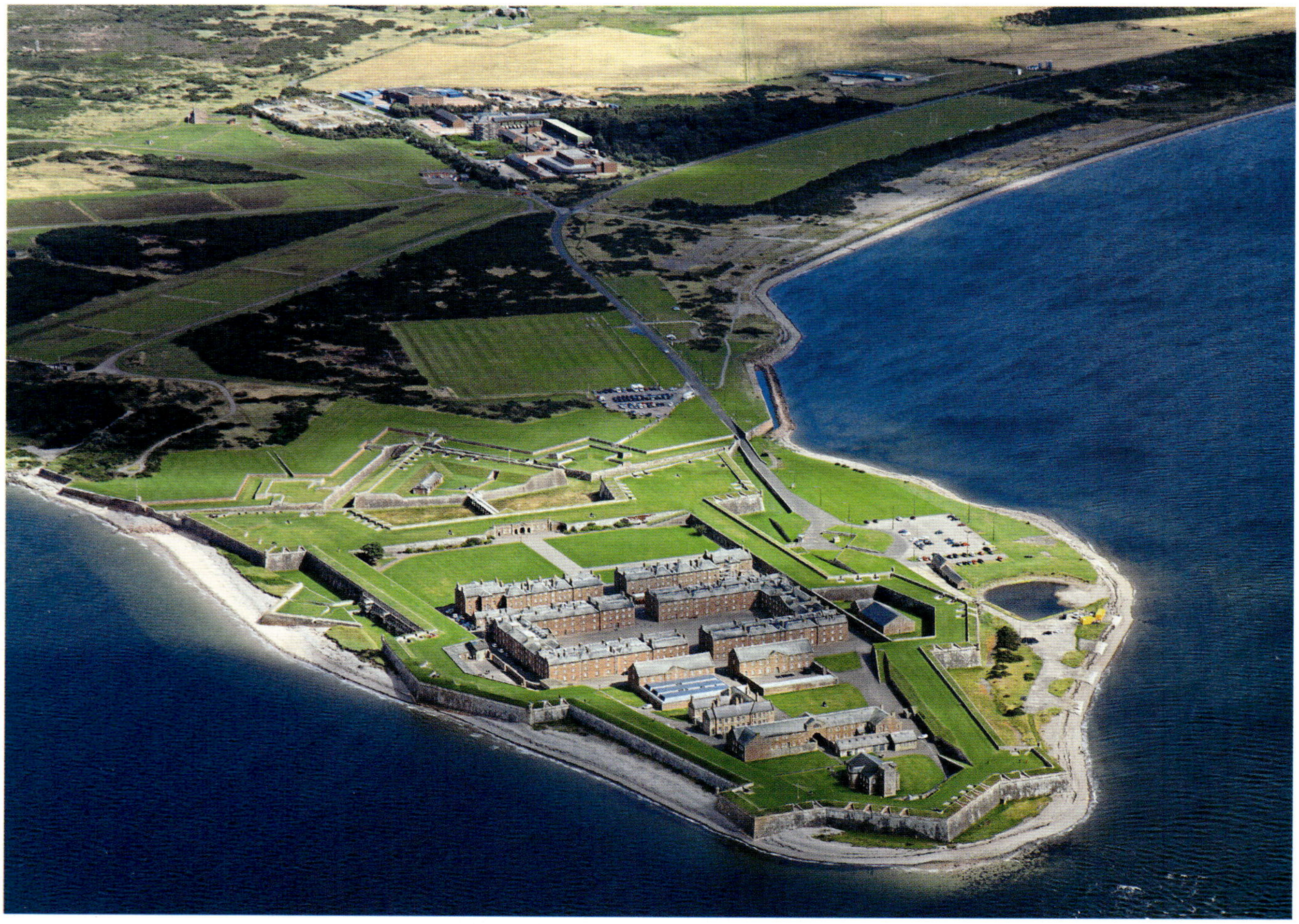

Sprawling across 42 acres, this massive fort was constructed with star-shaped walls to provide the best possible fields of fire for the cannon on its walls. The strongest defences faced inland to protect the garrison from marauding Jacobites. Still an active army base today, the fort's walls provide excellent views out to sea where bottlenose dolphins can sometimes be seen.

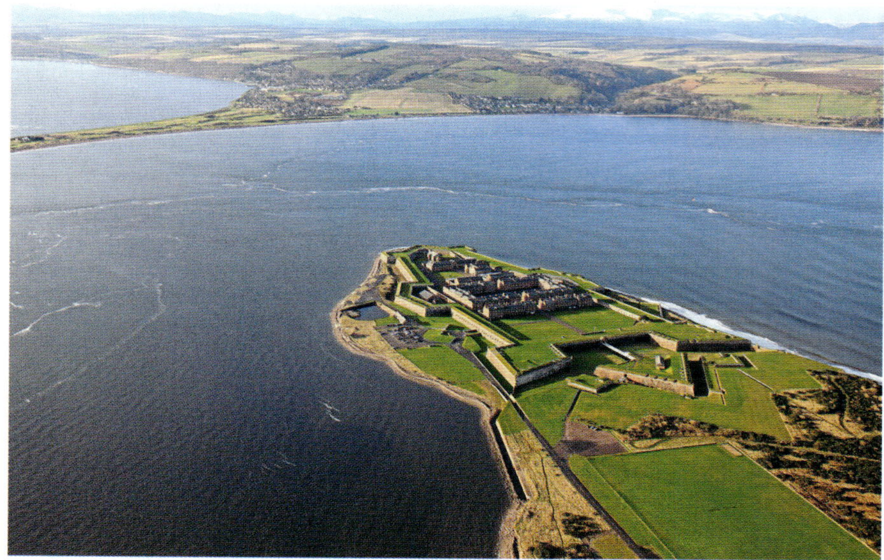

Visitor Details

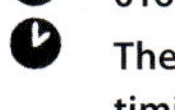
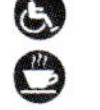

www.historicenvironment.scot/visit-a-place/places/fort-george

01667 460232

The fort is open all year with shorter hours in October to March, check website for timings. Check the website for details on outdoor events.

Disabled access surface levels only.

A tearoom on-site enables refuelling of thirsty tourists.

Some barrack rooms are open to show how they would have appeared at different times in history. Also on show are assorted weapons such as muskets and pikes. A loaned machine gun from a Zeppelin has also been noted. Many well-preserved massive artillery cannon line the fort walls and also some short range mortars are displayed. The regimental museum of the Queen's Own Highlanders is located here. The 42 acres give plenty of space for re-enactment groups to set up encampments with thrilling mock skirmishes. When budget permits, this also can include Spitfire, Mustang and Messerschmitt aircraft swooping low overhead.

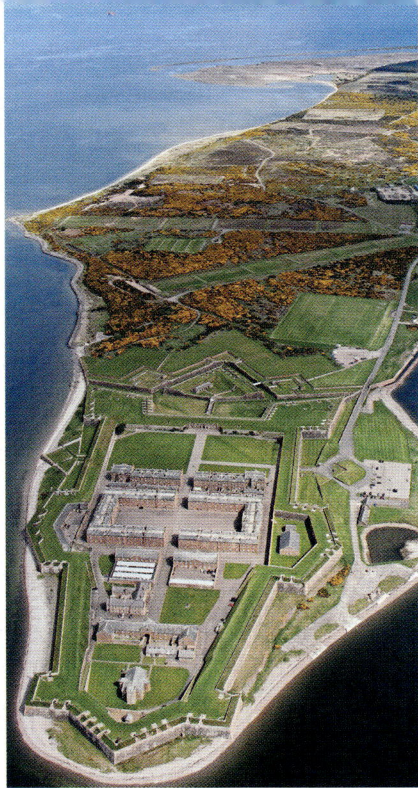

Location: Jutting out into the Moray Firth on a narrow spit of land eight miles NE of Inverness. Take the A96 main road to the Allanfearn crossroads then turn north-west onto the Ardersier road for four miles. You are following part of a former military highway originally built by the engineers under the command of Major Caulfeild which linked the Fort to Grantown, Corgarff and Braemar.

The attempts by Jacobite supporters mostly based in the Highlands and Islands to take control of the throne gave the government great anxiety. When the Jacobites marched into England, they caused panic in London with royals and nobles prepared to depart by barge along the Thames. These violent events between 1715 to 1746, culminating in the nearby battle on Culloden Moor, resulted in the building of three large stone forts along the Great Glen and a new road network linking the forts and several barracks. Only Fort George remains physically intact, the other forts being remembered in the names of towns Fort William and Fort Augustus. The first Fort George existed for a short time at Inverness near the river but was not defensible. The layout of Fort George followed the then-latest ideas on the placement of artillery. By combining ditches, ramparts, bastions and firing steps, all angles were covered using a star pattern. These aspects came from plans by Lieutenant-General William Skinner. The main defences face inland towards the potential threat but the fort also included a harbour to enable resupply if under siege. The seaward side was later reinforced to provide counter broadsides to any naval bombardment and to control shipping access to Inverness. The encircling walls are a mile in length which form a fine bracing walk with the potential for sightings of bottlenose dolphins which arrive daily to feed on fish in the tidal flows between the fort and the Chanonry Point opposite.

Architectural detailing came from the Adams family of architects. Followers of this Georgian style of building should also take time to visit the well-preserved Georgian town of Cromarty 10 miles north on the Black Isle.

Building started in 1748 and took 23 years to complete. More than 1,000 soldiers formed the workforce. As with modern projects, the costs soared from an estimated £92,673 to around £200,000 when fully fitted with more than 80 cannons, 2,672 barrels of gunpowder, other weapons, food for 2,000 men, a brewery and a chapel. This equates to almost £1 billion today or the cost of six F-35 Lightning jets or one third of the cost of HMS *Prince of Wales*, the aircraft carrier.

As part of the plan to pacify the Highland Clans, not all of whom were Jacobite followers, this unconquered remarkable redoubt sent a clear message of power. The threat from the clans became less of a concern as the fort neared completion. Ironically, such a costly investment found a use as a focal point for the recruitment of the Highlanders who maintained a proud history of military service to the United Kingdom.

Between 1881 and 1964, the fort served as the depot of the Seaforth Highlanders. The Fort is still an active army base with extensive firing ranges nearby visible on the accompanying aerial views. Fort George is currently the home of the Black Watch, the 3rd Battalion of The Royal Regiment of Scotland (3 SCOTS).

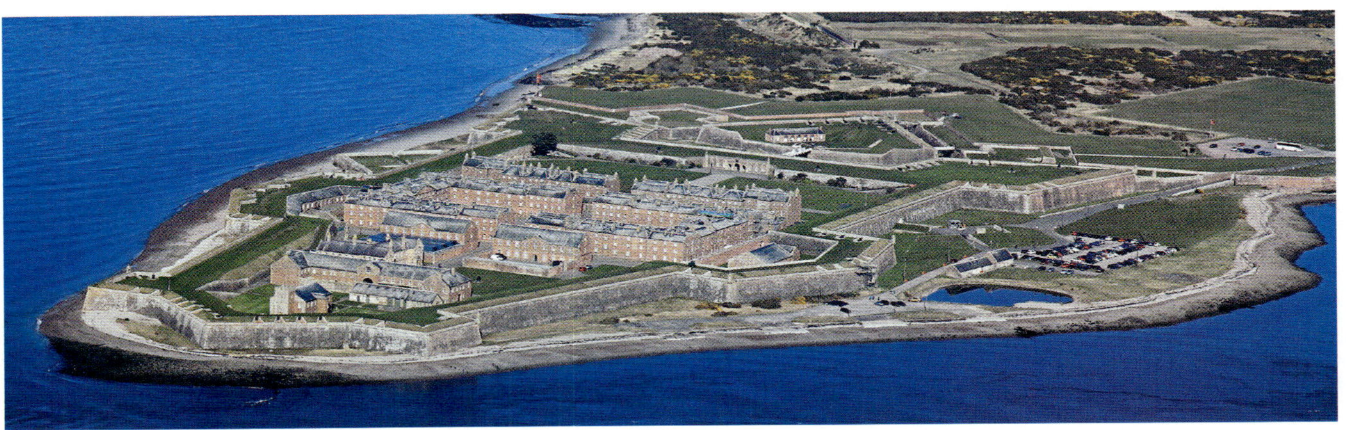

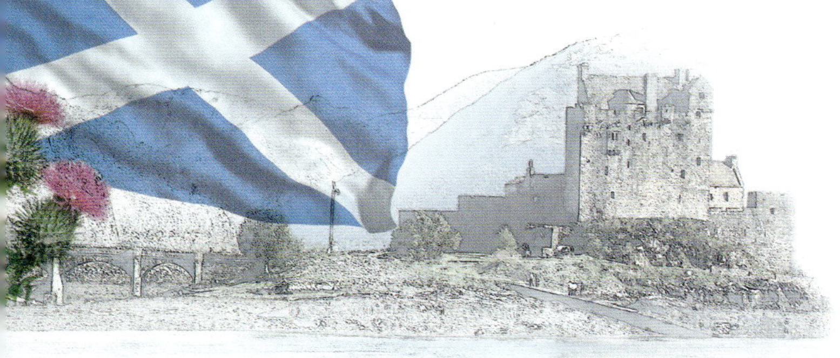

Foulis Castle

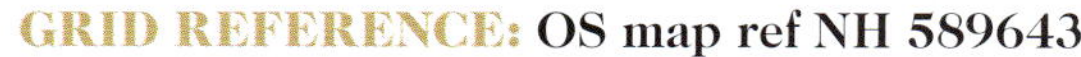

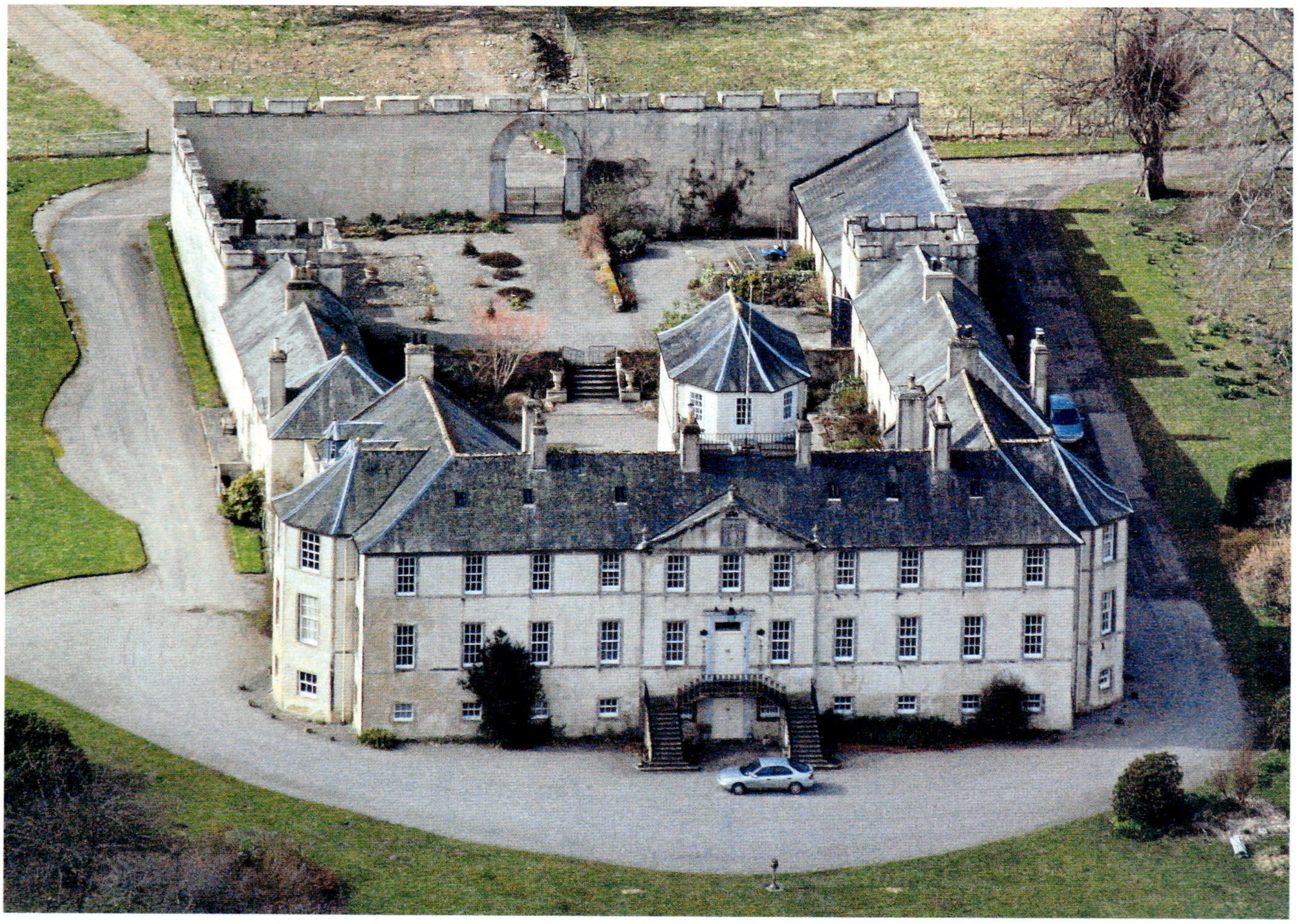

This fortified mansion house was constructed on the site of an earlier castle and today remains the home of Clan Munro. Visits are possible by appointment and beneath the comfortable and well-appointed Eighteenth Century exterior can still be viewed the original structure of a practical fortress from more troubled times.

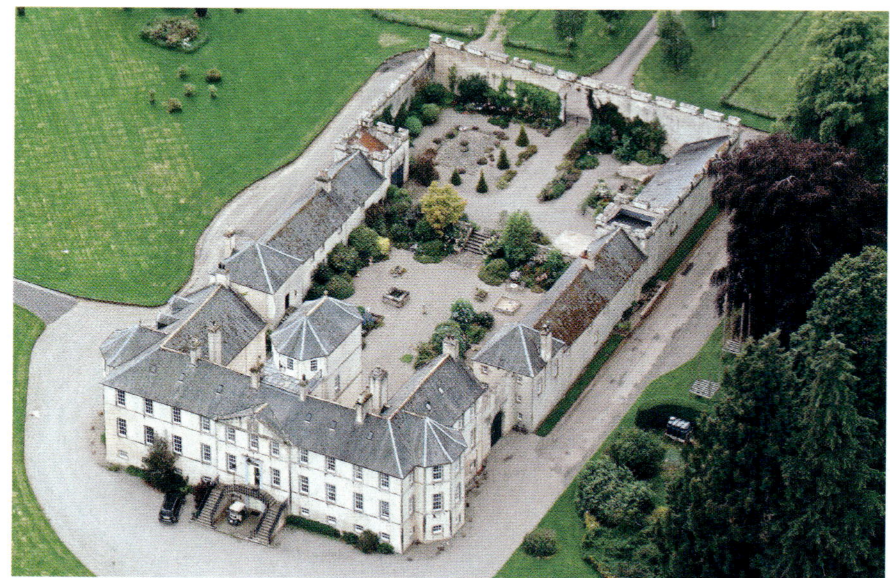

Visitor Details

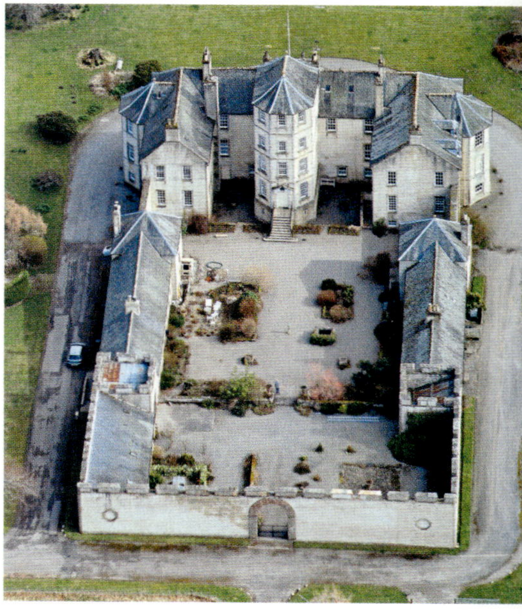

- www.clanmunro.org.uk/castle.htm
- No telephone.
- It is essential to make an appointment for a visit to Foulis Castle.
- Disabled access limited to surface levels.
- Refreshments in nearby towns.
- The Munro family have come together to welcome visitors to Foulis Castle. Tours are donation-based. A guide to the donation is £10 per adult, and a minimum of three weeks' notice is required.

Location: Foulis Castle is located in the district of Ross and Cromarty, two miles south west of Evanton on a minor road just north of the A9. Foulis Castle is not on a public transport route so a car or taxi is required. The easiest way to get to the castle from the south (Inverness) is to take the A9 road over the Cromarty Firth bridge, passing the Storehouse of Foulis Restaurant and Clansman Museum on the right (an great option for lunch) and then branch off to Evanton (B817). Just before entering the village take the road to the left (Drummond Road), at the next T-junction turn left and approximately one and a half miles later the castle should come into view. On the right there is a narrow road (signposted Foulis which can be easily missed) which leads to the beginning of the drive. The entrance has two pillars with eagles on top (symbols of Clan Munro).

Within the grounds are the remains of a mound which formed the foundation for a wooden fort, the Tower of Foulis. This is believed to date from the 11th century and was known as a motte. After this the Munro clan gained lands forming an estate including higher ground to the north. Part of the agreement was that they were bound to provide a snowball in midsummer if asked to do so. The place name Foulis is derived from the Gaelic 'Fo-Glais' meaning a streamlet; several of these drain the lands to the Cromarty Firth.

Mystery surrounds the exact form of the stone keep castle built in the 16th century. Almost hidden inside the current Georgian structure are gun loops, three arches and a tower dated 1754.

This tower was raised after Sir Harry Munro came home after opposing the Jacobites in the 1745 uprising. His castle had been attacked and burned by hostile clans.

After the defeat of the Jacobites at Culloden the chances of further clan warfare was much reduced, therefore much of his rebuilding took the form of a more continental style. The resulting mansion house forms the frontage of a large courtyard with a range of buildings including a bakery, coach houses, stables and a laundry.

Foulis Castle still remains occupied. It is the clan base of the Chief of Munro, Hector W Munro of Foulis-Obsdale, Baronets, although they live in London.

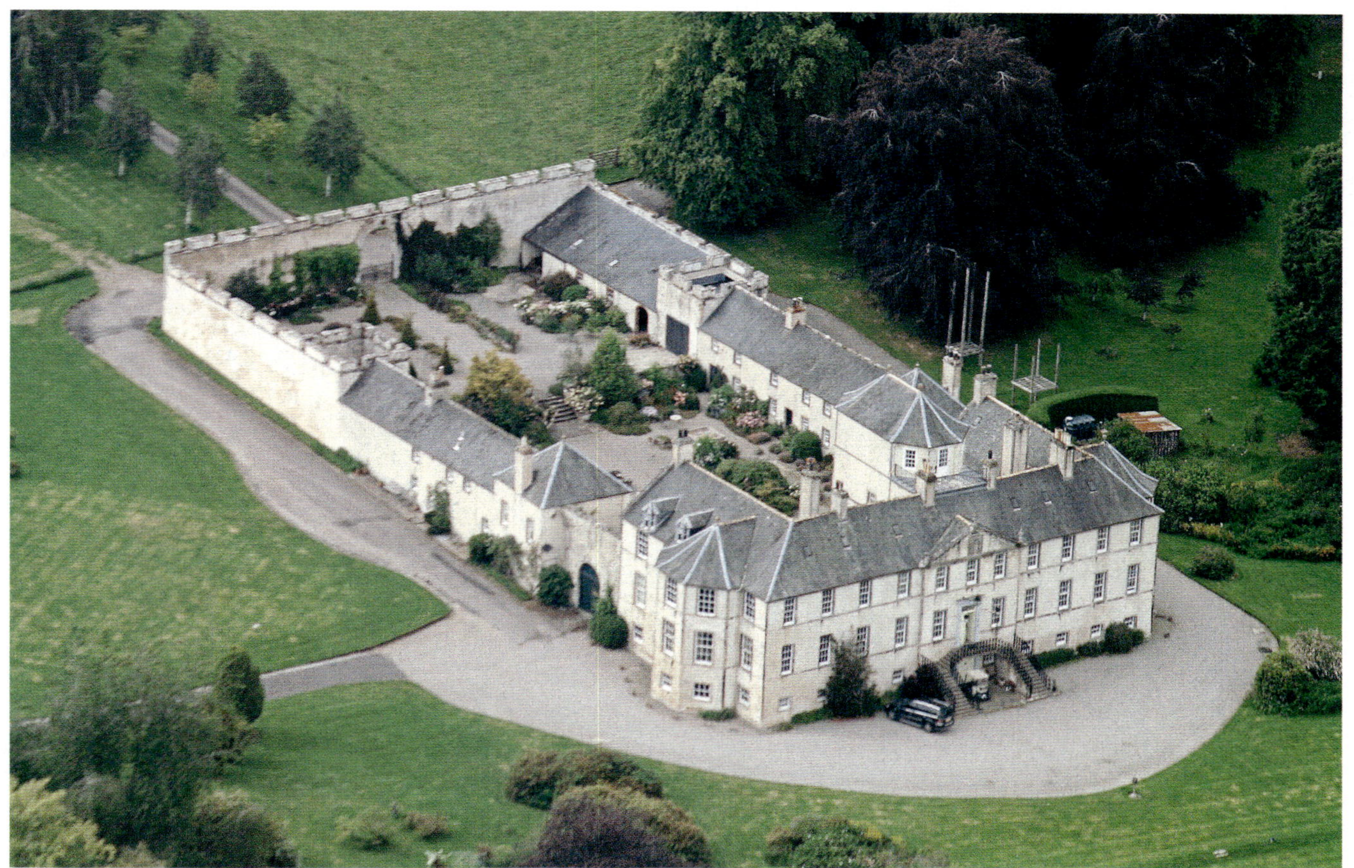

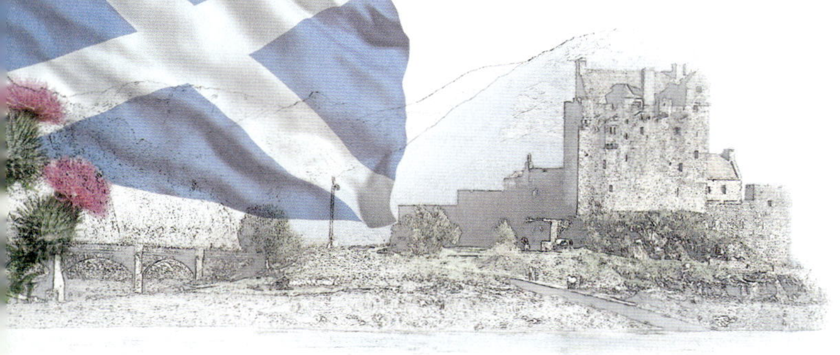

Fraser Castle

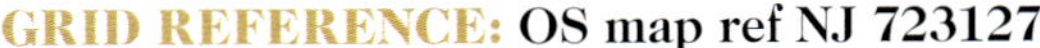

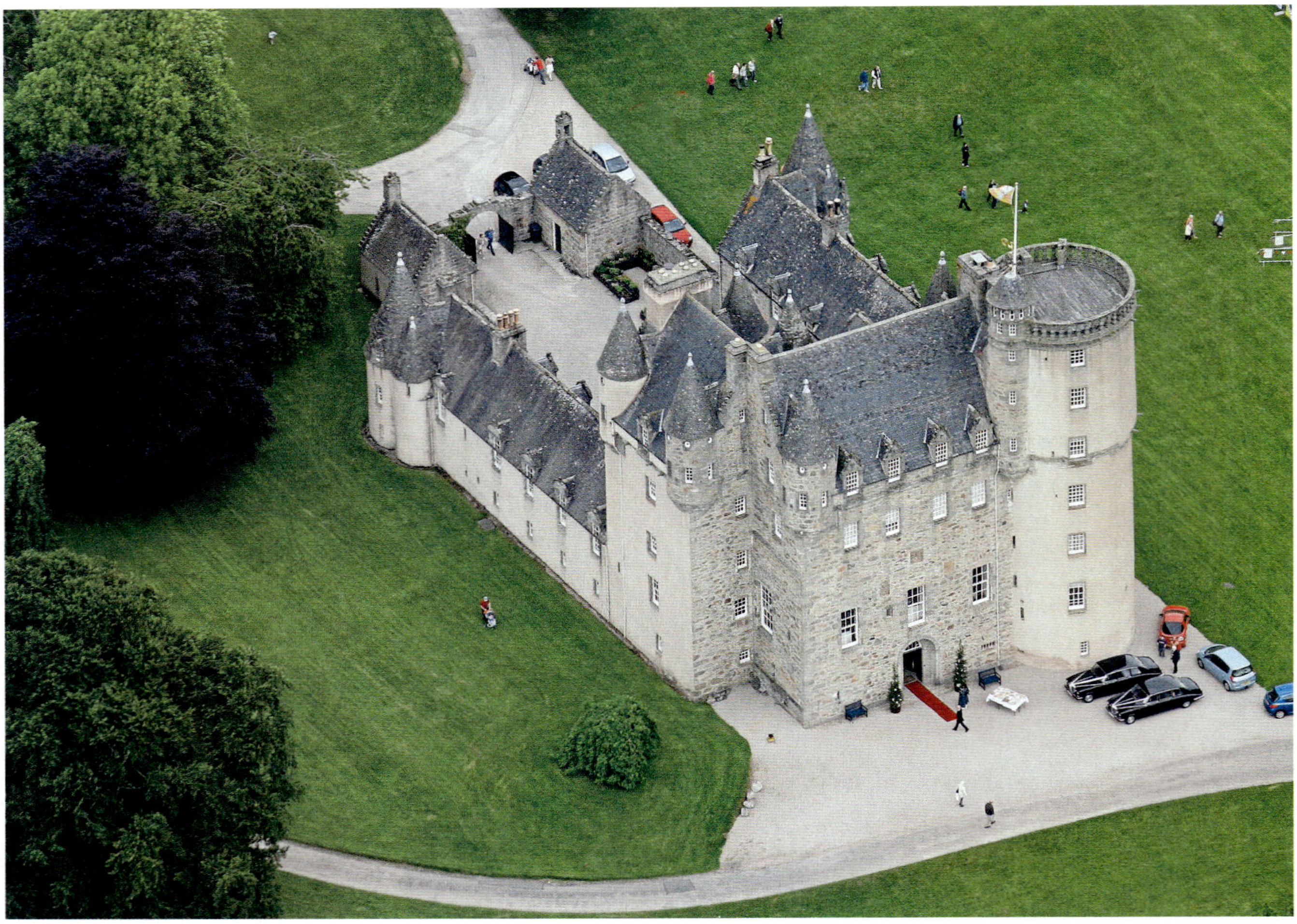

The great solid tower house seen today is a tribute to a skilled restoration. This was the base of Clan Fraser, who were besieged here several times, and there is much to explore inside, including secret rooms and trapdoors.Combined with the extensive grounds and gardens this is a gem that is well worth a visit. Now cared for by the National trust for Scotland.

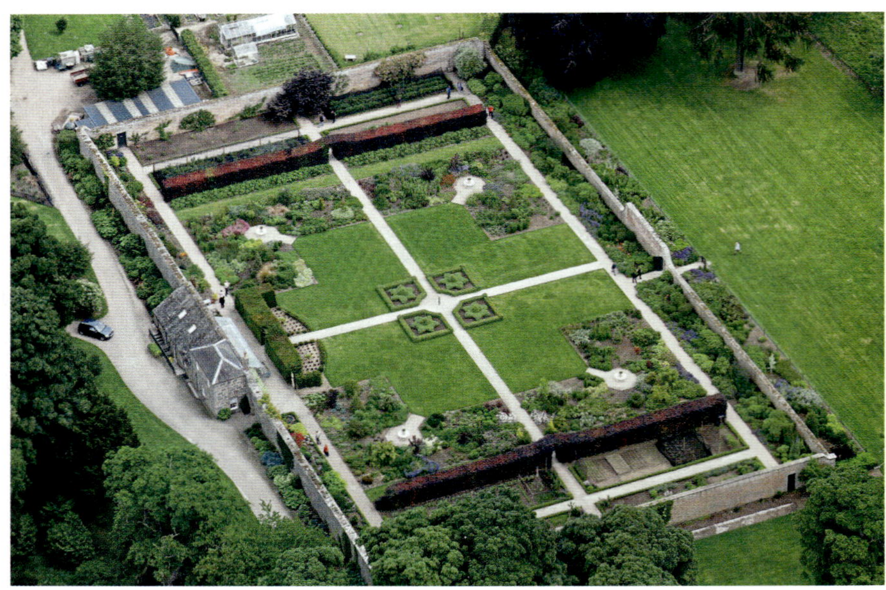

Visitor Details

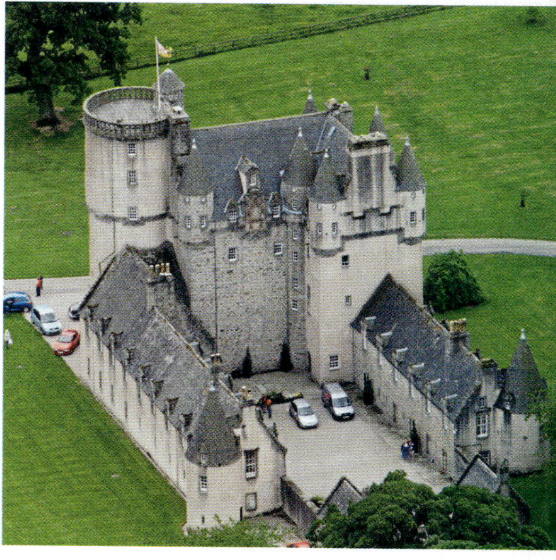

 www.nts.org.uk/visit/places/castle-fraser

 01330 833463

 The castle is usually open for most of the year; check website for times. Admission fee payable. NTS members have free entry.

Limited disabled access to the castle courtyard due to gravel. However, wheelchair access to the ground floor of the castle and the tearoom can be provided via the front door by contacting the number above. A digital screen in the reception area allows visitors to look at the upper-floor rooms in more detail. The scented walled garden and adventure playground are accessible for wheelchairs.

Tearoom and gift shop.

Many interesting rooms, antiques, portraits, hidden trapdoors, secret staircases and a spy hole.

Location: Castle Fraser is situated in the Aberdeen and Gordon district, six miles south west of Inverurie.

This is one of the best preserved Z-plan tower castles in Scotland because it was expanded outwards from the tower as the clan needed more comfortable accommodation. The rectangular tower was built for Thomas Fraser. The estate came to the Fraser Clan in 1454 as a method of ensuring loyalty to James II. For many years it was called Muchill-in-Mar castle.

Michael Fraser was keen to enhance the profile of the clan in the region and decided to make the castle a show piece. So he instructed mason John Bell to add two further towers to the corners of the keep, one of which is of a circular pattern. This resulted in a Z-plan fortress with ample room to live and entertain. Michael's son, Andrew, oversaw completion in 1618. By 1633, he had become a lord although this did not protect the clan from the conflicts to come.

The Frasers were Covenanters in opposition to the changes in worship imposed by Charles I. The second lord, another Andrew led the looting of the Bishop's Palace in Aberdeen. Soon after, the wrath of Royalist forces led by Lord Aboyne fell on the castle to lay siege. Frustrated by the strong defences they then took the easier option of destroying outbuildings and crops. The Marquis of Montrose arrived in 1644 with a more organised siege force which took the castle.

By 1674, the 4th Lord Fraser, Charles, had transferred ownership of the castle and estate to the Earl of Mar, John Erskine, a relative. Charles gained permission to reside in the castle. This deal also cleared the debts but bound the Frasers to Mar for life. In turn he had to support Mar in the Scottish Parliament vote for the Union in 1707 and ended up on the losing side in the 1715 Jacobite rising. Charles fell to his death from cliffs at Pennan while being hunted by government forces in 1716 after the rising failed. He had no male heirs and by 1787 Miss Elyza Fraser began improvements to the castle. Later efforts to maintain the massive buildings were made by Charles Mackenzie Fraser. He also added to the courtyard while in service as an officer in the Duke of Wellington's army.

In 1921, the castle was sold as a daunting ruin in need of restoration and became the home of Clive Pearson, the second son of Viscount Cowdray. After 25 years of hard costly work, the castle was given to his second daughter Lavinia and with her husband Major Michael Smiley (a Colditz castle escapee), they continued the project until 1976. The National Trust for Scotland became the current owners, later adding more land to ensure the castle surrounds could be improved to provide a fitting location for such a splendid castle. The grounds include an 18th century walled garden, lake, woodland and amphitheatre. Hauntings of this castle are many and include a lady in a flowing black gown, possibly Lady Blanche Drummond who died in 1874. Or perhaps she was the woman killed in the Round Tower's Green Room who is said to have been dragged down the stairs leaving a bloody trail which is now concealed by wood panelling. The large hall sometimes echoes to the sounds of piano music and voices when empty.

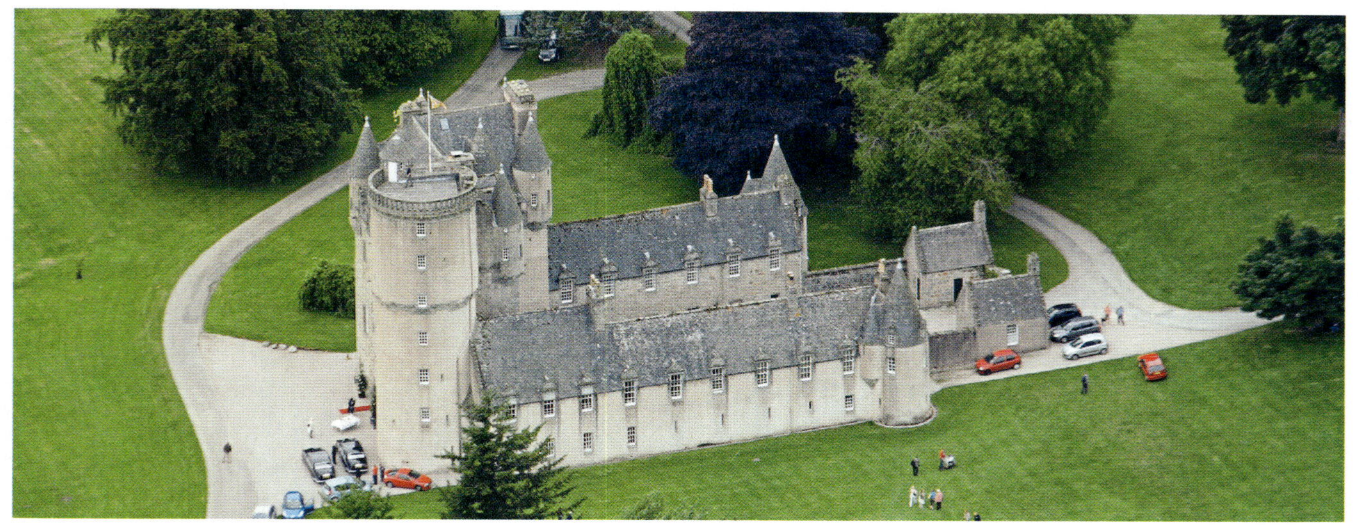

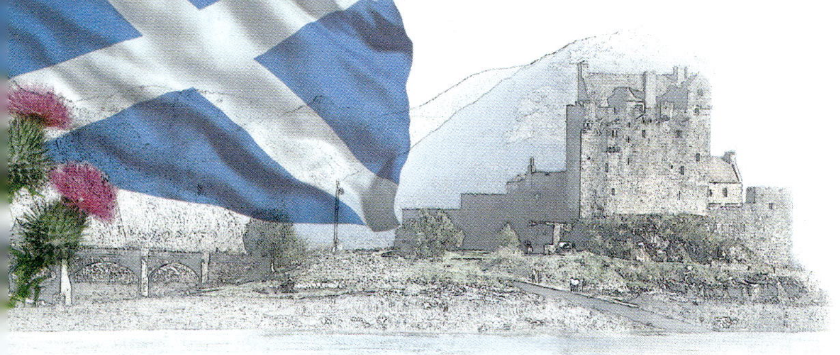

Fyvie Castle

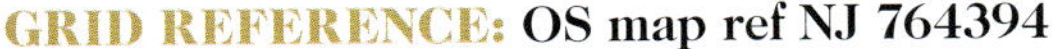

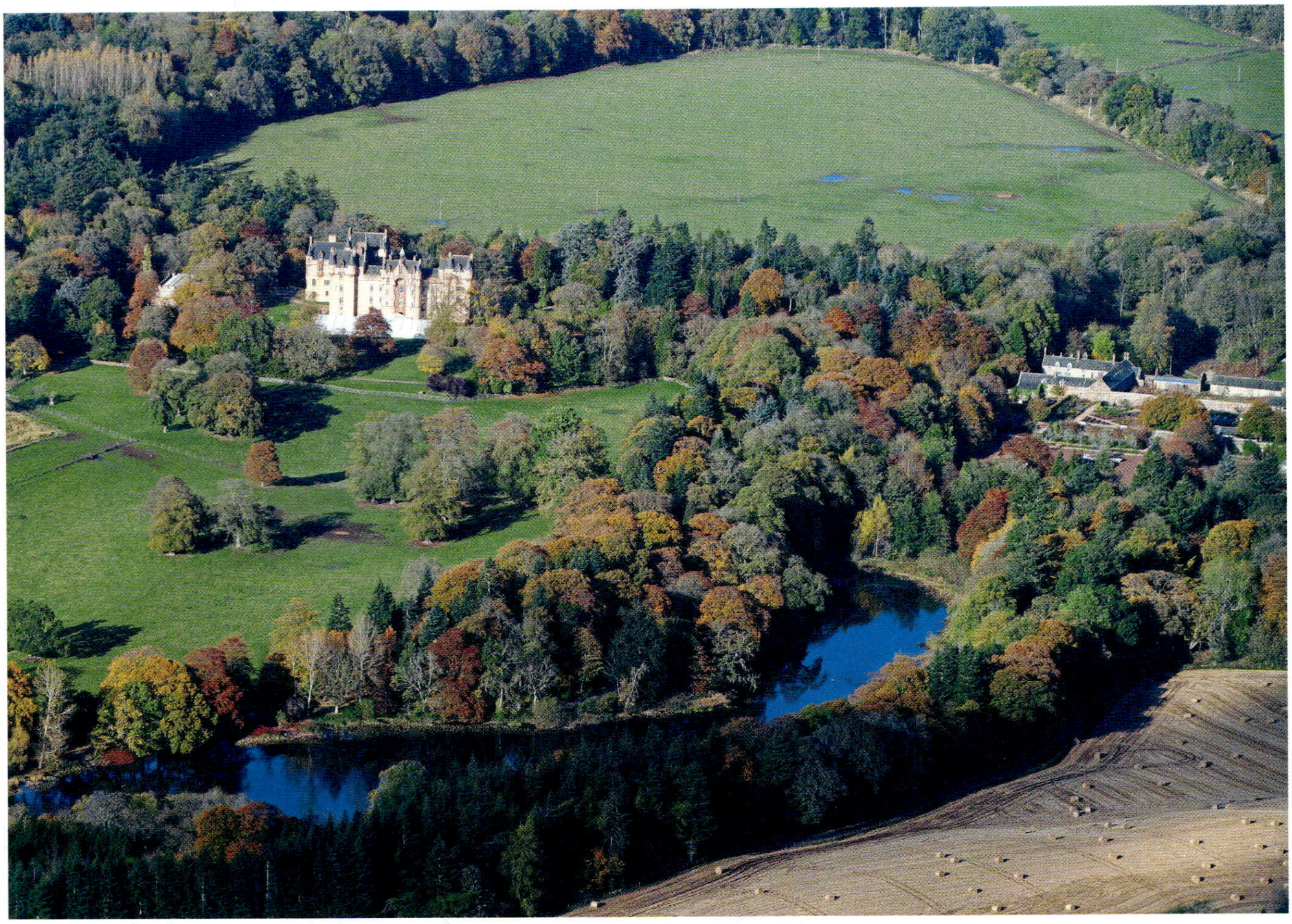

Soaring turrets, ornate arches and magnificent staircases are just a few of this castle's many outstanding architectural features. Inside, it is home to many historic objects and artworks. Over the course of its history it has changed hands many times and today its interior is decorated with the coats of arms of 22 noble families that have lived within.

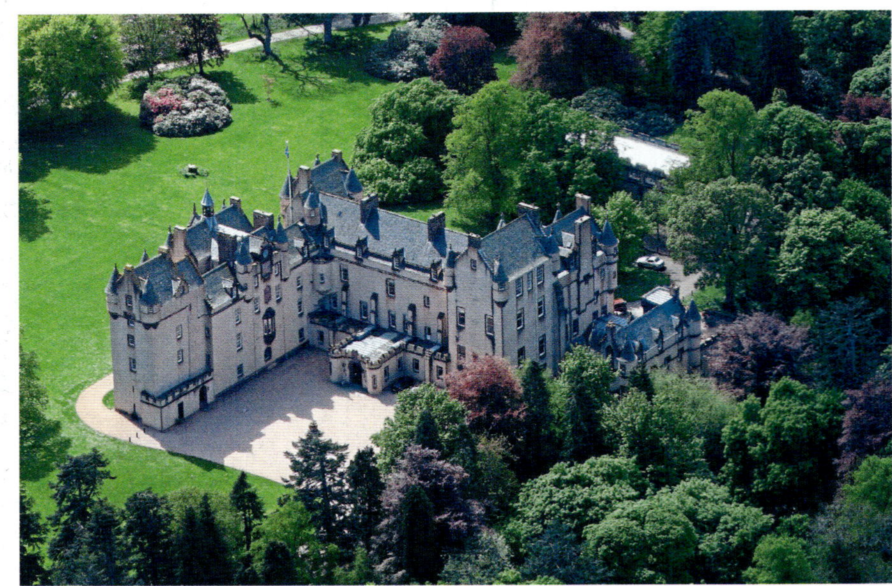

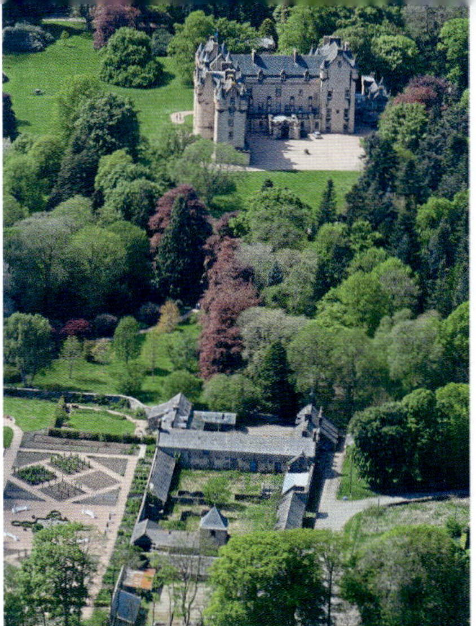

 www.nts.org.uk/visit/places/fyvie-castle

01651 891266

Entry to the castle is by guided tour. Pre-booking is suggested to save a wasted journey. Last admission to the castle is 4pm. The castle is open in the summer months. See detailed opening times on the website.

There is wheelchair access to the tearoom and toilet.

 The tearoom and gift shop open during castle hours.

The grounds and walled Scottish Fruits Garden are open daily from 9am to dusk.

Location: Situated in the Banff and Buchan district, Fyvie Castle is off the A947, one mile from Fyvie village, eight miles south-east of Turriff and 25 miles north-west of Aberdeen.

The earliest mention of a defensive structure at this site was in the 13th century and was likely to have been a wooden keep surrounded by a palisade. This took advantage of being inside a bend of the River Ythan which prevented advances from the west and left just a few access tracks across marshy ground to the east. Early royal visitors to this stronghold included William the Lyon, Robert the Bruce and Edward the First.

When the Battle of Otterburn was won by the Scots in 1388, many hostages were taken including the English knight Ralph de Percy. As part of a ransom deal, the King of Scotland, Robert III, granted Fyvie Castle to Sir Henry Preston as a reward for fighting in the battle. This marked the start of an ownership sequence of five clans who each added a new tower to the castle: Preston in 1390, Meldrum c.1440, Seton 1599, Gordon 1788 and Leith 1890. Few castles in Scotland have such an impressive appearance with soaring turrets, gables, finials and ornate entrance arches. Seton also had a lavish staircase added around 1600 and this is now decorated with 22 coats of arms of the many families connected to Fyvie.

Conflicts at the castle include the Marquess of Montrose gaining occupation by force in 1644 after a skirmish with the Covenanters and being taken by Cromwell's army in the 1650s. In 1694, the castle was forfeit to the crown after Seton's heir, the Earl of Dunfermline, supported the Jacobite cause. In 1733, the estate was bought by the Gordon Earls of Aberdeen. During this time, many changes were made to the layout of the castle and grounds including the parklands which can be seen today. The last major change to the castle was in 1890 when Alexander Leith added his tower after buying the estate, castle and contents. He was a wealthy business man and like Andrew Carnegie, another Scots born steel magnate, collected many historical items. The castle was filled with his paintings, furniture, tapestries and armour.

In 1984, the castle was bought with contents by the National Trust for Scotland. It is to be wondered how much extra they paid for the spectres? Such as the drummer boy, Andrew Lammie, who plays in advance of bad fortune coming to a clan. Or the Grey Lady said to have starved to death. In the 1930s, her skeleton was found in a wall cavity during repairs and haunting increased until the remains were replaced. Perhaps this is the same spirit as the reported Green Lady in a change of outfit? The former wife of Alexander Seton was said to be unhappy as she never gave the earl a male heir. He remarried quickly after her death in 1601. Her name, Lillies Drummond, appeared carved into the outside window sill of the castle room that the newlyweds occupied. The name is still visible, did she leave it?

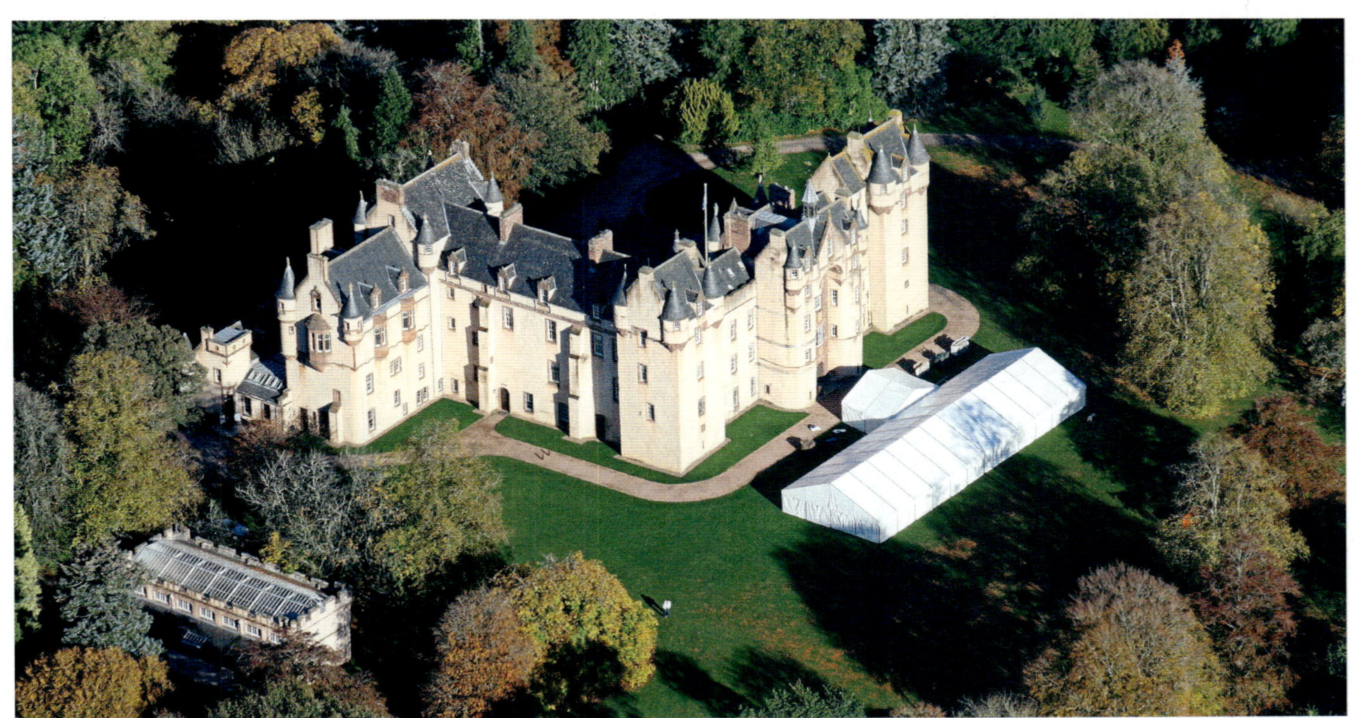

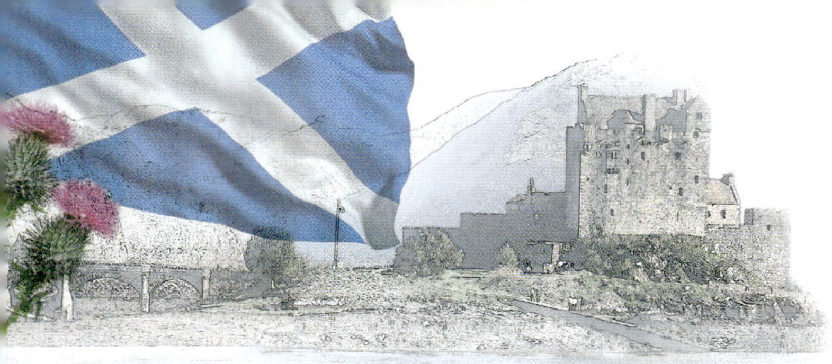

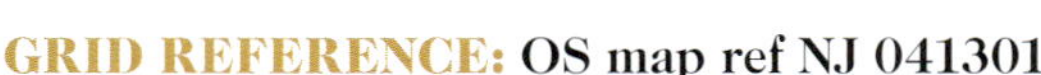

Castle Grant

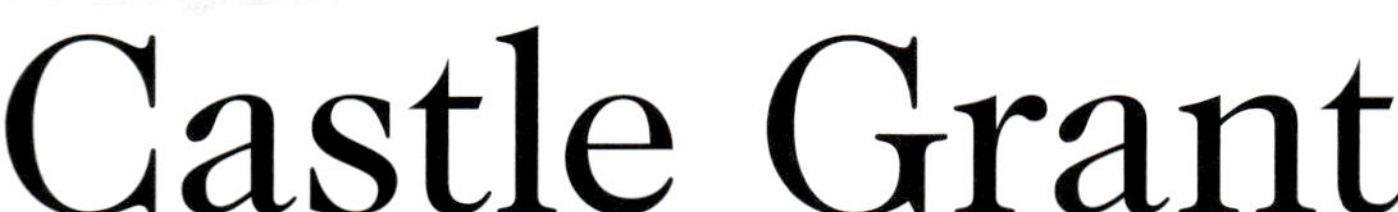

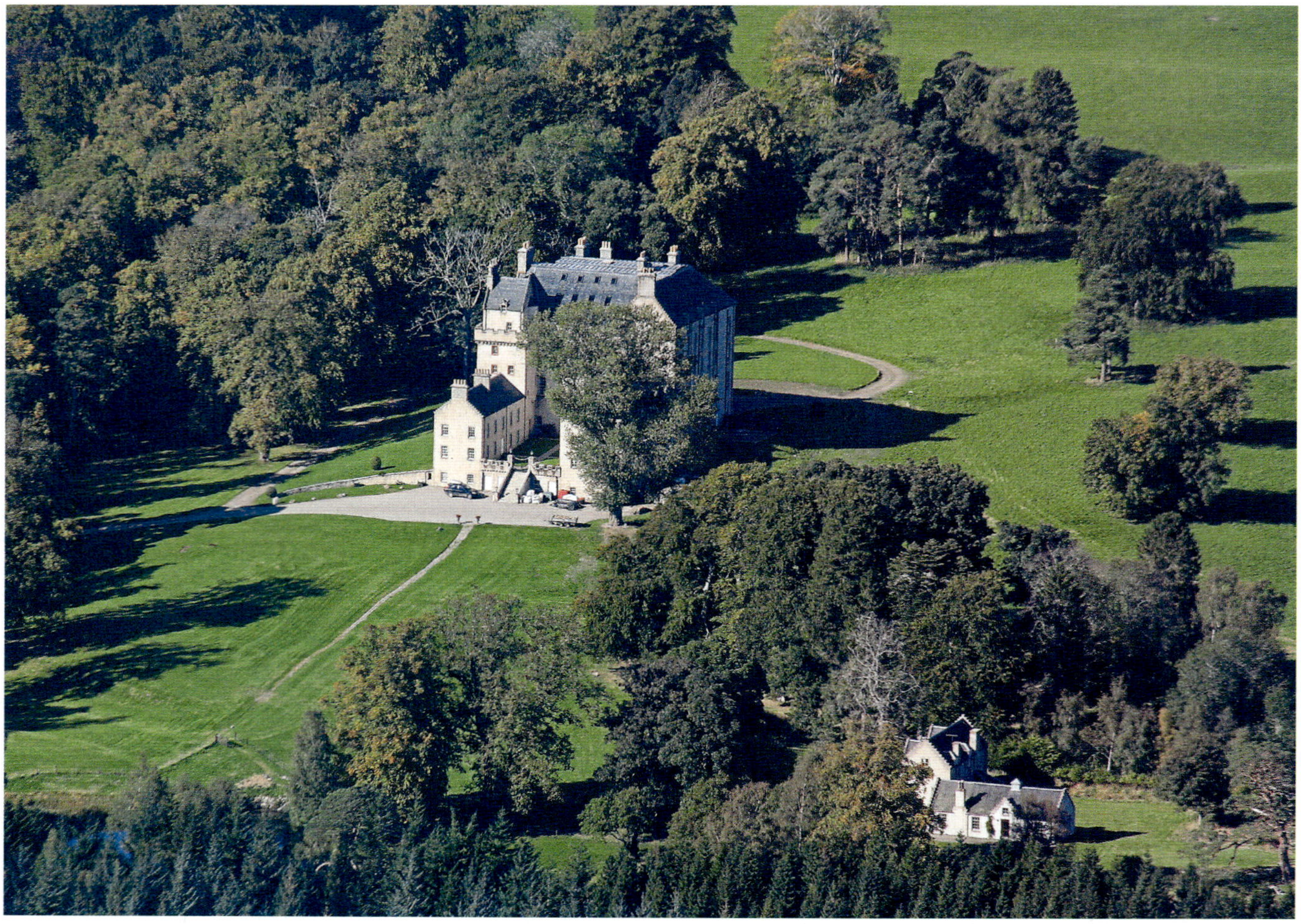

ABOUT THE CLAN

The story of the birth of Clan Grant forms part of the traditional tales told around roaring fires for centuries. These sagas tell of the Viking, Haakon Grandt from Norway settling in Scotland after time spent exploring Ireland. Early written references to the Grants record them as living in the area now called Stratherrick to the south east of Loch Ness. Sir Laurence le Grant was sheriff of nearby Inverness in 1263. They supported Robert the Bruce at the battle of Dunbar in 1296. Evidence exists recording the capture of Randolph and John le Grant there which was a sign of their importance, perhaps they were ransomed?

John survived to purchase lands at Inverallan, Strathspey in 1316 an area which became the clan's heartland.

The first clan chief was also the sheriff of Inverness in 1434, Sir Ian Grant. By 1493 the

Clan Grant

settlement in Strathspey had grown to justify a castle on the location known as Freuchie, started by Sir James Grant.

Clan feuds were inevitable but not constant. The Grants and Campbells joined forces to take up arms against the Gordons of Huntly in 1594. Another alliance was with the MacGregors; they were given safe haven at the castle when threatened.

During the civil wars in the 17th century the Grants supported the crown with their clansmen campaigning with the army of the Marquis of Montrose at Inverlochy.

In the 1715 rising the clan did not become tangled in the skirmishes and battles. After this unrest the government decided to form independent companies led by General Wade. The clans chosen for service as loyal to the crown were the Munroes, Frasers, Campbells and Grants. They became known as the Black

Visitor Details

Castle Grant is a private residence and not open to the public.

Location: Castle Grant is located two miles north of Grantown on Spey in grounds just off the A939 Grantown to Forres road. The ornate gatehouse on this road was also built to serve as a railway halt for the castle in 1863.

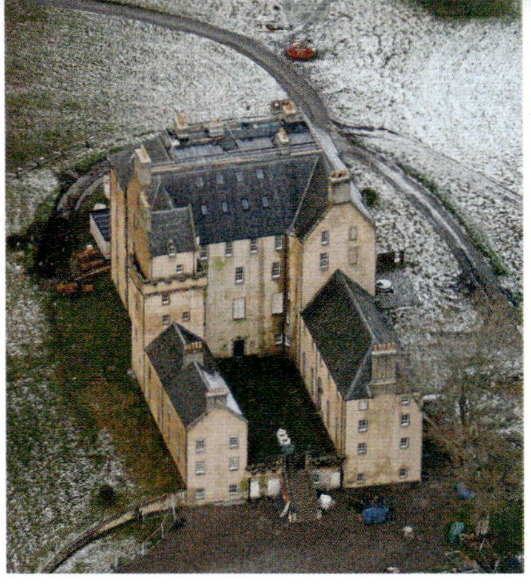

The early history of this location is the result of the castle building desires of the Comyn Clan. They had a castle on Freuchie Mound most likely made of timber close to the site of the current stone building. Clan Grant gained control of the tower structure by force in the 11th century and had created what became a stone Z plan tower house by the 15th century known as Freuchie Castle (the castle of the heathery place). By 1694, the Grant Clan had a good reputation as a supporter of the King and were granted a crown charter to legalise the ownership of the estate lands. This encouraged Ludovick Grant to change the name of the fortified home to Castle Grant and to add new family portraits to show their rising status to visitors. Supporters of the Bonnie Prince were unwelcome occupants of the castle in both Jacobite risings although no damage was recorded unlike another Grant castle at Urquhart bay on Loch Ness. Urquhart Castle was blown up by the Grants to deny its use by the Jacobites. Some Grants fought for the Jacobites at Culloden and survivors were encouraged to surrender by the Laird. Expecting fair treatment, they were transported to the West Indies instead.

An Independent Company of Grant clansmen failed to prevent the first Fort George at Inverness from being taken by Jacobites in 1746. The year 1750 marked massive improvements to the castle with extended wings, a courtyard at the rear and the enclosure of the tower. The basement was vaulted and a large hall with a massive fireplace

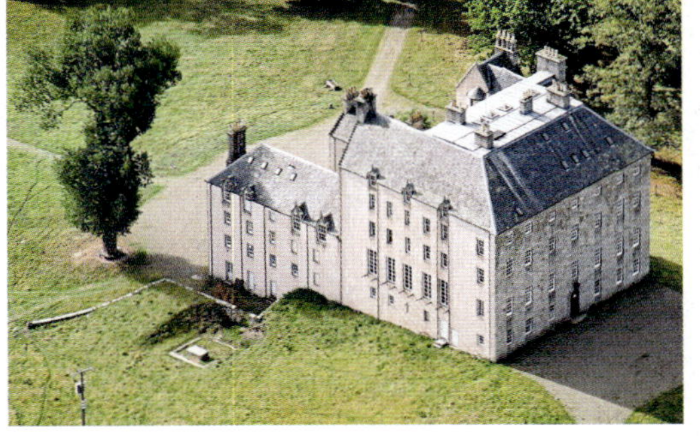

was created on the first floor. Access to the many upper floor rooms was now by a spiral staircase. When the Laird James Grant needed more craftsmen for his new planned town to be built nearby he used the castle works as a training area for masons. What is now called Grantown on Spey is a fine example of early town planning and his vision included establishing weaving with good housing. In the local region he had commissioned Thomas Telford to build more roads and bridges than General Wade. In her search for a Highland estate, Queen Victoria visited the castle in 1860 staying at the Grant Arms in the town. She was not impressed by the "factory-like appearance" of the castle and later chose Balmoral instead. Another person not impressed was the 16th century father of Lady Barbara Grant. She desired to be married to a person of reduced status. To prevent her elopement he locked her in a small closet in the castle tower. She would not give up her desires and is said to have died from a broken heart. Her ghost has been seen crying in that area now called Barbie's Tower. By 1811, the local Grant chiefs had been named The Earls of Seafield. The castle's upkeep proved too expensive so they moved to a mansion near Cullen on the coast. The family still owns much land and property in this region of Scotland. By the 1950s, the castle was derelict and since then, several owners have gradually renovated the structure.

The aerial views show work still in progress in 2018. The present owner is in a Russian jail.

Watch, appointed to keep law and order in the highlands.

Although the Clan Chief declared support for the British government in the 45 rising, not all branches followed his orders. The oldest clan branch around Glen Moriston supported the Jacobites at the battle of Prestonpans in 1745, helping to gain the victory for the Jacobites. This Jacobite branch also took the field on the marshy heath of Culloden in 1746. Other Grants were there fighting for the Hanoverian forces. The 'Good Sir James' was the honourable nickname given by locals to the baronet chieftain around 1765. He strived to treat his clansmen well and shield them from the hardships and clearances affecting the highlands. He arranged for extra food supplies to be distributed at his expense, created craft workshops and then had a new town built near his castle. Grantown is fine monument to him.

The Earls of Seafield were Chiefs of the Clan Grant from 1811-1915, when the 11th Earl was killed in the Great War.

The 27th chief of the clan had a dispute with his brothers in the 19th century. This resulted in the estate being split up. The Seafield Earldom was lost to the clan chief but the line continued with the title Lord Strathspey of Strathspey.

The Clan Grant Society was founded in 1897 see https://www.clangrant.org/

The home of the Clan Grant Society Worldwide is the old Church at Duthil, close to Grantown-on-Spey, and now known as the Clan Grant Centre. https://clangrantvisitors.org/listings/duthil-church/

Opening Times: The church building is open by appointment only. To arrange a visit call the Grantown Museum on tel: 01479 872478. The graveyard is accessible to the public at all times.

Motto: "Tenons ferme" which has become the well known clan war cry "Stand Fast Craigellachie" (from the crag above Aviemore where a beacon was lit to rally the clan to fight). Castles connected to Clan Grant which are detailed in this book. Grant, Loch an Eilean and Urquhart.

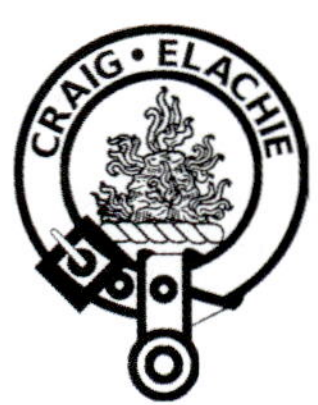

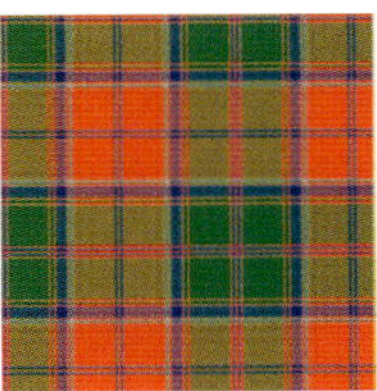

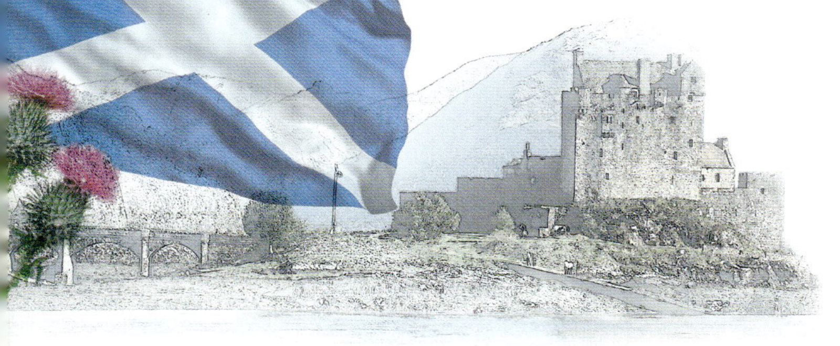

Gylen Castle

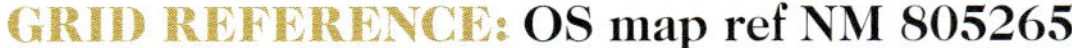

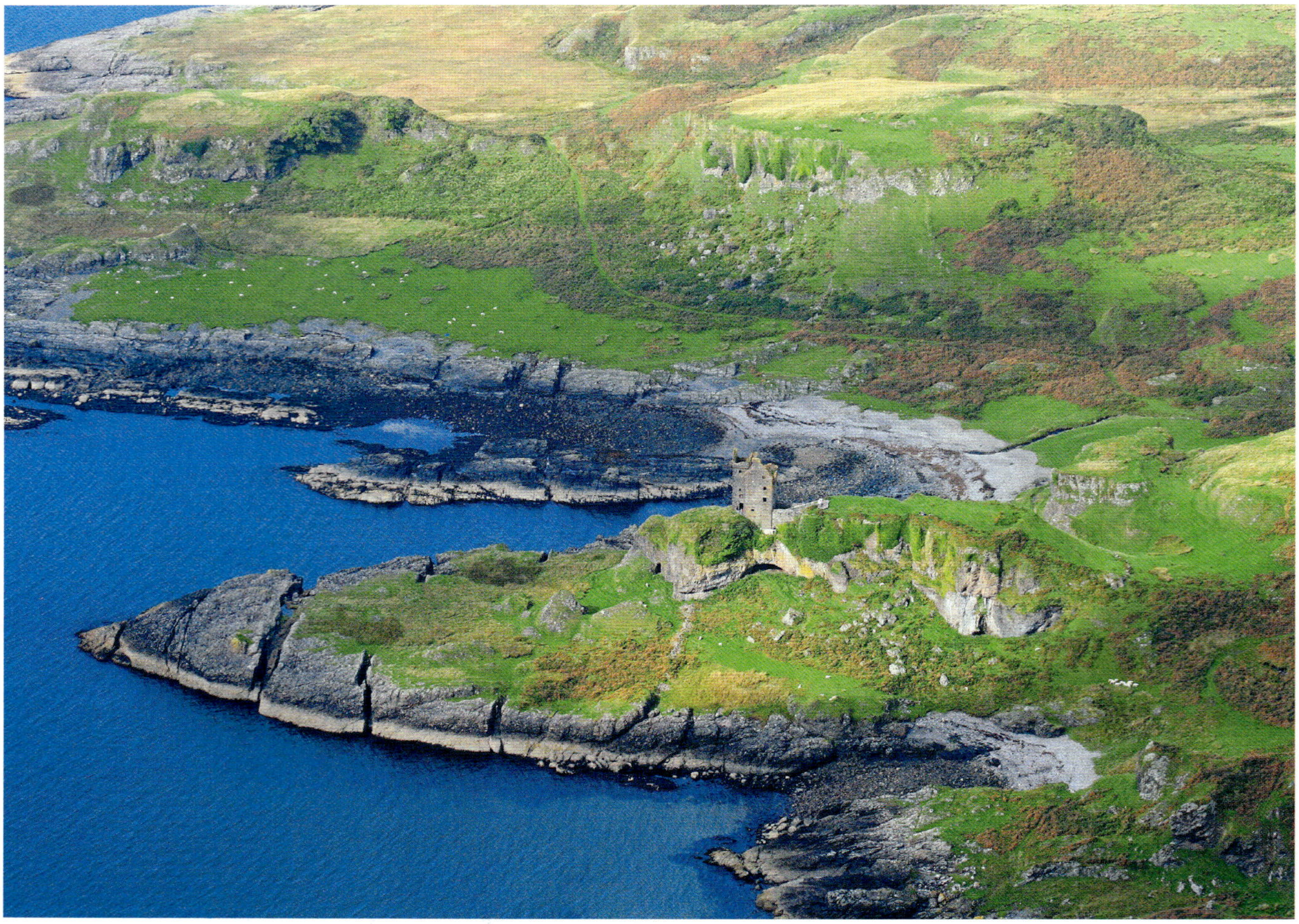

Located on the remote island of Kerrara, Gylen Castle was once a glorious white tower embellished with carvings. Surrendered to Covenanters in 1647, the garrison was slaughtered and the tower was torched. The remains still stand, perched on a rocky outcrop. Getting there requires a long journey but the spectacular views make it worthwhile.

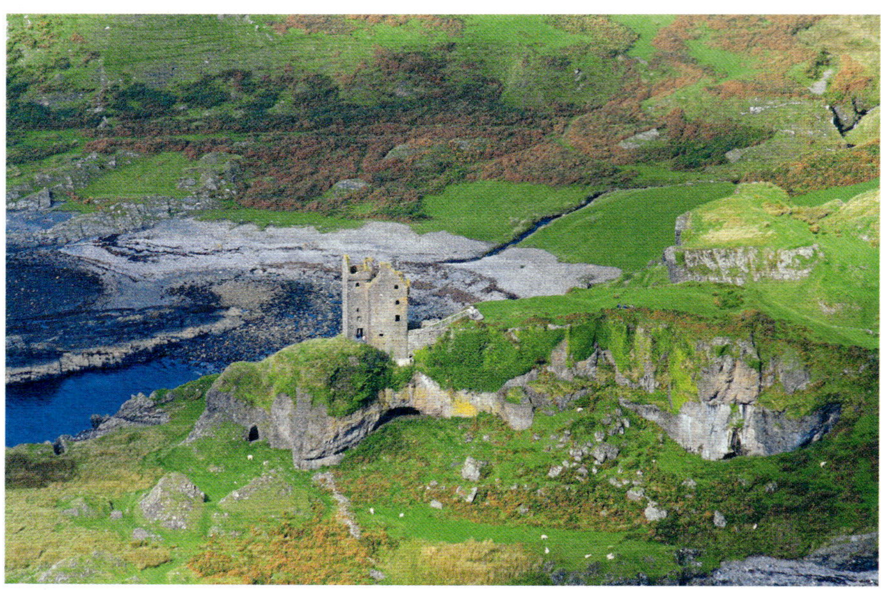

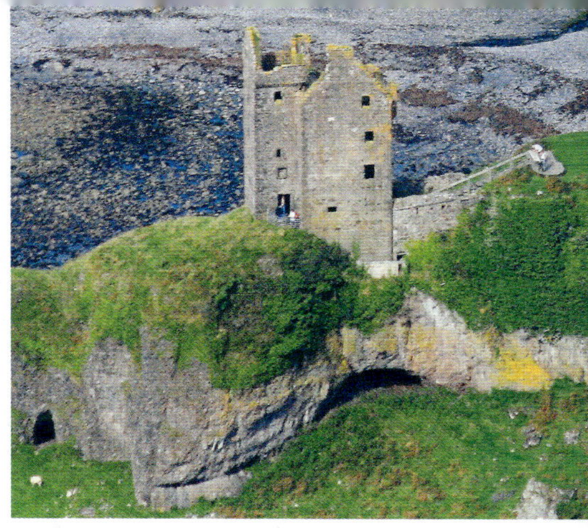

Website for nearby tearoom and bunkhouse: www.kerrerabunkhouse.co.uk

01631 566367

Open 24 hours, seven days a week.

Location: Gylen Castle is on the south end of the six mile long Island of Kerrara. This small island is between the Firth of Lorn and the Sound of Kerrara and is reached by a short ferry voyage from Gallenach near Oban. No visitors' cars are allowed. It is a four mile walk or cycle to the castle. Funding has been made to enable to upgrade the track linking north and south island communities.

Duncan MacDougall of Dunollie found a rocky coastal promontory here circa 1582 and decided to build a stronghold. Sea trading was very important, especially among the islands and inlets of Western Scotland. Therefore having a castle in the region extended the clan's influence and control. The L-plan tower house of four storeys was approached across a courtyard built to the cliff edges. Higher parts of the tower included gun loops, enabling shot to be rained down on hostile forces landing in the bay. Across the narrow approach, a curtain wall included firing positions and enclosed a spring.

Apart from a remaining decorative oriel window, it is not apparent that the castle was originally embellished with carvings and rendered in a white lime wash. This would have indeed impressed visitors, thereby enhancing the standing of the clan. The Clan MacDougall supported the Royalists in the Wars of the Three Kingdoms. Hence, the Covenanters' forces laid siege to the castle in 1647. Hoping for mercy, the occupants surrendered but in this case all were slaughtered except for a very young John MacDougal. The castle was sacked and burnt out, never to be restored.

Some castle stones now form part of Lower Gylen farm buildings. During conservation and stabilisation work by the MacDougall Preservation Trust around 2005, a mid-17th century copper turner coin with the letters 'NEMO' and part of a thistle pattern was discovered in the remains. This was likely lost during the time of the castle siege.

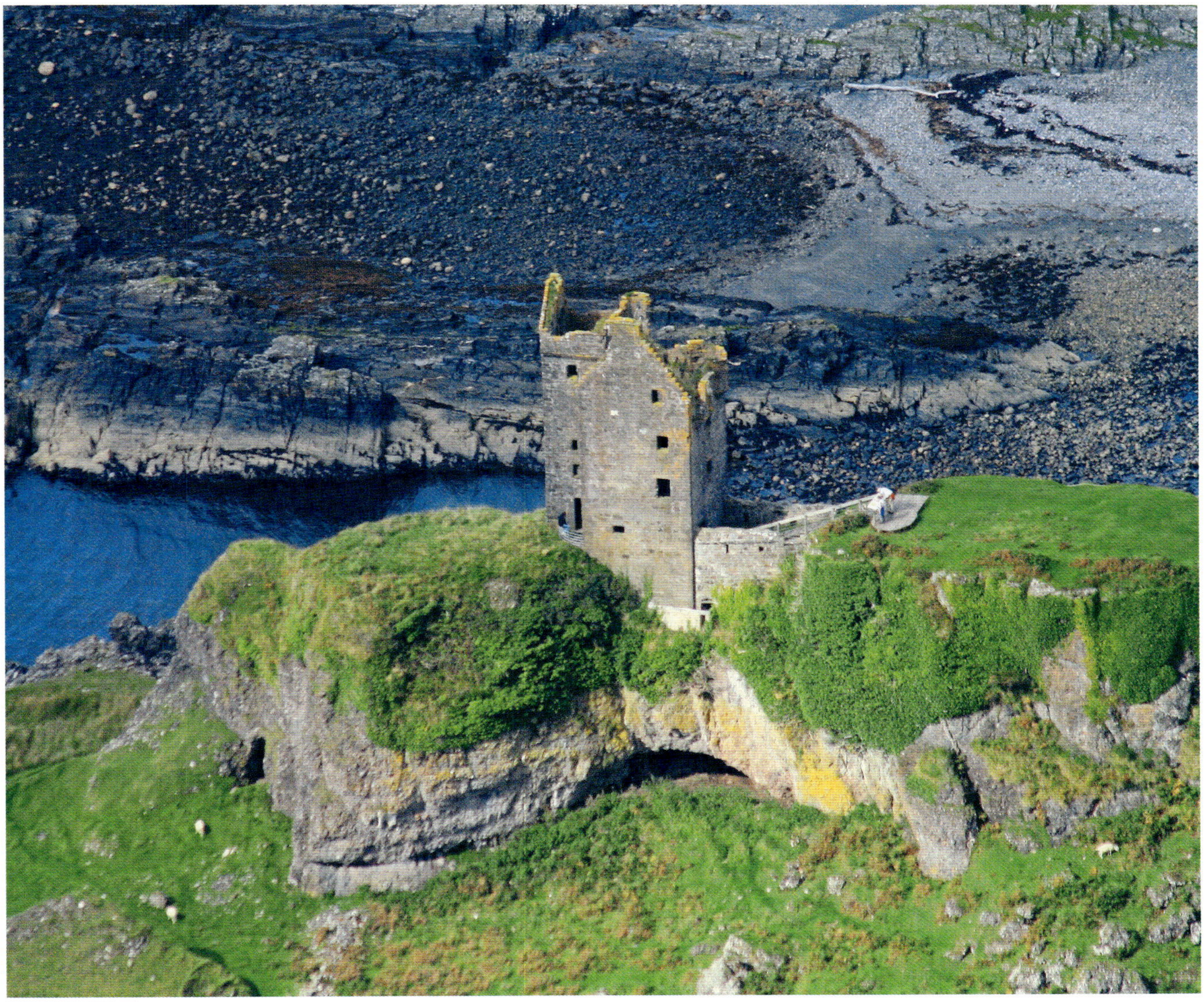

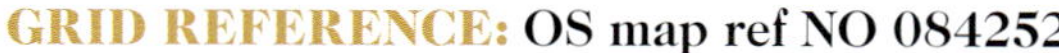

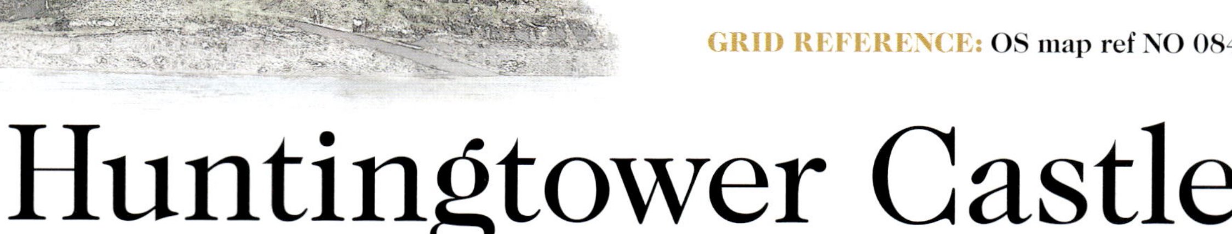

Huntingtower Castle

Originally named Ruthven Castle

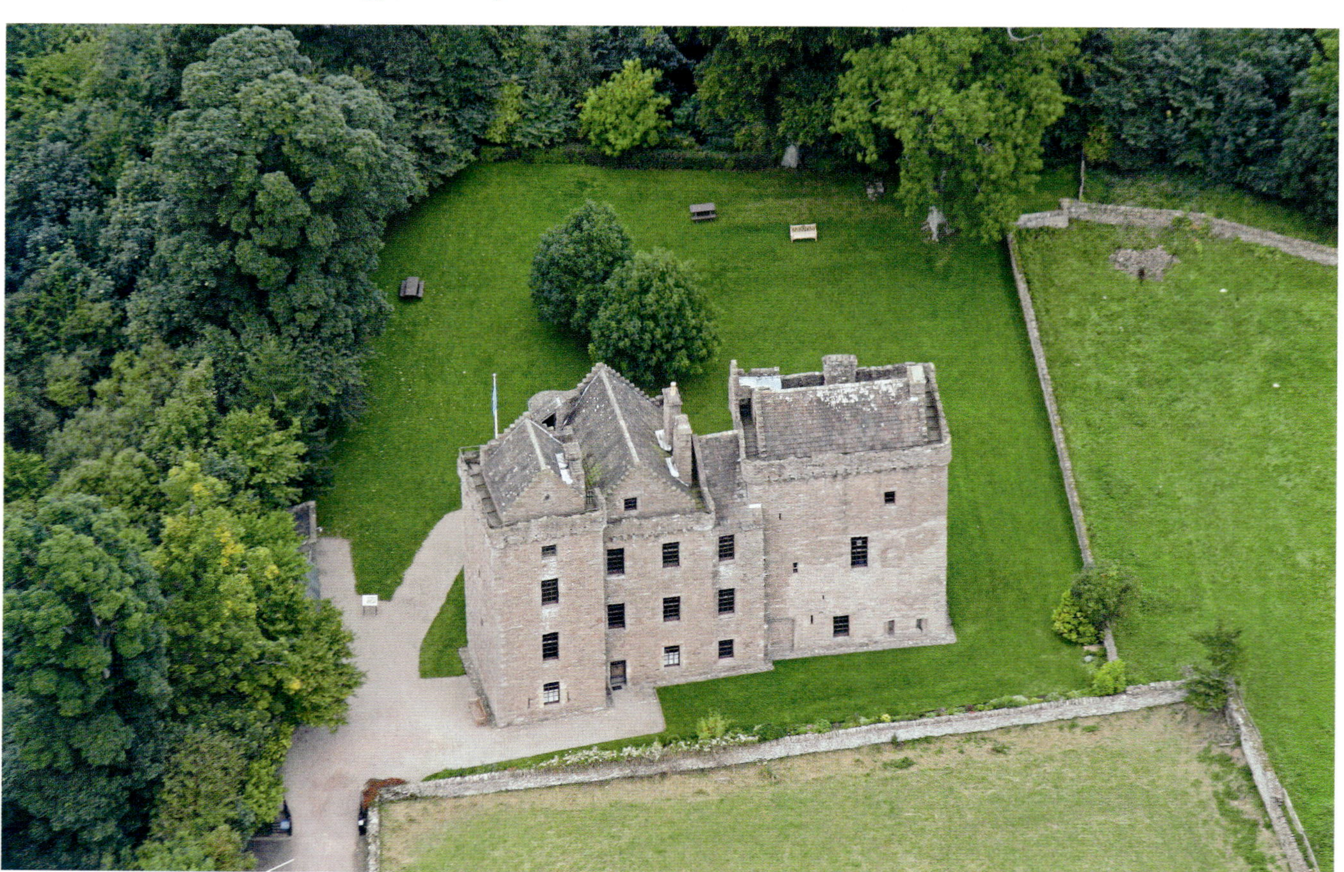

Originally built as two separate towers, this castle was the scene of a famous 'lover's leap' and the owners later used it to imprison a king. This extremely unwise move would ultimately lead to the destruction of the family, with their lands and possessions seized by the Crown. The two towers are now one and the castle is an excellent destination for those in search of some colourful history.

ABOUT THE CLAN

This is one of the few clans who can trace their origin back to a Viking line. The surname Ruthven was first recorded when Swain, son of Thor of Ruthven, granted lands to the monks of Scone around the year 1190. These lands in what is now Perthshire had the Gaelic name Ruadhainn which later became Ruthven.

The first Norse settlers had created a foothold in coastal areas around what is now Edinburgh. The fertile inland course of the River Tay marked the next area for settlement by them.

During the Wars of Scottish Independence, Sir William Ruthven decide to support Sir William Wallace, laying siege to Perth in 1297. This was the first instance of the Ruthven clan choosing to defy the English crown and being on the winning side. He campaigned with Wallace in the borders, re-taking Jedburgh. His reward in 1313 was to

Clan Ruthven

be appointed by King Robert I (The Bruce) as Sheriff of the Royal Burgh of St Johnstone, a local name preserved by the current football stadium. His land holding locally increased and Ruthven castle rose.

Hostage taking and kidnap were common methods of control and fund raising in the 15th and 16th centuries. The Ruthvens featured in both. Sir William Ruthven of Balkernoch, a very wealthy noble, had to survive three years being held as a hostage in England from 1424 for the ransom of James I of Scotland. Royal favour had been gained by his devotion to the king and in 1488 his great grandson became Lord Ruthven in parliament.

Despite having Ruthven Castle as a sturdy base, the Ruthven family had a long feud with the Clan Charterises of Kinfauns who were also rewarded with lands from The Bruce. When Lord Patrick Ruthven

Visitor Details

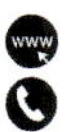 www.historicenvironment.scot/visit-a-place/places/huntingtower-castle

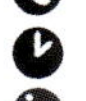 01738 627321

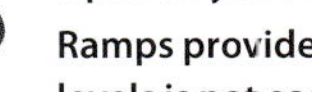 Open all year. For times see website.

 Ramps provide access into two ground floor rooms of the castle, but gaining the upper levels is not easy. Grounds and picnic facilities are suitable for visitors using wheelchairs.

There is a gift shop on location and a car park.

The nearby city of Perth has a wide choice of cafes and restaurants.

Location: Three miles west of Perth city centre, just off the A85 near the junction of the A9. Refreshingly easy to drive to, no need to negotiate twisting country lanes for hours. Also has public transport links to Perth.

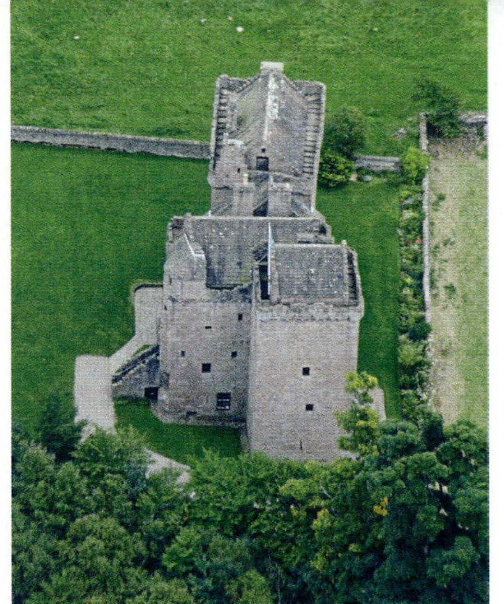

Clan Ruthven were staunch supporters of Robert the Bruce in the wars of Scottish independence. This politically adept lowland family gained additional lands as a reward. Having been made sheriffs of Perth in 1313, they also became lords in 1488. The growing family needed a convenient solid power base, so the first stone tower rose in the 15th century. This took the form of a keep of three storeys.

An L plan tower house was added beside it in the 16th century, rising slightly higher and being at first joined by a wooden bridge to the first tower. Further outbuildings once clustered near the towers, surrounded by a substantial defensive stone wall. When you visit, consider the view from the tower top and the tale of the Maiden's Leap. In one bedchamber the daughter of the first Earl of Gowrie was entertaining the attentions of John Wemyss. Hearing her mother was coming to disturb the dalliance, her daughter fled to the battlements and made a running leap to the lower tower across the gap. She survived to elope later that day and they actually lived happily ever after.

In 1581, William, Lord Ruthven was created Earl of Gowrie by the 15-year-old King James VI. The young King had Catholic advisors at the time: the Earl of Arran and the Duke of Lennox. A year later when the King was on a local hunting foray, he came to the castle to feast with his friends. In an attempt to influence him, the Protestant Ruthven family decided to place him under what we would call house arrest and this continued for 10 months until the King escaped while out hunting. Three years afterwards, the Earl of Gowrie was beheaded at Stirling, by Royal command.

The family were accused of plotting to kidnap the King again in 1600. When confronted by the King's supporters at Gowrie House in Perth, a fight erupted and John Ruthven and his brother Alexander were murdered. Afterwards they were found guilty of treason, the bodies dismembered and the remains displayed in four Scottish cities as warnings. This disaster brought to an end the favoured times of the Ruthvens with their land and properties seized by the crown and their coat of arms debased. The castle, now called Huntingtower, was gifted to Murray Earl of Tullibardine in 1633 by Charles I. Two became one when a connecting range with an internal stairwell joined the towers which added further accommodation.

Other occupants included the Duke of Atholl in 1676 and Lord George Murray, who later became Bonnie Prince Charlie's general in the Rising, was born here in 1694. Under the ownership of the Mercers in 1805, the semi derelict property housed labourers. And paying no rent was the ghostly Green Lady; with heavy footsteps and ornate clothing, she was said to be a portent of death by some and a helping hand by others. From 1912, the castle became a state owned property now overseen by Historic Scotland. Internally, there are many conserved features including a vaulted basement, a delicately painted ceiling dating from about 1540, painted plasterwork of a similar date and a secret hiding place used for Ruthven treasures – a cupboard within a cupboard, hidden behind a stone. While this is not a large scale castle, it deserves to be better known with huge helpings of history and preserved details to dwell on.

was appointed Provost of Perth he was replaced by a Charteris due to senior church interference.

The city refused entry to Charteris and after a skirmish between several clans the Ruthvens prevailed and he stayed as provost until 1584.

The history of Huntingtower Castle covers events around the kidnap and house arrest of young James VI. This led to the beheading of the Earl of Gowrie, Lord Ruthven. The later strange events and murders at Gowrie house led also to the Clan Ruthven becoming declared traitors with loss of properties and name.

In 1641, it became lawful for the Ruthvens of Ballingdean and their bairns to assume the surname. Further reputation of the clan was restored when Sir Thomas Ruthven gained a peerage as Lord Ruthven of Freeland in 1651 from Charles II of England. Patrick Ruthven,

1st Earl of Brentford fought in the Thirty Years War between 1618 and 1648.This terrible European war resulted in the deaths of over eight million people, including 20 percent of the German population, making it one of the most destructive conflicts in human history.

Patrick fought for the King of Sweden's army, being fond of battle but even fonder of alcoholic drink which he resorted to in huge amounts. He stayed sober while his fellow tipplers became hopelessly drunk. This enabled him to sway negotiations in his favour, making him popular with senior staff and the King of Sweden.

With such a negative image since 1600, it became common for clan members to change surnames. One branch in County Down are the Trotters.

When Alexander Ruthven became Governor General of Australia in 1936, he accepted a peerage on the condition that he was known as Lord Gowrie, thereby restoring a long lost title.

The present Clan Chief is Alexander Patrick Greysteil Ruthven, 2nd Earl of Gowrie, PC, FRSL. He is usually known as Grey Gowrie. He was a Conservative Party politician for some years, including a period in the British Cabinet, and was later chairman of Sotheby's and of the Arts Council of England. He has also published poetry.

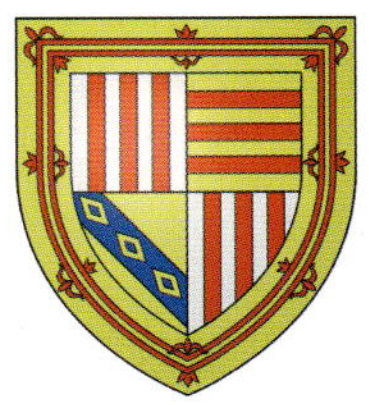

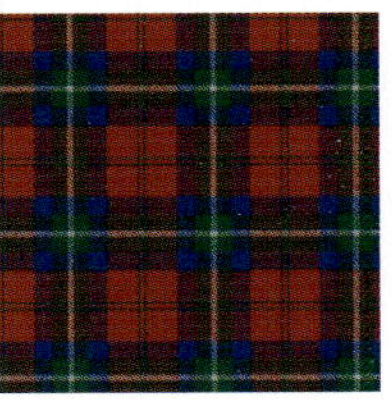

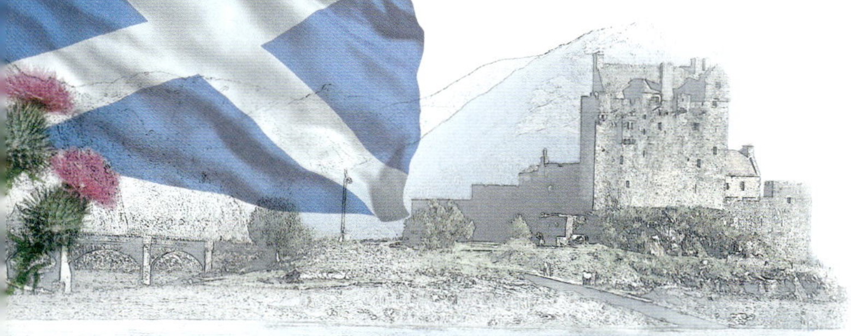

Huntly Castle

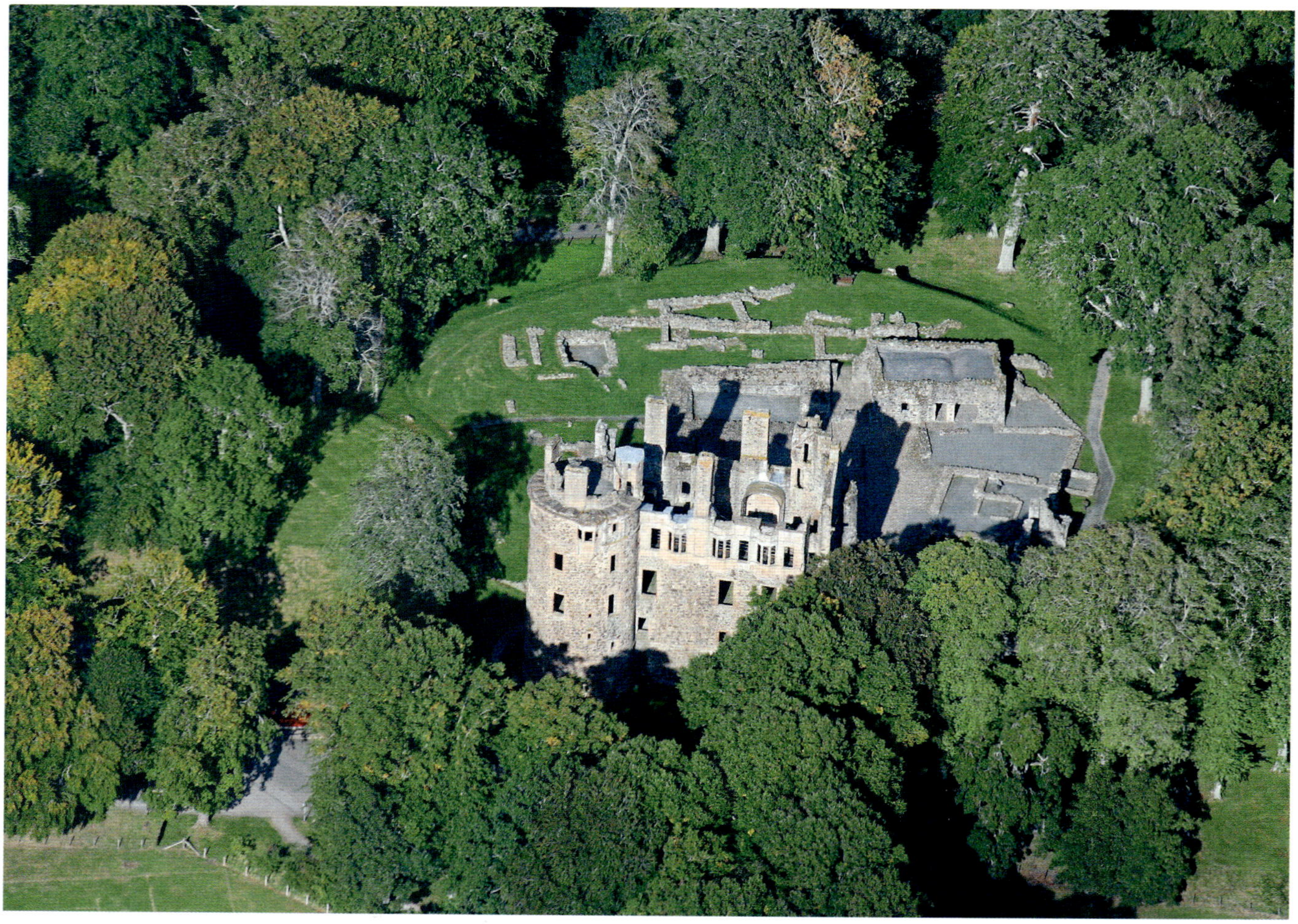

▮ ABOUT THE CLAN

Clan Gordon

The origin of the clan is said to have been
around the town of Gourdon in the Quercy
region of France. The first area of Scotland to
be settled by the family was in Berwickshire.
These lands were given to Adam Gordon as a
reward for supporting King Malcolm when he
defeated Macbeth at Lumphanan in 1057. A
legend tells the story of a Gordon knight who
faced then killed a monstrous creature which
had been bringing terror to the dwellers of the
Merse around that time.

The knight's grandson was Richard, Lord
of the Barony of Gordon in the Merse. The
monks of St Mary at Kelso were granted land
around 1155 by Richard who died shortly
afterwards, no doubt feeling assured of his
place in the afterlife. In the Wars of Scottish
Independence the Gordons supported Robert
the Bruce. Sir John Gordon perished during
the Battle of Otterburn when the Scottish

defeated the English in 1388. When a siege
forced surrender of the castle at Wigtown Sir
Adam Gordon became the governor. At the
battle of Homildon Hill near Wooler in 1402 Sir
Adam was killed leading the clan in what was a
disaster for the Scottish army defeated by the
dense rain of English arrows. His heiress was
his daughter Elizabeth. She married Alexander
Seton the son of the Seton clan chieftain. This
established a new line of Gordons because all
male descendants kept that name and could
also be Gordon chieftains. The clan by now had
become known as the House of Gordon, the
chief having gained the title Earl of Huntly.
Terror came to the Gordons castle at Huntly in
1452 when the Earl of Moray burned the castle
and destroyed the lands around. The Earl was
a supporter of the Douglas clan who were in
a power struggle with the king and his allies
making the Gordons a target. The castle rose

Visitor Details

- www.historicenvironment.scot/visit-a-place/places/huntly-castle
- 01466 793191
- Open all year. April 1 to September 30, daily, 9.30am to 5.30pm. October 1 to March 31, daily except Thursday and Friday, 10am to 4pm.
- There is a car park, gift shop, exhibition and disabled toilets.
- Huntly town has several places to eat, drink and shop.
- The castle can be explored from bottom to top. A spooky basement dungeon worryingly large enough for many inmates can still be accessed along a narrow corridor. The highest point is a lookout platform reached by a spiral staircase, giving almost aerial views of the castle layout.

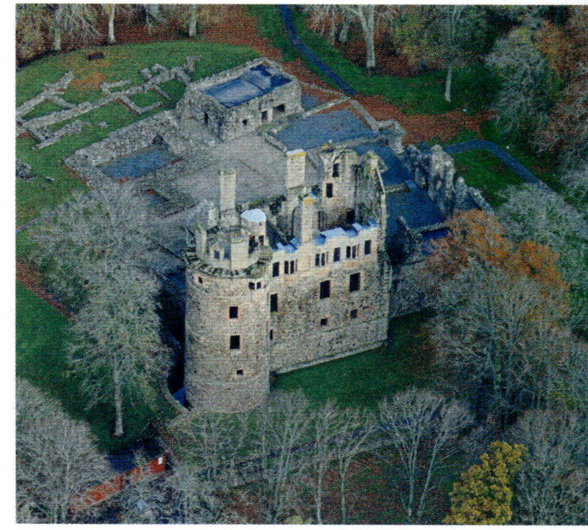

Location: This castle is located in the Aberdeen and Gordon district on the northern outskirts of Huntly town, just south of the River Deveron. From the A96 Huntly roundabout, head across the square in the town centre then under an arch. The castle is in parkland.

Huntly Castle is situated at the point where the Deveron and Bogie Rivers meet. This strategic location was where the first fortification was built in the 1100s. This timber bailey has disappeared under later buildings and the motte is now a grassed mound. The early building, known as the Peel of Strathbogie, enabled control of the estate by the Earls of Fife. Robert the Bruce visited in 1307 before winning a local battle against the Comyns of Buchan.

The Bruce also triumphed at the Battle of Bannockburn in 1314, however, the Earls of Fife were on the losing side. As punishment, the Earls were stripped of titles and lands. Sir Adam Gordon got the Strathbogie estate and this started the unbroken rise of the Gordon clan in the North East of Scotland.

Around 1410, the old wooden structure was removed and the first stone tower house added north of the bailey. Only the shapes of thick foundations are visible today. The first stone tower was destroyed by Douglas Earl of Moray in 1452 and the replacement was a strong rectangular keep.

From 1506, the name Huntly was bestowed on the castle and later on the town which grew nearby. The 4th Earl George continued to improve the castle until his death after the battle at Corriche near Aberdeen against the forces of Mary Queen of Scots in 1562. Her supporters included Lord James Ogilvie and the Earl of Moray, who plotted to gain greater land holdings. Confessions obtained by torture and statements twisted by envy

had been used to persuade Mary that the Earl of Huntly was a dangerous threat to her reign. He was certainly not one to follow Royal decrees despite supporting the Catholic cause. She also watched his son Sir John executed in such a manner that gave her nightmares for the rest of her short life. Further retribution followed: the castle was sacked and robbed of valuables including treasure from the Catholic church of St Machar. This was being kept safe by the clan and included altar cloths, vestments, gold and silver plates, and candlesticks.

The 6th Earl George and certain other clans rose against James VI, winning a battle at nearby Glenlivet in 1594. Some clans used the battle to settle inter clan disputes. Despite this partial victory in which many Catholic clan notables were killed, damages to the castle occurred afterwards and it was almost blown up. A major restoration took place after 1599 when he was pardoned and made 1st Marquis of Huntly. He commissioned much of the carved stonework that impresses today.

The Covenanter army occupied and spoiled the insides in 1640. By 1644, the army of the Marquis of Montrose took control but three years later General David Leslie captured and killed the garrison. The last military occupation was by Hanoverian troops in 1745, by which time it was longer fit for use as a home. After that it became a source of building stones. Clan Gordon owned it until 1923 when it became a scheduled monument maintained by Historic Environment Scotland.

again later from the ruins becoming even more splendid while the Douglas clan regrouped with Rosses and Crawford's clans supporting to make another try for power two years later. This time they were crushed between Huntly in the Highlands and the King in the Lowlands of Scotland.

The other neighbouring large clan were the Forbes however they were Protestants and this led to feuding with the Catholic Gordons. For example, in 1571, 20 Gordons were murdered at a feast inside the Forbes castle at Druminor. Revenge was swift with two clan battles following in the area and the burning of Corgarff castle with Forbes families trapped inside.

At the battle of Glenlivet in 1594 Clan Gordon formed part of a small mostly cavalry Catholic force which defeated a larger grouping of Protestant clans led poorly by the 19-year-old Duke of Argyll. Despite this victory the far

reaching power of Protestant King James resulted in the submission of many Highland chieftains after he burned down several of their castles. Although in the highlands and islands many clans might have pledged loyalty to the crown they still pursued their own feuds and raids. In a similar manner to other clans in the 1715 and 45 rising Clan Gordon had at times members fighting and falling on both sides. In the aftermath two regiments were formed from the clan to serve the army and named The Gordon Highlanders. The first was the Aberdeenshire Highland Regiment in 1777 which disbanded 6 years later. The Gordon Highlanders were formed in 1794 by the 4th duke Alexander and in 1994 became part of the merged Royal regiments of Scotland. They still recruit in the highlands and are based at Cameron barracks Inverness. Many heirlooms of the Gordon clan are

displayed at Brodie castle. Elizabeth Brodie was the last Duchess of Gordon. The current clan chief is Granville Gordon the 13th Marquis of Huntly. The family seat is at Aboyne castle.

Motto: Bydand, meaning Stay and Fight.

The Gordon clan are linked by an excellent website https://www.houseofgordon.org/ It has many active members.

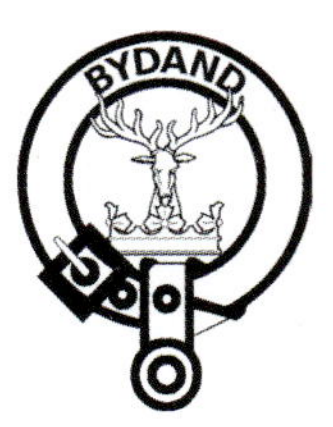
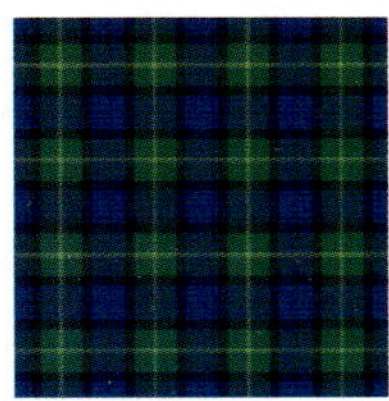

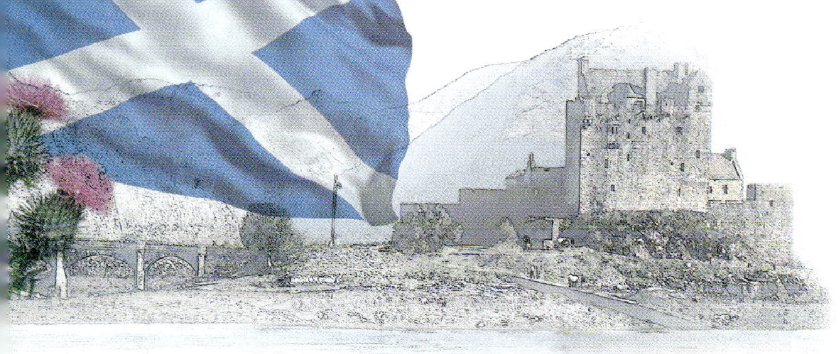

Inveraray Castle

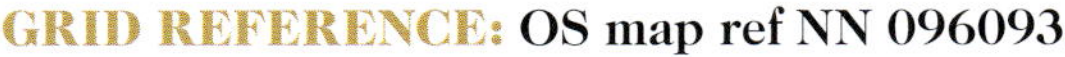

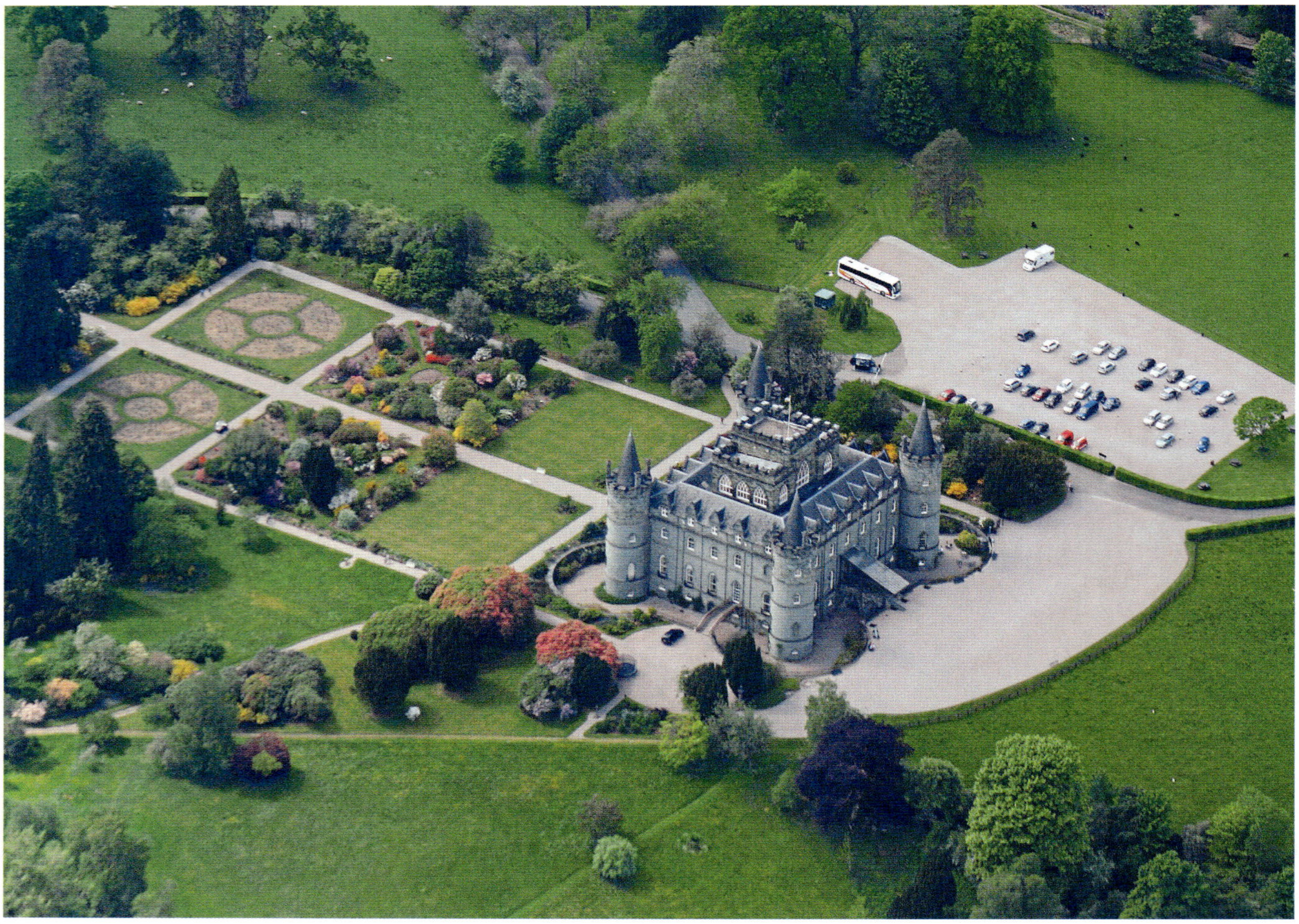

Within these walls the history of Clan Campbell is displayed and also conserved in the archive. Despite fires, sieges and changing fortunes the Dukes of Argyll have succeeded in keeping traditions and now manage a modern estate. The castle today has the appearance of a miniature palace, reflecting the power and prestige of the clan.

ABOUT THE CLAN

"Run, the Campbells are coming…" this warning cry was heard across much of Scotland many times. In equal measure would be the times assorted soldiers massing for a battle were reassured if they had the support of the mighty Clan Campbell on their side.

Campbell is still the eighth most registered surname in Scotland. That name may have its origin in the Gaelic words CAM meaning twisted and BEUL meaning mouth which is said to relate to the habit of Sir Cailean Mor of talking from one side of his mouth. This nickname Cambeul became the basis for the family name.

Argyll is the Campbell traditional heartland; records show that Archibald Campbell was made a Lord of Lochow Argyll in 1280. Sir Neil Campbell cleverly supported Robert the Bruce and married Robert's sister which led to their son John becoming Earl of Atholl. A well

Clan Campbell

connected successful marriage was worth more than one battle victory.

Later came Duncan Campbell born in 1390 known as Donnchadh Na-Adh (Duncan the Fortunate). He became the first clan chief and ruled for 40 years. During this time he claimed to be loyal to King James II however Duncan took risks to expand his power and landholdings in Argyll without the King's authority. He still impressed the King because by 1440 he was knighted and five years later became Lord Campbell of Lochawe. Perhaps a big influence on the king was that as the Clan chief Duncan commanded the largest private army in Scotland which grew as his land owning increased. Later they became the only clan that could bring artillery to battle.

Another reward came from James III in 1470 when the Campbells were granted Dunstaffnage castle. This joined the existing

Visitor Details

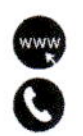

www.inveraray-castle.com

01499 302203

The castle is open from April to October. Guided tours can be booked.

Access notes from website: "Visitors should get guidance and help from kiosk or front door staff on arrival at the castle who will direct them, if appropriate, to park closer to the castle. The tour of the castle includes three floors and it is not possible to avoid stairs. Therefore, we offer FREE entry to blue-badge holders and one assistant as there is limited access due to the stairs and loose gravel around the exterior. We have two wheelchairs available for visitor use on request. We welcome assistance dogs in the castle and gardens, and also on the Estate. Please view our full accessibility guide on the website and contact the Estate Office if you have any further questions."

Tea room and gift shop.

The castle grounds have ample car and coach parking. The Clan Campbell room includes a display of weapons including 1,300 pikes, muskets, swords. Also on show are items once used by Rob Roy McGregor. Tapestries and paintings hang around themed rooms some decorated in neo classical style. Picnic area by the garden with woodland walks nearby.

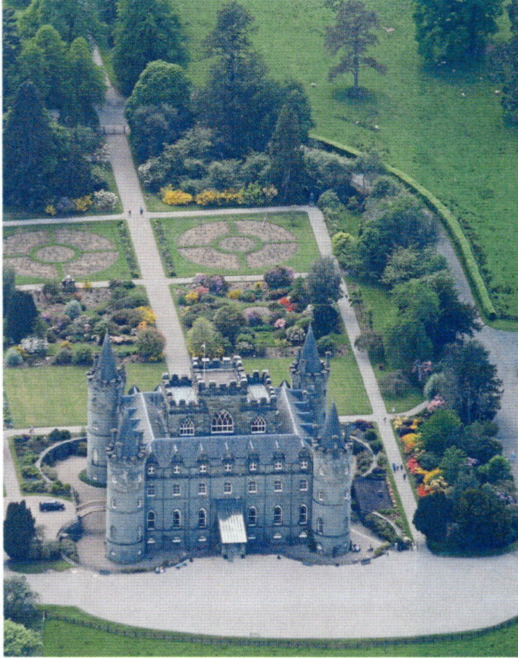

Location: Located in the Argyle and Dunbartonshire District, Inveraray Castle is one mile north of Inverary just off the A83 near the mouth of the River Aray where it flows into Loch Fyne.

The Campbells Earls of Argyll had created a substantial castle here in the 1400s with a tall keep and decorative features. The 1st Earl, Colin Campbell, was Lord High Chancellor of Scotland. The Marquis of Montrose attacked and burnt the castle in 1644. By 1743, the 3rd Duke of Argyll had the old castle knocked down to make way for a modern design as part of the desire for baroque gothic architecture.

A sketch by the architect Vanburgh was admired by the Duke and he commissioned Roger Morris and William Adam to make designs. He also decided that the village was blocking his view of the Loch. So he had it removed and rebuilt in its present location as shown in the aerial views.

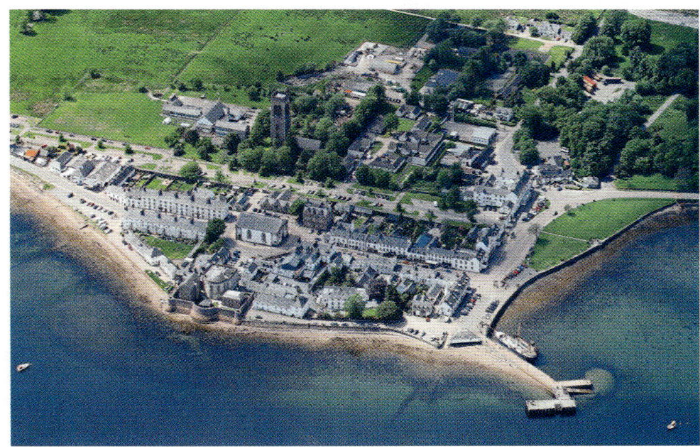

Originally the roof was flat but after a fire in 1877, a third pitched roofed floor was added with conical roofs on top of the four round towers.

Fire again attacked in 1975 and the Duke with his family had to live in the basement while repairs progressed, funded by clan members from around the world.

There are some stories of hauntings; the first by a harpist said to have perished in the fire of 1644. The library is where noises and objects falling down have been reported. On a road in nearby Glen Aray, the redcoats of Cumberland have marched past, long after the actual risings of the 45.

clan seat at a castle tower house, Innis Chonnell, near Inverary. With funds flowing in the clan chief had a new four-storey tower house with turrets built nearby.

The nearby settlement Inverary also prospered at the mouth of the River Aray, becoming a Royal Burgh in 1648. Roads met here and the adjacent Loch Fyne gave sheltered access to sea routes.

The fifth earl Archibald took command of the Mary Queen of Scots army at the battle of Langside in 1568. His side lost, mainly due to his insistence on classic clan battling based on using weight of numbers rather than clever tactics.

The Queen fled the scene south into exile. His brother however was on the winning side, a tactic used by many clans to ensure that family influence and some lands survived no matter who won a campaign.

Another Archibald, the 10th Earl, supported King William II of Scotland (William of Orange) His rewards included being made Duke of Argyll and Marquess of Lorne and Kintyre in 1703.

When the Jacobite risings took place the Campbells remained on the side of the crown. Combined with shrewd marriages this has enabled them to stay in power across their region of Scotland measured by holding 40 estates covering around one million acres under the control of the Duke of Argyll.

The current clan seat is the imposing castle at Inverary built in 1746. This is the location of a large collection of clan documents which have been studied by the Clan Campbell Education Foundation to create a detailed three volume history of the clan.

Motto: Ne obliviscaris (Do not forget)

For more information see https://www.ccsna. org/the-clan-campbell-history-project

Since 2001 the castle, the estates, and the role of MacCailein Mor or Chief of Clan Campbell have been in the care of Torquhil Ian Campbell, (born May 29, 1968), 13th Duke of Argyll. There is a very active Clan Campbell society based in North America with worldwide coverage, https://www.ccsna.org/

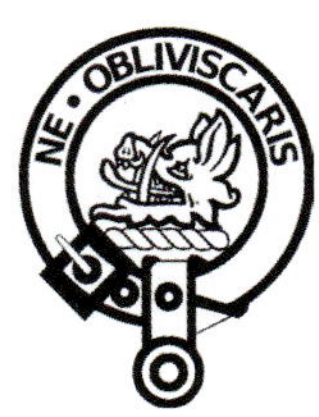

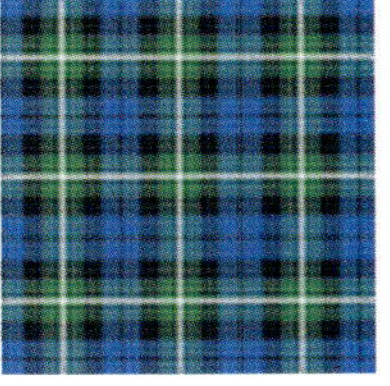

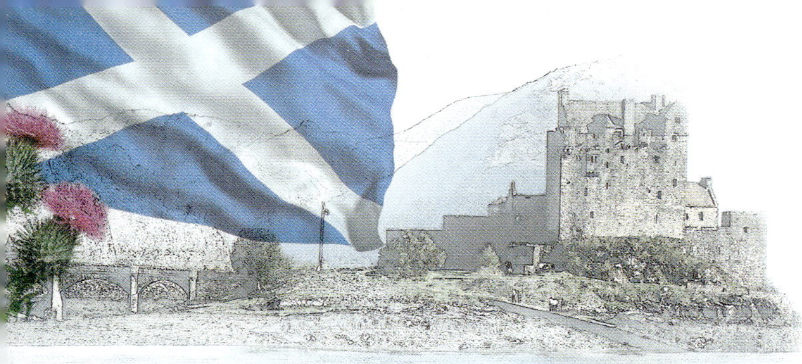

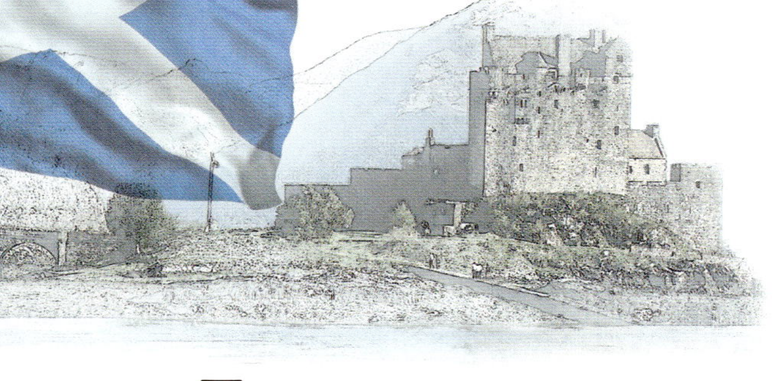

Invergarry Castle

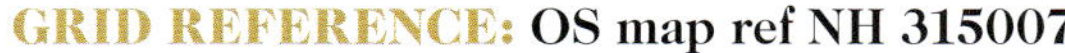

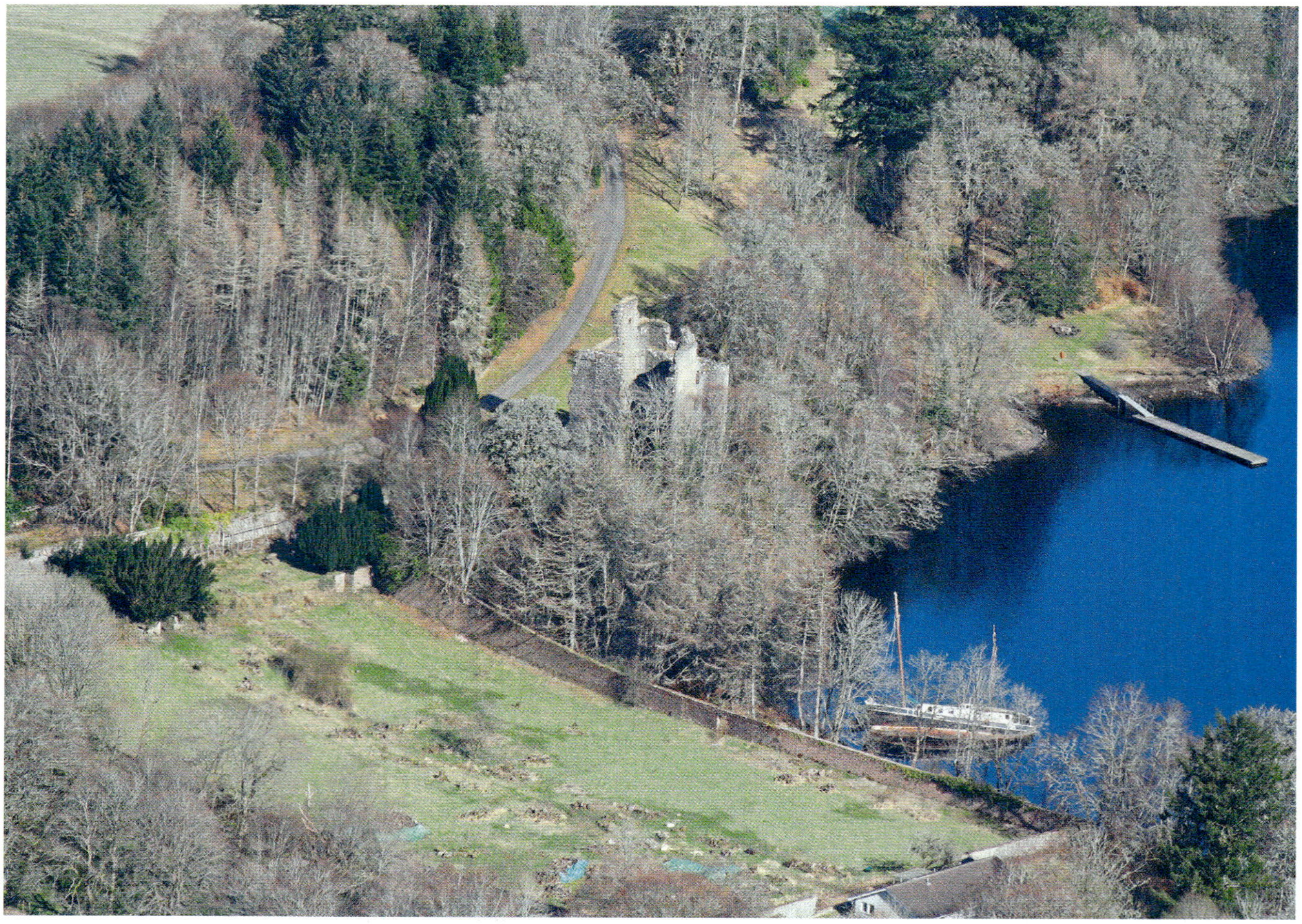

Supporting the Jacobite cause cost the MacDonnells the use of this castle. These ruins mark where they made a stand, fortunately they did survive but the crumbling castle did not. Now the remains, having been damaged by explosives laid by sappers during the conflict, sit on the shore of Loch Oich and are partially hidden from view by burgeoning woodlands.

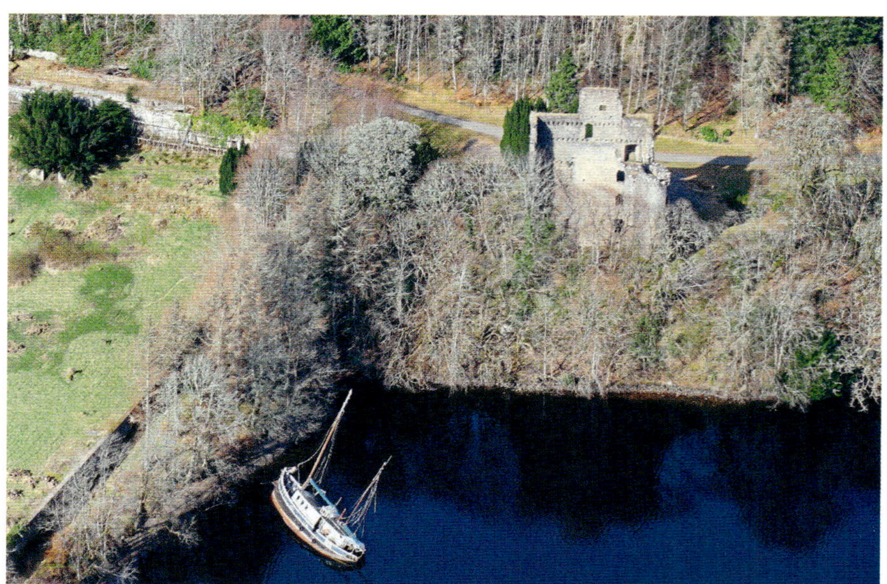

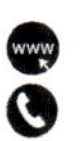

Visitor Details

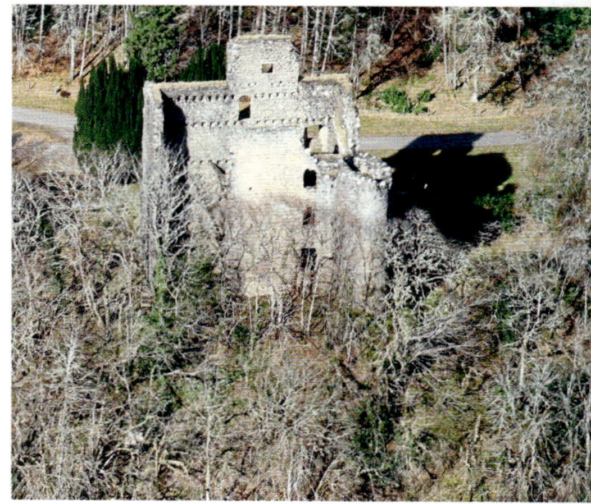

- Website of the nearby historic hotel: www.glengarry.net
- No telephone.
- This ruined castle is open all year.
- Outside viewing of ruin only.
- Food and drink can be purchased at the hotel.
- As shown in the air views, the ruin is almost hidden by forest. The castle ruin and hotel can also be visited by those using the Caledonian Canal which uses Loch Oich as part of its route. A public mooring jetty is available.

Location: Invergarry Castle is located in the Highland region 40 miles south west of Inverness. You can get there by driving about six miles south west of Fort Augustus on a small road east of the A82 overlooking the eastern bank of Loch Oich. Follow the signs posted for the Glengarry Castle Hotel.

Clan warfare in the 1600s was intense and the MacDonalds, also known as the MacDonnells of Glengarry, suffered when their castle at Strome was destroyed by the Mackenzies in 1602. On the shore of Loch Oich, a raised mound of hard stone attracted the attention of the clan chief. In Gaelic, it is known as Cragan an Fhithich or the Rock of Ravens. He decided a new castle was to be raised here; his clansmen passed the building stones hand to hand in a human chain from the slopes of Ben Tee. The design was six storeys tall; a tower house with a comfortable interior. This included a feasting hall and tapestry-lined bed chambers. It was not heavily fortified: it was designed to impress with a perimeter barmkin (low wall) which surrounded the necessary outbuildings such as the stables, bakery and brew house. In appearance, it would resemble Craigievar which is featured earlier in this book.

When Oliver Cromwell brought his civil war to Scotland, his troops led by General Monck fired the castle in 1654. They were trying to damage the power base of one of the largest clans in Scotland and failed because between 1688 to 1692 the restored castle held firm against the government of William and Mary. The clan preferred to support James VII of Scotland. They also firmly supported the Jacobite cause in 1715 and 1745. The castle was taken by the Hanoverian forces in 1716 but they did not stay because in 1745 Bonnie Prince Charlie was hosted by the Clan here as he started his recruitment drive. Lord John MacDonnell became part of the Prince's council. After the final defeat of the Jacobites at Culloden, the Prince stayed overnight as he made his escape westwards. John MacDonnell and his son were imprisoned by the Hanoverians. The destruction by explosives of much of the castle by Cumberland's sappers in 1746 made the resulting mess not fit for rebuild so the MacDonnell's promptly built the mansion of Invergarry house nearby. This has now become the site of the highly rated Glengarry Castle Hotel built in 1866-1869 by celebrated architect David Bryce.

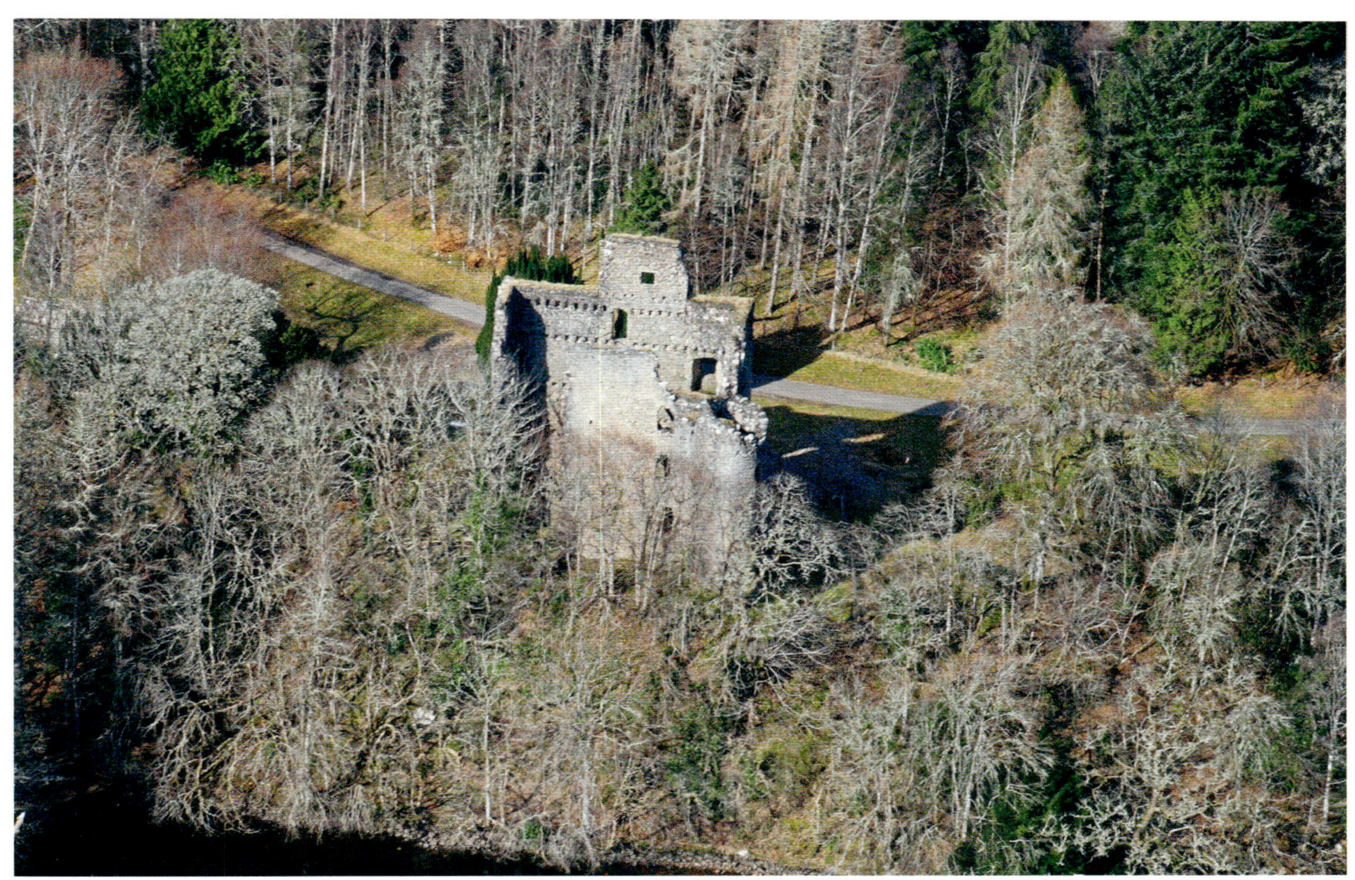

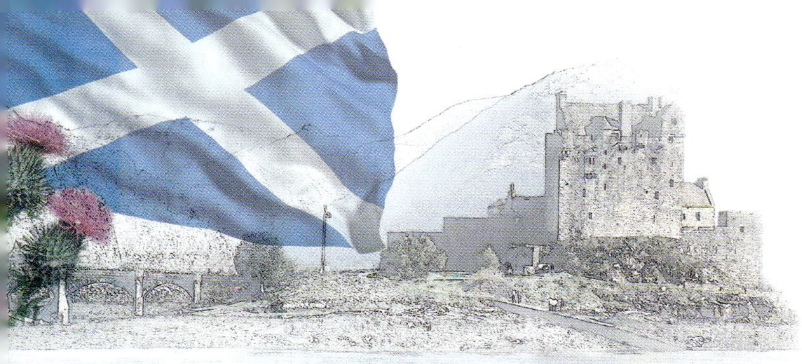

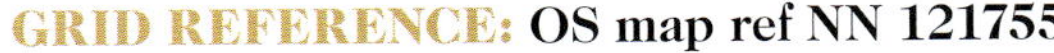
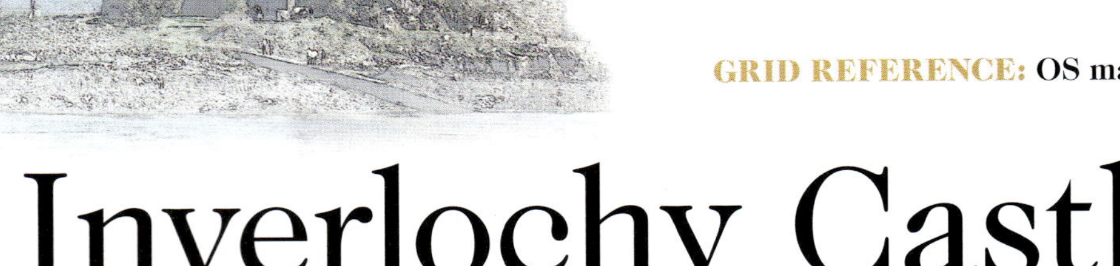

Inverlochy Castle

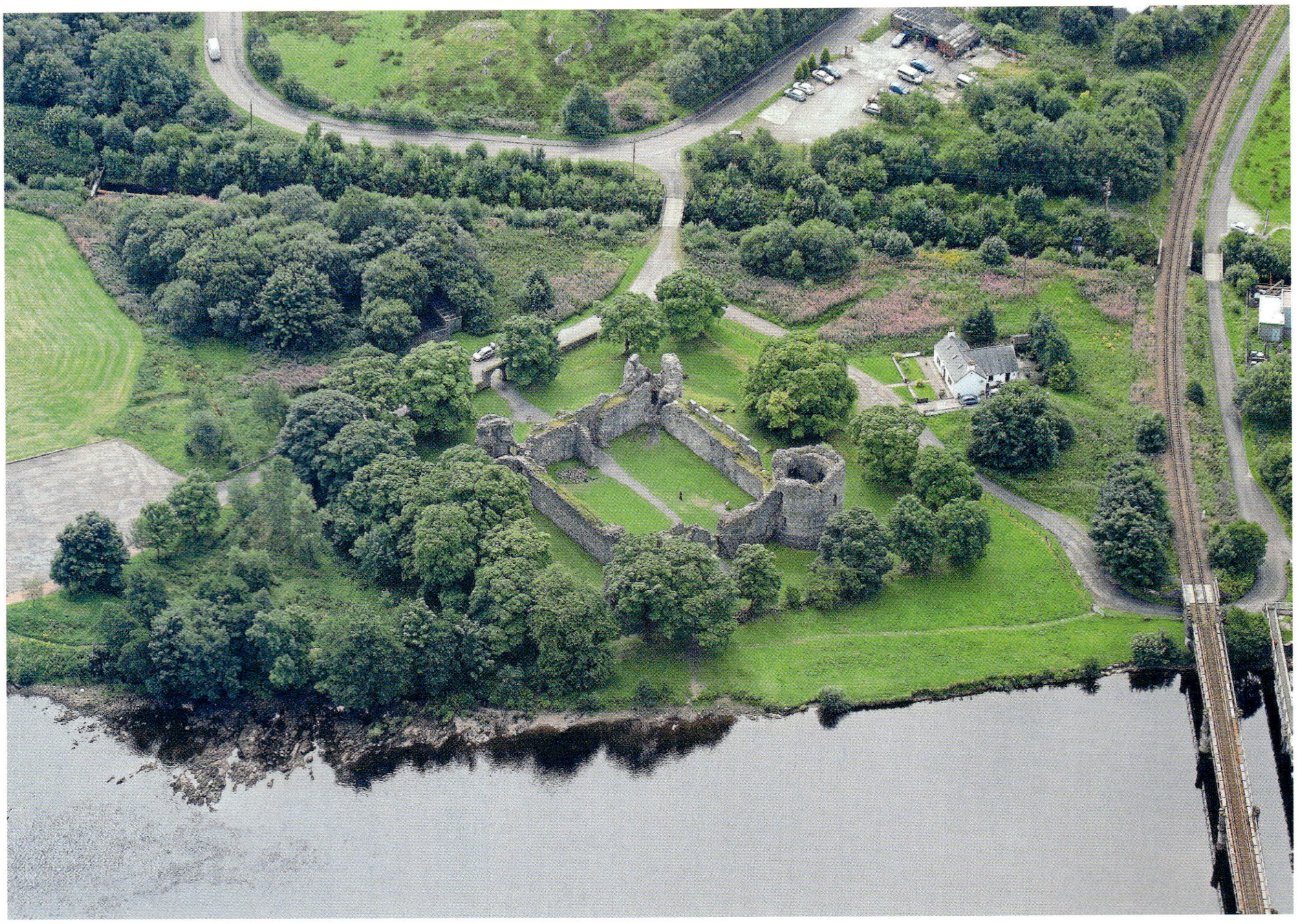

Guarding one entrance to the Great Glen this redoubt had a role as a rallying point for clans. From the battlements could be seen nearby skirmishes and ferocious clan charges. Queen Victoria called here to add to her thirst for knowledge of Scotland's past. Now it stands as a picturesque ruin beside the River Lochy.

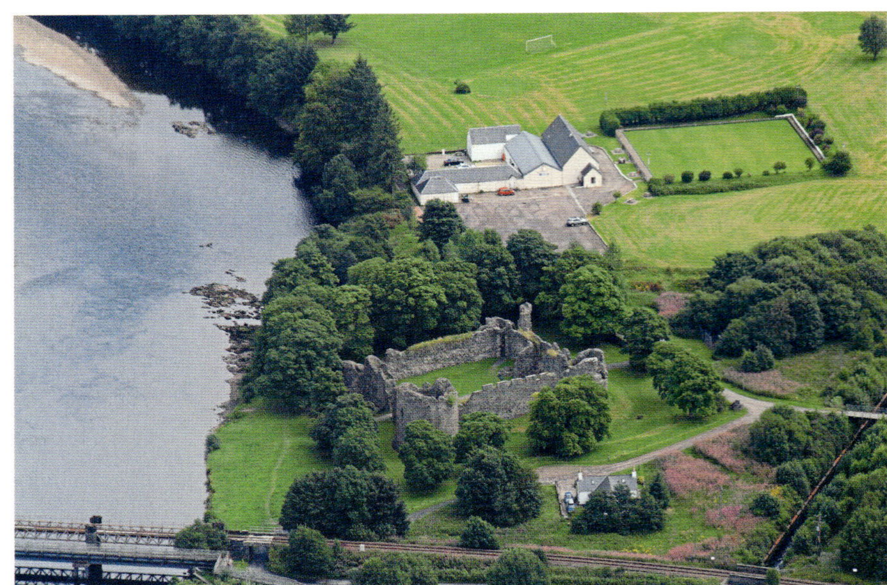

  ABOUT THE CASTLE

Visitor Details

- www.historicenvironment.scot/visit-a-place/places/inverlochy-castle/history
- No telephone.
- The castle is usually open daily and there is no admission fee payable. Take care when searching for more details of the castle online. Despite sharing the name, the Inverlochy Castle Hotel is not part of Inverlochy Castle.
- Outside viewing of ruin only. Gravel paths on flat grounds.
- Parking is adjacent but there are no facilities on site. However, there are plenty of places to eat drink in nearby Fort William.
- Keep a lookout during the summer for the regular daily steam hauled trains crossing the nearby bridge on the Fort William to Mallaig line, one of Scotland's most scenic rail routes. For details including maps of the second battle see also www.battlefieldsofbritain.co.uk/battle_inverlochy_1645.html

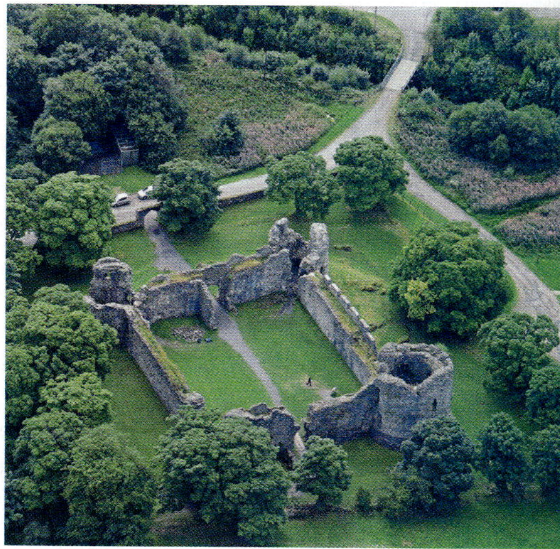

Location: Inverlochy Castle is situated two miles north-east of Fort William off the A82.

The shape of these ruins is reminiscent of many toy model castles: stout walls enclose a courtyard with a round tower on each corner of the rectangle. One of the towers is larger and could have been the keep. There was also a surrounding ditch. Each entrance was guarded by a portcullis. The river provided additional protection as well as fresh water.

The castle was constructed around the end of the 13th century by the Lord of Badenoch and Lochaber, John, 'the Red' Comyn. He had great ambitions and held many castles in his lands. Clan Comyn was defeated as a major power by Robert the Bruce after he became king in 1306, with castles including this one ravaged and reduced to ruin. The Bruce also murdered John Comyn at Greyfriars church Dumfries. The clan survivors had to rename themselves and became the Cummings. Nearby the castle in 1431, the army of King James I was defeated by a smaller force of clansmen led by The Lord of the Isles, Alexander MacDonald. The Gordons of Huntly became the owners in 1505 taking over from the Clan Cameron, the temporary custodians. The King James IV only gave the castle to the Gordons because they agreed to make repairs to make it fit for a garrison.

In the February 1645, a second battle took place at the castle. It was being held by about 1,500 Campbell clansmen led by the Earl of Argyll who was a Covenanter. Against them were the Royalist forces of James Graham, the Marquis of Montrose. It was expected that the Royalists would approach from the direction of Inverness down the Great Glen which was being carefully watched by Campbell lookouts. Despite the winter conditions and rough mountain terrain, a tiring tricky route march was made by Montrose's men heading into the hills south of the Great Glen valley. This enabled them to make a surprise attack on Inverlochy Castle from the slopes of Ben Nevis. This caused the already injured Earl of Argyll to panic and flee from the castle by sea. So it was left to Duncan Campbell of Auchinbreck to defend their honour. He fought to his death in a skirmish line while his musketeers fired from high points on the castle. Eventually 1,500 Campbell Covenanters were crushed in brutal clan combat while the few survivors scattered into the hills. In 1654, the castle was abandoned in favour of Cromwell's new timber fort further down the River Lochy at its mouth where it joins Loch Linnhe. By 1690, this was also replaced by a seaside stone artillery fort of which only a few walls remain. They can currently be seen opposite Morrison's supermarket in Fort William town.

The last consolidation at Inverlochy Castle was a tidying-up with minor masonry repairs in readiness for the visit of Queen Victoria in 1873 when she was a guest of local landowner, Lord Abinger.

 ABOUT THE CLAN

Clan Cumming

The records show that the clan were known as the Comyn family of Norman origin. In 1066 one of the knights with William the conqueror was Robert of Comyn. Robert survived the landings and battle to later become the Earl of Northumberland in 1069. Wilhelmus Comyn, Bishop of Durham in 1124 was another Comyn appointment made by King David I of Scotland later also becoming chancellor. Keeping the family in high positions was a fine way of prospering so the bishop ensured his nephew Richard followed into that role.

With lands already held in Tynedale and Roxburghshire Richard married Hexstilda grand daughter of King Donald Ban. His sons later brought further lands via marriage, William became Earl of Buchan and another son gained the Earldom of Mentieth and Lordship of Badenoch. A measure of how powerful they had become was that between them the family held 13 Earldoms by the 13th century. John Comyn, Lord of Badenoch and Alexander Comyn, Earl of Buchan were two of the six 'Guardians of the Realm'. They had good reasons to claim the throne when King David died in 1286 however it went to King John of the Balliol clan. When the King was deposed his clan left Scotland shortly afterwards because the power now belonged to the Comyns. Notably Red Comyn became the uncrowned ruler with many castles in his domain and men at arms on call. He favoured his own interests and at times fought for the English then switched to the Scottish side. This did not ensure trust from Robert the Bruce. They met inside a Dumfries church in 1306. An argument broke out and in the resultant violent fight Robert fatally stabbed Red Comyn and his uncle. During the following wars of independence Bruce destroyed many Comyn properties. By the time he became King soon afterwards the power of the Comyns had been removed. One of the results was that the clan members changed their surname to Cummings.

A branch became established at Altyre in Moray descended from a brother of the Black Comyn although they still had to defend themselves locally against raids by the Chattan and Brodie clans. The lands of nearby Gordonstoun came into the family with the marriage of the 13th chief of Altyre to the Gordon heiress. In turn the family took the surname Gordon-Cumming. The clan home is now centred on the Altyre Estate.

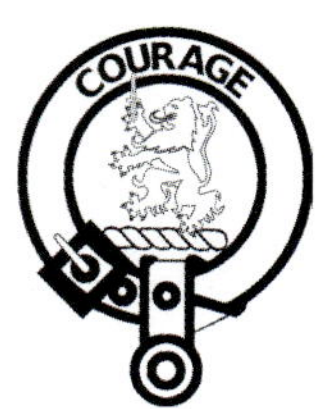

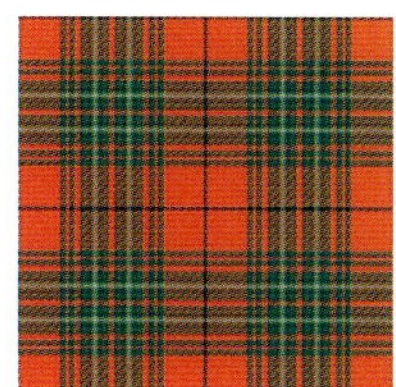

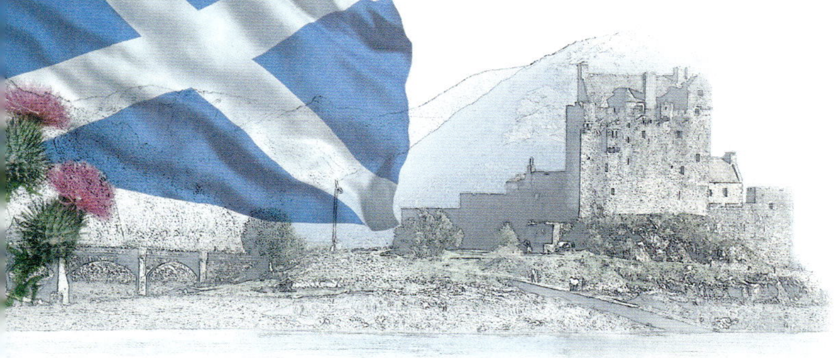

Inverness Castle

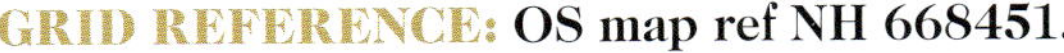

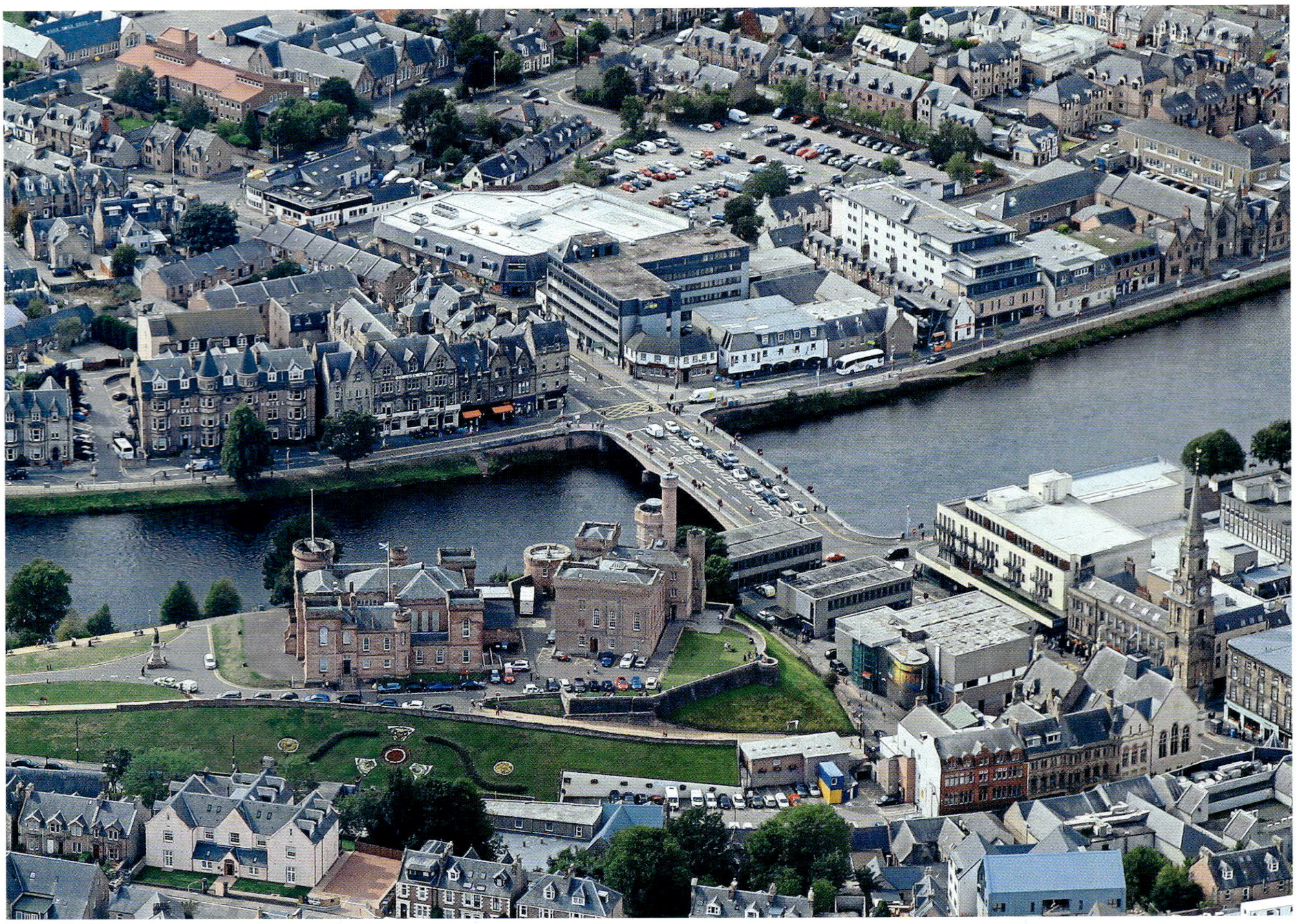

Although the modern town nestles next to the castle the open views from alongside the river make this an impressive creation to ponder. Inverness witnessed many tumultuous events at this location which will be highlighted in a new visitor centre being established on the site of the old sheriff court inside. Some of these events are detailed here.

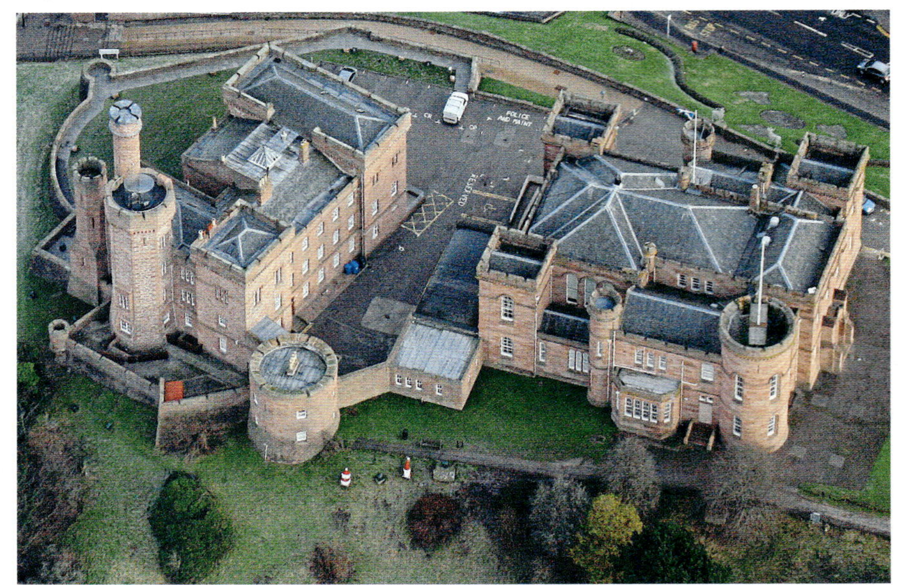

Visitor Details

www.highlifehighland.com/invernesscastleviewpoint/castle-viewpoint-2

01349 781700 (High Life agency for council leisure locations)

Opening times for the viewpoint are on the website link above.

There is access for wheelchairs only on the ground floor. Access improvements will be included in the conversion of the castle interior when it becomes a visitor attraction.

There are plenty of food and drink outlets nearby.

The castle interior is due to open after new displays are completed in 2024.

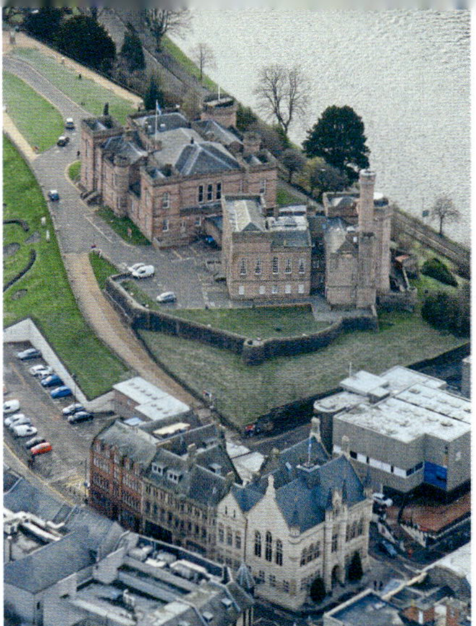

Location: Situated on the east bank of the River Ness, Inverness Castle is in the city centre a quarter mile south of the railway station on top of a small hill. There is a car park adjacent to the Eden Court Theatre just across the river from the castle and then it is a 10 minute walk. Multi storey car parks are also available near the train station.

A series of castles have topped this sandstone hillock since around 1057. Originally a steep cliff protected the side closest to the River Ness. The first castle here was likely to have been commissioned by Malcolm III while other sources suggest David I. This castle was later captured by Robert the Bruce in 1308 and suffered significant damage. By 1362, rebuilding was under way with records showing sheriff's court sessions taking place on site. This legal tradition continued here until 2020. Stone walling and turrets were added by the Earl of Mar between 1412 to 1415, written proof of the costs incurred is still to be seen in exchequer rolls surviving from that time.

The power of the Highland Clans concerned King James I so he invited 50 clan chiefs and close family to a parley at the castle in 1428. He betrayed their trust because they expected a peace treaty with terms. Instead he had them imprisoned in chains in solitary confinement, executing some within days. Lord Alexander, for example, was held in bad conditions for 12 months. His fury was great and after his release he returned to Inverness with 10,000 clansmen to sack and then burn the town's properties which were made mostly out of wood and thatch at this time. To his frustration, he could not take the castle so his tormentors escaped his wrath.

The third Earl of Huntly held a position of power in Scotland as a Justicar. Effectively he was the prime minister of Scotia north of the Clyde. So he was instructed in 1508 to update the castle by adding a hall, kitchen and a chapel. No progress had been made by 1514 when his heir George took over and he was also slow to make progress. Perhaps the funding had been diverted to improve their own lavish castle at Huntly. By 1540, the improvements had been incorporated at Inverness plus the addition of a tower. By now, George the 4th Earl of Huntly had also been appointed constable of Inverness Castle and it may be surmised that he desired a comfortable residence when away from Huntly. The scene was set for an extraordinary clash.

In 1562, Mary Queen of Scots arrived with her retinue and demanded entry to the castle. There was time for gift shopping as well, 15 tartan plaids and barrels of gunpowder being on her list. The Earl of Huntly, acting as constable, refused admission due to his family being in dispute with the queen despite both being of the Catholic faith. She had already made efforts to have his Huntly Castle residence seized.

When clans in the local area, notably from the Frasers and Munroes, heard of her poor treatment they joined forces at Inverness Castle and overwhelmed the castle garrison. The Queen had the Earl executed then hung from the castle walls. Mary had little experience of the complex political situation in Scotland and her revenge was likely to have been encouraged by one her close advisers, the Earl of Moray. The threat from the risings of the Jacobites in 1715 resulted in the castle being enlarged with a barrack block for 600 men, officers' quarters and a governor's house. When General Wade took over command of the army in the north, he had new forts built and also a road network. Inverness Castle was renamed Fort George in honour of the King and surrounded by a curtain wall.

During the 1745 uprising, the Jacobites took control of Fort George/Inverness Castle and Fort Augustus but failed to win Fort William. They withdrew from Fort George after the winter of 1746 and blew up the fort but sadly all this achieved was the accidental loss of a French Sergeant sapper killed by his own explosives detonating early. His dog was blown across the river but survived.

As with many castle ruins in towns, the remains became a handy source of building stones. To discourage further uprisings, the Hanoverian government built a new Fort George on the coast east of Inverness (see section on Fort George).

The dramatic sandstone building now seen towering above the river was built between 1843 and 1846. A few traces of earlier structures remain: a well, an outside stairway and part of a rampart wall above Castle Street.

By 2020, the law court and associated cells were no longer in use due to the new justice centre being opened at Longman, Inverness.

An inside renovation is estimated to be completed in 2024. This will then enable the castle to open as a visitor attraction showing in detail the history of the site. Meanwhile, the adjacent museum and art gallery are well worth a visit.

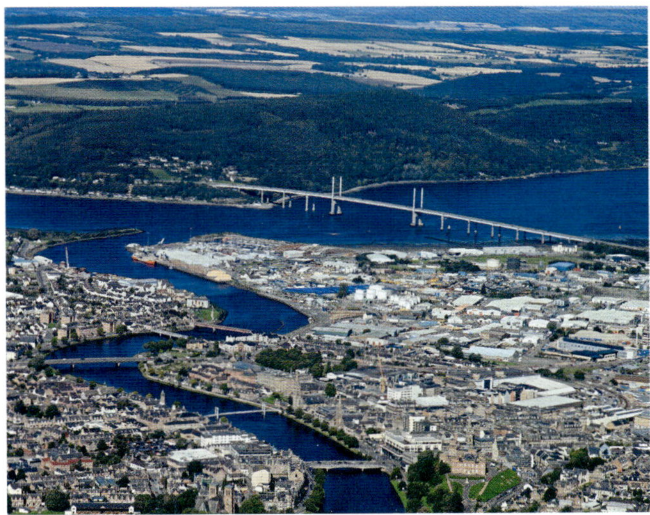

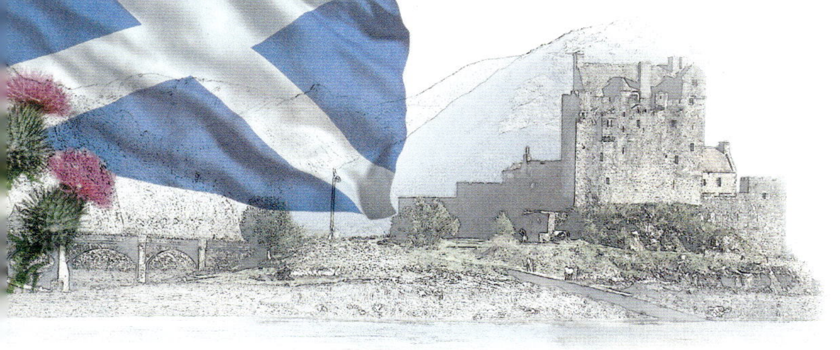

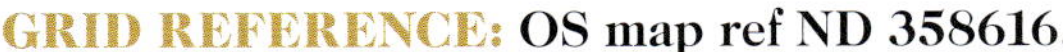

Keiss Castle

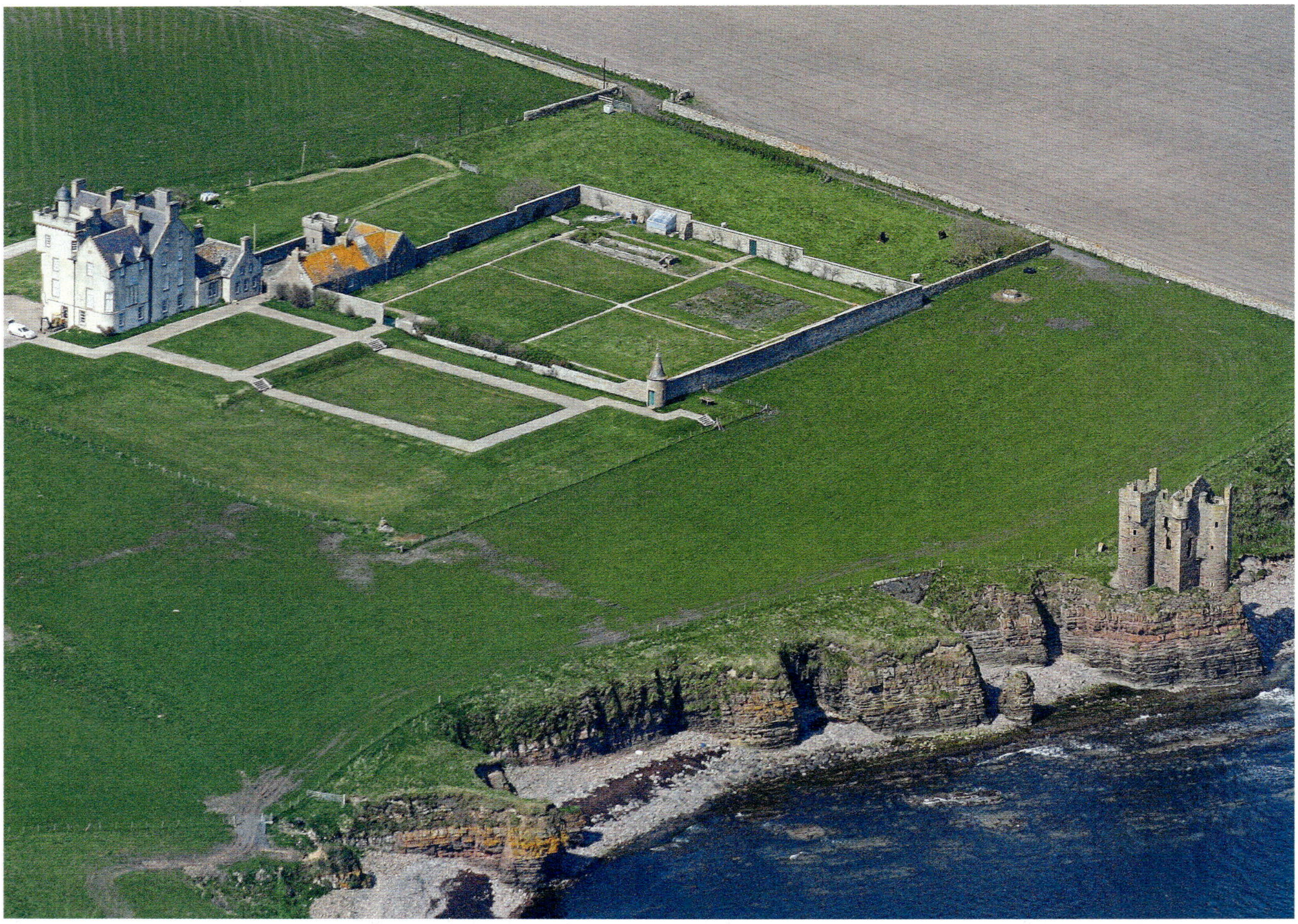

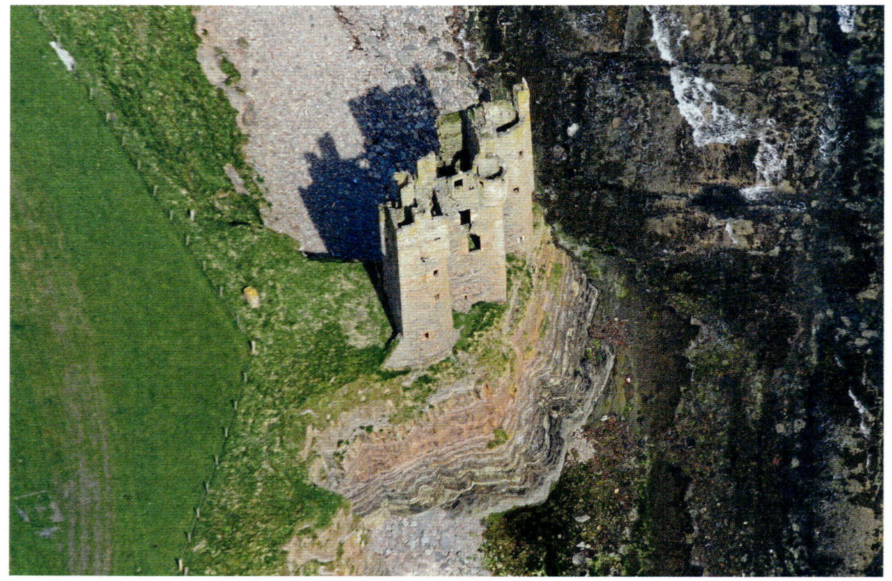

Fulmars, pigeons and gulls now nest inside the shattered tower perched precariously above the shore near Keiss. This is another monument to the ambitions of the Sinclair clan, the adjacent Bay is named after them. Today this historic defensive structure, allowed to decay because its owners moved to a comfortable mansion nearby, faces an implacable foe in the form of coastal erosion.

ABOUT THE CASTLE

Visitor Details

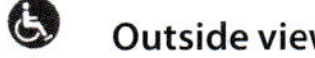

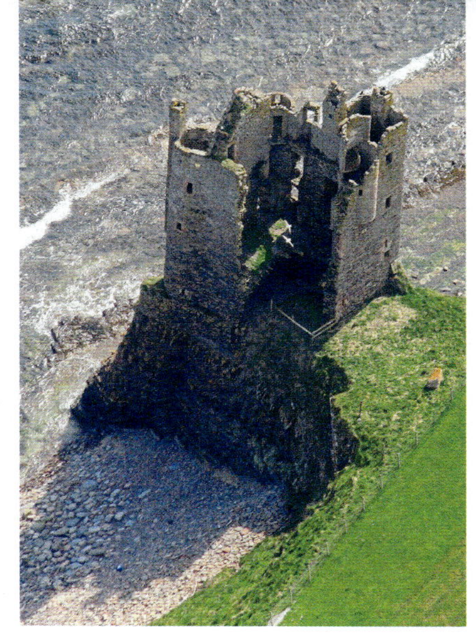

- Open 24 hours a day, seven days a week.
- Outside viewing of ruin only.
- The location is a fine place for night skies photography especially when the Northern Lights appear. This link will help with forecasts http://www.glendaleskye.com/aurora-alerts-app.php

Location: Situated in Sutherland and Caithness, Keiss Castle is about six miles north of Wick. Park at Keiss harbour and walk north for just under a mile. Look out for the remains of broch structures on the way. The castle is perched on a crumbling cliff top above the beach.

This is one of the three castles built by the Sinclair Clan on the edge of the bay which now has their name. The other two are Girnigoe and Ackergill which are also covered in this book.

It is likely that an older Pictish fort had occupied the outcrop chosen by the castle builders.

Construction is attributed to the 5th Earl of Caithness, George Sinclair, around 1600. The design is a Z-plan tower house but very narrow for its type although it still contained four floors, an attic and basement. In its short history of use, it was not attacked.

When threatened, the occupants gave up the building without a fight. The 7th Earl died at the castle in 1698 and then the property was neglected in favour of a large mansion being built nearby. This appears in some of the air views and is called Keiss House. By 1755, this mansion was the chosen home of Sir William Sinclair, the 2nd Baronet of Dunbeath.

The ruined tower house is a wonder to look at but do not venture inside due to unstable masonry; leave it to the nesting birds. Coastal erosion is now threatening the future of the tower.

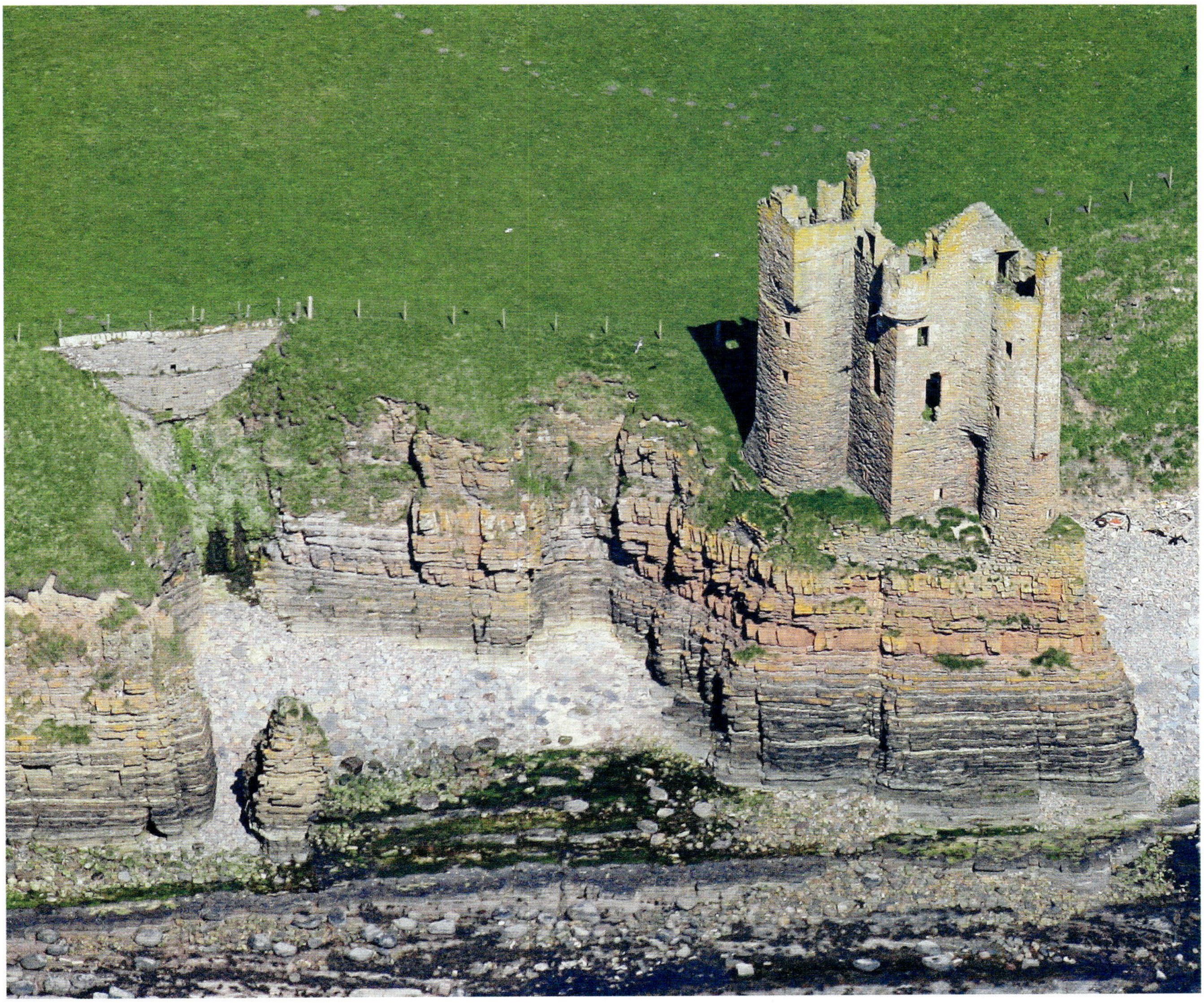

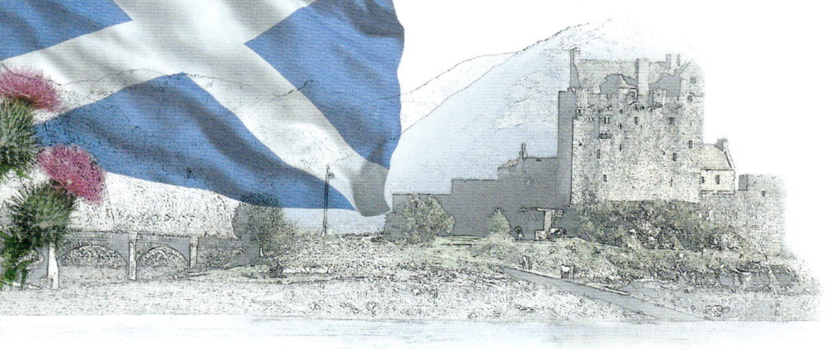

Kelburn Castle

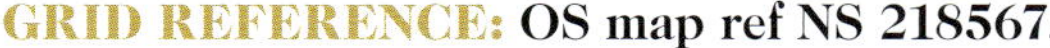

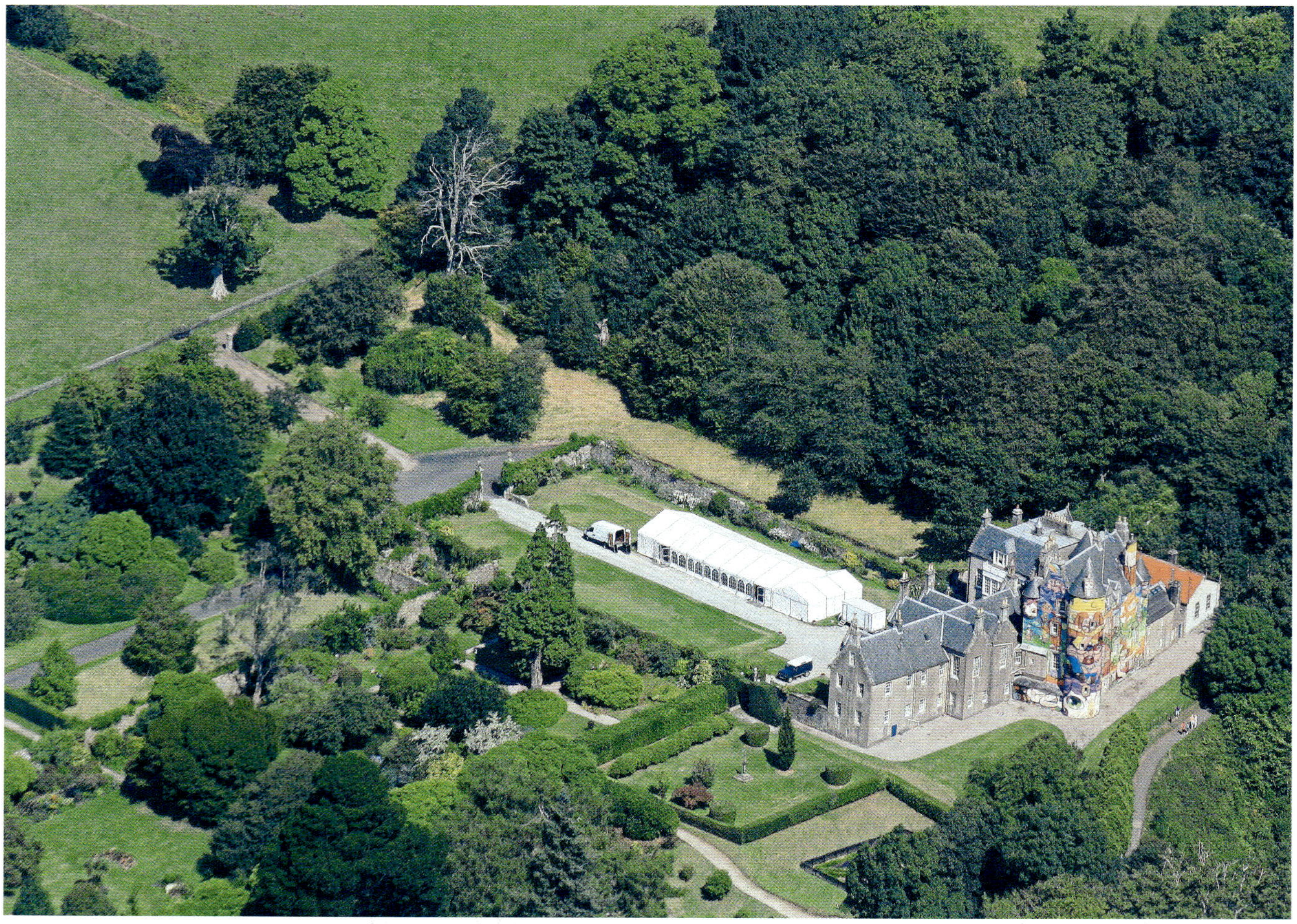

Brightly adorned by modern artists' murals, the castle walls shout for attention. This recent interpretation of an old idea (adorn your castle to stand out proudly) has been controversial but it is a fitting means by which to celebrate the Boyle clan, who maintain the castle and estate despite the many challenges involved in such a mammoth undertaking.

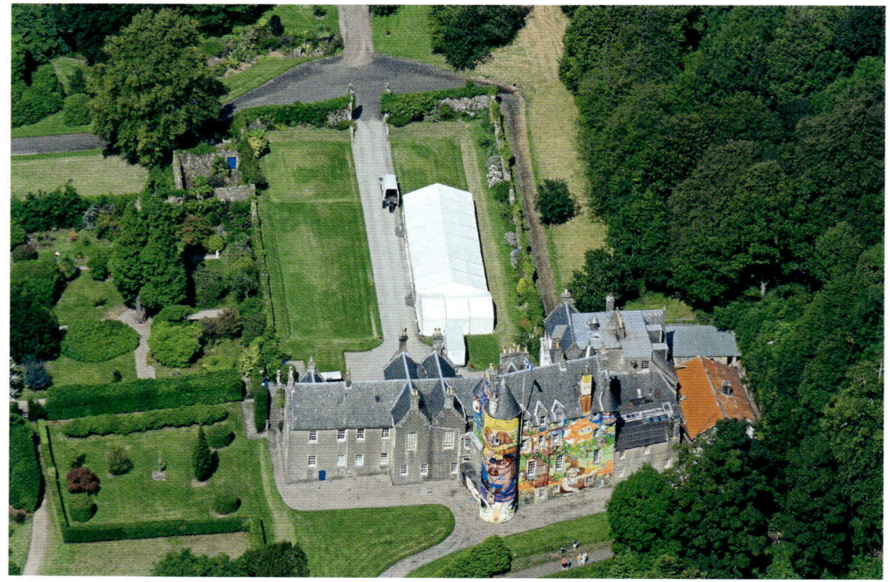

◼| ABOUT THE CASTLE

Visitor Details

 www.kelburnestate.com

 01475 568685

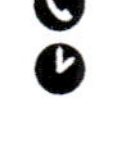 The castle is still the private home of the 10th Earl of Glasgow, Patrick Boyle, and his family. Due to this reason, the castle is usually only open for tours on set dates. The grounds are open daily 10am-6pm from Easter to October with shorter hours through the winter.

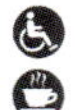 Disabled parking is available but the estate has many gravel paths and steps.

A cafe and gift shop is on site.

The grounds are free to visit but there is a car park fee of £5 payable on entry. There are three outdoor play areas including the Secret Forest which is a fairy tale trail through the woodland. There is also the Wild Wild West Saloon and the Adventure Course.

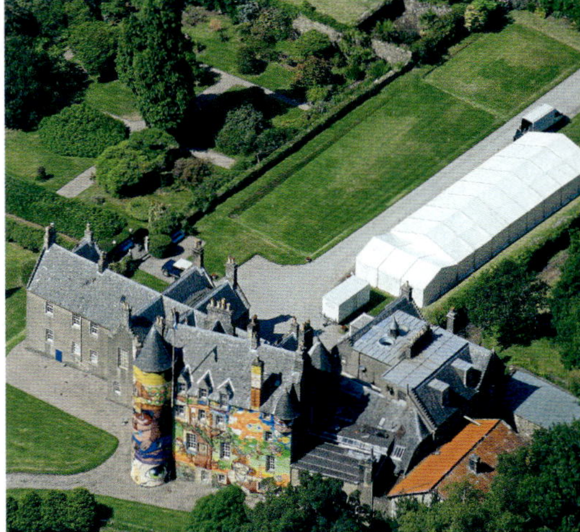

Location: Kelburn Castle is located in Ayrshire two miles south of Largs on minor roads off the A78 at the Kelburn Country Centre.

The Boyle Clan still occupy the castle which is probably the longest unbroken castle residency by any family in Scotland. The name Boyle comes from the Norman town of Beauville near Caen. In 1164, David de Boivil appears as a witness to a charter. By 1275, Richard de Boyville held the lands of Kelburn. The first defensive building on this site was a wooden tower and palisade. This was recorded in the accounts of the Battle of Largs nearby in 1263 when the Scots beat off a sea-borne landing by Viking raiders.

By the 1200s, a stone building in Norman style had replaced the timber fort. The traditional Scottish tower house appeared in the late 16th century and still includes parts of earlier stone works. When David Boyle MP became Earl of Glasgow in 1703, he added a new north west wing. He commissioned expert mason Thomson Caldwell to design and build a mansion house style extension onto the castle.

Meanwhile, the castle estate grew with orchards and gardens as well as areas for food production. In 1880, the 6th Earl added further improvements. The Kelburn name is also known in New Zealand due to the 7th Earl becoming governor there in 1892. The castle and museum have many items displayed from his time in that far away land.

Many castles were not left as bare stone. They were painted bright hues to proudly stand out and protect stone work from the ravages of the climate. Kelburn has taken this a stage further with world-renowned murals swirling across the castle. These were added by Brazilian artists in 2008.

Following the opening of the grounds to the public in 1977, the estate buildings and stables were converted in 1980 to provide a tea room, shop and visitor information. A separate equestrian centre has been created and weddings are catered for with a large tented pavilion on site.

◼| ABOUT THE CLAN

Clan Boyle

As mentioned in the history of Kelburn castle, the name Boyle comes from the Norman town of Beauville near Caen. In 1164, David de Boivil appears as a witness to a charter. By 1275, Richard de Boyville held the lands of Kelburn. By 1291 Henry de Boyville was in charge of castles at Dumfries, Wigtown and Kircudbright. Richard and Robert de Boyvil are listed in the 1296 Ragman Roll declaring their allegiance to Edward I. Around this time a further allegiance was made when Richard Boyle married a daughter of Sir Robert Comyn. John Boyle, his descendant, was killed at the Battle of Sauchieburn just South of Stirling. He was one of the nobles, with King James III leading 30,000 Royalists but they were defeated by 18,000 rebels led by his son Prince James. The King died on the battlefield after a fall from his horse. The Boyle family lands were confiscated but his son had them restored by James IV of Scotland (formerly Prince James).

Mary Queen of Scots was supported by the Boyles against Elizabeth I and later the clan changed sides again by favouring the rule of Charles I from London. This did not make the clan popular with other Scottish Nobles. The power of political office was attractive to the Boyles with John Boyle of Kelburn gaining a seat as a Commissioner of Parliament; his

eldest son also held a seat and his appointment as a privy councillor followed. By 1699 he became Lord Boyle, soaring to the position of Earl of Glasgow in 1703. With this background it is not a surprise that in the 1715 rising he supported the Hanoverians by funding recruitment of new troops locally.

The 3rd Earl John was wounded at the Battle of Fontenoy in Belgium 1745. After this clash of over 100,000 men the French were regarded as victors. With huge numbers killed and wounded on both sides, the allies lost control of channel ports and much of the low country. The allied army opposing the French was led by an inexperienced Duke of Cumberland who hastened back to Scotland to lead the last stages of the defeat of the Jacobites. The French army was committed to fighting this war of the Austrian Succession in mainland Europe and this was one reason that they did not send troops to support the Jacobite cause.

In 1747, John the 3rd Earl was again wounded at the battle of Lauffeld near Maastricht. another French victory in the same campaign. This also marked another defeat for the Duke of Cumberland, his career finished in 1757 and his father the king never forgave him for this and other mistakes. After these military misadventures

Earl John of Glasgow took a senior Church of Scotland position for the next nine years. George Frederick Boyle in the mid 1800s also became involved in the church. However he lavished family funds on renovating churches across Scotland and indulging his love of art and design. He also had work completed at Kelburn castle including purchasing expensive Pre Raphaelite artworks.

By 1888 his cousin David Boyle had to provide funds when the estate became bankrupt and parts were sold off. In 1890 David became the 7th Earl and served for five years as governor of New Zealand, rising to the peerage in 1897 and becoming Baron Fairlie. The current clan chief is the 10th Earl and was a Royal Navy Reserve Officer and lives with his family in Kelburn castle. The clan motto is Dominus providebit ("The Lord will provide").

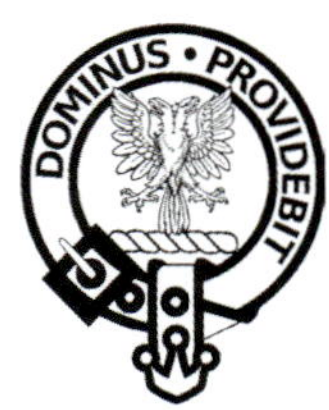

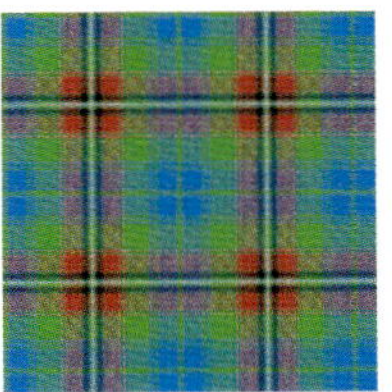

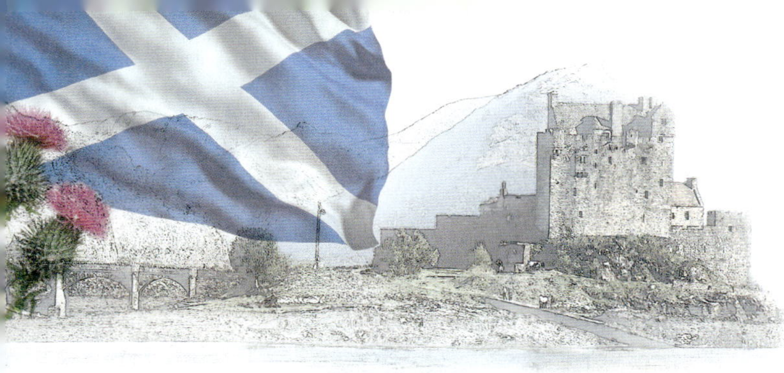

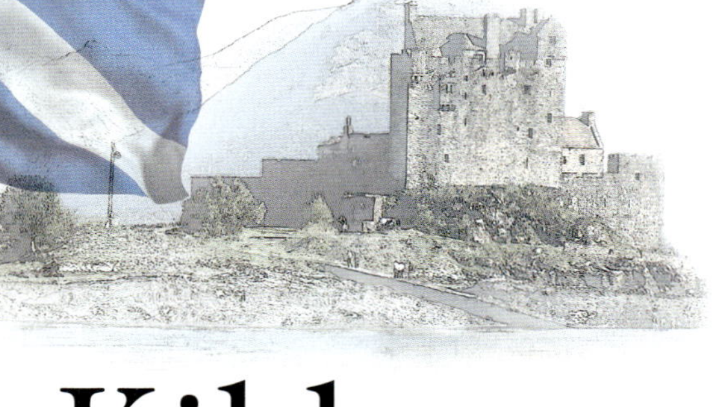

GRID REFERENCE: OS map ref NJ 455164.

Kildrummy Castle

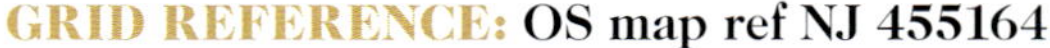

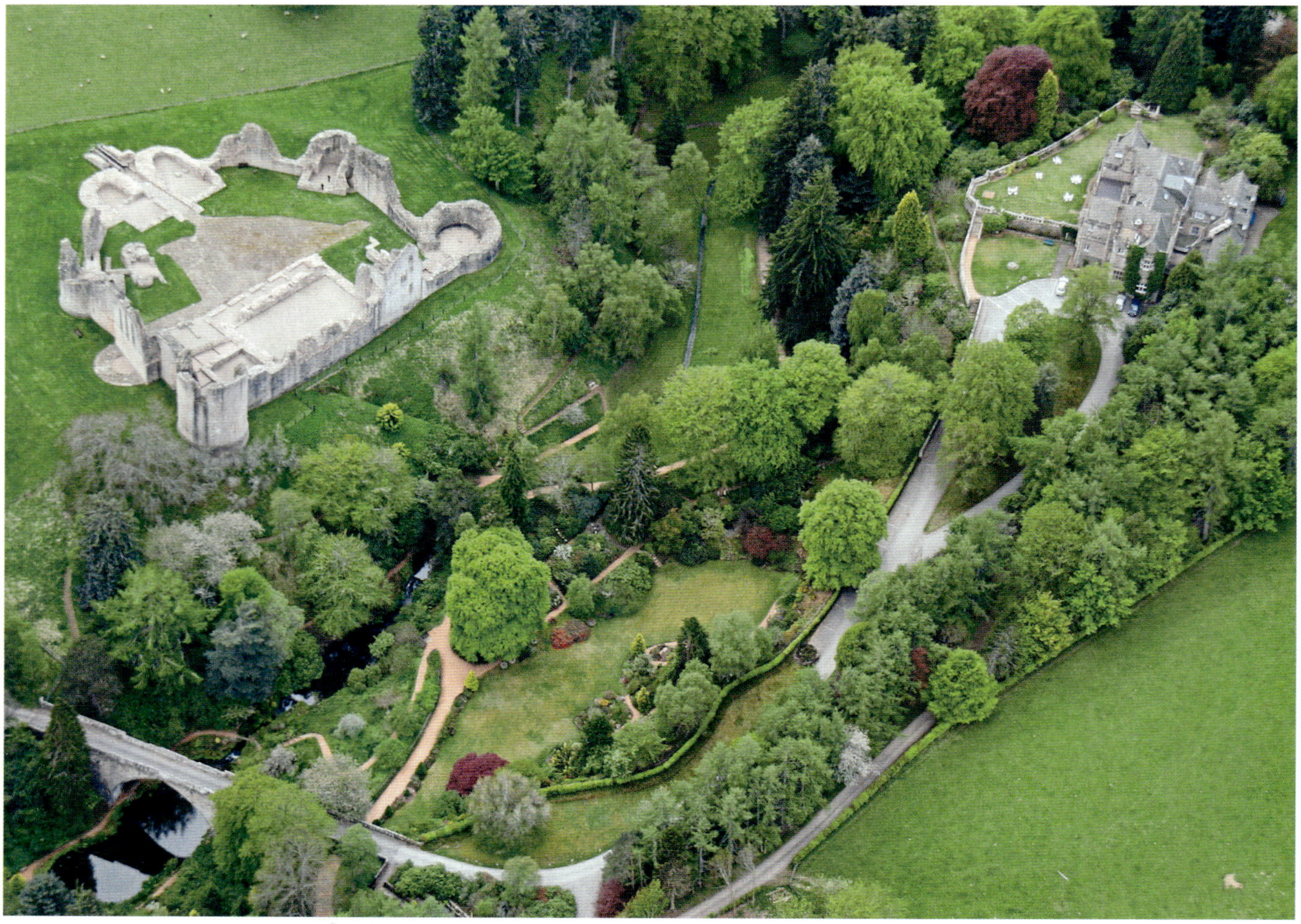

Once a massive and imposing fortress, this castle was held by Robert the Bruce's younger brother Nigel until it was betrayed by a traitor on the inside. Nigel and his men were all hung but an even grislier fate awaited the unfaithful carpenter who had brought about his demise. More sieges followed, and gang warfare, until the wrecked castle eventually ended up being used as a quarry.

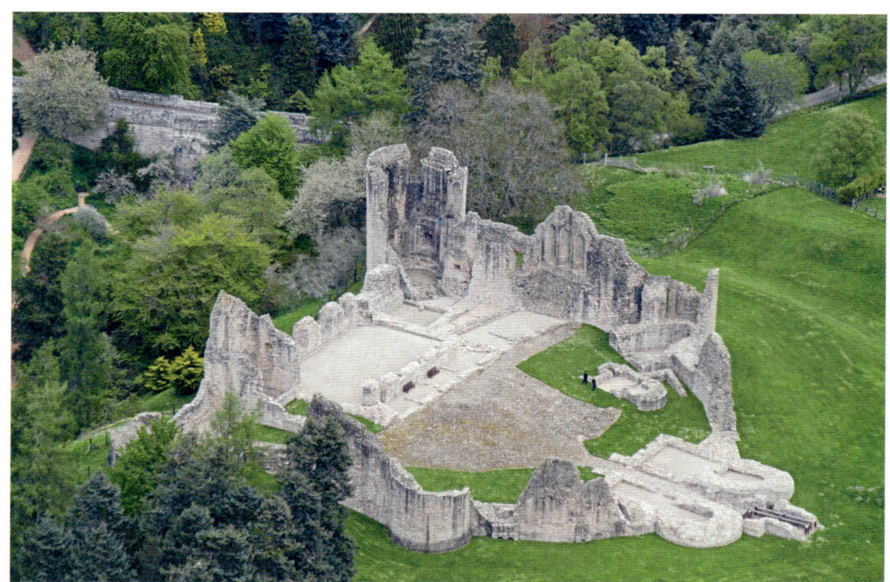

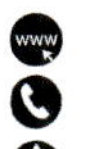

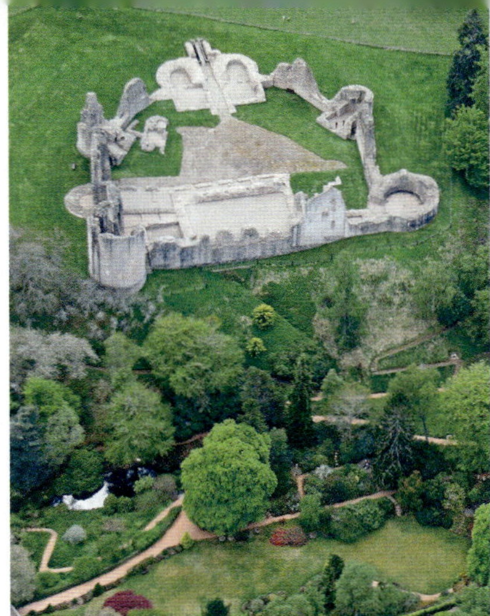

Location: In the Aberdeen and Gordon district, Kildrummy Castle is 20 miles south of Huntly just off the A97. The car park is next to the main road and then it is just a short walk to the castle. An alternative route can be found from Alford (six miles east) on the A944/A97.

In the 13th century, Gilbert de Moravia (the Bishop of Caithness) decided to place a castle here so that he could control several cross country routes. On one side, the castle was protected by a natural valley. Steep-sided ditches were dug below the high castle walls on the other sides. The gatehouse was protected by two towers. The main curtain wall had six round towers on the corners and the inside held a large courtyard. The hall building was a substantial two-storey creation, much of which survives today. The three tall lancet windows still soar above the foundation of the chapel.

Such a substantial strategic castle was the target for many sieges. The forces of King Edward I of England were the first to take control in 1296. They lost it to Nigel Bruce sometime after that. Nigel probably had support from his older brother, Robert the Bruce. In 1306, treachery enabled the English to retake the castle. During the siege, a traitor inside the castle set fires using his knowledge as a carpenter to weaken the defences. The entire garrison were hung, including Nigel, which was unusual as often hostages were released after ransoms were paid. The traitor was rewarded with gold but because he was seen as a threat, the gold was melted and poured down his throat.

During the Second War of Independence, the castle was retaken from the English. The Earl of Atholl laid siege in 1335 attempting to gain it for the English. The castle defences were organised by Lady Christina Bruce (sister of Robert the Bruce). Her husband, Sir Andrew Moray, with his force of around 4,000 clansmen including 800 knights from Lothian rushed north to her aid. With local knowledge from his clan, he chose to make his battleground by a forest, stream and loch at Culblean, 12 miles south of the castle. Here on St Andrews Day, using clever tactics including a fake retreat he defeated the Earl of Atholl and his 3,000 men. The Earl of Atholl was killed alongside Walter and Thomas Comyn having refused to surrender.

This battle and siege marked the final attempt to re-gain an English outpost in Scotland by Edward Balliol. His summer invasion plans were destroyed here along with his desires to conquer and rule Scotland. A tall stone monument marks the battle site in a woodland clearing at Culblean, midway between Aboyne and Ballater.

King David II of Scotland had the Earl of Mar removed from the castle in 1363 after another siege and it stayed in royal hands until 1368. The Wolf of Badenoch, Alexander Stewart, gained the castle and title, Earl of Mar, around 1400 by forcing Isabella Douglas to marry him.

After the death of the Wolf in 1435, it was claimed back by King James I cutting the Erskine Clan out of rightful ownership. They tried to take the castle by force in 1442 but failed. Then the Cochranes and Elphinstones joined the growing list of clans who

had short residences at Kildrummy. They yielded to legal claims in 1626 and the Erskines, Earls of Mar, moved in.

John Strachan, the Younger of Lynturk, had by the year 1526 gained a bad reputation in North East Scotland. He joined in with members of the Forbes Clan to spread murder and mayhem with their mercenary gang. In 1530, his attack on Kildrummy left it burned and sacked. He just escaped execution and fled to France.

Cromwell took the castle in 1654 to deny its use by Royalist supporters. Fire raged in 1690 when Viscount Dundee made it of little use to government forces. However, by 1715, repairs were good enough to enable the last Earl of Mar to base his Jacobite sympathisers there while he planned the uprising. After the failed rising, the government used the castle as a quarry preventing re-occupation. Colonel Ogston, the owner between 1898 and 1931, tidied up some of the rubble remains. In 1951 the state became custodians the department responsible currently is Historic Environment Scotland.

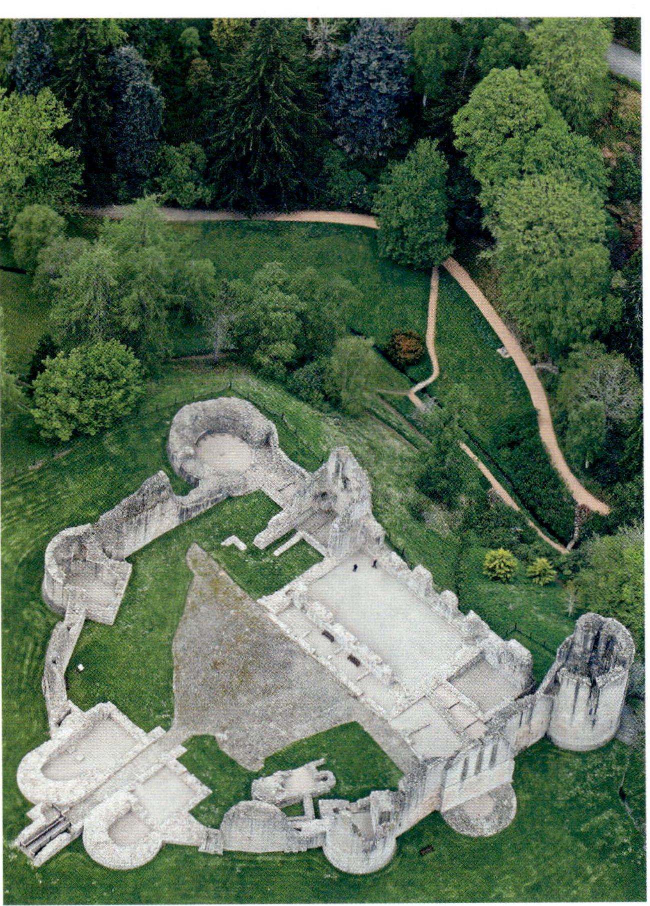

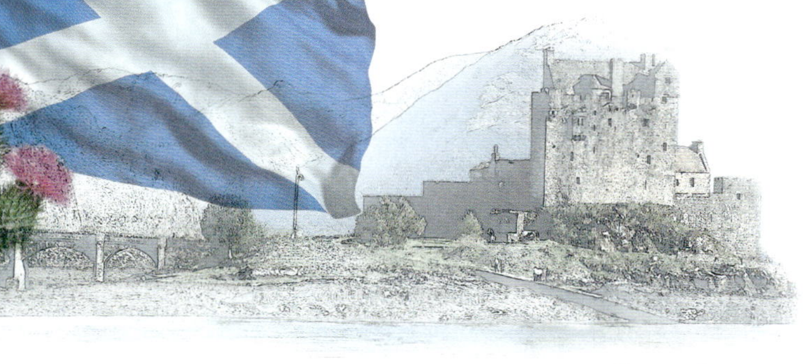

Knockhall Castle

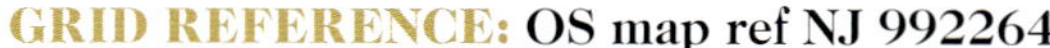

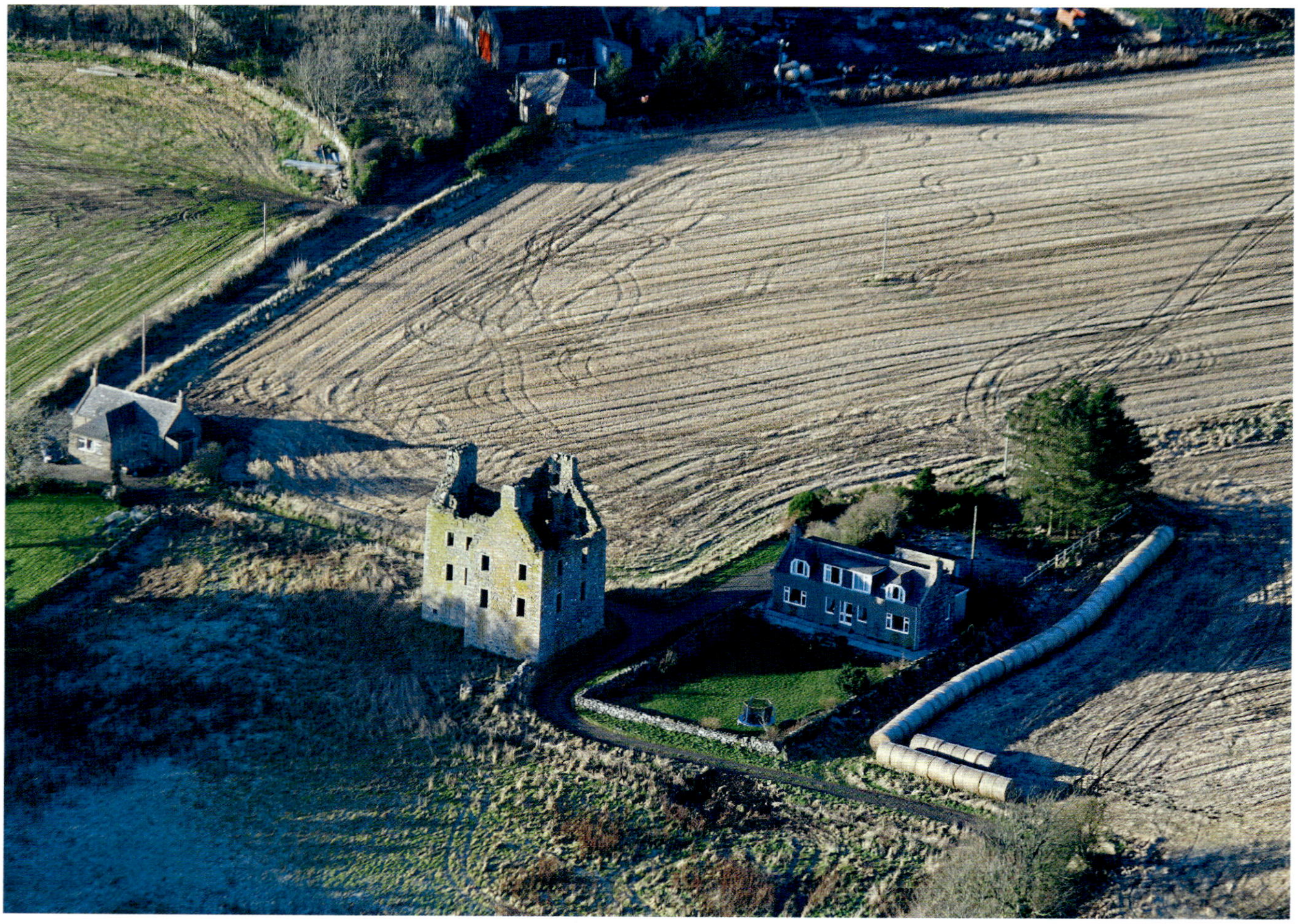

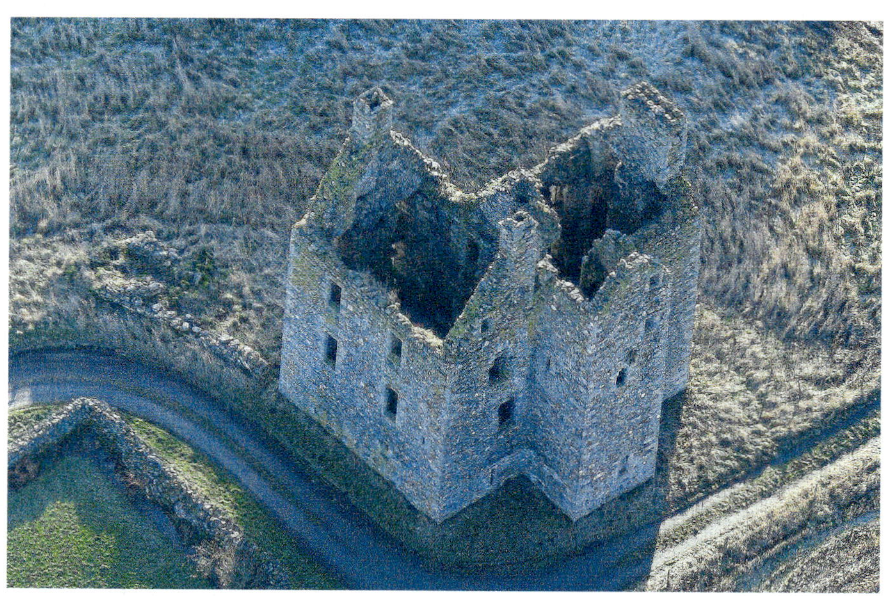

Fire raged out of control in this compact and once comfortable little castle during the 1700s but who would save the family? The answer is funnier than you might imagine. And afterwards, just move to your spare castle, leave this one to crumble. Today it can be viewed from the exterior only, unless the viewer feels rich enough to purchase the site.

Visitor Details

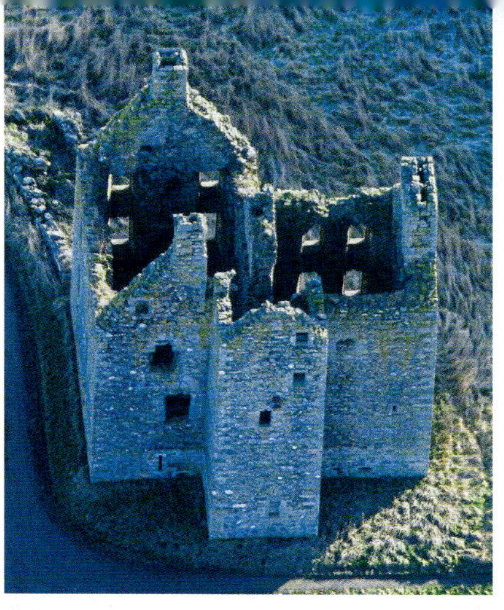

🕐 Open 24 hours a day, seven days a week.

♿ Outside viewing of ruin only.

Location: This castle is located in the Aberdeen and Gordon district one mile north-west of Newburgh and west of the A975 on minor roads near Mains of Knockhall.

This L-plan tower house was built around 1565 by Lord Sinclair of Newburgh. He was related to the wealthy Sinclairs of Caithness. In July 1589, the Lord was honoured when James VI stayed at his fine residence. He feasted in the hall on the first floor; his food was prepared in the basement kitchen. Above the hall were the chambers which were made comfortable with an open fire and built in latrine.

Clan Udny became owners in 1634 and suffered upheaval when Earl Marischal forcibly took the tower for the Covenanters in 1639. The clan moved back in soon afterwards. However, in 1734 a terrible fire broke out and the castle was gutted. Luckily the family survived thanks to the laird's jester, Jamie Fleeman, who got them to safety. Instead of rebuilding the stone shell of a tower they stayed in their other property in the area at Udny Castle. The stabilised ruin has been listed for sale with Savills since 2017 for offers over £130,000.

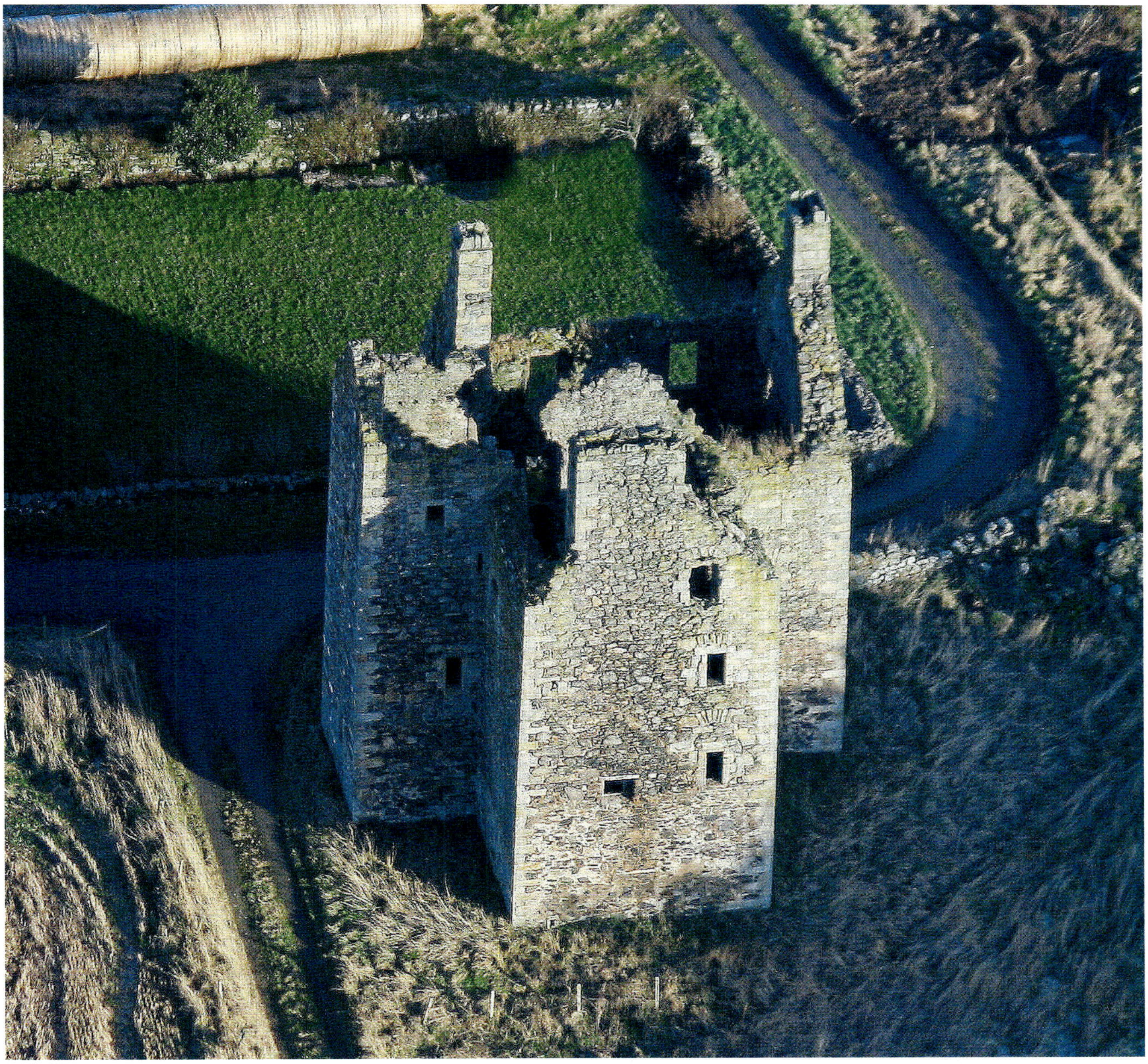

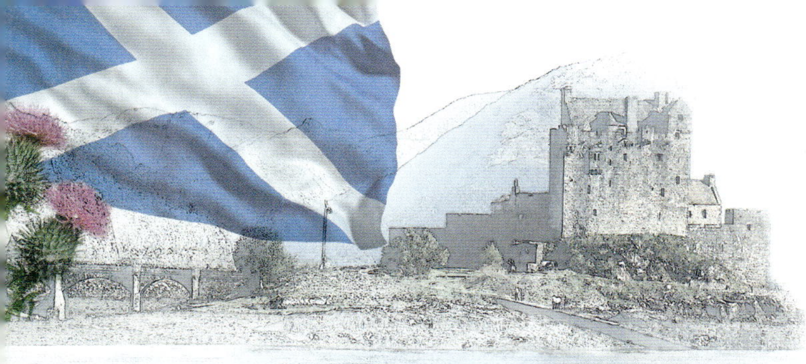

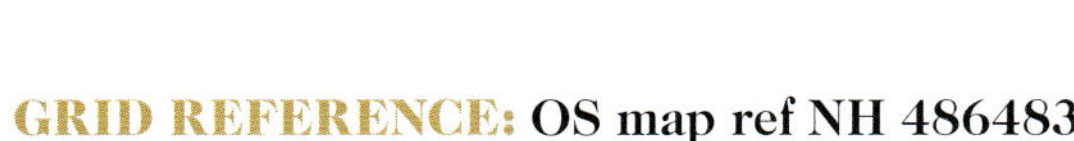

Castle Leod

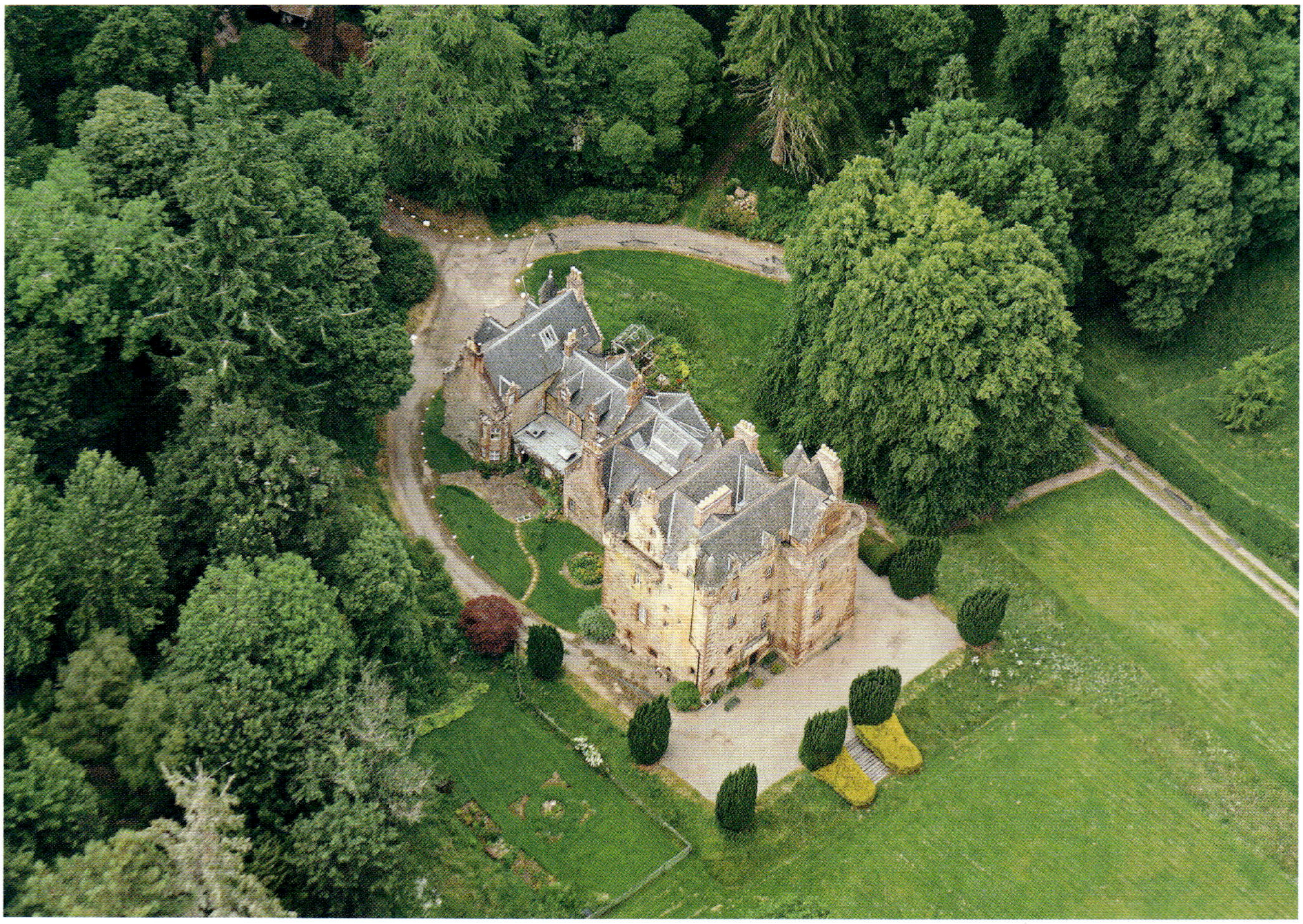

◼ ABOUT THE CLAN

Some Mackenzies settled in the Inverness area but they also spread across both coastlines of the North and inland. They were found in Kintail, around Loch Duich centred on Eilean Donan castle. Before then they were present as part of the Kingdom of Dal Riata, sharing ancestors with Clan Matheson and Anrias. These ancestors were the Gillean of the Aird giving a solid Celtic background rather than Norman.

By dedicating their military services to the Kings of Scotland the clan became very powerful mercenaries. Eilean Donan castle was a gift of the king to Colin Fitzgerald, son of an Irish Earl; he changed his family name to Mackenzie.

By 1362 lands in nearby Kintail were granted to Murdoch Mackenzie by King David II. At the battle of Blair Na Park by Strathpeffer circa 1490 the clan, with support from Clan

Clan Mackenzie

Brodie, had become strong enough to beat the MacDonalds, thereby ending the expansion attempts by the Lord of the Isles. This resulted in the Royal reward of more lands in the North West.

King James IV also sent them to punish the Macleods on the remote Isle of Lewis; a nasty affair where the Mackenzies forced the Macleods to surrender a stronghold by threatening to drown their captive Macleod maidens on tidal rocky islands. This resulted in yet more land rewards from the king. By 1607 all the lands from Ardnamurchan to Strathnaver were held by the Mackenzies. In the 1715 rising the clan chief led 3,000 men for the Jacobites against a smaller government force at Alness which retreated. This caused several weeks of local clan revenge raids and the Mackenzies holding Inverness were forced to surrender to the

Visitor Details

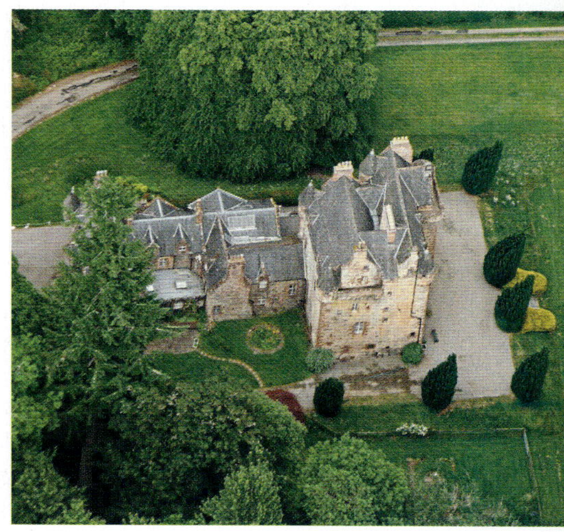

- www.castleleod.org.uk
- No telephone.
- Private, open by arrangement only. Public open days are held annually with a small parking fee payable which helps the building trust fund.
- Contact the trust for more information.
- Refreshments at nearby Strathpeffer town.
- Private tours for small parties may still be available by special arrangement with the Trust. These are conducted by the Mackenzie Clan Chief, John Mackenzie, Earl of Cromartie, or by approved tour guides. The tours can be for the grounds only or possibly extended to include a tour of the house. For more information contact projectadmin@castleleod.org.uk

Location: Castle Leod is in the Ross and Cromarty district four miles west of Dingwall and one mile north of Strathpeffer. By road, you can find it just north of the A834.

The castle occupies an area of high ground which may have been the reason it was chosen by the Picts for an earlier fort. 'Leod' is a Viking name which can be traced to an uncle of the mighty Norseman Thorfinn, Jarl of Orkney and Caithness. Later, the Norse earls in the 11th century created a stone keep on the site to replace the first wooden structure. Ships could reach the head of the Cromarty firth just four miles away. Around 1610, Sir Roderick Mackenzie of Coigach started the unbroken line of occupation by the Earls of Cromartie by building the five storey high L-plan tower house. This castle is an outstanding example of its type because it has not been greatly changed since the 15th century although the pitched roof was added later.

The Victorian and Edwardian additions are clearly separate. The tower is decorated with conical bartizans and parapets. Many gun loops and arrow firing slits pierce the thick walls. Another indication of a strong defence are the iron grills preventing entry via the windows. The exterior ground level has been raised since the completion of the castle because the entry door used to be on the first floor and could only be reached by ladder. That door is now at ground level with some firing slits at ankle height, clearly not the original intention.

George Mackenzie, the 3rd Earl, supported the Jacobites in 1745 and as a result of their defeat and his capture nearby, he lost his estate. He almost joined three other Jacobite lords destined for execution but his brave wife, Isabella Gordon, fainted at the king's feet having presented him with a petition to save her husband's life. With help from the Prince of Wales, the Earl was instead imprisoned in the Tower of London for three years then exiled to Devonshire. He later moved to London and became destitute. His son managed to get their lands back in 1784. However, the estate was in a poor financial state so by 1814 the castle had become a ruin. Repair work was carried out by the Hay-Mackenzies after Anne married the Duke of Sutherland in 1861. This also heralded the return of the Earldom of Cromartie. A detailed account of the continual restoration plan can be found here https://www.castleleod.org.uk/project/

The grounds contain many fine specimen trees including a Spanish chestnut possibly planted in 1550 for the mother of Mary Queen of Scots, Mary of Guise. It has a huge spiralling trunk. Also nearby are two giant sequoia, one being the largest tree in Britain by bulk. The current owner has continued the tradition of planting and is part of an international conifer conservation programme.

This castle was the inspiration behind the creation of Castle Leoch which was occupied by Jamie's uncle, Colum Mackenzie, and his clan in the Outlander series of novels.

The real Mackenzie family are still residents and have this to say: "Castle Leod is surely one of the most beautiful, romantic and unspoilt castles in the Highlands." There certainly seems little reason to disagree.

Frasers and Munroes. In the 45 rising the clan fought well at Falkirk, captured Foulis and Dunrobin castles but were ambushed at Littleferry and so never took the field at Culloden.

Other Mackenzies formed part of Government independent companies. The Earl of Cromartie was captured at Dunrobin, stripped of his title and some lands forfeited as a temporary punishment. The fighting spirit of the clan was soon harnessed by the British army. Units included the Highland Light Infantry raised in 1777, Seaforth Highlanders 1778 and Ross shire Buffs 1793. Predicting the future in a series of enigmatic riddles was the skill given to the Brahan Seer who was a Mackenzie.

For example, in the 17th century he foresaw ships travelling across land North of Tomnahurich hill Inverness. The building of the Caledonian Canal realised that dream. He met an awful end in a burning tar barrel. Canada saw many Mackenzies arrive; Sir Alexander explored its far north, trading fur and reaching the Pacific coast around 1772, the first to make the land crossing.

Two Prime Ministers of Canada were Mackenzies.

Whisky Galore and Monarch of the Glen were some of almost 100 books written by Sir Compton Mackenzie. He has the deserved reputation of weaving a tale which will have the reader in stitches; humour always threads the stories. These have featured in film productions and TV series.

Castle Leod, near Strathpeffer is the Seat of Clan Mackenzie, their Chief, John Ruaridh Grant Mackenzie, 5th Earl of Cromartie, and his family. It is featured in this book as well as Eilean Donan.

Motto: "Luceo non uro" (I shine, not burn). Also used is the Gaelic motto "Cuidich 'n righ" (Help the king).

A very active society links clan members across the world https://clanmackenziesociety.co.uk/

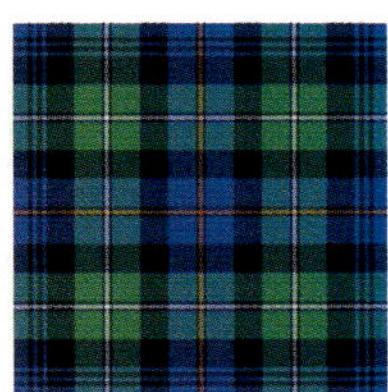

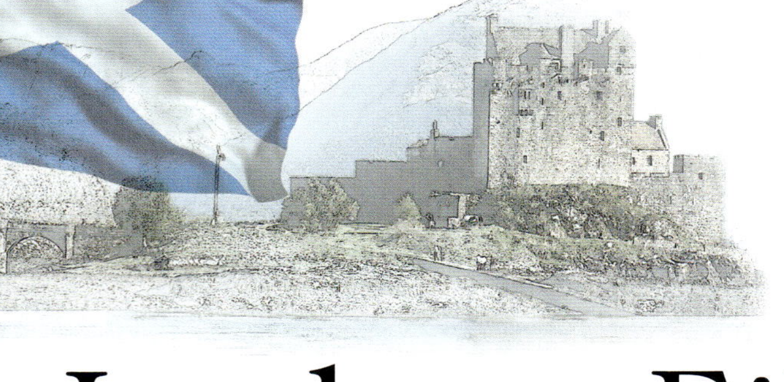

Loch an Eilein Castle

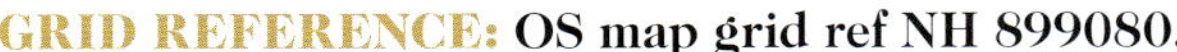

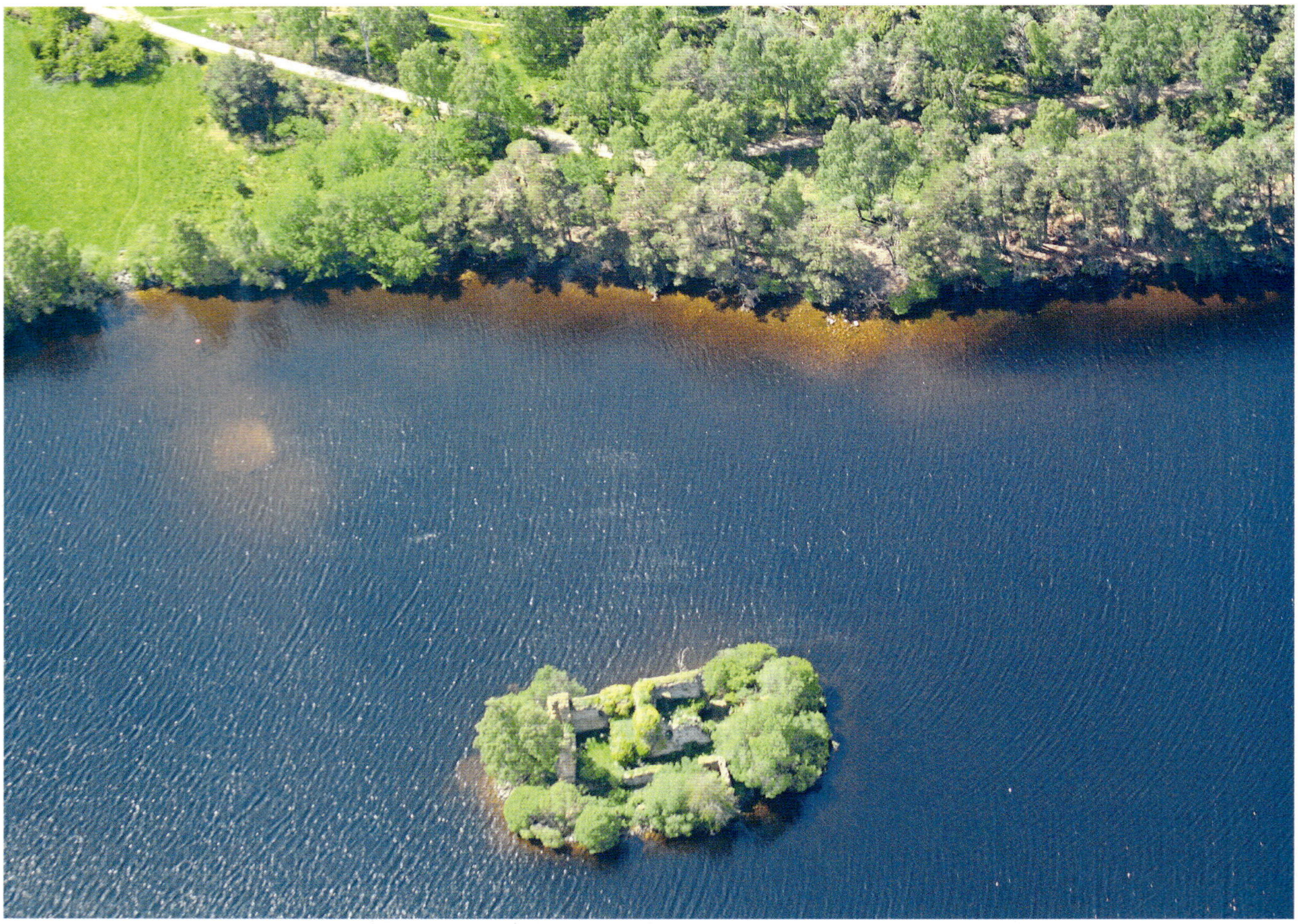

A small ruined castle perched on top of a tiny island in Loch an Eilean, this building served as a prison for the gentry at one time. However, more recently it has attracted film-makers with its remote and romantic nature. It can only be viewed from the shore, however, the old causeway having sunk. The nearby shore and forest is a great place for picnics and walks.

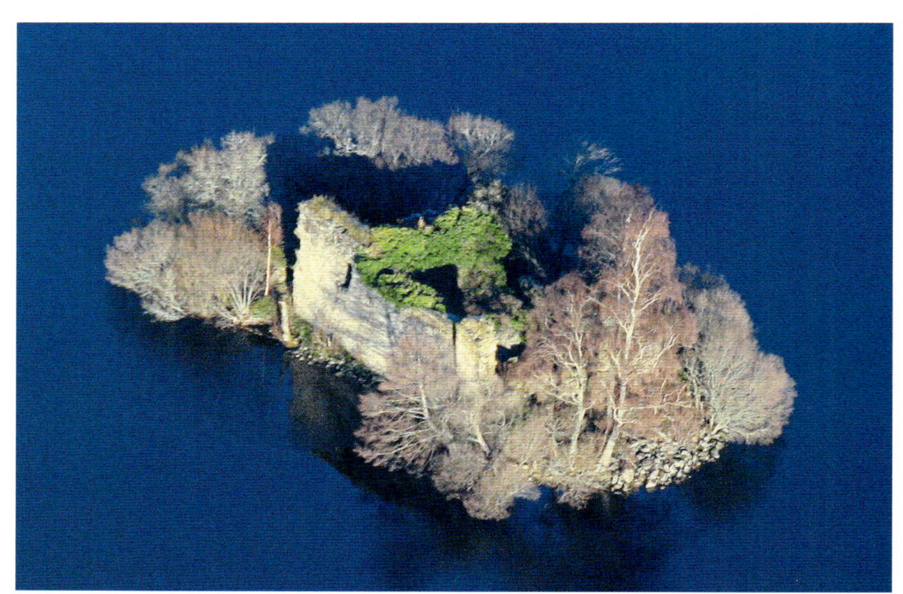

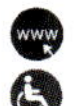

Visitor Details

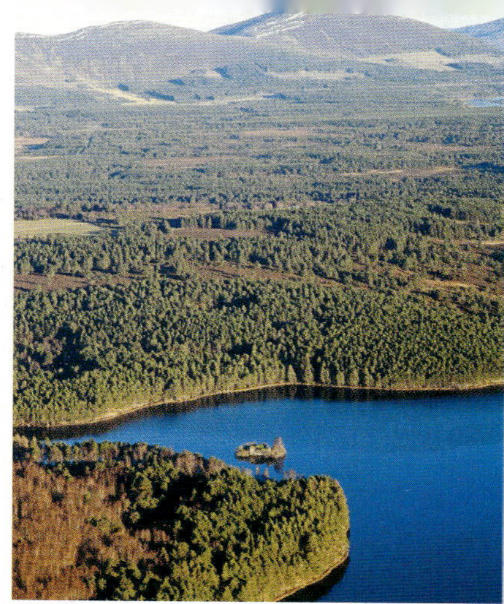

Ruin on island.

Outside viewing of ruin only.

There is a large car park on the estate land with a cafe and visitor centre on site.

The car park is not free. This is a very popular picnic spot with a circular walk around the loch. The castle is visible from the shore. This was the last osprey nest site from 1916 until 1954 when a pair bred at Loch Garten six miles north east from the castle.

Location: Loch an Eilean Castle is on a small island in the loch of the same name three miles south of Aviemore. Follow the minor road from Rothiemurchus ('the Ski Road') which is sign posted to the Loch.

Before the loch water level rose, possibly due to timber transport operations, the castle island was linked by a causeway to the nearby shore. The busiest castle builder in this region was known as the Wolf of Badenoch, Alexander Stewart.
He became tangled in warfare with the church and burned sections of Forres and Elgin Cathedral in 1390. He is therefore most likely to have ordered the castle to be built on an island due to him being responsible for another castle to be built in the same way on Lochindorb. The aerial views show that the castle likely consisted of a keep, hall and surrounding courtyard protected by a curtain wall.

Several clans held the castle including the Gordons, Mackintoshes and the Grants. In 1690, Jacobites gave siege to the castle but the defenders led by Dame Grizel Mor Grant held out against them. The last recorded use was in 1715 when a local noble was detained there to prevent him raising his Mackintosh clan against the Jacobites.
Film appearances include the BBC TV series Monarch of the Glen as an island graveyard. The surrounding shore and forest provided backdrops for the Outlander series. The most recent filming here for Outlaw King involved the creation of a medieval village along the beach mobilising 200 crew and 31 horses.

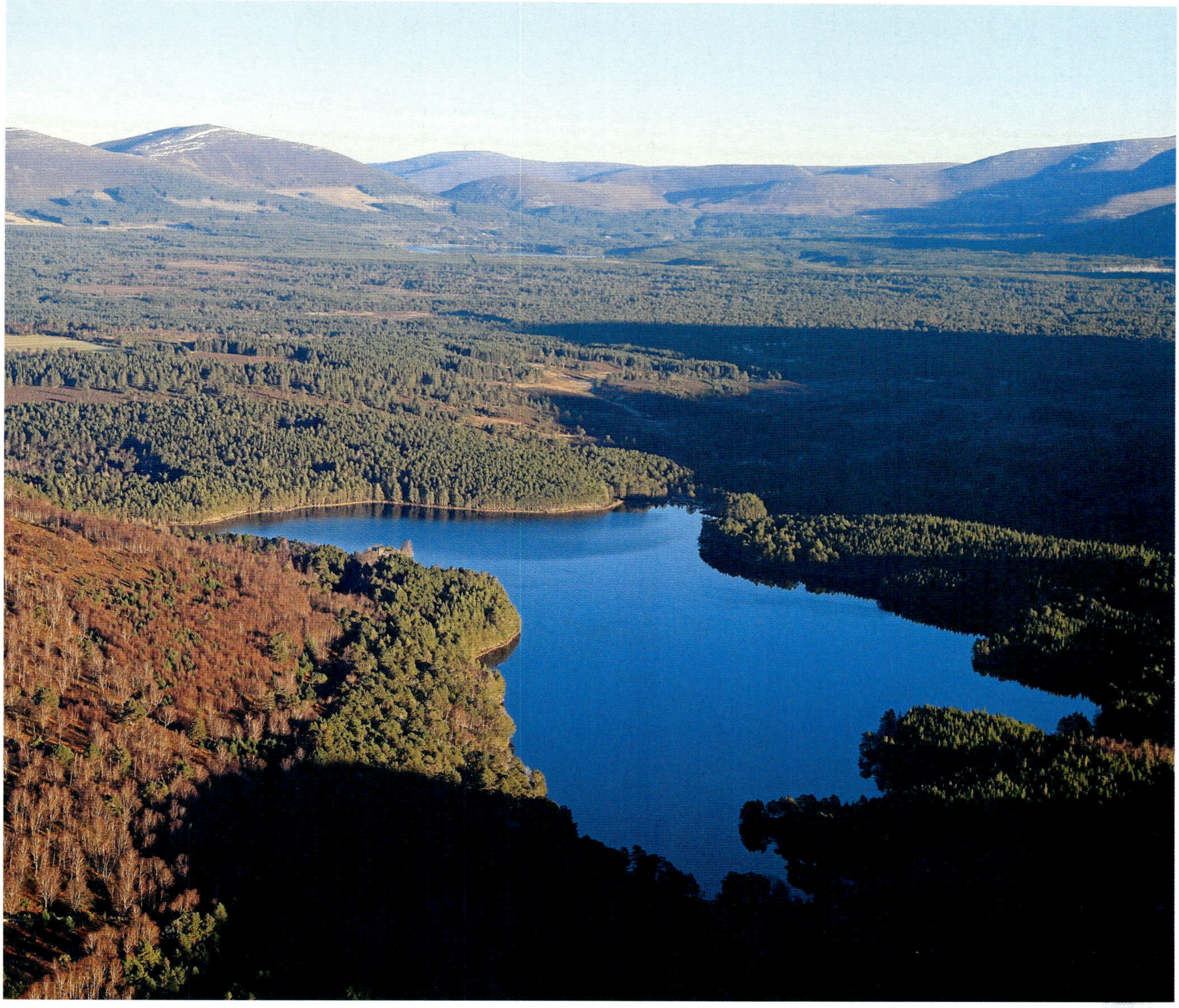

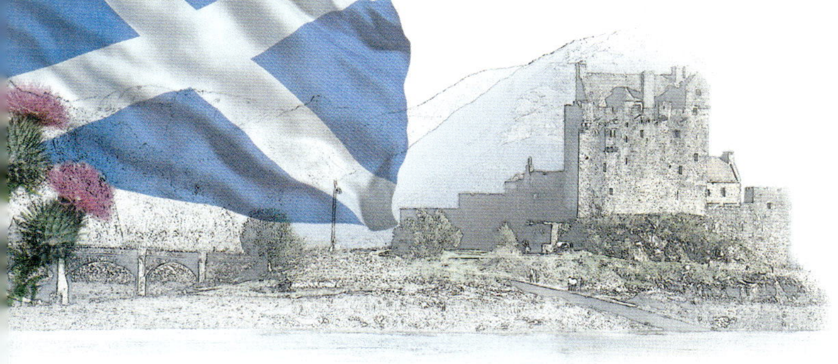

Lochindorb Castle

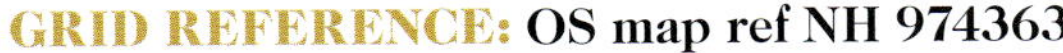

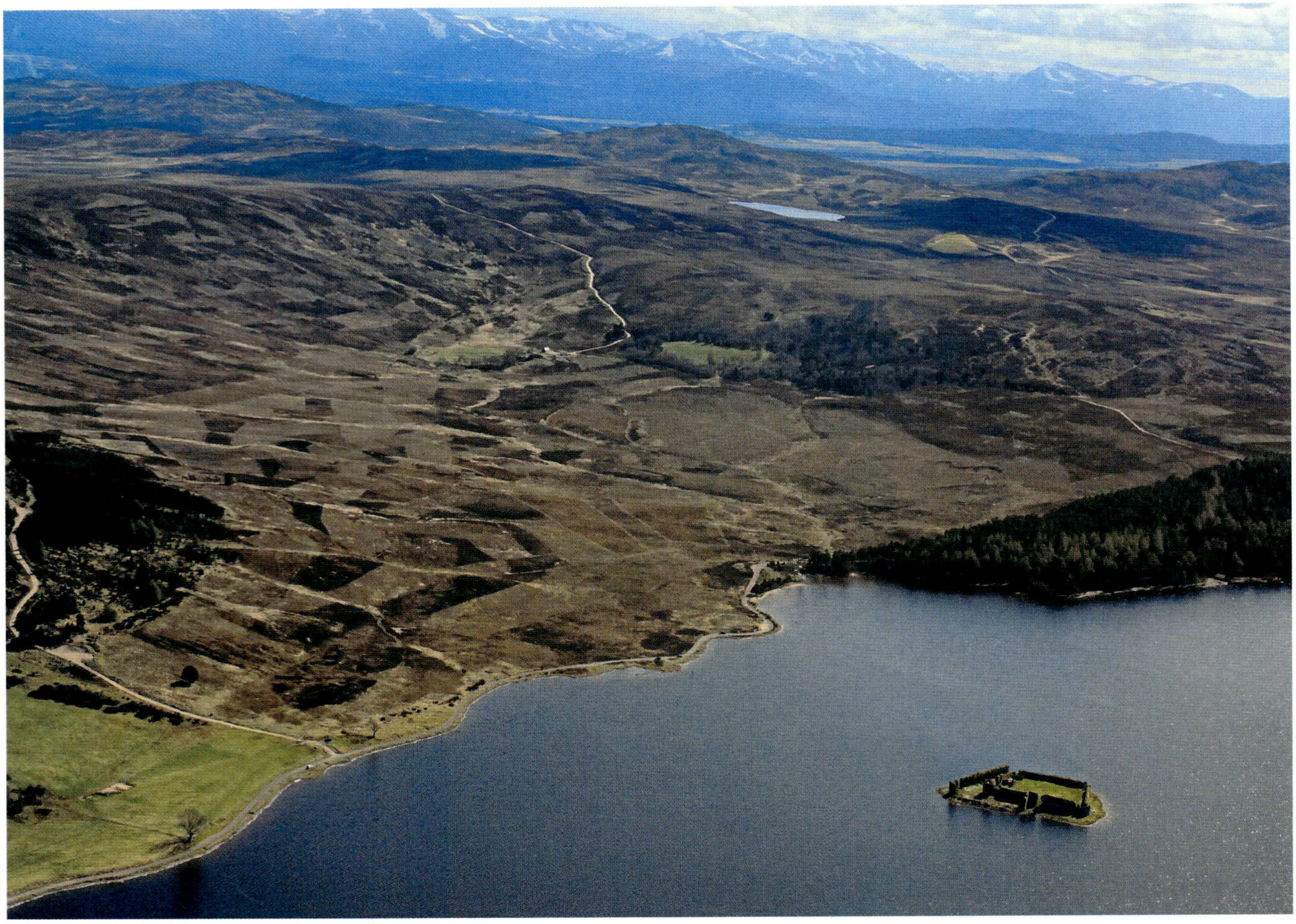

This castle, which may have been constructed on an artificial island, has a warlike past. One of its occupants, the Wolf of Badenoch, spread fear across a wide area of the North; destruction often followed his gang of ruffians. Today this is one of the most peaceful castle ruins, being located several miles away from the nearest town.

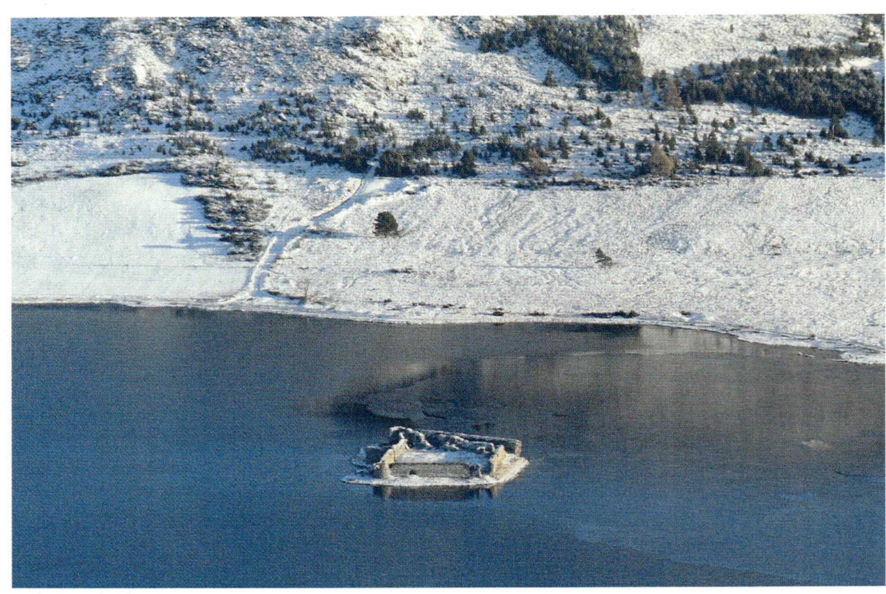

Visitor Details

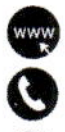 https://her.highland.gov.uk/Monument/MHG6778

 No telephone.

Available to view 24 hours a day, seven days a week.

Outside viewing of ruin only.

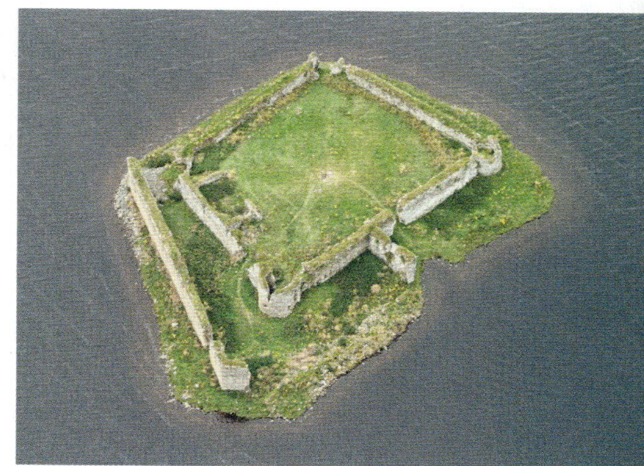

Location: Lochindorb Castle is located seven miles north west of Grantown on Spey. It occupies a small island. A loch side viewpoint can be reached by following a single track road for three miles from the junction on the A939 Grantown to Forres road. Apart from the lodge and castle ruin there are no other buildings here, just the noises of water lapping on the shore and the calls of the moorland birds. In contrast at the time of the occupation of the castle the surrounding lands were covered by forest.

Sir John (the Black) Comyn and his clan built the castle on the island which might be artificial. The design resembles another Comyn castle still visible at Inverlochy. Within the walls there is evidence of a hall and chapel. The Comyns at their strongest occupied over 25 castles in North Scotland.

Lochindorb castle was captured by forces of Edward I in 1303. Andrew Moray tried to recover it from the English by siege in 1335 but retreated as the approaching army of Edward III threatened to overwhelm his forces.

The most famous and feared occupant was the Wolf of Badenoch the nickname given to Alexander Stewart, Earl of Buchan. From 1372 his clansman harassed the region and this included the burning of Elgin cathedral and parts of that town.

Archibald Douglas, Earl of Moray was recorded as being the owner in 1455 but just a year later he fell in battle at Arkinholm near Langholm in the Scottish borders. This small battle was a victory for James II and marked the end of the powerful Black Douglas clan as opponents to the King. The castle became royal property and orders were given for it to be slighted. This was done by the Thane of Cawdor in 1458 and that marked the end of its use. He salvaged the iron Yett (gate) and had it installed at his nearby castle where it can still be viewed.

Underwater archaeologists have recently recovered a large intact 15th century jar and several stone balls which were likely fired by a trebuchet during a siege. No evidence of a causeway was found.

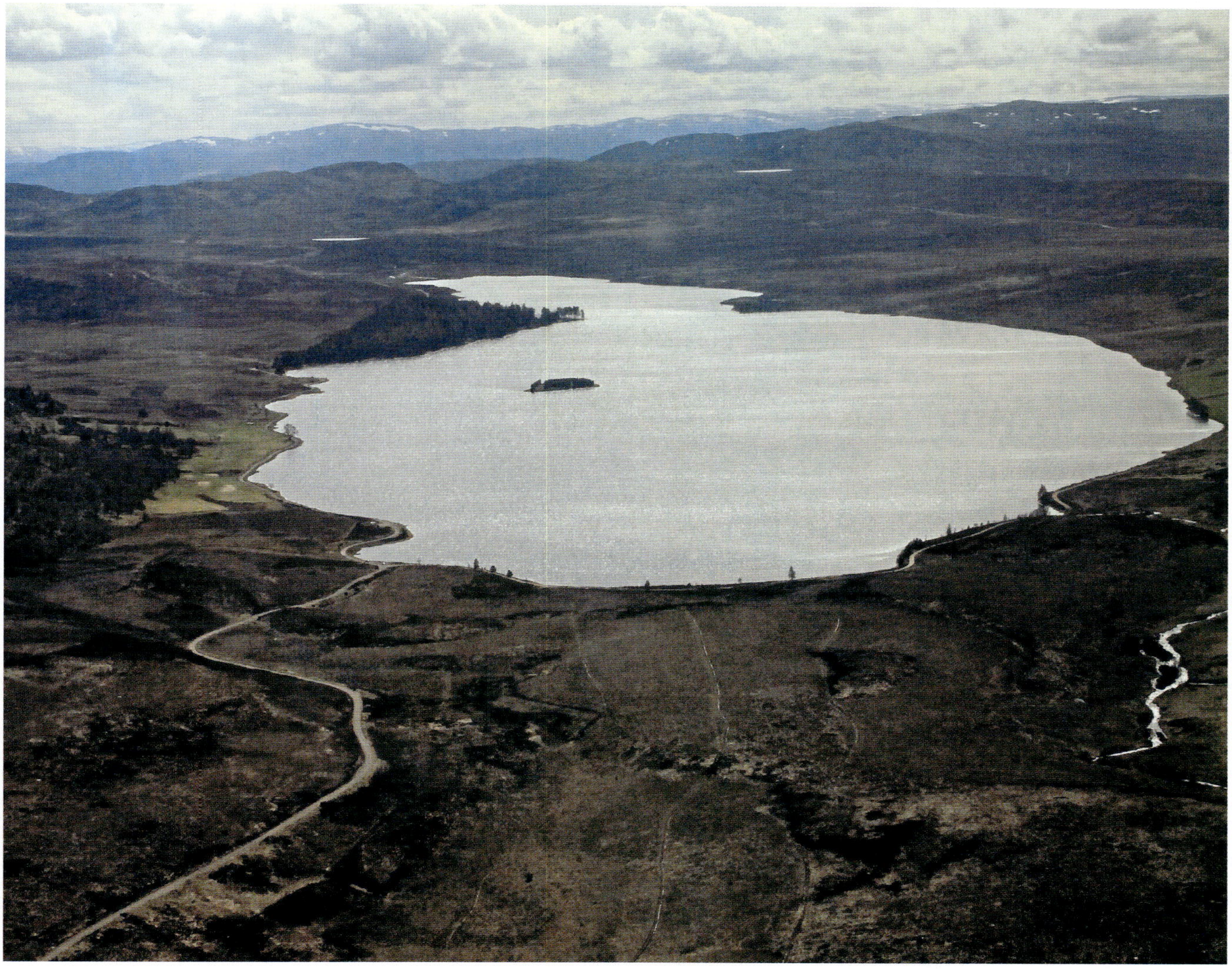

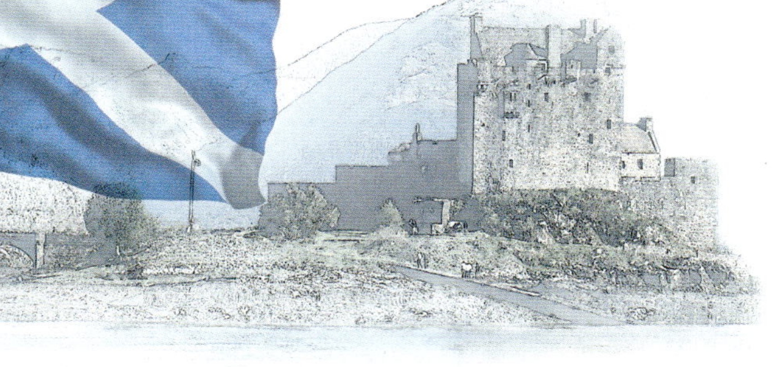

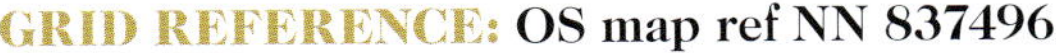

Castle Menzies

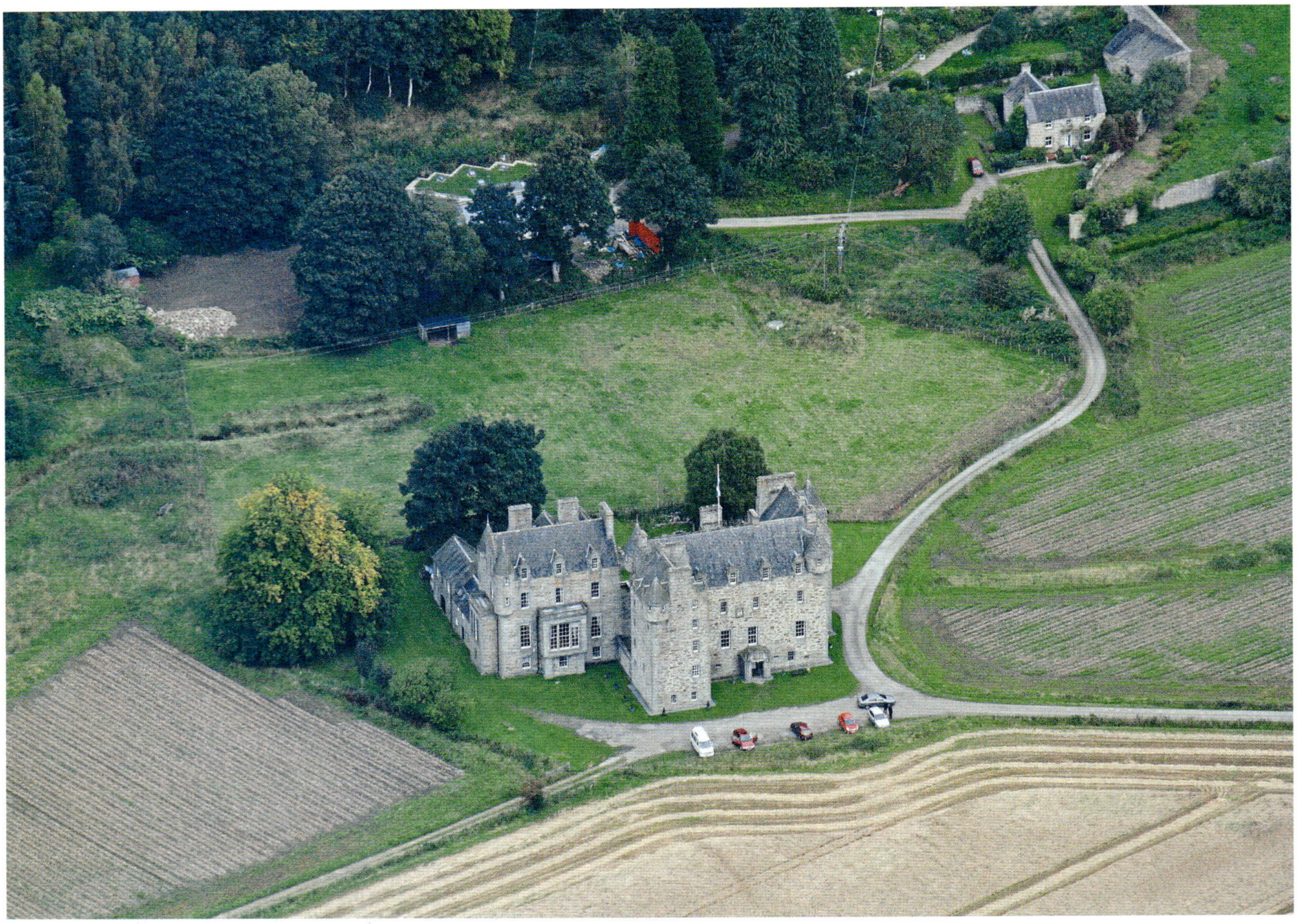

The clan members from across the world have united to rescue this important redoubt from ruin. Having fallen to the level of military supply depot during the Second World War, it has been fully restored to become a modern day clan headquarters which now provides a recreation of how the Menzies chieftains originally lived.

▮▮ ABOUT THE CLAN

The origin of early family members was in Normandy after the area called Mesnieries. In the court of King Alexander II the role of chamberlain was gained by Sir Robert de Menzies in 1249. But you would hear him spoken about as Mingis, which is accepted as the way to pronounce Menzies. He was awarded lands with his son in Rannoch, Glen Lyon and Weem, all in Strathtay.

Robert the Bruce took his son as companion in arms, later gifting him lands in what is now Perthshire and Dumfries. The Declaration of Arbroath was made in 1320 and included the signature of Thomas de Meineris.

The islands of Shetland and Orkney were governed by David Menzies in the early 15th century on behalf of the Norwegian owners. Later in that century the 8th clan chief, Sir Robert Menzies, built the Place of Weem in

Clan Menzies

1488 close to where the current castle Menzies stands. Royal approval was bestowed on the Menzies in 1510, when the lands became a barony. Hence the title of Baron became attached to the landowner and still exists in Scotland.

Trouble with neighbours was common, then as now. However violence broke out more often. The Stewarts of Garth took Fortingale castle from the Menzies and wrecked it. And clashes with the Campbells also occurred.

By the 17th century the Menzies fought alongside the Campbells in the covenanters conflicts and the civil wars against Cromwell's henchmen.

During the first Jacobite rising in 1689, clansmen were found on both sides but Major Duncan Menzies of Fornock is listed as leading an effective charge against government troops at Killiekrankie.

Visitor Details

    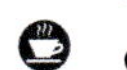 

www.castlemenzies.org

01887 820982

The castle is run by a trust on behalf of the Clan Menzies Society. The castle is usually open from Easter to mid-September but check website for changes.

There is disabled access to the ground floor.
Car and coach parking is adjacent to the castle.

Gift shop, tea room and clan museum.

The entire old castle interior can be viewed.

Location: Situated in the Perth and Kinross district two miles north-west of Aberfeldy. Castle Menzies stands between Weem and Dull just off the A827. It is also worth visiting the Scottish Crannog Centre on Loch Tay five miles west of the castle while in the area.

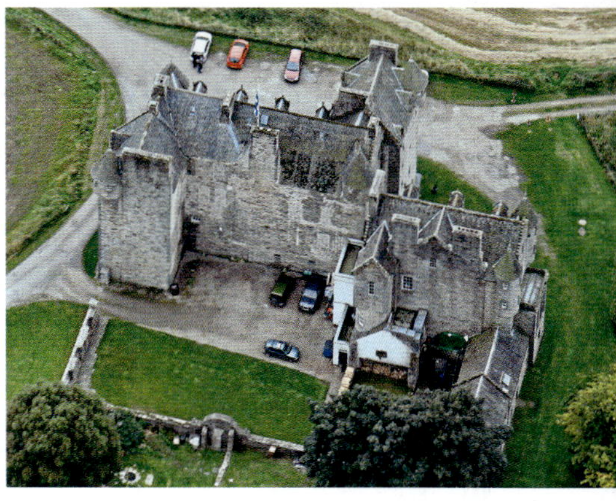

When the Clan Chief, Sir Robert Menzie, built a fortified mansion on this site below Weem Rock in 1488, it became known as the Place at Weem but was burnt down by a hostile neighbour in 1502. The replacement was a Z-plan tower house designed to defy the march of time, although it has needed lots of repairs over the centuries.

A need to feel secure led to the highest levels including battlements and two towers giving an aspect of strength to deter aggressors. Perhaps one was for bells and the other for a lookout. In 1577, the ornate dormer windows were added and the towers removed.

General Monck took the castle in the 1650s as part of Cromwell's campaign in Scotland. The Menzies here did not support the Jacobites in 1715 and as a result the castle was forcibly occupied by the Jacobites during that rising.

In 1746, Bonnie Prince Charlie stayed briefly on his way north but was encouraged to move on. Just a few days later the Menzies had to vacate the castle while the Duke of Cumberland's forces made use of the buildings.

In 1840 a new wing was added to the rear of the castle. This enabled a more comfortable lifestyle as the threat of siege warfare had gone. The wing included bedrooms, bathrooms and guestrooms for hospitality.

The castle was sold in 1914 and the series of owners that followed were unable to keep up with repairs. During the Second World War it was a Polish army medical supplies depot. By 1957 it was a ruin and at the first meeting of the Menzies Clan Society

that same year it was decided to buy the ruin and start a long process of restoration. It is probably unique for modern day clan members to own and restore their own castle. They are also restoring the nearby garden.

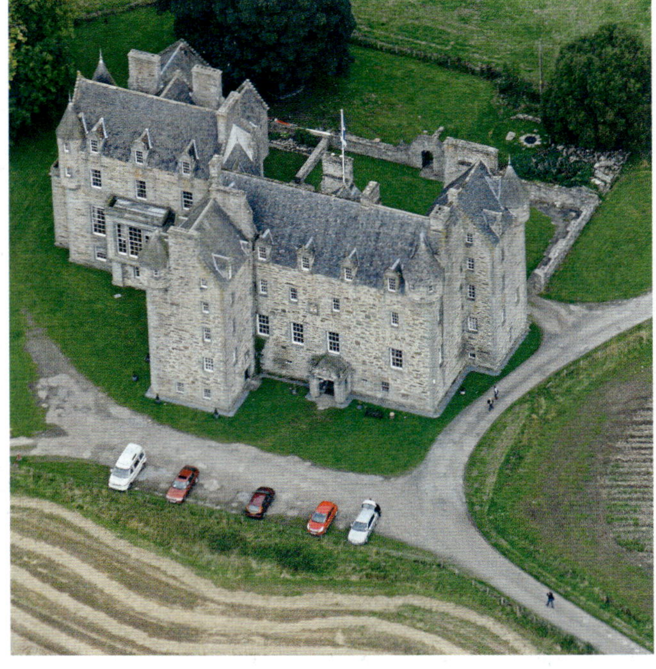

Although the clan chief claimed to support the government, his factor Archibald Menzies of Shian had other ideas. He raised the clansmen in 1745 for the Jacobites and they were present at all battles, fighting alongside the Atholl men. At Culloden Archibald Menzies commanded the First battalion of Atholls brigade under a white flag with red saltire. They were on the right wing and took part in a fatal charge which resulted in bloody hand to hand combat, Archibald being one of the many killed on the moor. Many Menzies battled afterwards to protect the retreating wounded and able survivors from cavalry attacks.

Canada was a popular destination for many highlanders seeking better prospects, some did indeed prosper there. In 1665 Sir Alexander Menzies became a baronet of Nova Scotia having escaped a Scotland

ravaged by civil war during which he was badly wounded. His brother died at the battle of Worcester in 1651 fighting for the Royalist cause. The Larch tree arrived in Scotland from Austria's highlands in 1737 thanks to the Weems branch of the Menzies and has flourished across the nation since. Visitors will have noticed the many Menzies shops in Scotland which have grown from a few bookshops started in Edinburgh in the 1860s. These merchants now purvey a wide variety of comestibles, beverages and printed matter to travellers of discerning tastes.

Sir Robert Menzies became Prime minister of Australia in the 1950s; his Scottish ancestor had been part of the earlier gold rush to that distant land, an indication of the pioneering Menzie spirit. Other pioneers include members of the Menzies Clan Society who

purchased the ruin of Castle Menzies in 1957. It is now a finished castle restored to closely represent the original. A charitable trust has been established to host clan gatherings and many other events such as weddings are held. Clan archives are available for research at the castle. This is the link to the society website https://clanmenzies.org/

Motto: "Vil God I sal" which means "With God I shall".

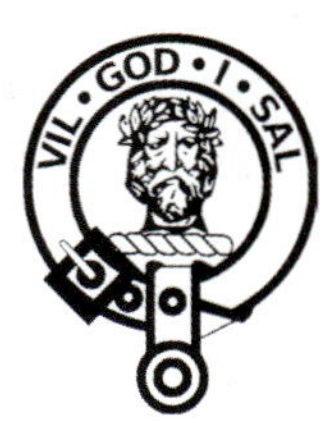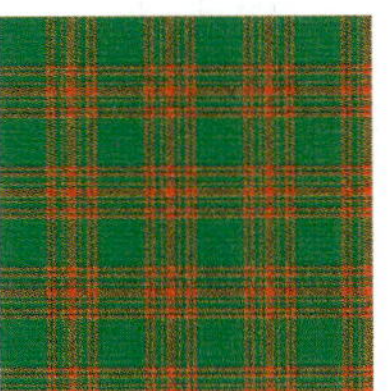

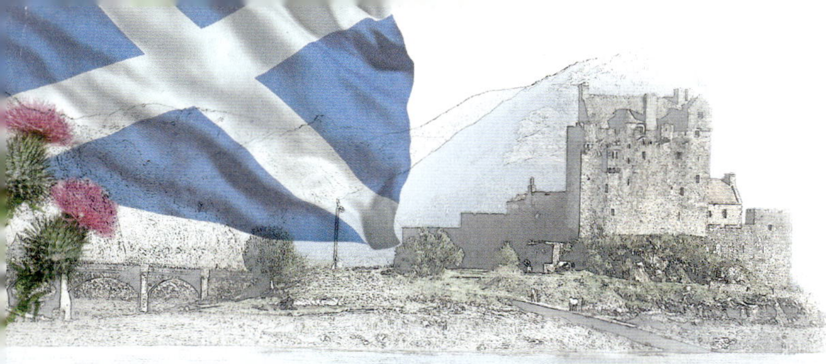

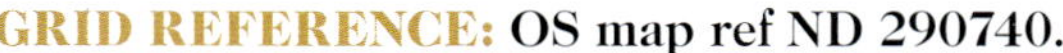

Castle of Mey

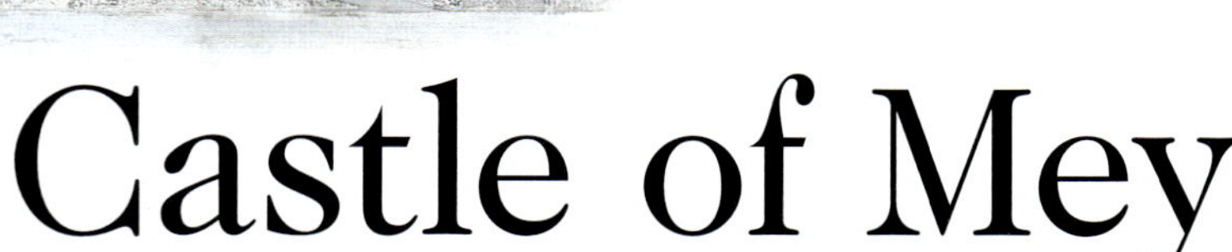

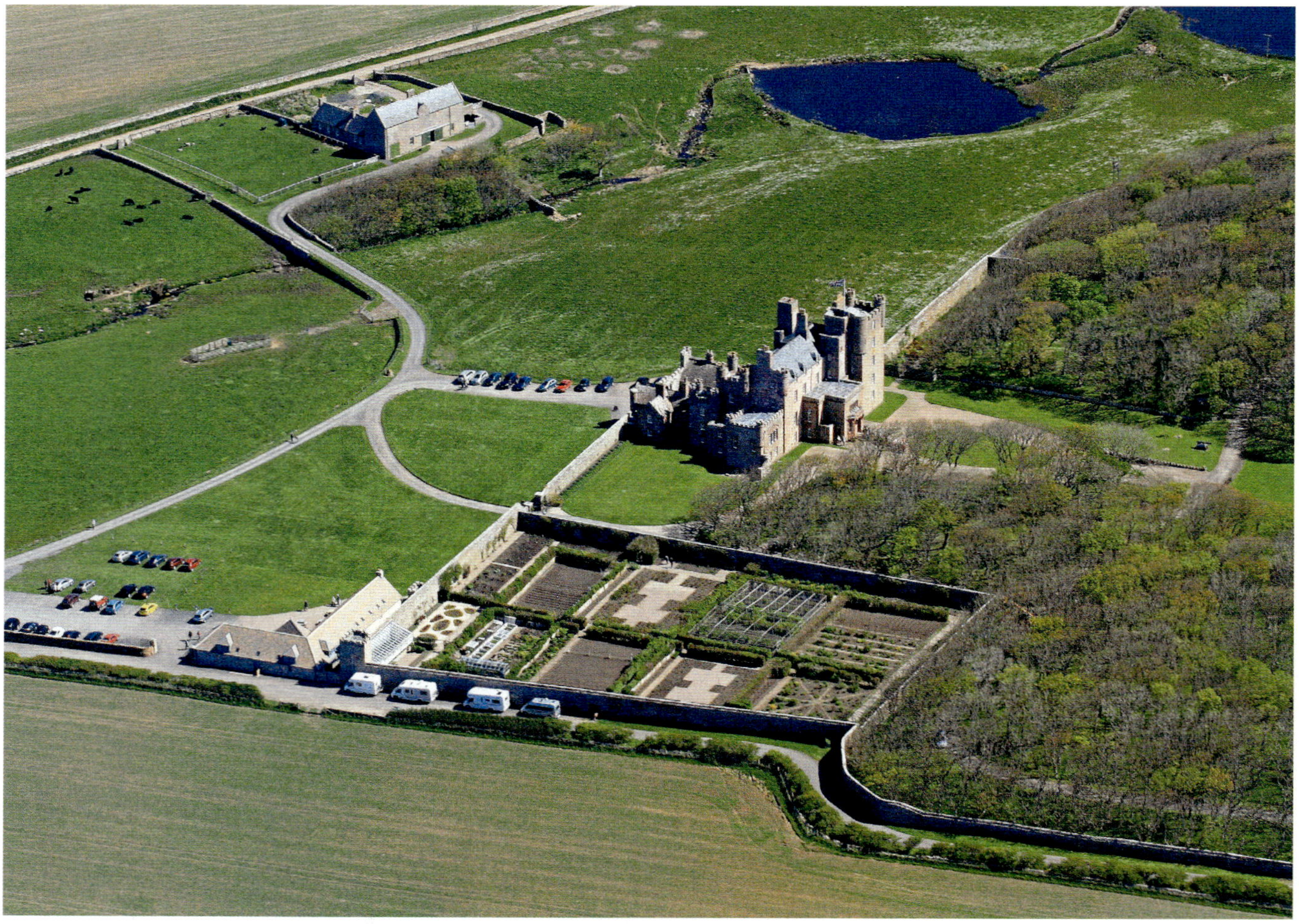

This tower house may have crumbled away after the family ran out of heirs to inherit, had it not been for the intervention of Her Majesty Queen Elizabeth The Queen Mother in 1952. The tower was given back its old name, restored and modernised with electricity and running water. Today it is maintained by the Prince's Foundation, which was established by Prince Charles.

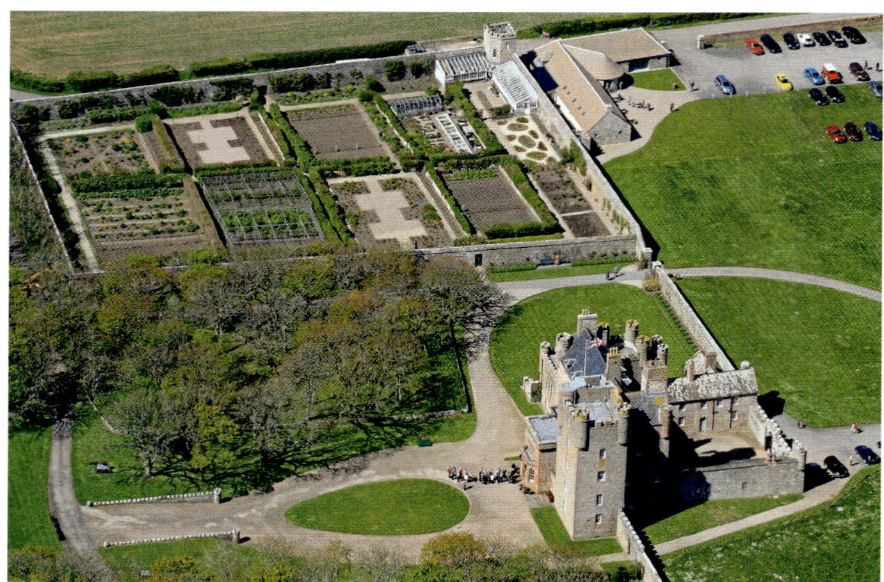

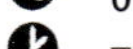 www.castleofmey.org.uk

01847 851473

This castle is open to the public from May to September.

Access for the disabled is to the principal floor only.

 The tearoom, shop and toilets are completely accessible at the visitor centre by the car park. Email: enquiries@castleofmey.org.uk

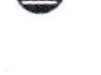 The castle is now run by a trust, the Prince's Foundation.
A list of the many aims of the trust can be seen here...
https://www.castleofmey.org.uk/about/the-castle-of-mey-trust/overview

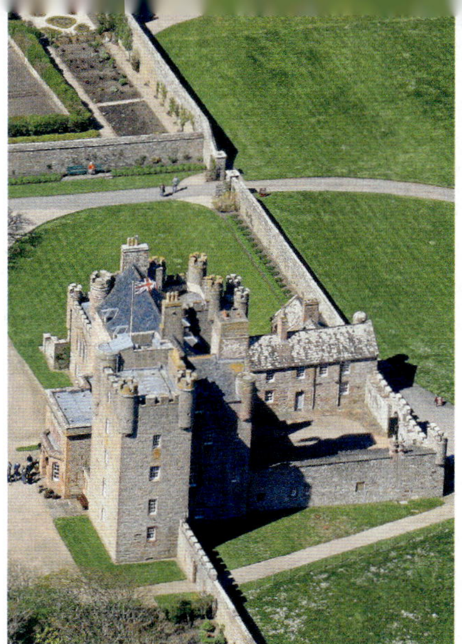

Location: Castle of Mey is situated in the Sutherland and Caithness district 15 miles north of Wick and five miles west of John O'Groats. Turn off the A836 at Mey village and follow the minor road for about two miles north.

In 1566, the Sinclair Earls of Caithness purchased the lands of what is now the Estate of Mey from the Bishops of Caithness. By 1572, a three-storey Z-plan tower house had been built here by George Sinclair, the 4th Earl. On both sides of the tower were tall ranges to the sides and rear. This created a three sided courtyard open to the sea in the north. When the castle passed to his younger son, William, the castle was renamed Barrogill and gradually extended. During 1819, renowned castle designer William Burns added Tudor Gothic style decorations including corbelled bartizans crowning some corners. This was also when the grand entrance and the dining room were added.

On the death of George, the 15th Earl, the castle left Sinclair ownership due to the lack of heirs. He left the castle to his friend F G Heathcote on condition that he changed his name to Sinclair.

His widow eventually sold it to Captain F B Imbert-Terry. By 1950, the estate farms were sold and the tower was almost derelict. Her Majesty Queen Elizabeth The Queen Mother purchased the property in 1952. Despite its poor condition, she set about renovating and restoring the castle, gardens and parklands which extended to about 30 acres. In addition, she added the first ever supplies of electricity and running water. She also returned the castle's original name, changing Barrogill Castle back to the Castle of Mey.

It may be wondered if she encountered the ghost of the Green Lady? She is said to be the wandering spirit of Lady Fanny, daughter of the 5th Earl. In the 1600s, her father imprisoned her in an attic room as she planned to elope with a ploughman. In despair, she made a death dive from the rooftop.

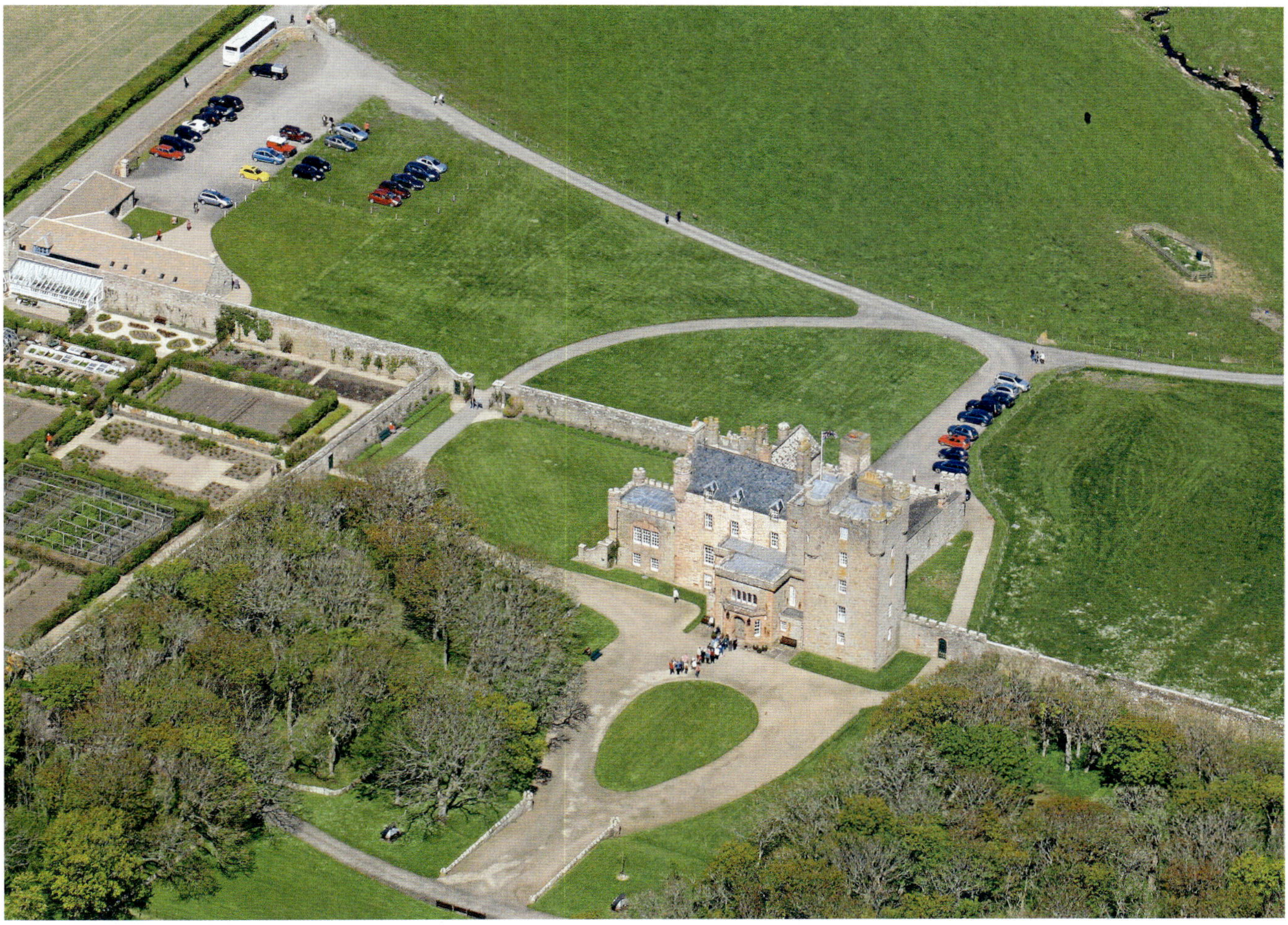

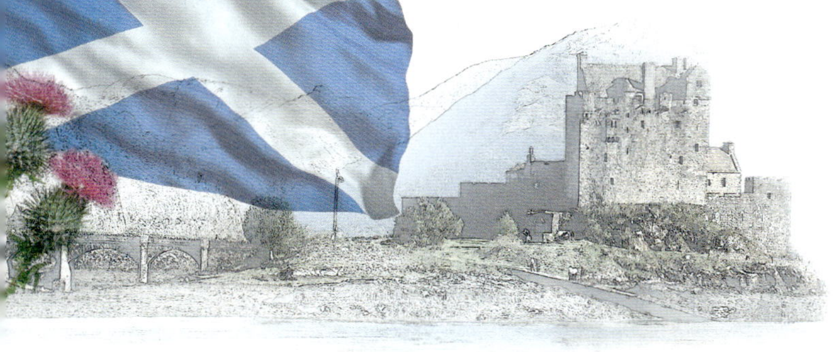

Neidpath Castle

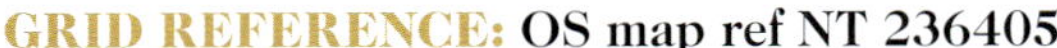

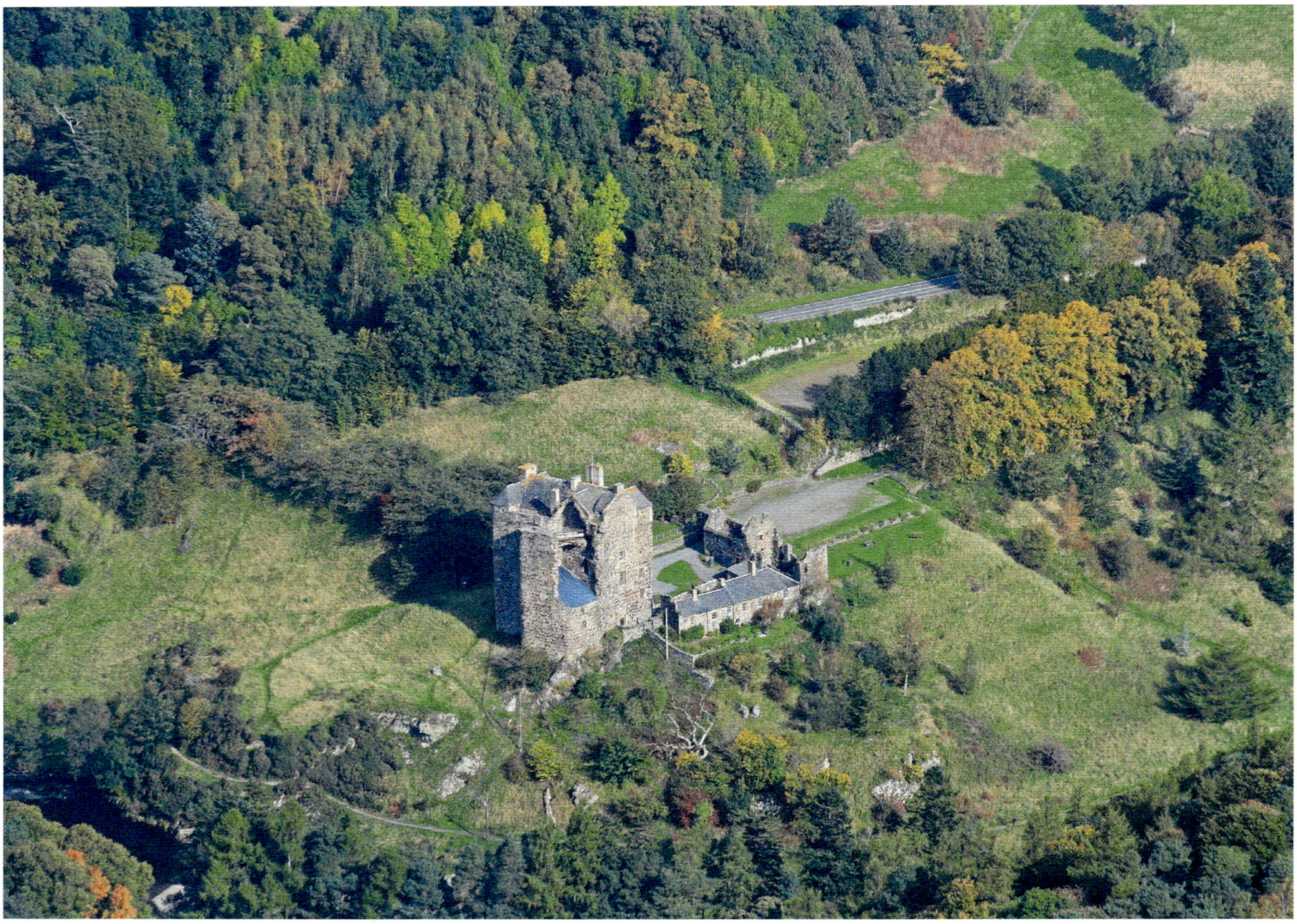

Firmly planted on the edge of the borderland of Scotland and England, Neidpath Castle has as a result been attacked many times over the course of centuries. Now visitors can stay in the estate cottages and arrange to view inside the castle, following the footsteps of both royals and famous writers.

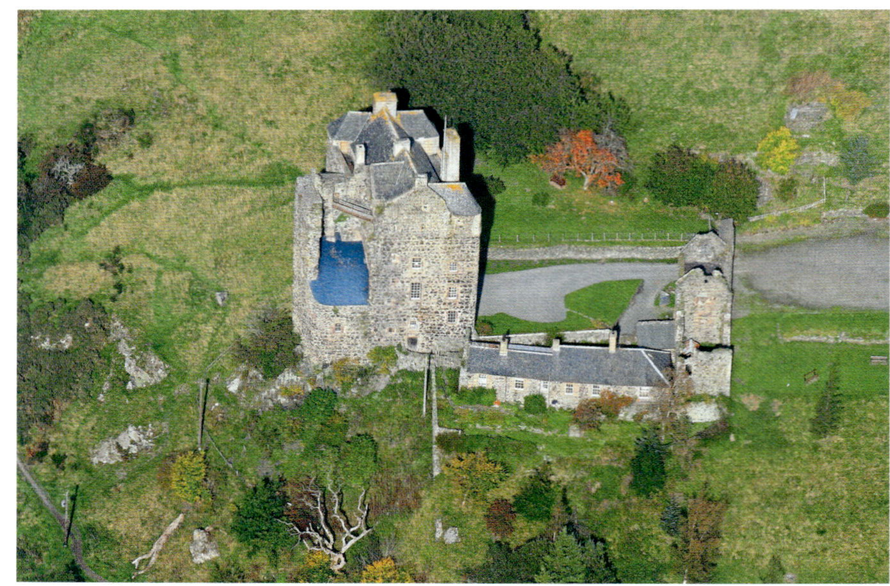

ABOUT THE CASTLE

 www.neidpathcastle.com

 01721 720333

 Neidpath Castle is open by appointment all year round. Email enquiries@neidpathcastle.com or telephone to book. Additionally, there are some open days each year.

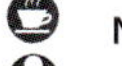 Gravel paths.

No shop.

Events and self catering accomodation can be booked. For details see the website.

Location: This castle is in the Borders district next to the A72, one mile west of Peebles.

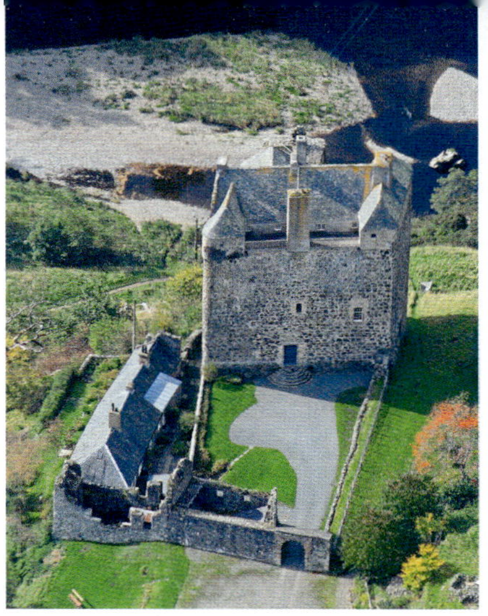

Located just above a steep gorge formed by the River Tweed, this large L-plan keep was built by Sir Simon Fraser around 1263 on the site of an earlier fortress. A marriage enabled the Hay family to gain the Barony of Neidpath in 1312. Sir Willam de Haya then oversaw the building of the lower parts of the keep which stand today. Royal visitors included Mary Queen of Scots in 1563 and her son James VI in 1587.

In 1645, the Hay castle owners stood against the forces of the Royalist, the Marquess of Montrose. A year later, John Hay was made 1st Earl of Tweedale by King Charles II to obtain his loyalty. By 1650, the Hay Clan solidly supported Royalist causes and held the castle against Oliver Cromwell's troops for a long time until artillery bombardment badly damaged the tower and west wing, forcing surrender. In the 1660s, the 2nd Earl altered the upper castle storeys, repaired the damage, added outbuildings and improved the estate grounds which included the planting of an avenue of yew trees. This exhausted his finances so Neidpath was sold in 1686 to William Douglas, Duke of Queensberry. He passed the castle on to his son in 1693 and over the next 100 years alterations were made. By 1780, the occupants were tenants but neglect resulted in the collapse of the upper storeys of the wing

in 1790. The castle became a well-known historical attraction. William Wordsworth and Walter Scott visited Neidpath in 1803. There is no doubt that the setting inspired them both to write tales of chivalry and carnage.

On the death of the Duke in 1810, the castle, along with the Earldom of March, was inherited by the Earl of Wemyss. Neidpath is still in possession of the Wemyss family.

OWNER'S COMMENT...

"Across the centuries, Neidpath has been home to generations of the Fraser, Hay, and Douglas families. And for over 200 years, the estate has been privately owned by the Wemyss family. The true beauty of Neidpath is that very little has changed over the years. The rugged stone walls, hidden staircases, and beautiful views from the battlements would all be very familiar to its formers residents. Outside, the ancestral emblems are clear to see in the archways and carvings around the castle. Inside, the burnished wooden floors bear the indents from the spurs of the gentlemen's boots."

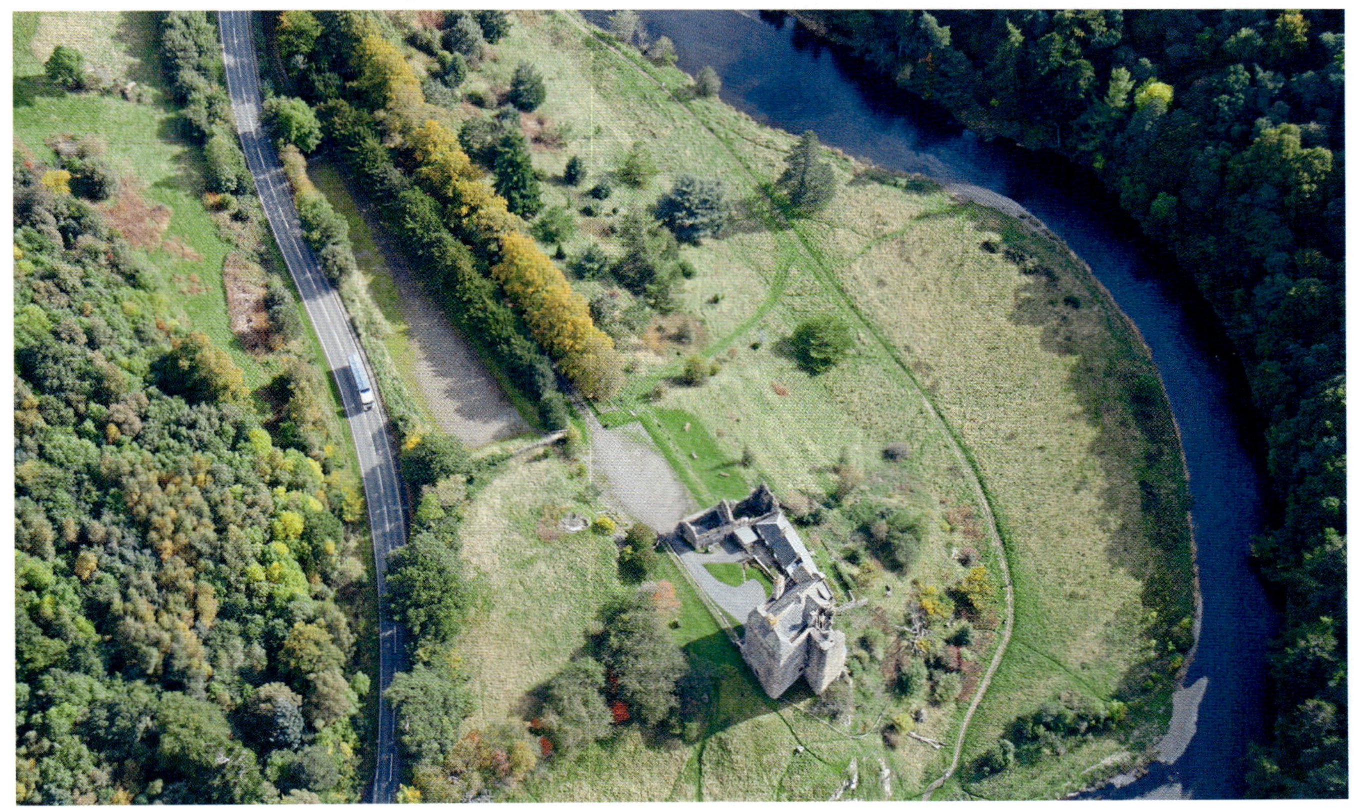

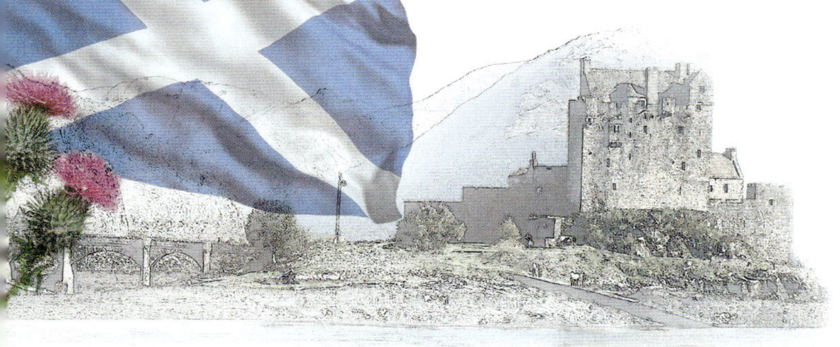

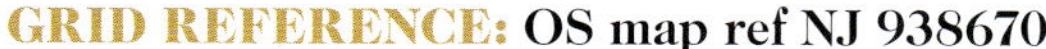

Pitsligo Castle

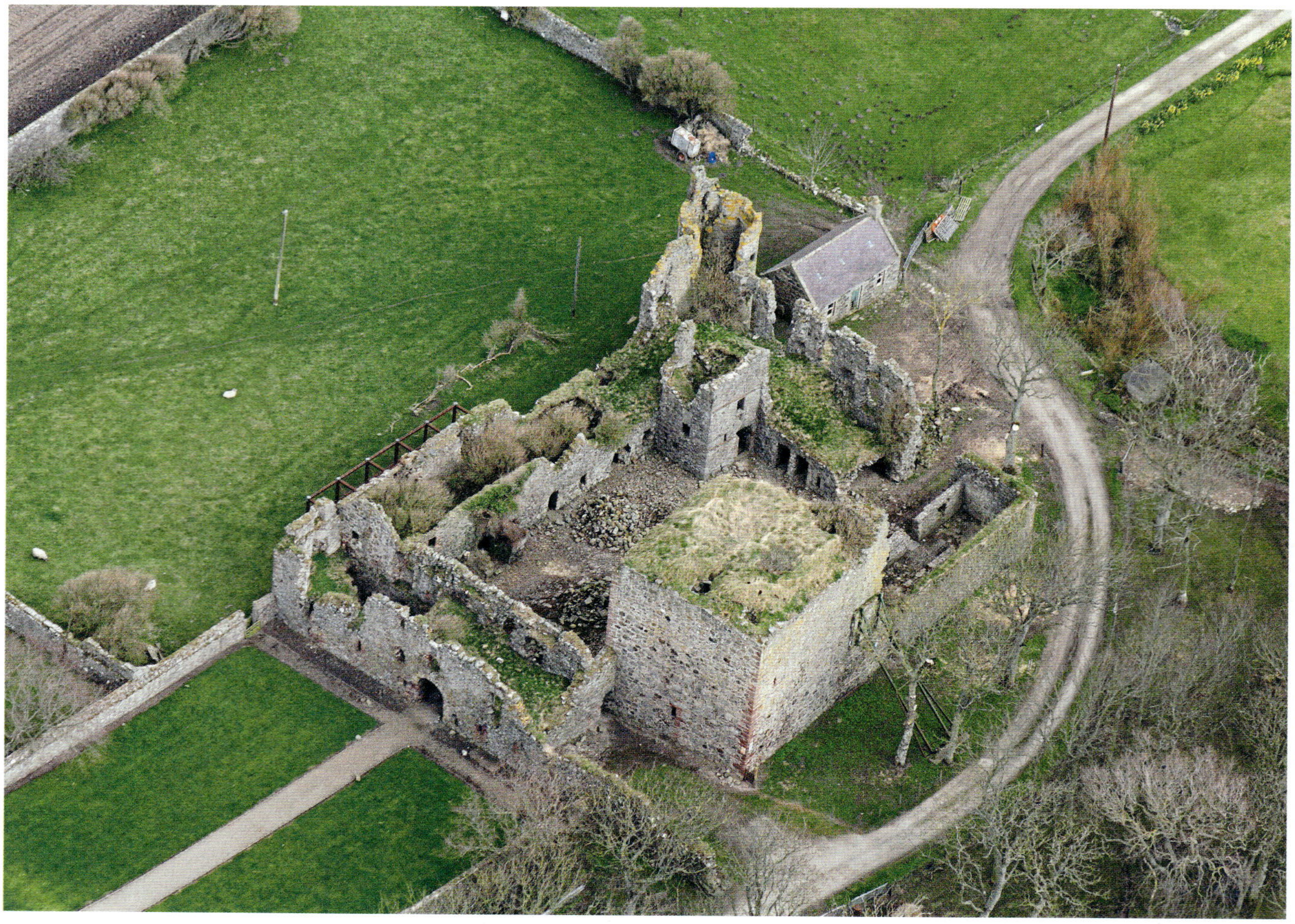

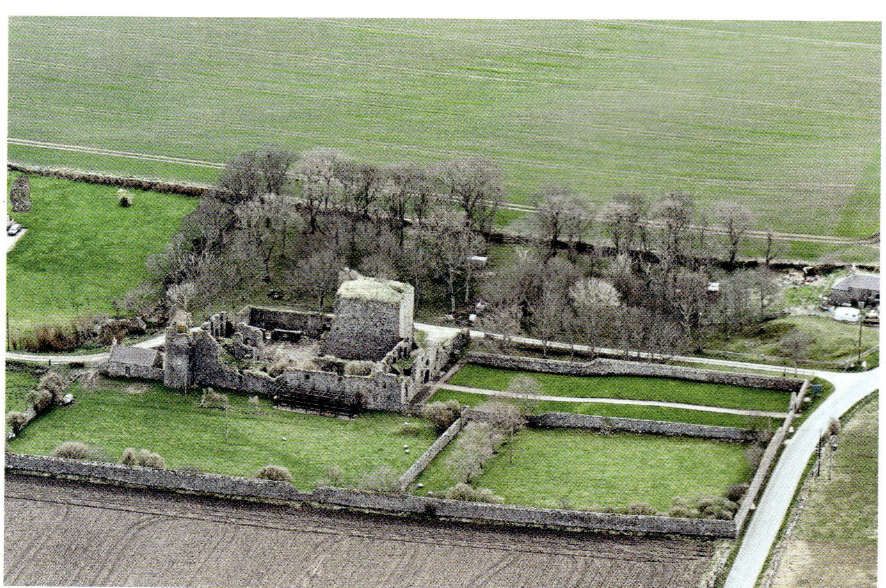

Clan Forbes resided here when this castle was in its heyday and their history is tangled with tales of shipwrecked treasures. Their Jacobite Lord was hunted by Royalists with a reward offered for his capture. There were many in London who wanted to see him brought to England in chains for a beheading. Did he manage to survive?

Visitor Details

- Open 24 hours a day, seven days a week.
- The extensive ruins can be viewed from farm tracks. They have not been made totally safe, therefore caution is advised and pets and children should be kept under control.
- Fraserburgh has many shops, eateries and a lighthouse museum.
- The beach at Rosehearty is one mile away for exercise and fun.

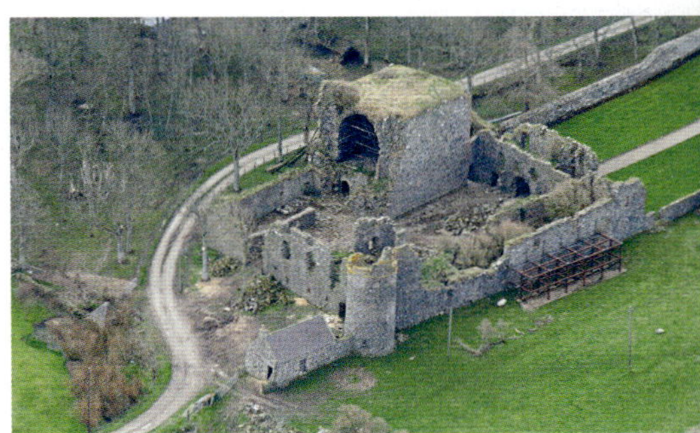

Location: Situated in the Banff and Buchan district, Pitsligo Castle is three miles west of Fraserburgh. It is just south of the B9031 and off a minor road which links with the village of Rosehearty and its harbour.

The lands which include the site of the present castle were slowly but surely acquired by William Forbes starting in 1423 when he married Agnes Fraser. He gained Aberdour from her family and by 1429, owned enough of the local estates to approach King James I for the title of Sir William Forbes. His large stone keep was the start of a series of building projects from 1424 onwards which grew to include a courtyard and ornate arched gateway. He became Lord Forbes of Pitsligo in 1433.

In 1566, early trade contacts were formed between Queen Mary Tudor and the Russian Tsar, Ivan the Terrible. A ship called the *Edward Bonaventure*, bound from Russia to England, was laden with fine furs, gifts for the Queen and other valuables. It also carried the first Russian Ambassador en route to London. The ship sought shelter in Rosehearty bay due to a fierce northerly gale But the ship was smashed onto the shore; hundreds were drowned apart from the ambassador.

He later complained that locals had looted the wreck. Despite Royal commissioners calling at Pitsligo Castle under instruction from Mary Queen of Scots, nothing was recovered. This is not a surprise because the Forbes were no friends of Mary and shipwreck flotsam was regarded as a free for all.

Clan Gordon and Forbes men fought at the Battle of Craibstone in Aberdeenshire in 1571. The Forbes supported King James while the Gordons supported Mary, Queen of Scots. Both sides fielded around 800 men and lost around 200. Later the Gordons attacked Pitsligo, resulting in the need for repairs to masonry. The greatest damage to the castle happened after the Jacobite risings: most of the roofs were removed and the contents ransacked on government orders. Lord Alexander Forbes had supported the cause of the Bonnie Prince. After the final disaster at Culloden in 1746, Forbes was made an outlaw and the government sent many troops into the area around Pitsligo to arrest him. They planned to transport him to London for beheading. However, he escaped before capture ensued. The locals gave him food and he lived rough for many years, sleeping in a cave, under bridges and in woods.

He boasted of being a cobbler as well. This happened when troops arrived suddenly in a village. He sheltered in a cobbler's and when they came inside he pretended to mend shoes. He later also watched them march past as he crouched by the roadside begging. Never betrayed, he died aged 84 in 1762. This unexpected lifestyle shows that he was held in high regard by his former tenants and how much they despised the Hanoverian authorities.

The castle ruins were neglected and the adjoining grounds became a market garden. In 1989, a descendant of Malcolm Forbes, who had become a wealthy publisher, gave funding to enable the ruins to be stabilised. After his death in 1995, his children passed the castle and nine acres of former gardens into the care of the Pitsligo Castle Trust.

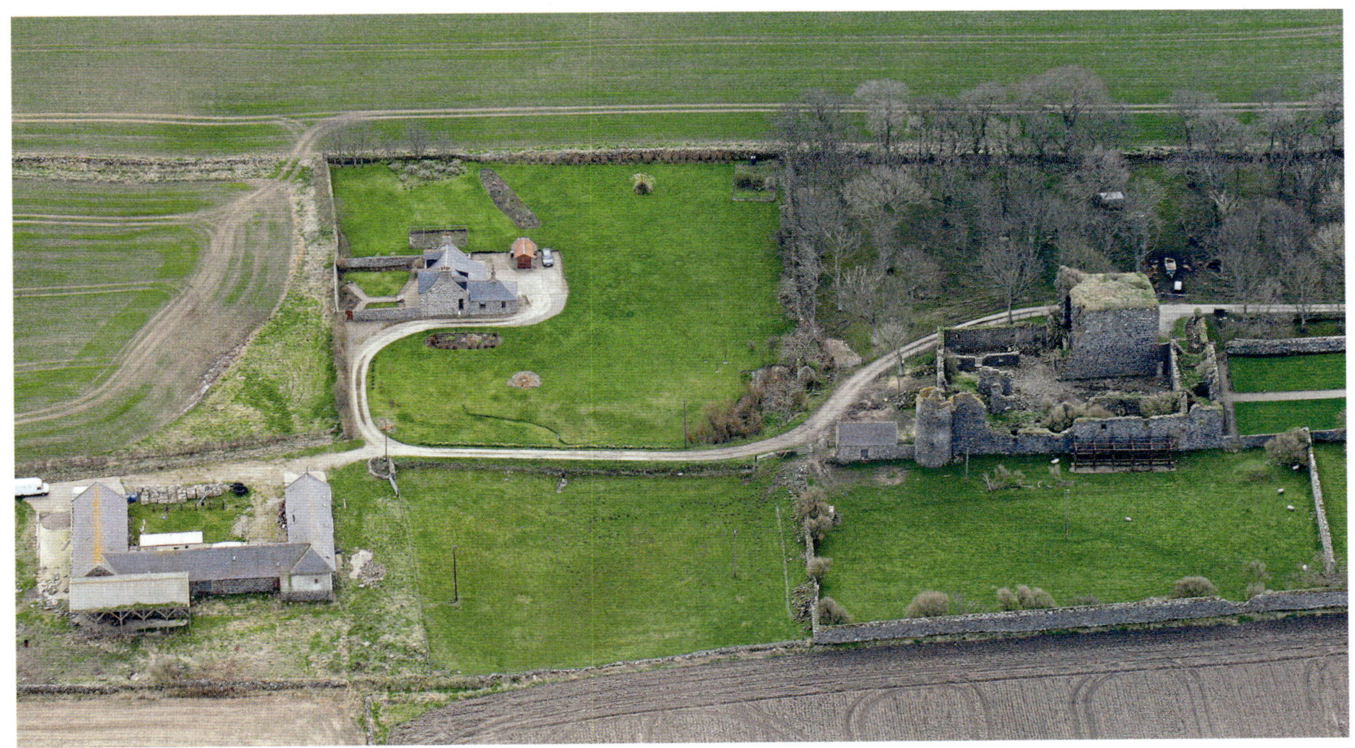

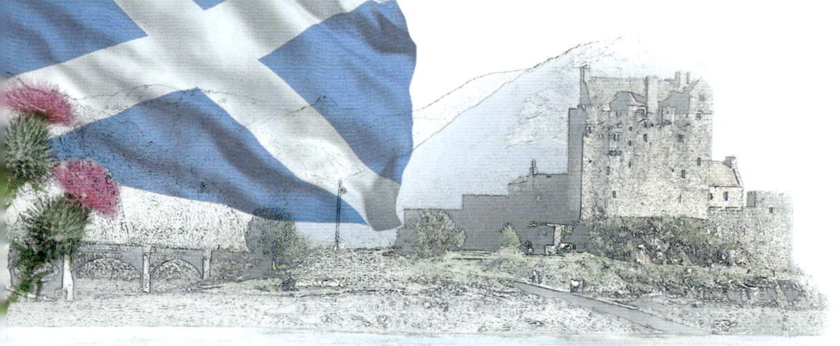

GRID REFERENCE: OS map ref NH 924526.

Rait Castle

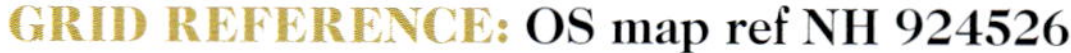

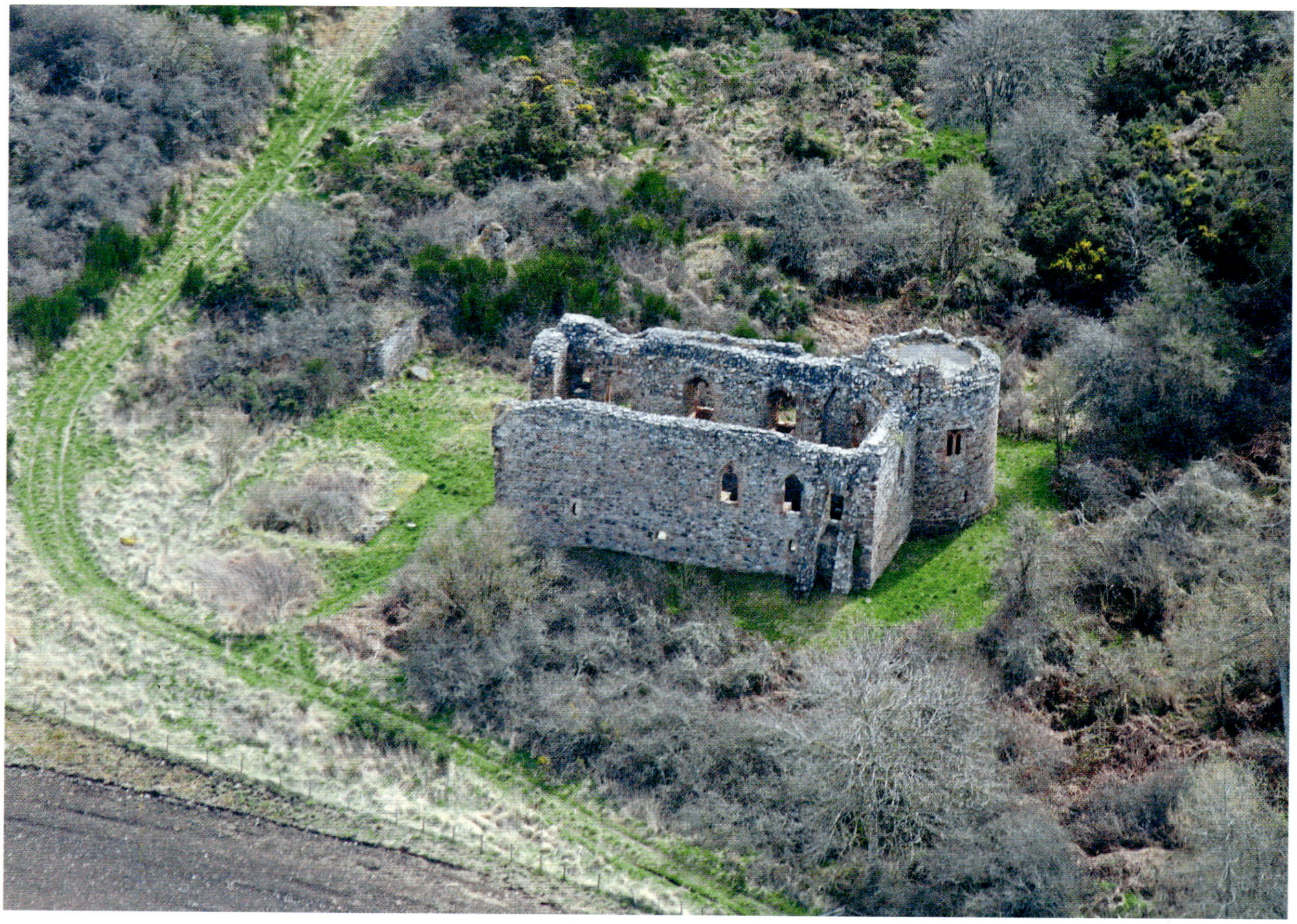

A small castle that was held by the de Raits, part of the Comyn Clan, this overgrown ruin was reportedly the scene of a bloody treachery, a slaughter and the mutilation of a daughter by her own father. Today it is accessible via rough tracks through the rugged surrounding scenery. A campaign is under way to see this ancient tower house preserved.

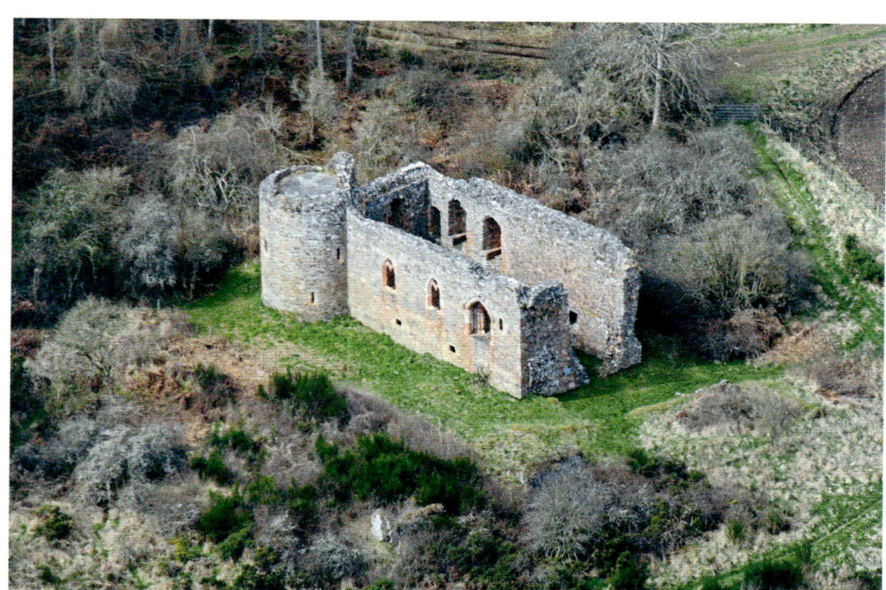

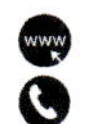

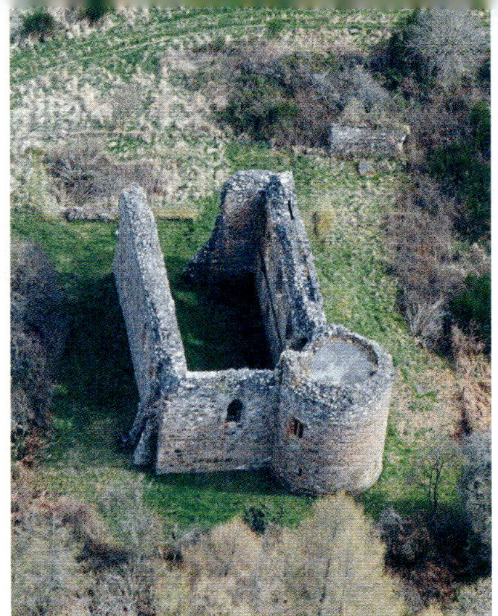

- www.saveraitcastle.org/Index.htm
- No telephone.
- The castle is open all year but follow the country code regarding gates and dogs being kept under control.
- Ruin, rough tracks give access.
- For food, drinks visit nearby Nairn.
- A fine beach and play areas visit nearby Nairn.

Location: Situated two miles south of Nairn very close to the B9101 Nairn to Grantown road, Rait Castle can be reached by a farm track, signposted Rait Castle Farm. The ruin is on an area of rising ground.

Some courtyard walls remain rising to 9ft tall, enclosing the foundation of the Chapel of St Mary of Rait. The castle has two storeys and a basement which is not vaulted. Some say the basement was used for livestock, but this is doubtful because the smell would have been awful. Physical evidence exists to show that the castle was built as a comfortable home that could be easily defended. There was no access from ground level, that is another reason why the basement probably was not used for livestock. The entrance was via a removable bridge from the higher ground to the first floor guarded by a portcullis with the addition of stout removable bars held in wall slots. The windows were protected by iron yettes.

An outstanding feature of this small castle was the high standard of sandstone carving and designs which can still be seen. This ornate Gothic type is more usually found in churches and monasteries of the period and is absent from local castle keeps such as Cawdor Castle. The main tower also has a vaulted roof of intricate pattern. The builders of the 13th century hall house were the de Raits, part of the Comyn Clan. Sir Alexander Rait gained notoriety when he murdered the 3rd Thane of Cawdor (the Clan Calder chief) around 1395. He fled to Hallgreen House, Mearns near Aberdeen. In the Statistical Account of Scotland for the Parish of Croy and Dalcross collated by a local parish minister in 1799, the tragic incident circa 1442 which led to the abandonment of the castle was first related in print...

"The story is to the effect that Comyn of Rait, under the guise of a desire to bury former animosities and establish friendly relations, invited the Mackintosh and his followers to a grand banquet at Rait. The invitation was accepted; the Mackintoshes, never doubting, prepared to attend. They were, however, timely warned that the Comyns in this had planned a foul plot and that at a given signal each Comyn would rise and slay his defenceless guest. Old Comyn had put all his household under a solemn oath that they would not reveal the plot to any person, but his daughter, anxious for the safety of young Mackintosh, who was her lover, found a way to disclose the plot. She went to a large boulder some distance from the castle, and told the whole story to the stone, but she knew her lover was behind it, as it was their usual trysting place, and he would hear every word. The stone to this day is called The Stone of the Maiden.

The Mackintoshes, notwithstanding the warning, resolved to attend the feast. When the night of the banquet came, each Mackintosh hid his dirk in his plaid, but gaily took his seat around the festive board of Comyn of Rait. The revelry ran high, and the walls of the old castle resounded with the mirthful shouts of the carousers. At length the toast is given, "The memory of the dead." This was the signal agreed upon for the slaughter of the guests. The Comyns rose and were about to draw their swords, but the Mackintoshes, being forewarned were forearmed, and with a yell of derision sprang to their feet, drew their daggers and thrust them into the hearts of the Comyns.

Among the few who escaped death, it is said, was the Chief of the Comyns, who flew to an upper chamber where his daughter was, whom he believed to have given the information, as he knew the girl and the young Mackintosh were lovers. Seeing the maddened state of her father, the young lady sought to escape from him by leaping out of the window, but before she could do so, he cut off both her hands with a broadsword. From the night in which the tragedy was enacted, the bloodstained walls of Rait have been tenantless. So runs the tradition."

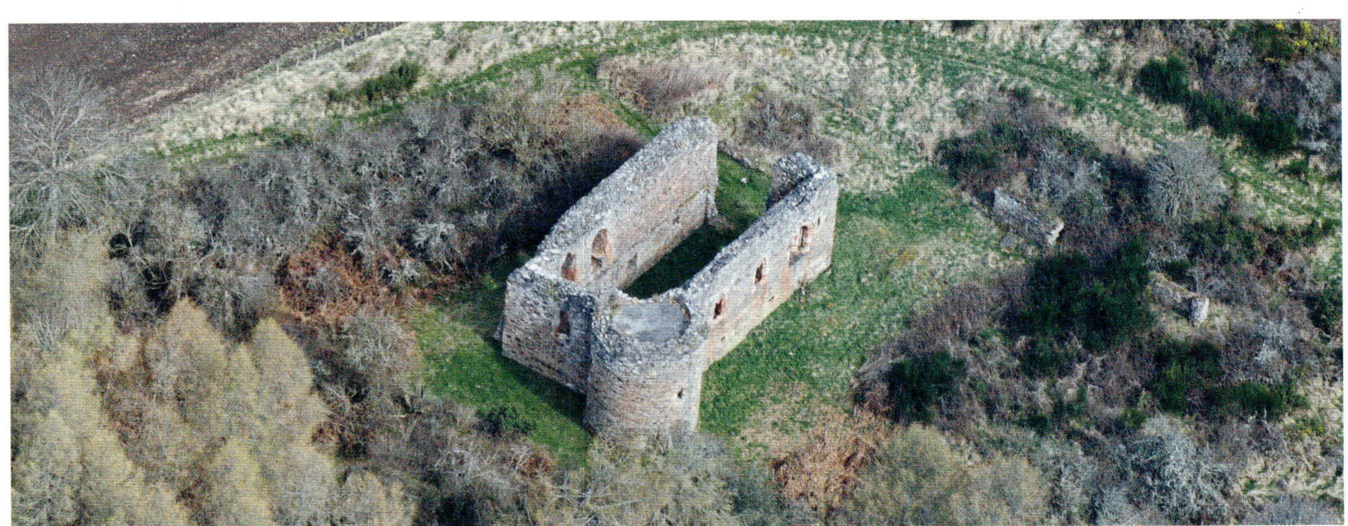

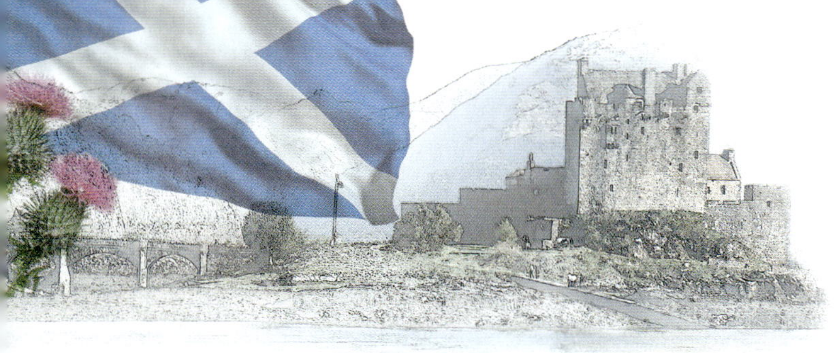

Rosslyn Castle

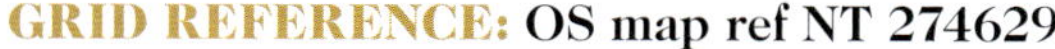

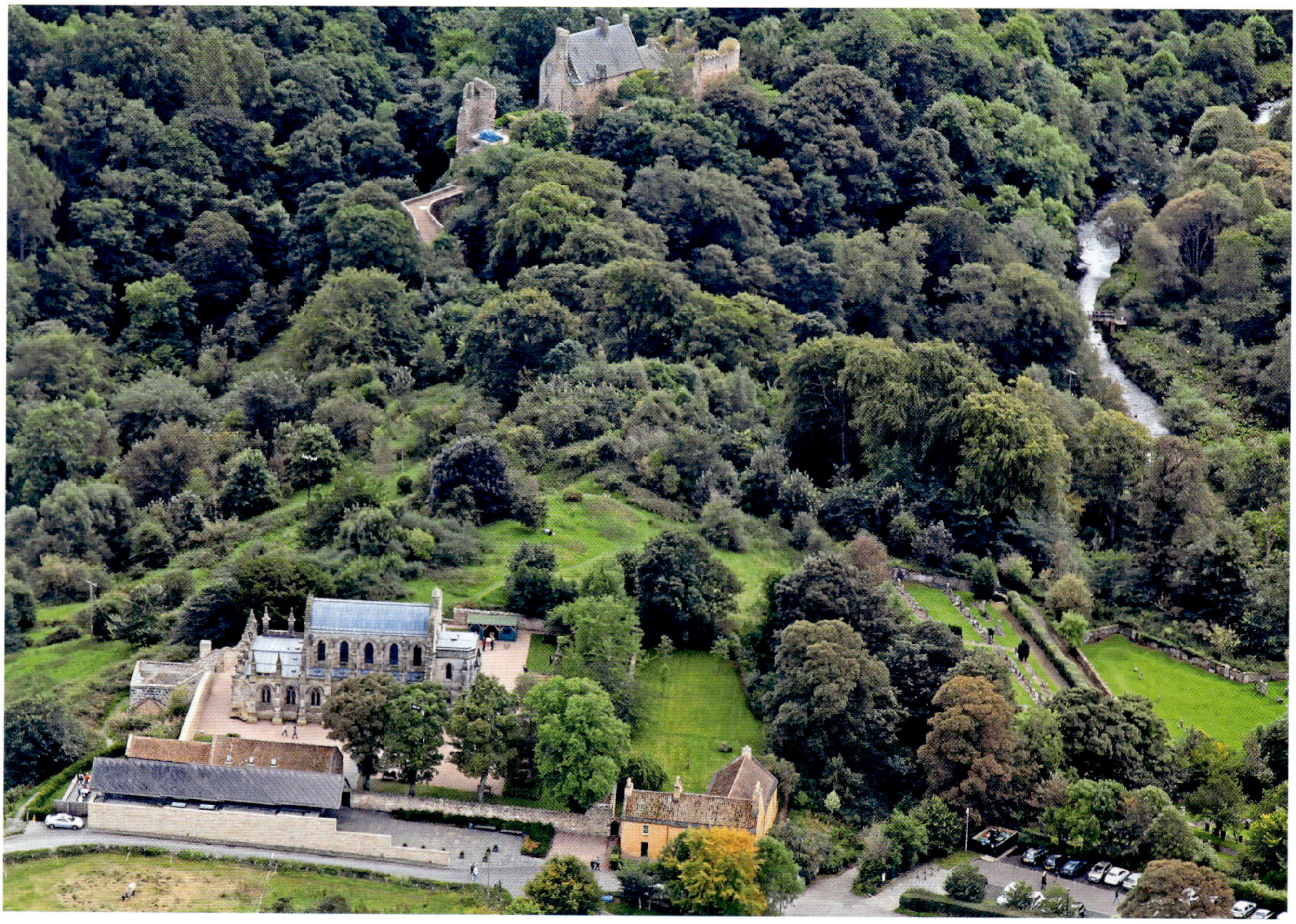

Connected to Shetland and Sutherland, Rosslyn Castle was ravaged by Cromwell's men but has now been restored and is available for holiday stays rented from the Landmark Trust. Explore the chapel nearby and ponder the Da Vinci code clues hidden within. Rosslyn offers an opportunity to experience Scottish Castle living in person.

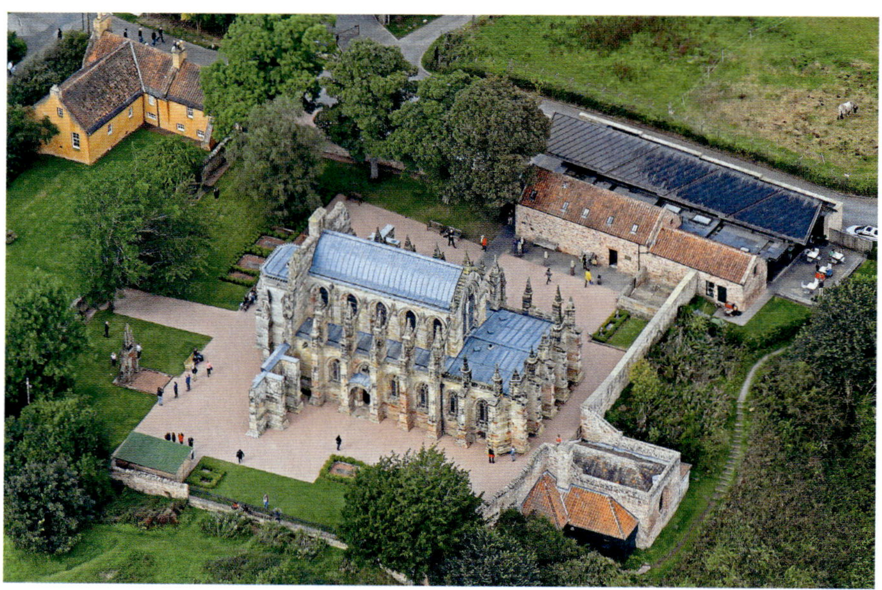

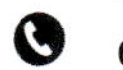 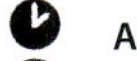 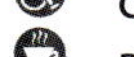

www.landmarktrust.org.uk/search-and-book/properties/rosslyn-castle-13940/#Overview

01628 825925

Access via booking accomodation.

Contact the trust for more information.

Refreshments at nearby chapel visitor centre.

Please note that the castle interior is only open to guests of the Landmark Trust.

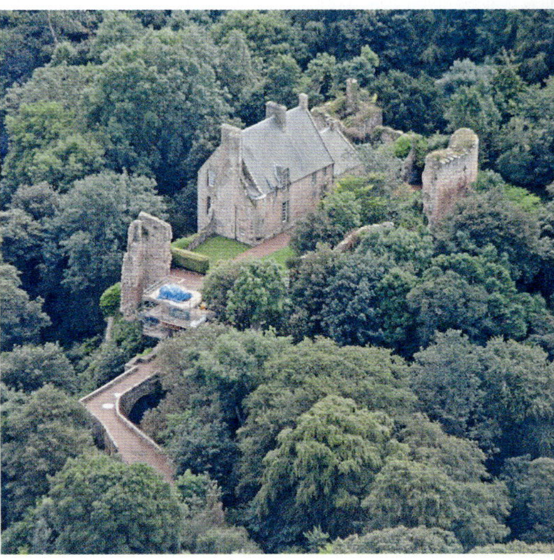

Location: Rosslyn Castle (or Roslin Castle) is in the Lothian district two miles south of Loanhead. It is situated half a mile south-east of Roslin village on a minor road just south of the B7006. Rosslyn Chapel is close by. You can start your walk to the castle from the chapel car park via footpaths and a track.
The walking guide is here: https://www.walkhighlands.co.uk/lothian/roslin-glen.shtml
An alternative way to the castle is from the car park at the Rosslyn Glen Country Park just off the B7003. The footpath takes visitors across a footbridge then up some steps to the castle approach road and bridge.

Perched on top of a promontory above steep cliffs in a bend of the river North Esk, the original access to the castle was by use of a drawbridge spanning an artificial ditch. This led into a small courtyard with buildings crowding around. The Sinclair Earls built the first castle here between 1280 and 1350. The wealthy Henry, Earl of Orkney, also named Baron of Roslin and Lord of Shetland, was the first in line of ownership which has continued to the present day with the Sinclair-Erskines, including the Earl of Rosslyn.

Around the year 1400, Henry's son built a rectangular keep in the south-west corner. Fire ravaged the castle in 1452 due to an accident and almost a hundred years later, the Earl of Hertford pillaged the castle and set fire to it again. This left a ruined wall of the keep still standing.

In the late 16th century, the bridge was rebuilt with a stone arch. A stout gatehouse was added and an impressive five-storey east range built into the side of the rock face. This range included a bakery, kitchens and dungeon. Around 1622, renovations included the addition of fine renaissance detailed carvings to the door and window surrounds in the east range.

The rampage of Oliver Cromwell's forces across Scotland did not leave out this castle: their artillery barrages caused damage in 1650. By the 18th century, it was in poor condition although the east range was still inhabited. The Earl of Rosslyn title was granted to James Erskine in 1805 by inheritance along with the local estate. The current owner, the 7th Earl, leases the castle as holiday accommodation via the Landmark Trust after the east range was restored between 1982 to 1988.

The nearby Rosslyn chapel was founded in 1444 by Sir William St Clair and took 40 years to complete. Practically every surface inside and outside this unique building is carved in an outstanding display of craftsmanship, including angels, Green Men and the famous Apprentice Pillar. The vault contains ten of the earlier Sinclair Clan including knights originally interred in full armour. Both the chapel and castle are important plot points in the Dan Brown book The Da Vinci Code and were used as locations for the feature film. For current opening times please check the website https://www.rosslynchapel.com/visit/

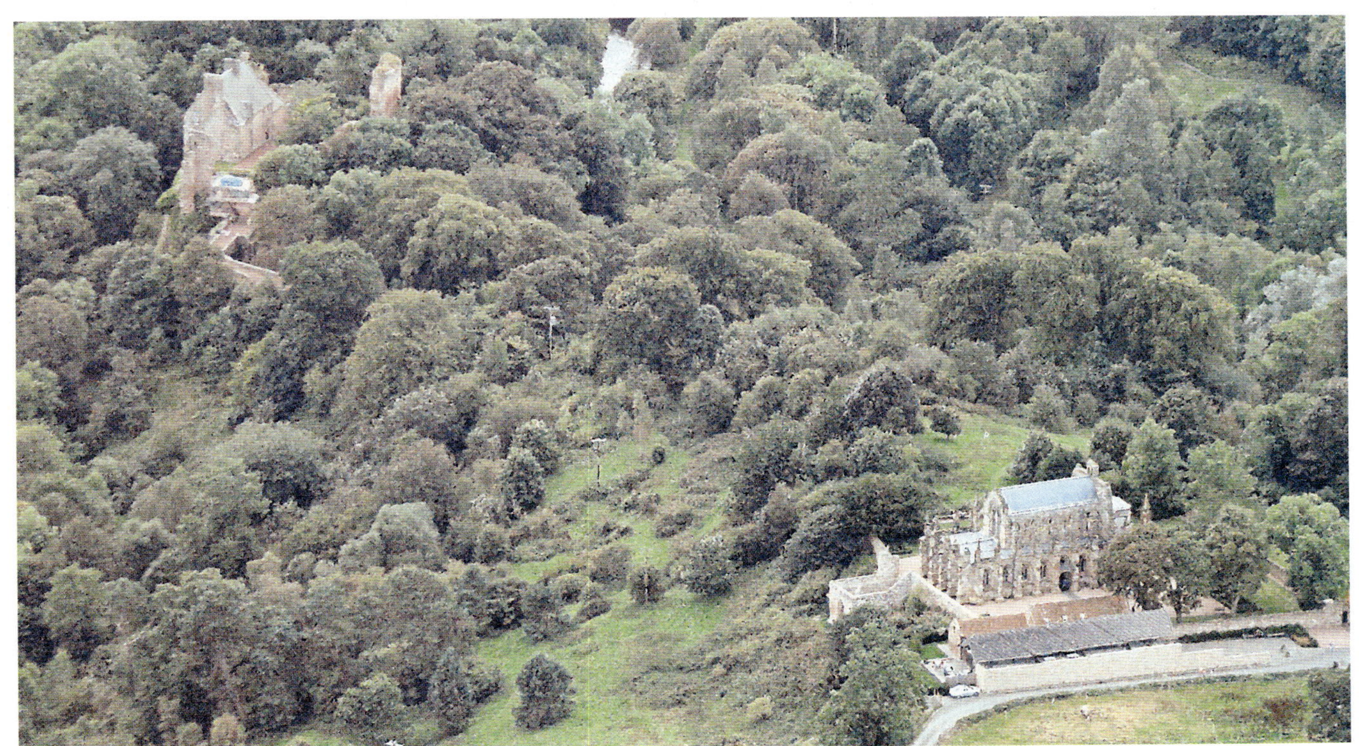

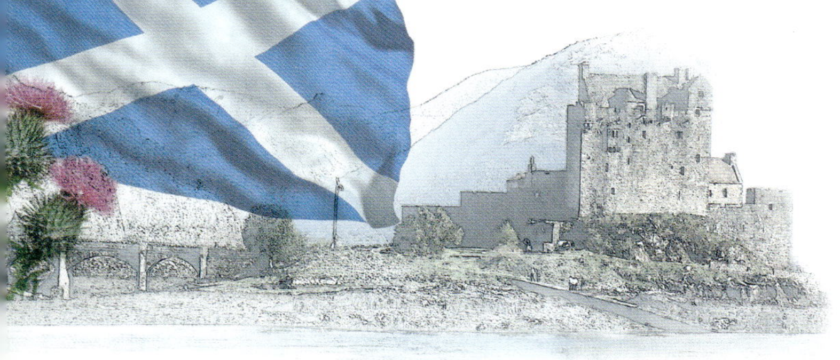

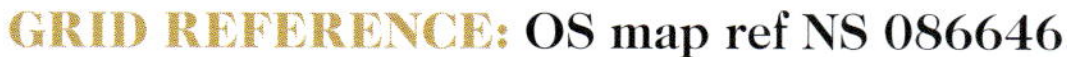

Rothesay Castle

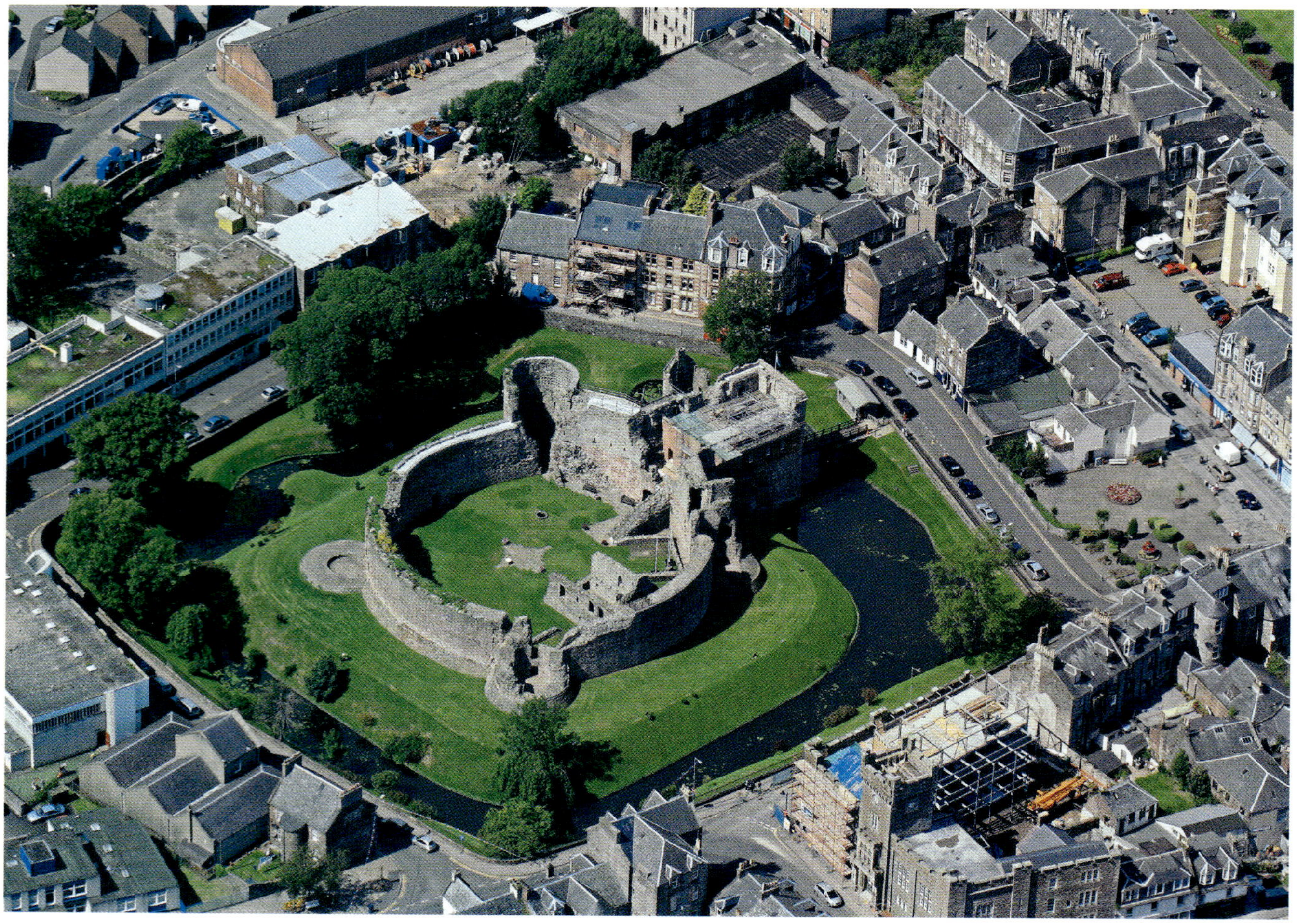

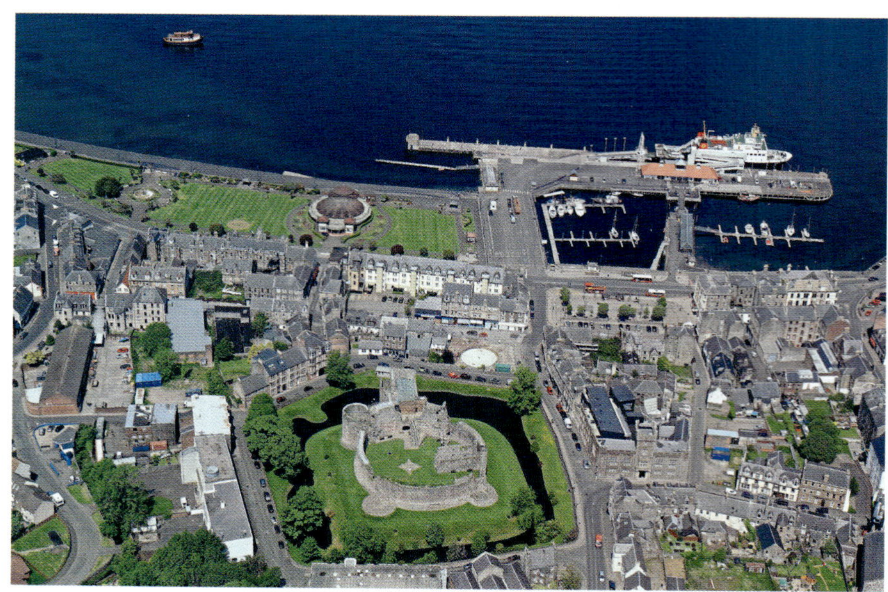

This royal fortress was constructed to defend against invasion by the kings of Norway and withstood numerous siege attempts. However, it proved unable to resist the cannon of Oliver Cromwell's forces and was wrecked. Years of dereliction followed till clearing and restoration works preserved what remained during Victorian times.

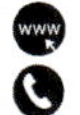 www.historicenvironment.scot/visit-a-place/places/rothesay-castle

 01628 825925 / 01700 502691

 Usually open all year but check the website for the current opening times if planning a visit.

 The nearest adapted toilet is at the Rothesay ferry terminal, about 200m away. Refreshments at many local town cafes.

The visitor centre has ramped access. Access to the dungeon is down a metal ladder of ten rungs. Upper levels in the gatehouse are reached by two sets of stairs.

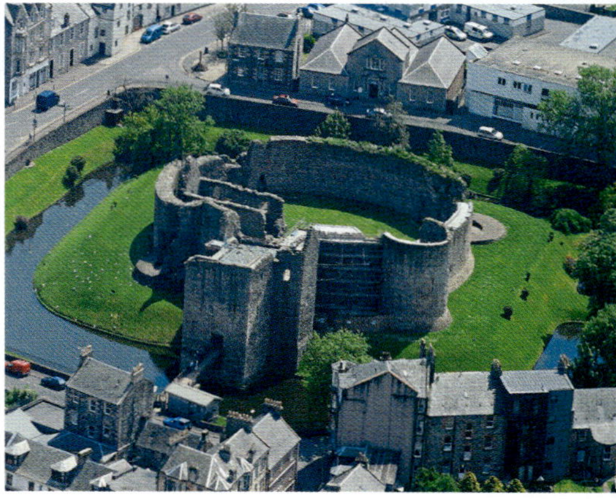

Location: In the Argyll and Dumbarton district, Rothesay Castle is in the centre of Rothesay town on the Island of Bute. CalMac Ferries link the island to the mainland from Wemyss Bay.

The Kings of Norway had, by 1098, forced King Edgar of Scotland to give them the Hebrides, including the Isle of Bute, after 200 years of sea-born Viking raiding. By 1200, the High Stewards of the King of Scotland had retaken Bute and decided to build a castle at Rothesay. The first fortress on this site was a timber castle perched on top of a motte. The sea and beach were originally very close: a good choice for replenishments but a bad choice when the enemy ships arrived. This fort was built by the 3rd High Steward around 1200. He reinforced the defences by adding a stone curtain circular wall. The Stewards later became known as the wealthy Stewart Clan.

In the 1230s, a siege lasting over three days was led by Uspak, King of Man and the Isles. It was a bloody affair with the defenders harassing the attackers by pouring hot oil over them from above while the Vikings, sheltering under shields, hewed a gap in the soft sandstone wall with axes. They took the castle but had to retreat soon afterwards when more Scots arrived by sea.

In 1263, King Haakon IV of Norway voyaged with a thousand ships and warriors to the west coast of Scotland. He effortlessly took Rothesay Castle by surrender and then landed other forces along the mainland coast at Largs.

Meanwhile, the rulers of Scotland used diplomatic delaying tactics to slow down the planned invasion by the Norwegians. The autumnal storms then smashed many of the longboats into driftwood. The Viking fleet was scattered and skirmishes on land around Largs did not go well for them. The Norwegian king decided to withdraw his forces and fleet to his Orkney base for the winter where he fell ill and died. Three years later, his son Magnus handed back the Hebrides to Alexander III although the agreed sale price was never paid in full. This was the end of the attempts by the Norwegians to regain the Hebrides by force.

A 19th century folk song tells of Lady Isobel: her family was killed by the Vikings and she refused to marry one of the invaders. She stabbed herself and her blood-soaked ghost has been seen on steps near the chapel on the castle grounds. The next attack was home grown: Sir Robert Boyd of Cunningham wrested control of the castle from the English in 1306, but they returned in 1334 to regain control. However, the Scots were back inside before the English settled in. Those rising stars the Stewarts made it to Kingship in 1371 and both Robert II and III enjoyed seaside stays at the castle by the shore. By now, the water-filled moat surrounded the wall, which prevented tunnelling attempts and made axe-wielding attacks impractical. Four towers were added to the curtain wall. This enabled the defenders to fire arrows down on those close to the wall. When the King was not residing he allowed relatives to look after the castle. The title Duke of Rothesay was bestowed on the next in line for the throne, a

tradition which has continued with Prince Charles. In 1462, the last Lord of the Isles, John of Islay, failed to take the castle. The 12th century shell keep was not considered large enough for comfort by James IV so the larger rectangular four-storey keep and gatehouse were added and completed by James V after 1541. This still displays the royal court of arms above the door. Having crossed the drawbridge, the entrance follows a long vaulted passage. Set into the passage floor there is still a trapdoor above a prison pit dungeon that reminded all visitors of the punishments at hand for those who wronged the King. Above the passage are the great hall and lavish rooms that were for the king and guests. The only building inside the motte which survives is a small chapel. The north west tower is called the Pigeon Tower because nest boxes are built into the outside wall.

The Master of Ruthven laid siege in 1527 and failed to gain entry but he destroyed much of the surrounding Burgh of Rothesay. In 1544, the Earl of Lennox managed to get inside of the castle with the support of a force of 18 ships and 800 men provided by King Henry VIII. The relentless invasion forces of Oliver Cromwell took the castle from royalists around 1650 and decided to base troops there. They left the fortress as a wrecked shell in 1660. Further destruction happened in 1685 when supporters of the 9th Earl of Argyll rebelled against James II. They used fires to torch remaining timbers and scorch walls. Between 1816 to 1817, the 2nd Marquess of Bute had many workman clear vast amounts of rubbish and rubble from inside the walls. His successor, the 3rd Marquess, continued improvements from 1871 to 1900 with plans provided by his architect, William Burges. They had already rebuilt Cardiff Castle and Castell Goch in Wales. While visiting Bute, try to find time to visit Mount Stuart House, an extravagant gothic manor also resulting from their partnership.

In 1961, the castle was donated to the care of the state and is now managed by Historic Environment Scotland.

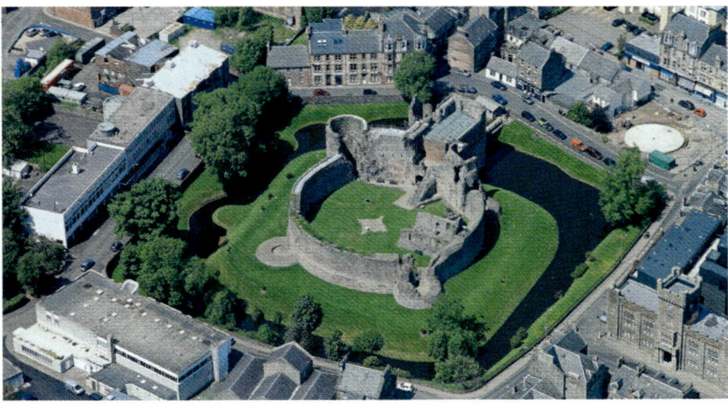

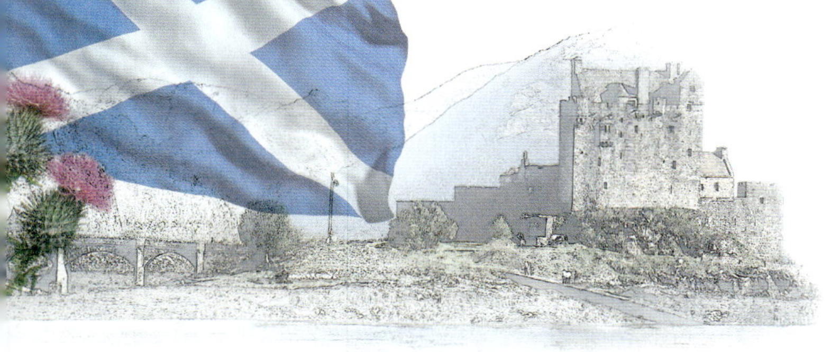

Castle Roy

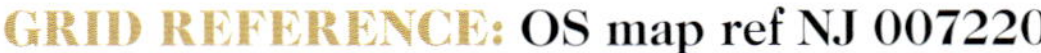

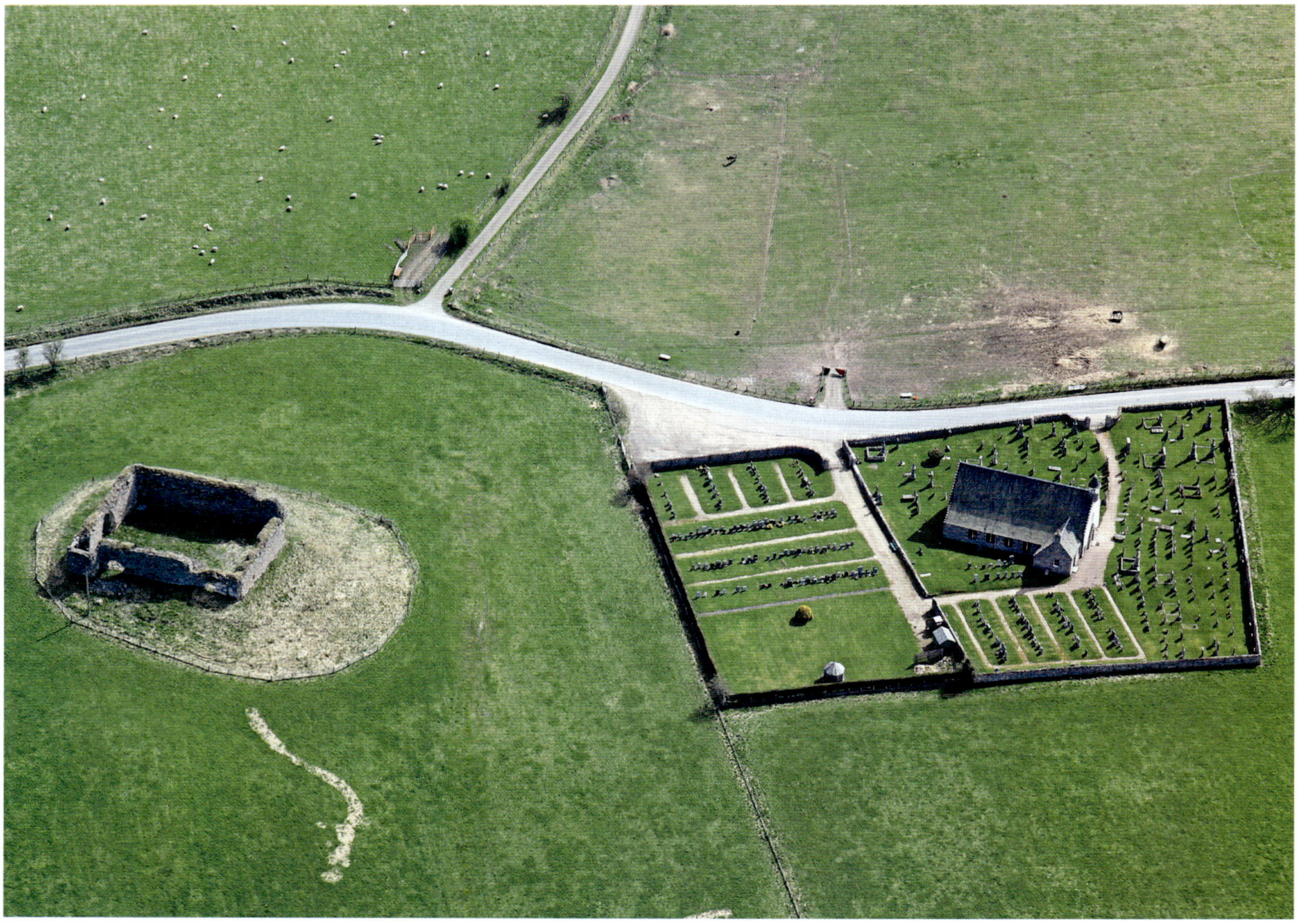

The ruination of this small castle has exposed structural features which would normally have remained hidden from view. When it was built it formed part of the substantial Comyn networks of defensive structures. Today it is in the care of a trust which seeks to stabilise its remains and educate visitors about its extensive history.

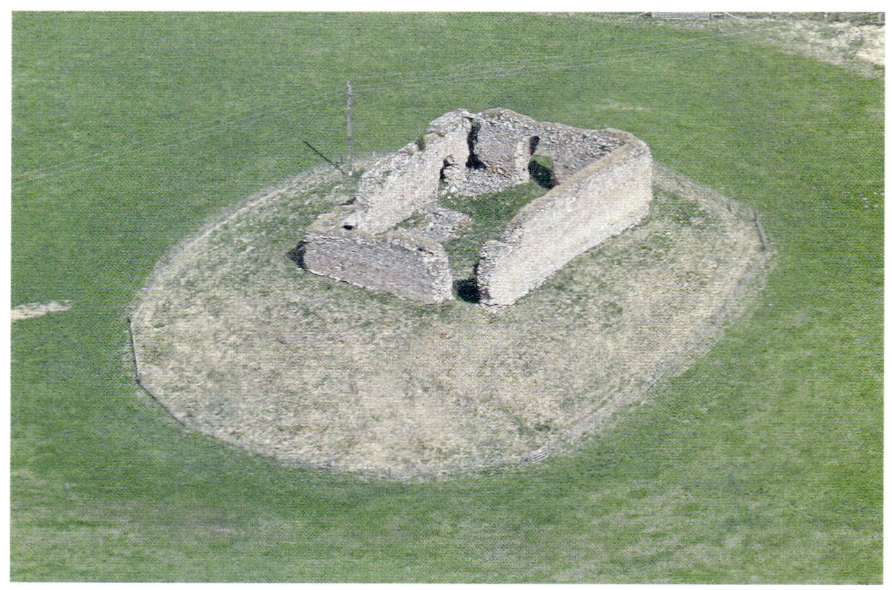

- https://castleroy.org.uk/
- No telephone.
- Castle Roy is open all year.
- Ruin access by short path.
- Nethybridge village has several shops and places for refreshments.
- Donations to the trust are welcomed.

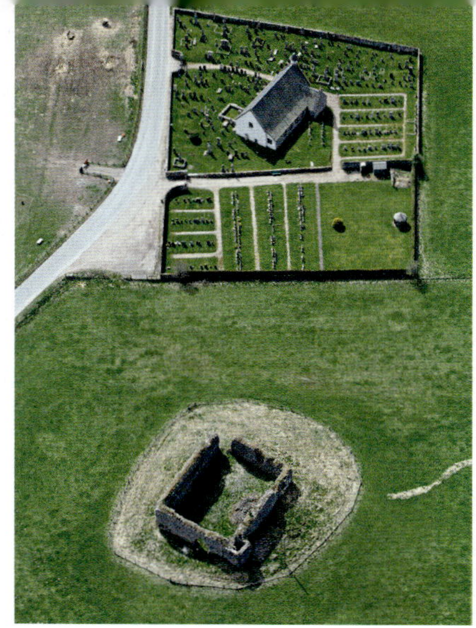

Location: Castle Roy is in Strathspey, four miles south-west of Grantown-on-Spey. It is next to the B970 which links Grantown to Nethybridge. The castle can also be reached by leaving the Aviemore-Grantown road at the Broomhill junction over the River Spey. Cross the historic wooden bridge to Nethybridge village. Turn left at the T-junction. There is parking adjacent to the Old Kirk.

The name Roy is not connected with a clan name: instead it is from the Gaelic Caistel Ruadh meaning red castle. It forms part of a network of castles built and held by the Comyns. Other examples nearby can be found at Freuchie Hillock (the later site of Castle Grant), Lochindorb, Loch an Eilean and on the mound at Ruthven before the barracks were placed there. The Comyns were of Flemish origin settling here in the 13th century.

The castle was placed just above the flood plain of the nearby River Spey on the edge of the former Great Wood of Caledonia. It was a handy location for hunting, fishing and keeping a watch on who was coming and going along the tracks which followed the river. In its earlier years, the castle would have seen visits from the Earls of Mar, the Stewarts and finally the Grants. The corner tower had two floors and the courtyard was likely to have contained timber buildings. The substantial walls are made of local glacial rubble stones still held together by the original lime mortar. Two entrances are built into the walls, unusual for such a small building. One could have been used by VIPs, such as the Clan Chief. The Castle Roy Trust took over in 1994; its aim is to preserve the castle, as it stands, for future generations. The trust also endeavours to make it a free, all-abilities, visitor and education centre and to create a community venue for the outdoor performing arts and other events, such as weddings and family parties.

The trust has been working to stabilise the walls since taking ownership of the castle. The tower foundations were supported and repairs have been done to stop any further movement. The website link gives further details.

The adjacent Old Kirk is not quite as old as the castle and no longer the parish place of worship. It is now run by an association of volunteers for the benefit of the community. It has a beautifully preserved interior with great acoustics.

Here is the website link with information on opening times. https://nethybridge.com/out-about/abernethy-old-kirk/

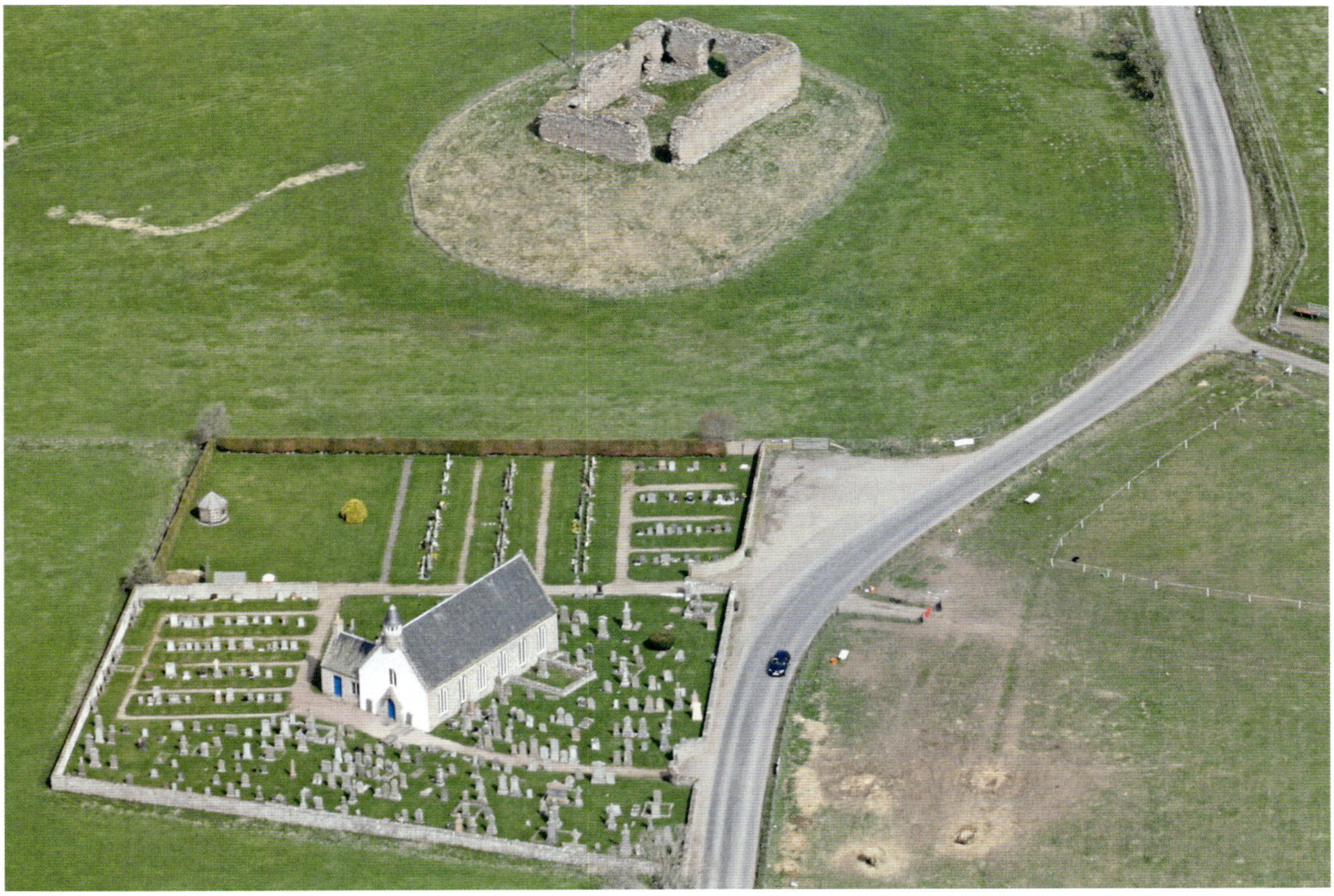

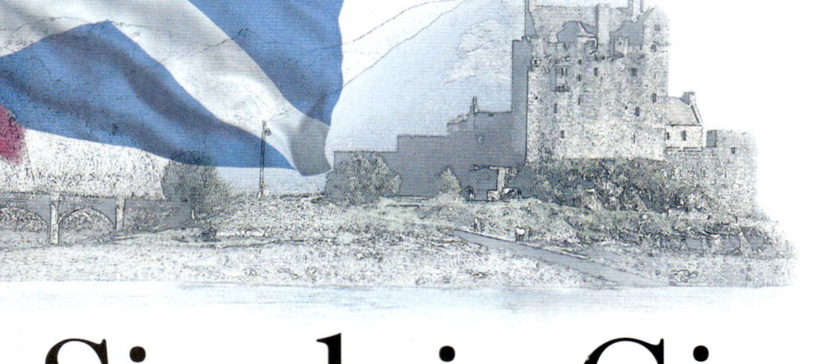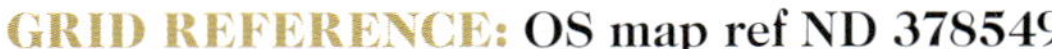

Sinclair Girnigoe Castle

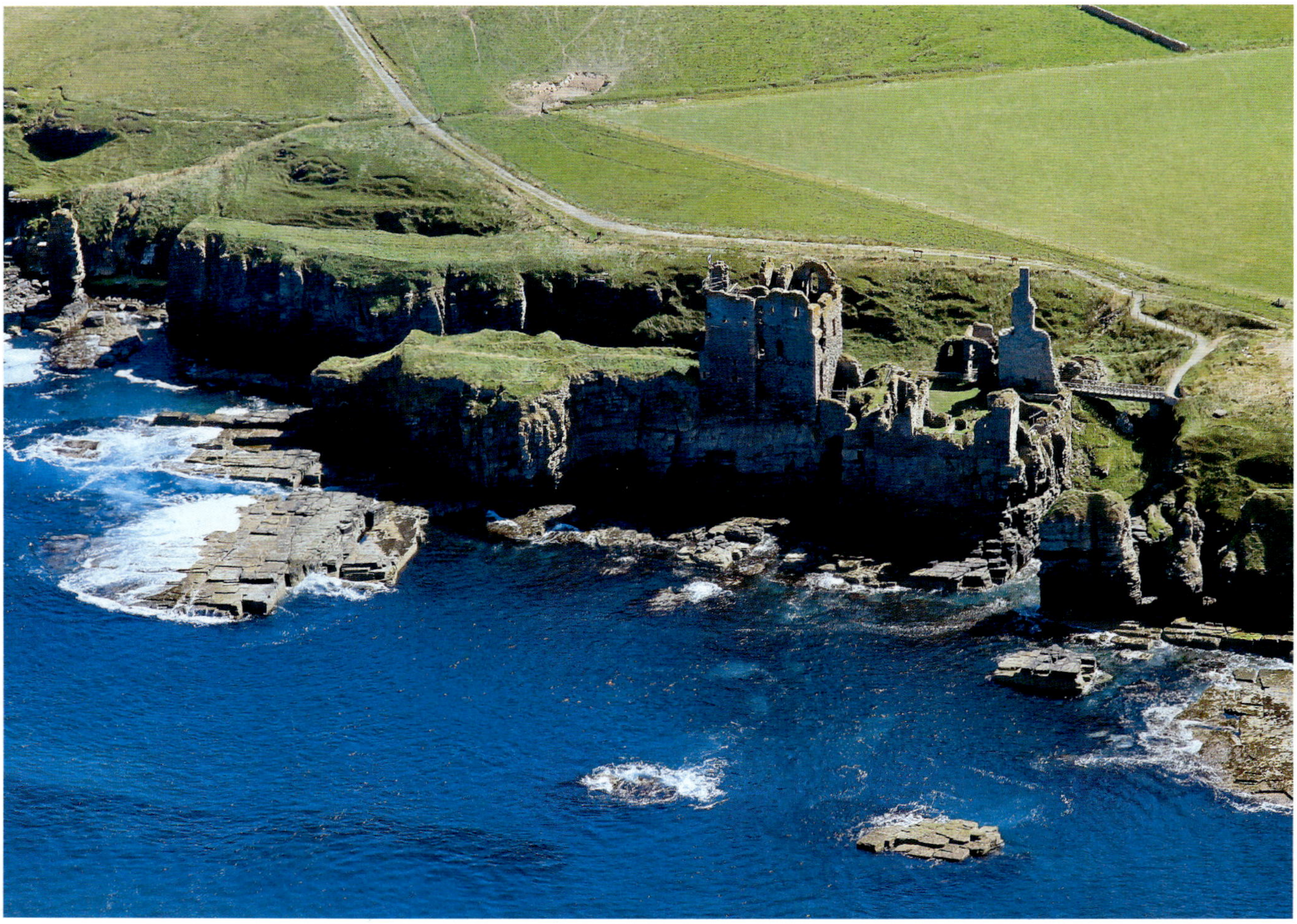

At times a wild place with an equally wild history which includes the Sinclair chief leading warriors into the biggest battle but never returning. There would also be torture for the chief's son and a narrow escape for his friend. The last great clash of the clans, against the Campbells, happened nearby. Recently funding has been provided to protect the ruin from further collapse.

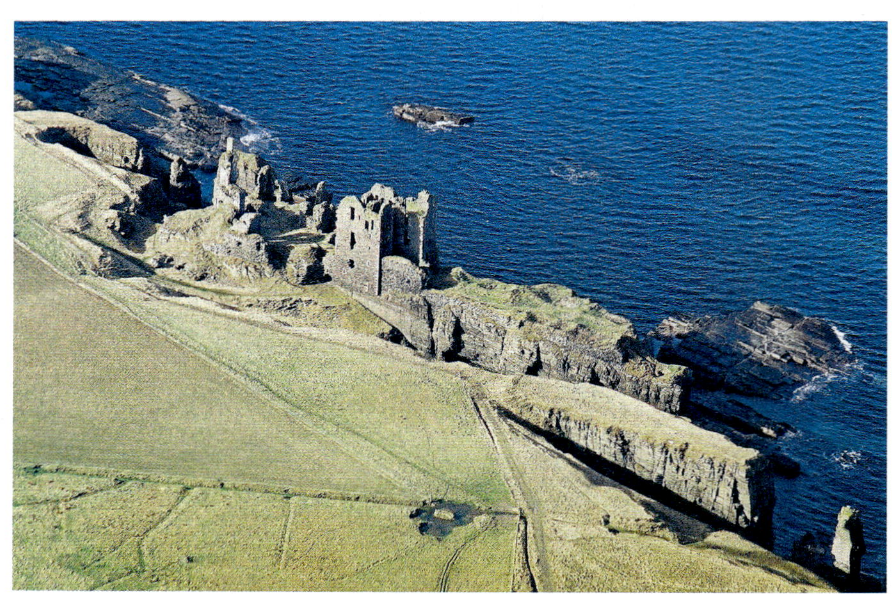

Visitor Details

 Website in development at the time of writing.

 No telephone.

 Open all year but avoid in severe weather as there is little shelter.

 The modern bridge, which is in place of the original drawbridge, can be easily crossed to the ruins. Although now stabilised, the ruin can only be viewed from ground level.

Carry your own refreshments as there are no facilities at the ruins, apart from picnic tables.

Strong footwear and warm clothing are advised as there is often a sea breeze. Should weather and tides permit you can descend to the small beach below the castle cliff.

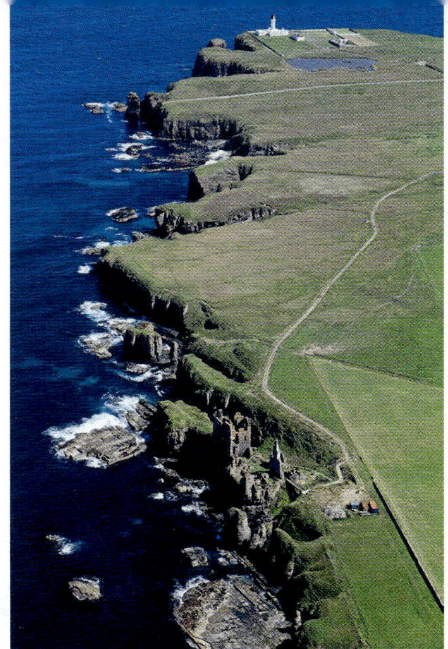

Location: On the southern cliffs of Sinclair's Bay, three miles north of Wick in Caithness and Sutherland. Head along the small coastal road on the north east side of Wick, via Staxigoe where a sign is posted for Noss Head. After about two miles, stop at the small car park on the right just before the Noss Head Lighthouse driveway. From here the level track heads north west taking about 20 minutes to the castle ruins.

Fortifications along the rocky cliff promontories of Scotland's coast were at one time commonly seen but the earlier ones built by the Picts have seldom survived due to extreme weathering or being hidden beneath later castles. Excavations have found indications of an early defensive stronghold beneath the current castle ruin here. The King of Norway had appointed the Sinclairs (aka the St Clairs) as Earls of Orkney, which was still a Norwegian possession. The influence of those early settlers was recently proven when some of the male population of Orkney, Shetland and Durness were DNA tested and found to have the strongest Viking Norwegian ancestry in Scotland.

When James III of Scotland married Margaret of Denmark, her father, Christian the first, King of the Kalmar Union (Denmark, Sweden and Norway), was unable to immediately provide a dowry. Instead, he said that he would provide the dowry at a later date, and pledged the Orkneys and Shetland as security for his promise. With no coin or treasure arriving by 1472, James decided that the islands were his by default. He asked William Sinclair to step aside from his Earldom and granted him lands in Caithness and Fife to compensate him.

The second Earl, William, located a defensible site for his castle with clear sea views because in those times when the sea was the route of traders and raiders, keeping a lookout was essential. The first stone castle under the name Girnigoe occupied the further end of the rocky cliff top finger and was completed around 1496. William perished in the Battle of Flodden Field in 1513. Casualties were heavy for the Scots and among the 10,000 killed were nine earls, 13 barons, five heirs to titles, three bishops, two abbots and King James IV. See http://www.flodden.net

Next to live at the castle was Earl John Sinclair. He also died in a battle at Summerdale in Orkney in 1529 while unsuccessfully attempting to put down a local rebellion.

The fourth Earl of Caithness, George, achieved notoriety in 1577. He had the power of life or death across all of Caithness and Sutherland, holding the appointment of Justicary from the King. He became a tyrant despised by commoners and nobles alike. He suspected his son, John Master of Caithness and his friend, Mackay of Strathnavar, of plotting against him. So after tricking John into visiting Girnigoe with no bodyguard, the earl had his son imprisoned in the dungeon where he was treated badly. His friend escaped on horseback before the trap was sprung. After seven years of torture, John died having been driven mad by the final five days of starvation, followed by being given salted beef and then no water. The narrow finger of land restricted room for the essentials of a comfortable lifestyle. The poultry needed

space to roam and guests had to be impressed in a great hall. In 1606, the gatehouse, curtain wall and drawbridge formed part of the extension commissioned by the 5th Earl, George. He also gained permission from parliament to change the castle name to Sinclair in line with modern practice. The L-plan tower house had five storeys including the expected secret chamber, this time hidden in the vaulted kitchen ceiling.

The campaign by Cromwell's army in the 1650s resulted in the castle being occupied by General Moncks' troops. Recently excavated debris has revealed their disregard for the owner's property. To repay a debt, the sixth Sinclair Earl of Caithness transferred the castle to his cousin, John Campbell of Glen Orchy, in 1672. Four years later the Earl died with no heir and Campbell married his widow, thereby claiming the title Earl of Caithness. This move did not meet with the approval of George Sinclair of Keiss who felt he deserved the title and the castle due to being a first cousin to the sixth Earl. In 1680, George's forces stormed the castle after a siege of firing floors and roof and wrecking walls. He was destroying the castle that he claimed was his.

With support from government troops, Campbell's clansman marched across rough ground to approach Altimarlach near Wick to confront Sinclair's clan in July 1680. This was the last battle of the Clans on record and resulted in the Sinclairs losing around 300 men, many of whom drowned in the Wick River with just a few lost on the Campbell's side. After this clash, the rule of law via the Privy Council took account of both claims and allowed George Sinclair to hold the title Earl of Caithness. The castle and lands were awarded to Campbell with a new title as compensation, Earl of Breadalbane. The castle remained derelict.

The Sinclair family purchased the ruin in the 1950s from the Dunbars and it was donated to a trust set up for its preservation in 1999. Most of Sinclair Castle was completely ruined; only a chimney, some outer walling, and an access passage remained and were in need of repair to continue standing. The ruins of the tower house were also in danger of falling into the sea. The cliff walls supporting the castles were collapsing.

The World Monument Fund listed the castle on the 2002 Watch List highlighting its importance. With help from the Clan Sinclair Trust, Historic Scotland, Caithness and Sutherland Enterprise, the Highland Council, and the Heritage Lottery Fund, the WMF provided a grant in 2003 for the survey, documentation, and stabilization of the castle. In 2007, the WMF made more funding available for the immediate and long-term conservation of the castle. The work included the building of a bridge to facilitate construction and visitor access to the site and emergency repairs.

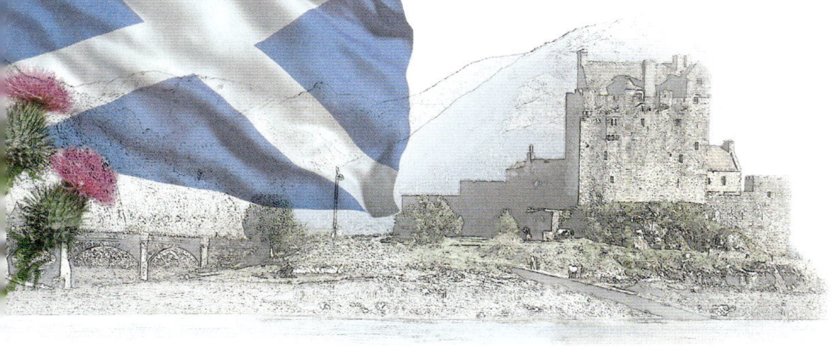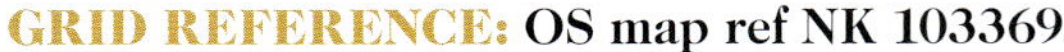

New Slains Castle

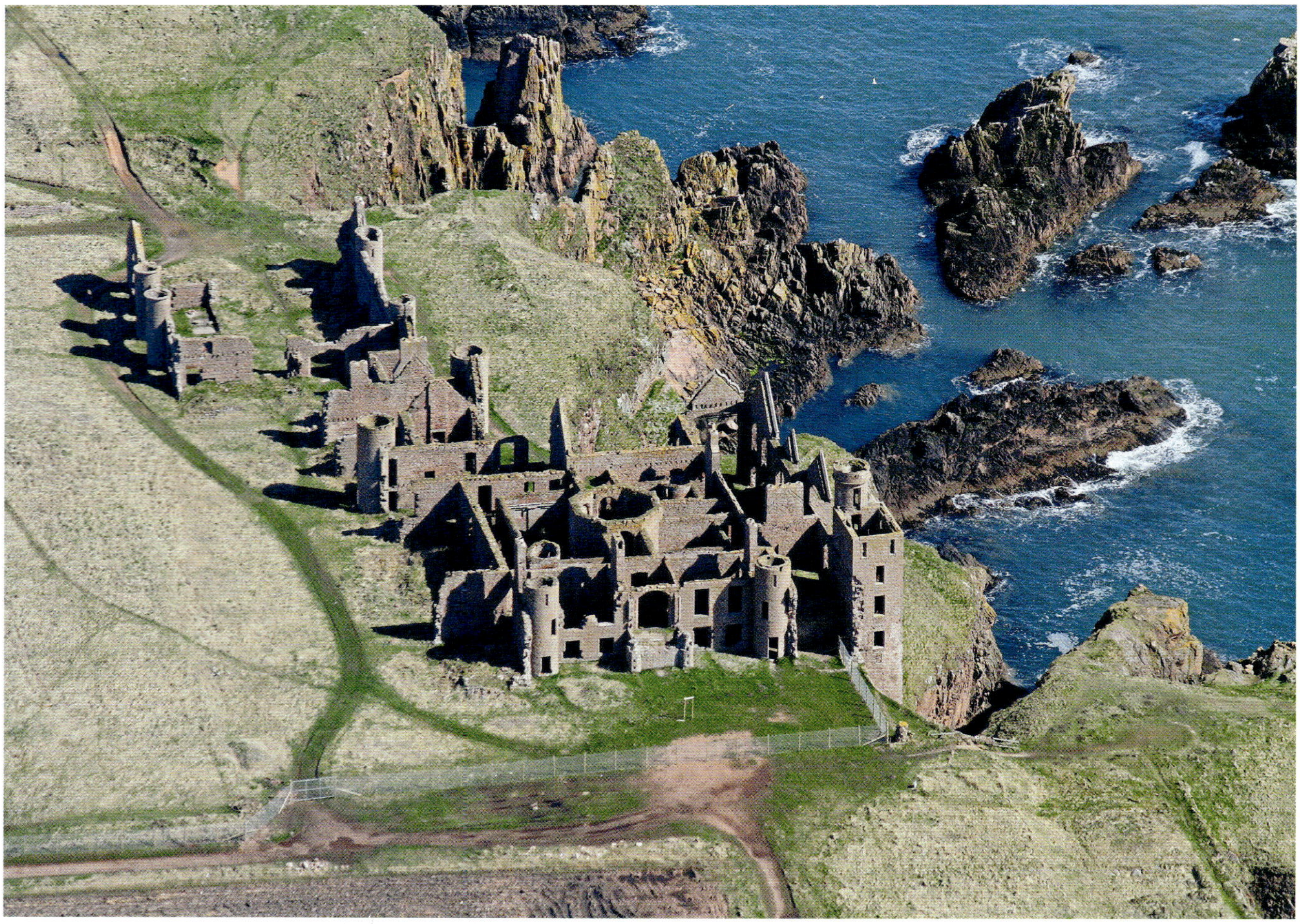

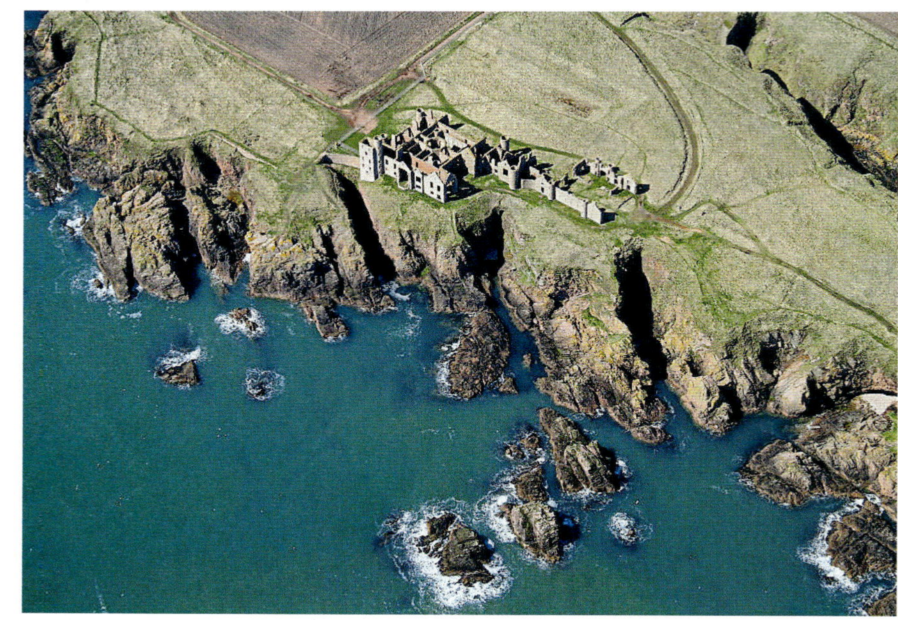

Once the home of a powerful clan, these forlorn ruins bear testament to the rise and fall of a shipping empire, as well as the devastating decisions of its reclusive owner.
In better times, Dracula author Bram Stoker drew influence from the nights he spent at this clifftop location, surrounded by wave wracked seas storming ashore.

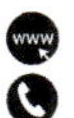 No website.

 No telephone.

 Open 24 hours a day, seven days a week.

No facilities.

Take your own picnic.

No. Ruins are fenced off. Next to public coastal footpath. Fifteen minutes' walk from Cruden Bay.

Location: Slains Castle is found off the A975 to the east of Cruden Bay. There is a small car park adjacent to the main road followed by a walk of just under a mile to the castle ruins. Note that cars can be taken right up to the ruins but a very robust suspension is required.

Visitor Details

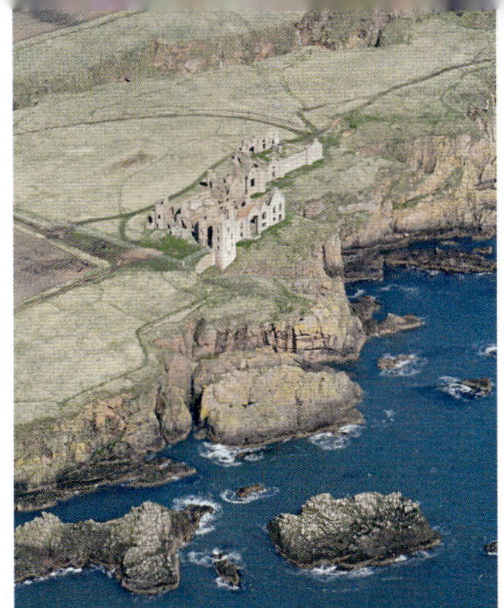

High above the wave lashed cliffs of Cruden Bay, the crumbling New Slains castle once echoed to the sound of lavish balls and many feasts.

The first castle on site was built in about 1600 by Francis Hay 9th Earl of Errol the leader of the most powerful local Clan Hay.

By the 1830s this draughty crumbling castle was not a practical home for the 18th Earl and he commisioned a lavish baronial style mansion of impressive stature.

Bram Stoker had become fond of nearby Cruden Bay as a holiday destination away from his work in London theatreland. The Earl in 1894 invited him to enjoy his hospitality at New Slains, the candlelit mansion perched above the North Sea and this influenced his settings for Dracula.

Perhaps the charismatic Earl became the model for the Count of the novel, mixed

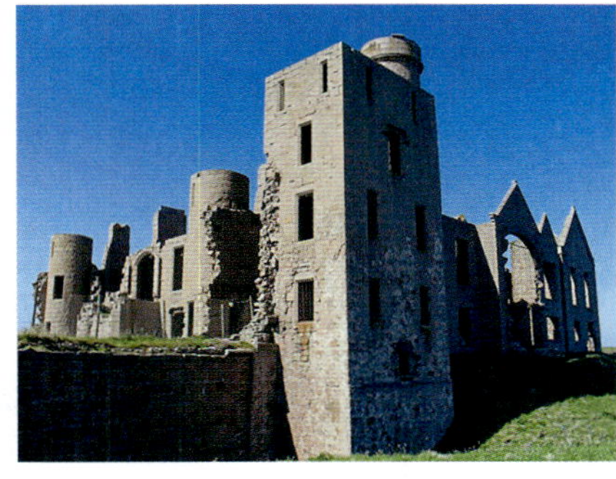

with the folk tales of Hungary and blood seeking vampires?

The castle passed from the ownership of the Hay clan in 1913 to the reclusive owner of the Ellerman Lines shipping dynasty but by 1925 Sir John Ellerman ordered the roof to be removed to avoid taxes. This hastened the decline of a once grand castle into a ruin. There a re plans for a restoration and letting as holiday flats.

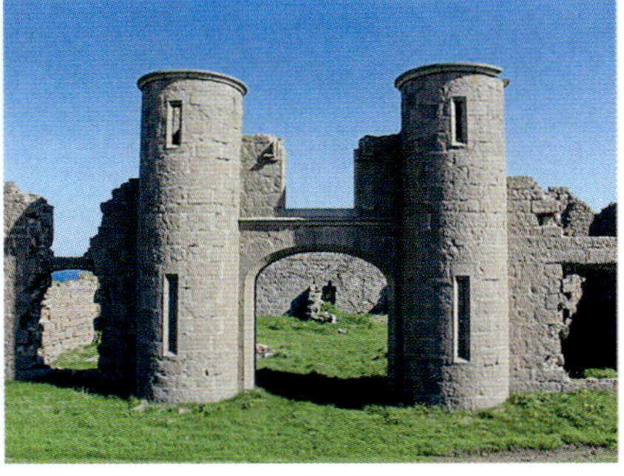

CASTLE FACTS

A castle keep could shelter about 100 people with livestock on the ground floor. Later designs with a bailey wall could shelter up to 500 dependent on food and water supply.

Medieval castles cost around £475 per square foot and could take three to six years to complete.

ABOUT THE CLAN

Clan Hay

The Hay Clan originated in Normandy, arriving in Scotland by invitation after the Normans residing in England impressed the Scottish Kings.

They envied the Normans' castle-building skills and formalised administration of land ownership.

Among those joining the Hays from Normandy were the Oliphant, Comyn, Balliol and Bruce families. These newcomers also encouraged the Scots language at court which supplanted Gaelic – the latter eventually only surviving in the North and on the Western Isles.

King Malcolm IV had the court position of Cup Bearer filled by William Hay II in 1160. By marriage to Eva of Pitmilly, a Celtic heiress, he started the lineage of Clan Hay. The king clearly valued his loyalty because in 1178 he was made first Baron of Errol. The fifth Lord Errol joined Robert the Bruce, helping him to victory in the Battle of Bannockburn in 1314. His reward was the role of Lord High Constable of Scotland. Nowadays, titles involve ceremonial duties.

However, the combats of old demanded a price often paid in blood. The chieftain of Clan Hay was also Commander of the Royal Bodyguard which formed rings of steel around the king in battle. Sadly, this led to the demise of many Hay chieftains.

In August 1513, James IV, King of Scots, gave one month's notice of his plan to invade England. This chivalrous gesture enabled the English to prepare. The Battle of Flodden took place near Branxton, Northumberland involving over 100,000 soldiers. The notables of Scotland included earls, knights, clergy, chieftains and the king – many of whom stayed at the front of the battle lines and most perished including those of Clan Hay. By contrast the English notables watched from the relative safety of the baggage area at the rear. The folk song Flowers of the Forest marks the great loss of Scotland's sons in this terrible defeat.

The Hays chose to support the Jacobite uprising using Slains Castle as a meeting place for plotting and fundraising between 1708-1745.

Having picked the losing side, the Hays then became one of many subdued clans, never challenging the state again.

When King George IV made a state visit to Scotland in 1822, the cost of lavish entertainment organised by Sir Walter Scott nearly bankrupted the Hays.

The 19th Earl supported fishing communities in Aberdeenshire and founded the village of Port Erroll which provided housing at low rents.

The Clan Hay Centre has been established at Delgatie Castle near Turriff.

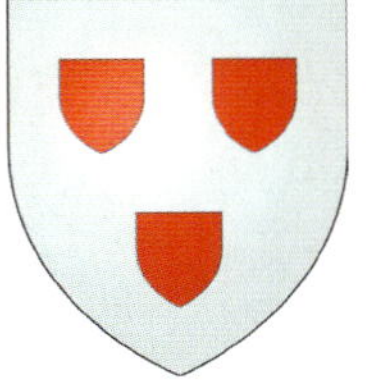

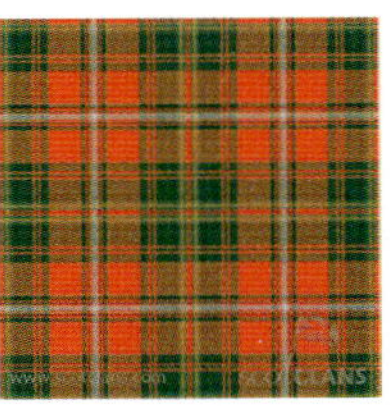

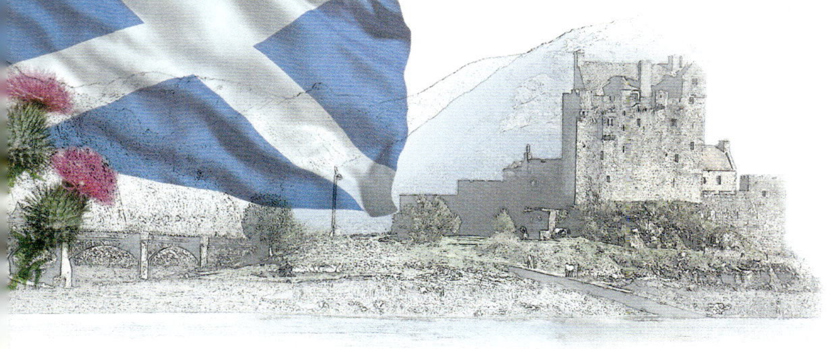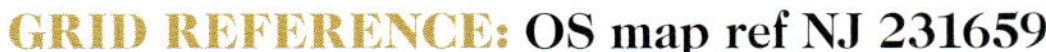

Spynie Palace

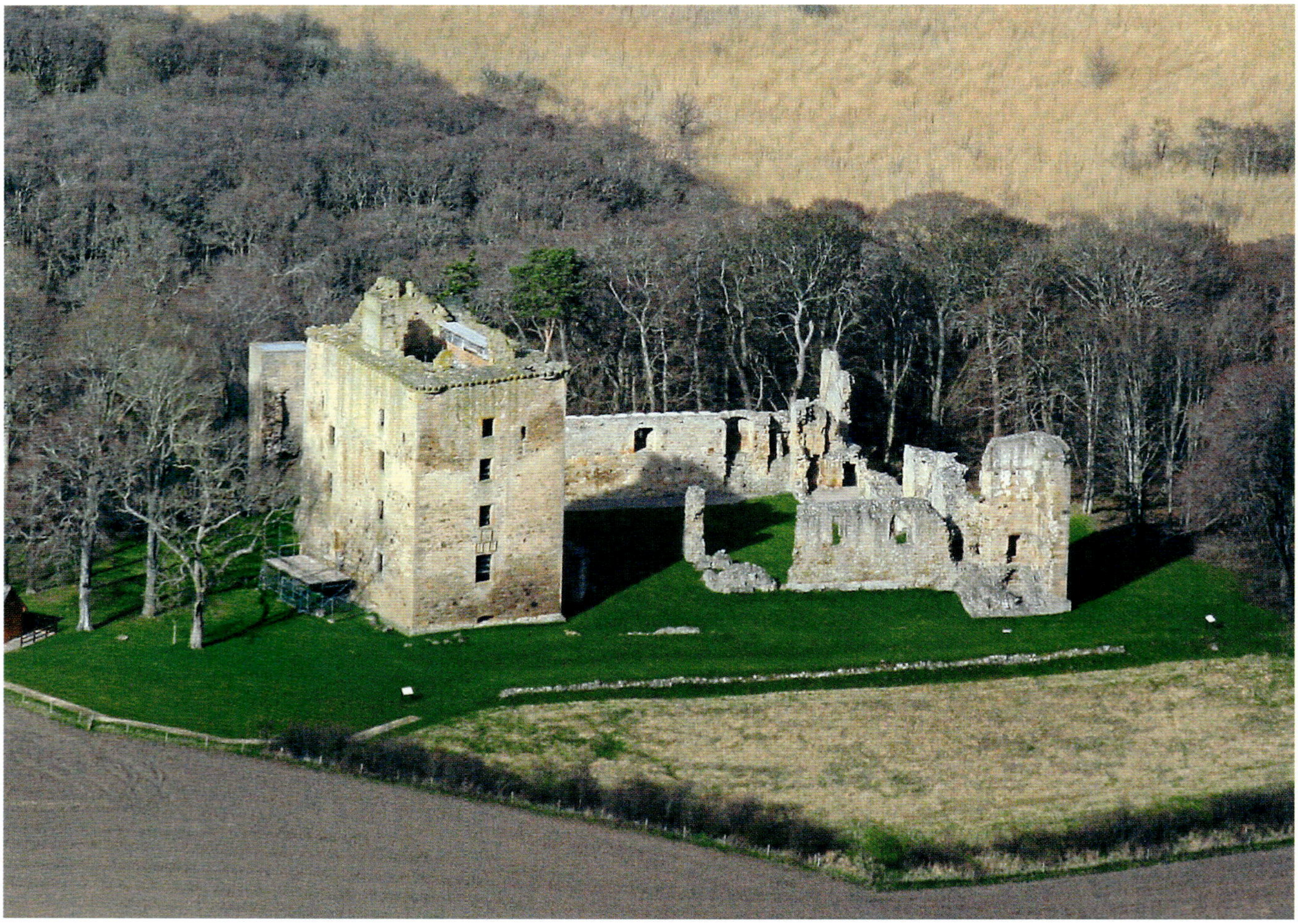

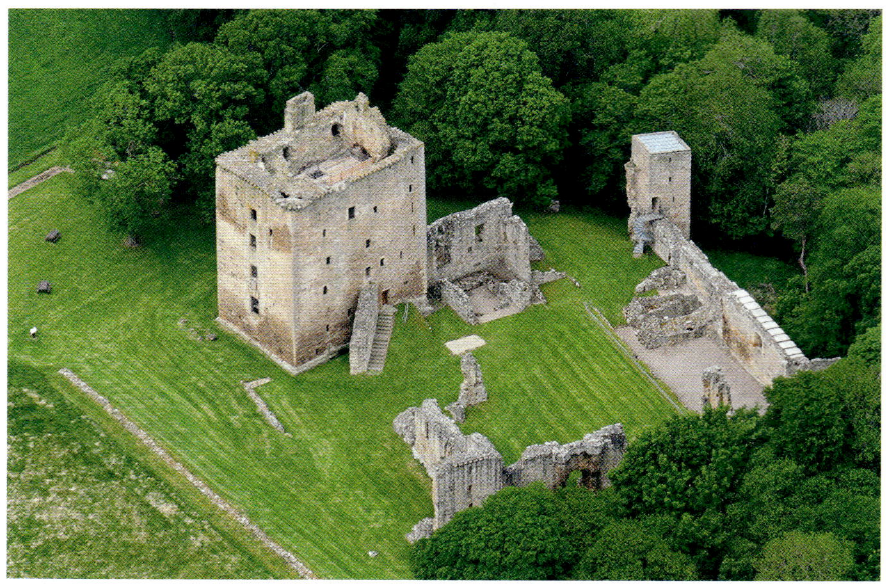

 www.historicenvironment.scot/visit-a-place/places/spynie-palace

 01343 546358

Spynie Palace is usually open daily from April to September and only at weekends from October to March. A joint ticket with admission to Elgin Cathedral is available in summer.

 Access to upper levels is via an historic stone spiral staircase. There is an adapted toilet in the shop area. There is a small shop on site with step-free access. The car park is 40m from the castle on gravel paths.

The nearby towns of Lossiemouth and Elgin have a range of cafes and general shopping.

 At ground level are the ranges and kitchen remains. The basement of David's Tower is reached down an uneven stone staircase which can be very dark.

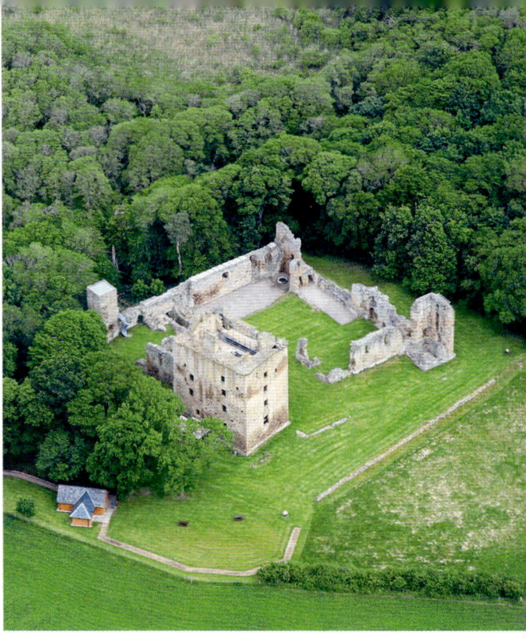

Location: Spynie Palace is situated in the Moray district two miles north of Elgin just off the A941 Elgin-Lossiemouth road. You can find it in a wooded area on the edge of Spynie Loch and Canal.

Many medieval bishops who hailed from nobility had their own castle palaces and led the life of aristocrats; the first bishop to own Spynie Palace being no exception.

A promontory on Spynie Loch was chosen as the location for this castle and the nearby cathedral because it was the main port for Elgin. The loch was larger in those distant days and connected to the sea. Building materials could be brought by sea from the sandstone quarries at nearby Hopeman. The castle had a sea gate and cobbled lane to the loch side harbour.

Travel overland to and from Elgin was restricted to the south by the mountains. The Spey and Findhorn Rivers to the east and west were hard to cross. This channelled trade to Spynie on the Moray coastline. The first small cathedral church was established at Spynie by Bishop Brice as part of the growing settlement there around 1207. Later, the new cathedral soared skywards in Elgin but the bishops remained at Spynie enjoying the comforts of the largest bishop's palace in Scotland.

By 1226, the locals and visitors could view the huge cathedral taking shape at Elgin. To see four men working a treadmill crane to hoist stone blocks 200ft into the air would seem almost magical. Even today when you view the substantial remains it is still a marvel to imagine the impact this had on the people in medieval times. The palace was known as the Lantern of the North throughout the kingdom.

The cathedral attracted the vengeance of Alexander Stewart, the Wolf of Badenoch. This vile brigand attacked and burned buildings in Forres, Pluscarden Abbey and in Elgin he razed the cathedral, hospital and many homes of the clergy to the ground during 1390. He had particular hatred for the church which had refused to allow his divorce. Conveniently for him, his older brother, Robert III, was next in line for the throne so just before he was crowned, he asked Alexander to be repentant, pay some fines and then pardoned him, which naturally he did.

Bishop Innes created the first ranges of the palace buildings just after these attacks, wisely not trusting that the Wolf had truly reformed. Inside a tall defensive wall remain two ranges with first floor halls, possibly a chapel building, and the basement foundations of a substantial circular tower which could have been the first main accommodation block. These are all overshadowed by the massive tower house known as David's Tower, six storeys with a first floor entrance. It is named after Bishop David Stewart who had started its creation around 1465. The high and mighty liked to call on the bishop and enjoy the feasting with wines from the cellar. These included James IV, Mary Queen of Scots and James Hepburn, 4th Earl of Bothwell. In 1589, General Munro terrified Bishop Guthrie into surrender after threatening siege and had him thrown in jail. Later in 1645, the Innes and Grants clans held out for the covenanters at the castle against a siege by Gordon, the Earl of Huntly. By 1686, the last bishop to reside at the castle died there. In 1688, Bishop Hay was removed from his position and the castle fell into ruin. The state took over Spynie Palace in 1973 which has enabled the ruin to be made safe. But they have not stopped the sightings of a ghostly piper, strange music and unexpected lights.

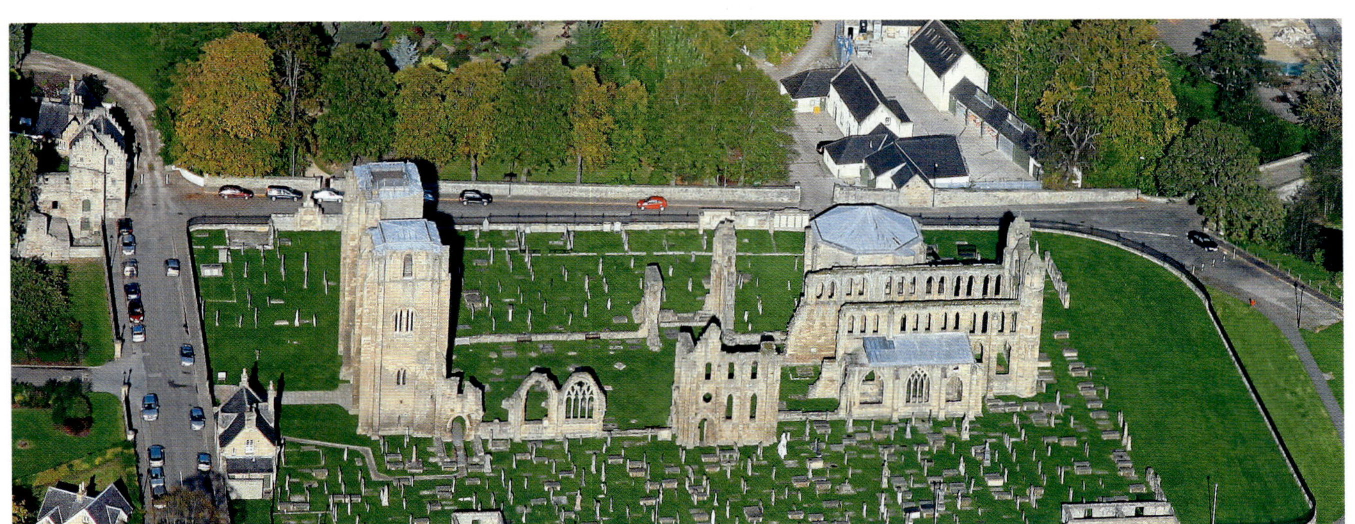

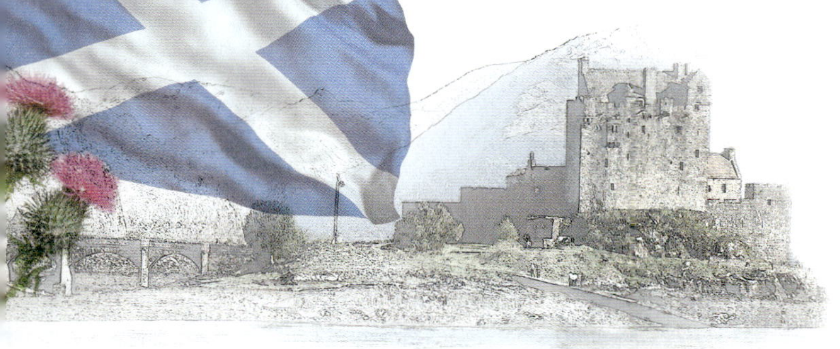

GRID REFERENCE: OS map ref NM 921473.

Castle Stalker

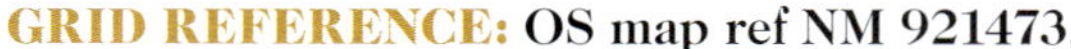

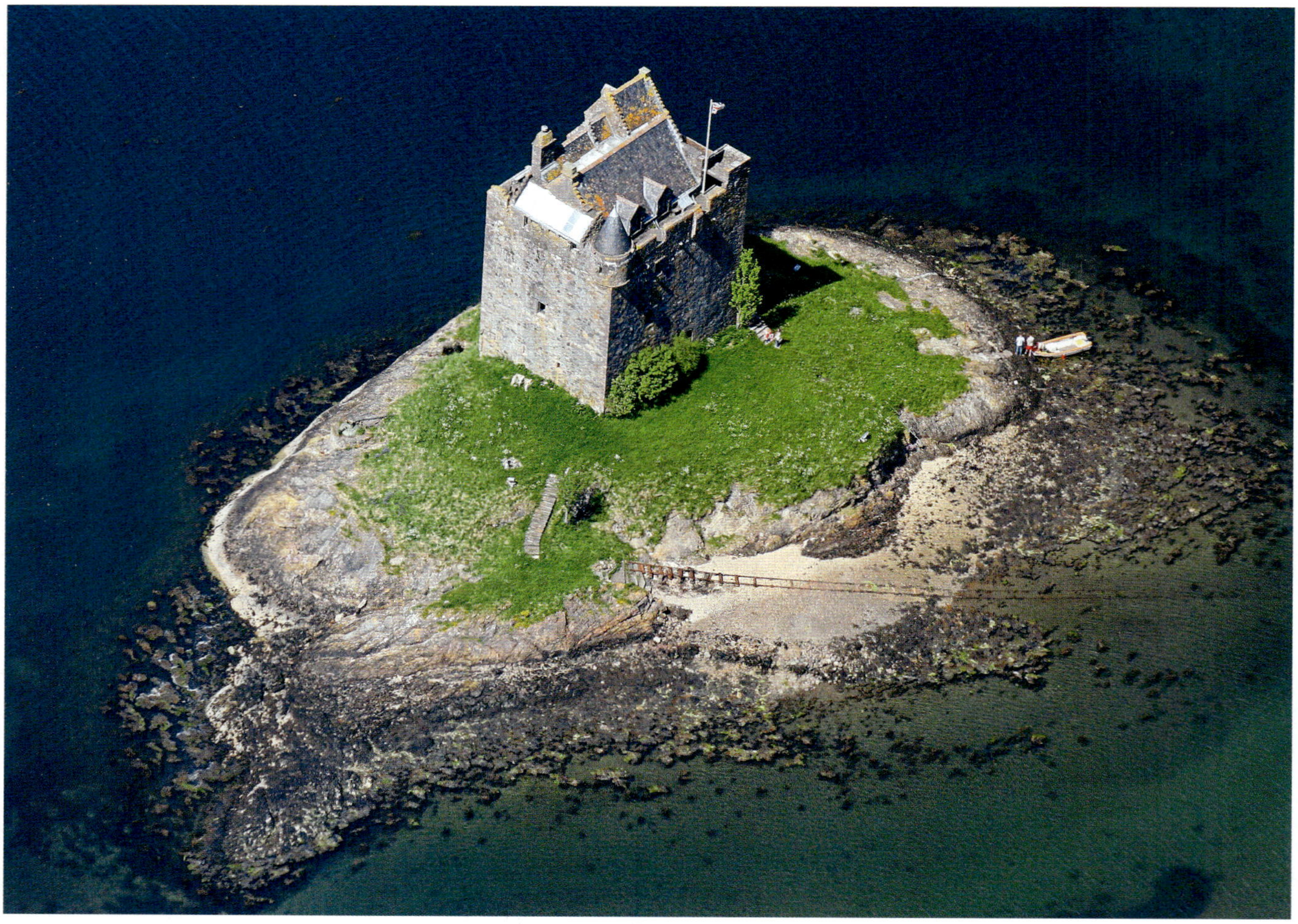

Probably the smallest island castle to survive intact this restored bastion has had a greater part to play in Scotland's history than its isolated location might suggest nowadays. It has also had several small parts in films. Visitors will need to board a ferry boat if they wish to take a tour of this compact but attractive tower house.

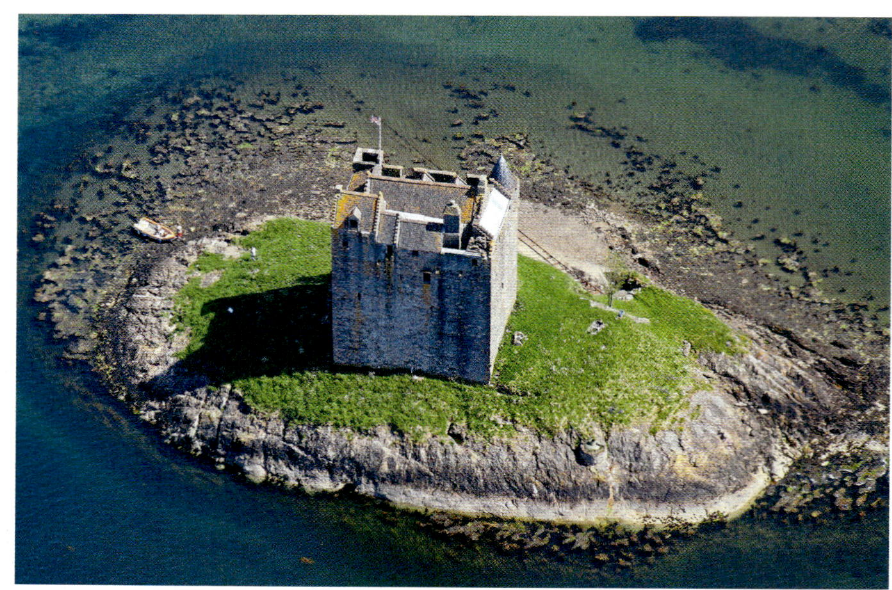

Visitor Details

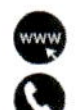 https://www.castlestalker.com/wp/

 01883 622768

Open by pre-booking only.

Agility is needed to scramble ashore and use the steps inside the castle. Full details are on the website.

No refreshments.

The owners arrange pre-booked tours inclusive of the ferry boat.

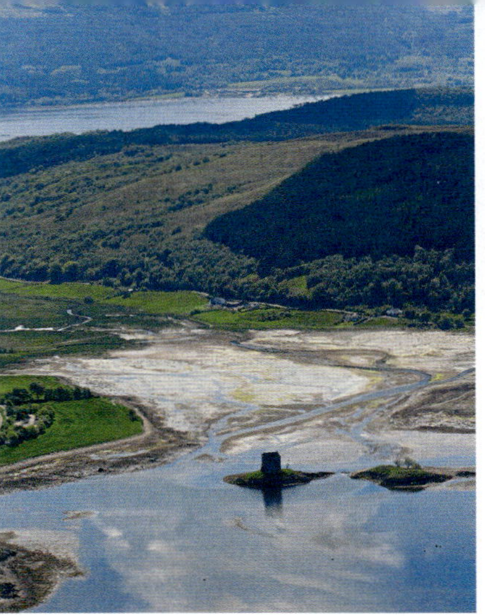

Location: Castle Stalker is in the Argyll and Dumbarton district on an island situated on the tidal Loch Laich just at the meeting point with the larger Loch Linnhe. The nearest viewpoint is from the A828 road at nearby Portnacroish.

The Stewarts of Appin were awarded Chamberlain of the Isles around 1388 by King James IV for helping defeat MacDonald, Lord of the Isles. They had the large tower house built in the 1440s with four storeys and a garret. At ground level is a vaulted basement which includes a prison room. The outside stone steps lead to the first floor hall with living rooms on the floors above. Around 1620, some sources say a drunken bet led to the loss of the castle to Clan Campbell, others say it was fairly sold. Civil war in 1688 led to the Stewarts retaking the castle but after the Campbells laid siege in 1690, the Stewarts surrendered.

In the 1745 rising, 300 Appin clansmen attacked but made no progress against the 60 Campbells holding the fortress. The Jacobites' small cannon could not penetrate the thick walls which left the castle with the Campbells. The castle became a useful stop for the government forces on the supply route between Inverary and Fort William during the rising.

The chief sold the castle and lands in 1765 but it fell into decay from 1780 and became roofless in 1831.

The ruin was stabilised by Charles Stewart financing works in 1908 but the final restoration had to wait until Lt Col D R Stewart became the owner in 1965. He dedicated himself and his family to ten years work to bring it back to its present fine condition. This included finding ways to lift heavy beams without the aid of cranes. In July 2013 a different type of lift happened at the Castle. A visitor became ill on the island and a Royal Navy Sea King helicopter used a winch to lift the stretcher and casualty from the top of the castle.

The final part of the comedy film Monty Python and the Holy Grail was filmed at the castle which was named Aaaaaargh by the Monty Python crew.

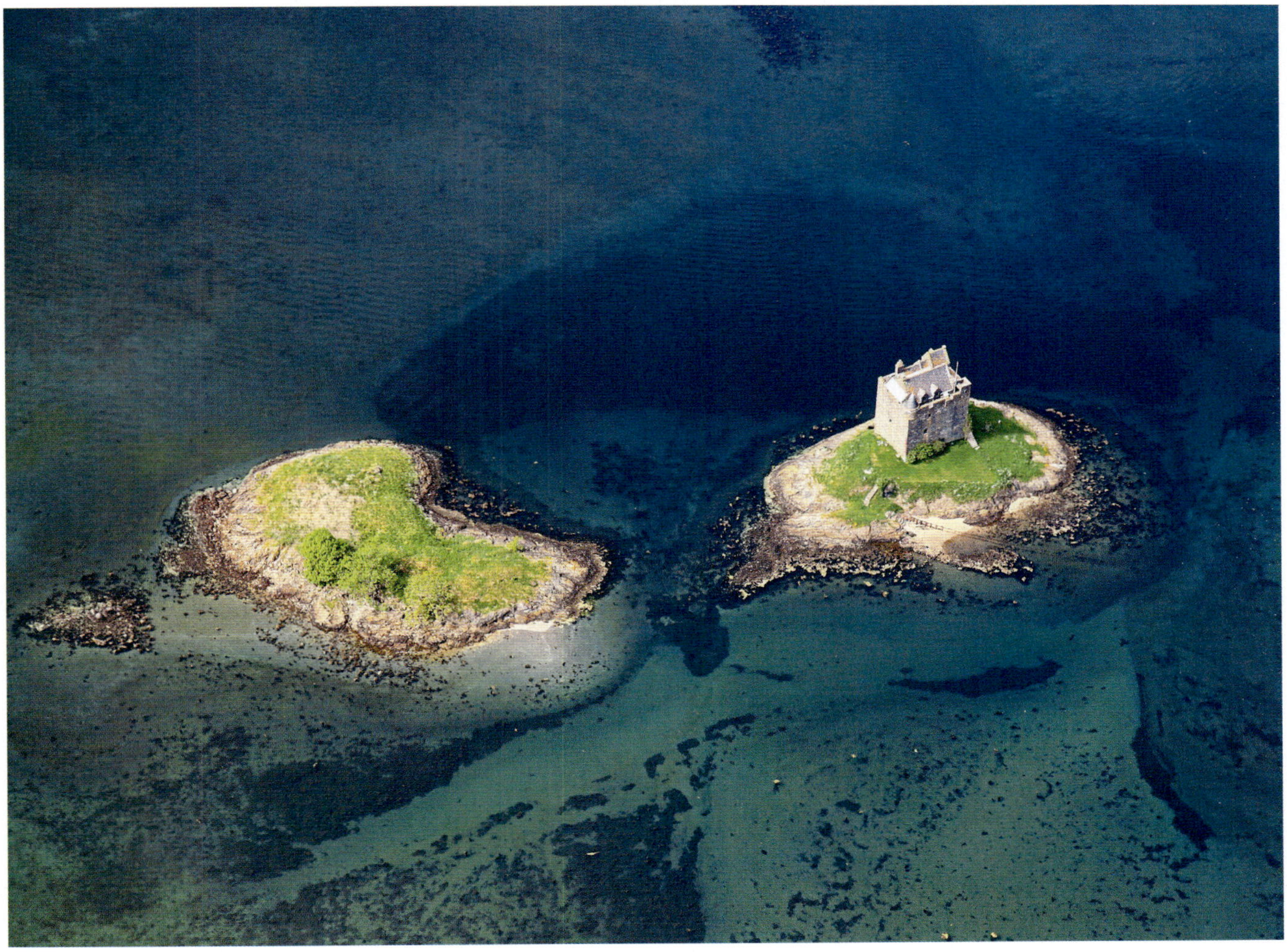

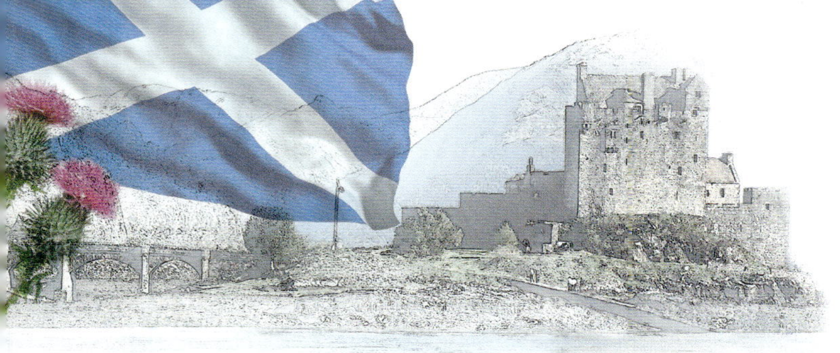

Stirling Castle

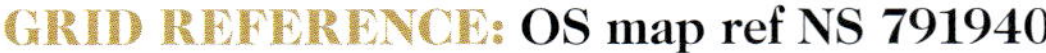

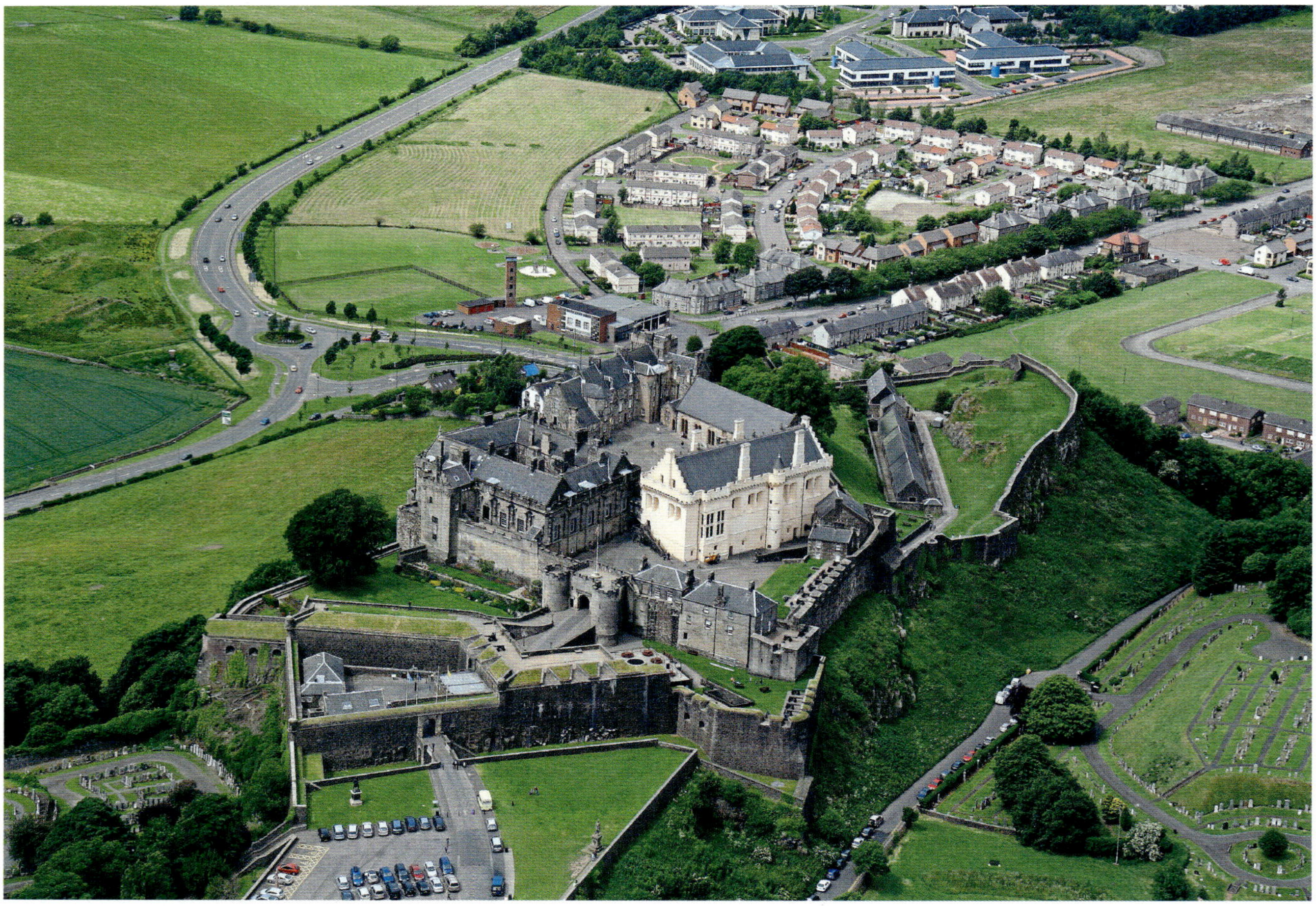

This massive monolithic fortress, the second largest in Scotland after Edinburgh, grips the rocky outcrop firmly. In our times we flash past by car, train and plane but it is worth at least a day investigating what happened here and how those events shaped the modern nation. If Edinburgh castle is the lock then Stirling is the key to the kingdom.

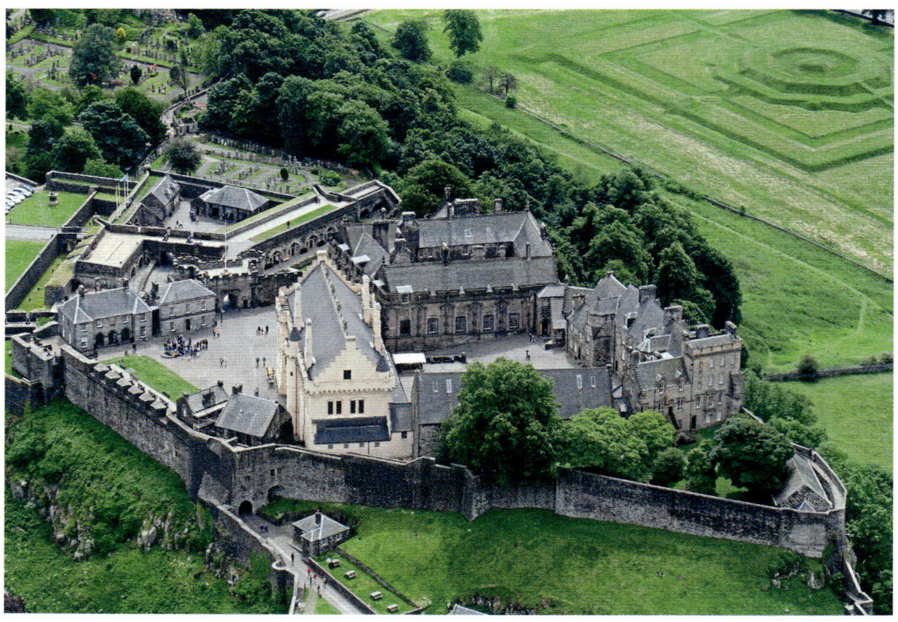

 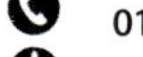 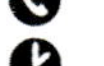 www.stirlingcastle.scot/

01786 450000

The castle is open all year: 1Apr to 30 Sep – 0930 to 1800, 1 Oct to 31 Mar – 1000 to 1600
You will need to book on line in advance for admission tickets.

 Full accessibility details are available on the website.

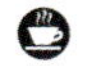 On site shop and cafe.

Both Stirling Bus and Train Stations are within walking distance of the castle, it is situated
up a steep hill. If you are arriving by car, you will also need to book a parking space.

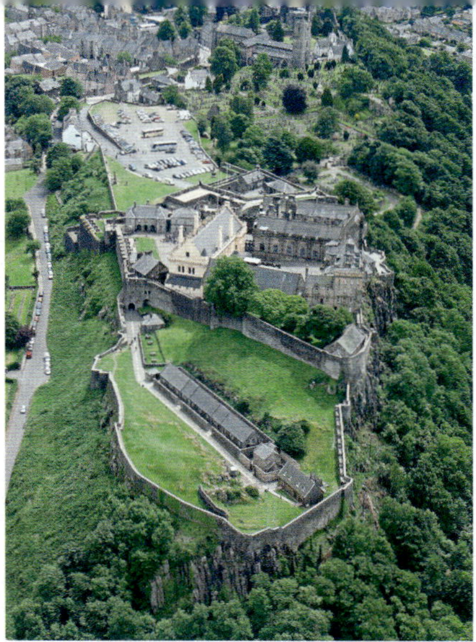

*Location: This impressive castle is situated in Stirlingshire district in the city of Stirling. It
lies west of the A872 and south of the A84 – one mile south of junction 10 on the M9 motorway.*

This solid stone fortress sits astride the Stirling Sill Crag surrounded by steep cliffs. It is one of the largest in Scotland – only matched by Edinburgh Castle. From the heights, it was easy to observe the lowest crossing point of the River Forth. Regular patrols by mounted horsemen would have made it difficult to pass by unchallenged. The old fords and later bridges were the scenes of large decisive battles.

The first castle here was built in the 11th century by Malcolm Canmore in a courtyard style. Various Scottish kings and queens lived and died in Stirling Castle. For example, Alexander I died in 1124 and William the Lyon in 1214. Births included James II in 1430 and James III in 1451. It was James II who tricked the 8th Earl of Douglas into attending the Royal Court at the castle in 1452, and then he had him killed and thrown down the cliff. A happier event was the crowning of Mary Queen of Scots in 1543.

An epic siege took place from April 1304 when Edward I arrived with large forces and 12 siege engines. These trebuchets were used to launch stone balls, lead lumps and burning bombs. These crashed into the walls and flew over into the castle grounds. Despite this the 30 men inside led by Sir William Oliphant held out for four months. His offer to surrender came when they watched a massive new trebuchet being assembled, The 'Warwolf' was the King's project and he smashed the gatehouse with it. After that he accepted the surrender and did not kill the Scots garrison but banished Sir William to the Tower of London. William Wallace later had the Scots back in control of Stirling Castle only to have it retaken by the English until the aftermath of the nearby Battle of Bannockburn in 1314. The English commander, Sir Philip Mowbray, surrendered the castle to Robert the Bruce and joined his future campaigns.

The Bruce had the castle slighted (damaging the defences to deny its use to invading forces) and it was then abandoned.

The English returned and had made such good repairs that when Sir Andrew Murray attempted to retake the castle for the Scots in 1337 he failed. Between 1571 and 1585, the castle was besieged three times by Scots factions during the reign of James VI. In 1651, Oliver Cromwell's forces led by General Monck captured the castle during his attack on Scotland.

By then, the use of cannon bombardments was an effective way to force a surrender – in this case, causing the garrison to mutiny. The last siege was in 1746 when Prince Charles' Jacobites unsuccessfully tried to take the castle. A standing army garrison then became a long term feature of castle life after the risings were subdued. The needs of a larger army garrison resulted in the redesign of the insides of many historic buildings to form barracks. An armoury, ammunition store and firing range were built into the remote north end of the castle grounds. The army left in 1964, however, the castle is home to the regimental museum of the Argyll and Sutherland Highlanders which is located in the King's House. This has recently been completely redesigned to reflect the regiment's strong connections with North Scotland. It was reopened by Her Majesty the Queen in June 2021.

After the barracks were empty, renovations were commissioned by Historic Scotland, the new custodians. This included restoring the beautiful hammer beam roof of the Great Hall of James IV. During the work, the sounds of footsteps were heard echoing around the hall, but no one was there apart from the workers who hastily left and were not keen to return. Several locations now represent the medieval period including the chapel and kitchen. It is possible to walk around the battlements and enjoy the fine views including the shape below of the large Kings Knot ornamental gardens. To the north-east is the tower of the Wallace Monument on the mount of Abbey Craig.

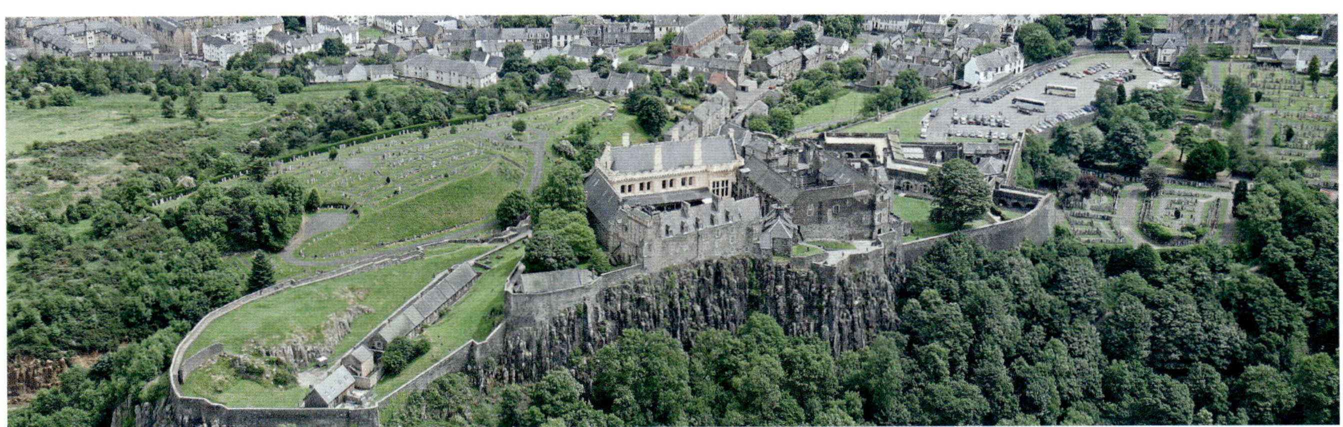

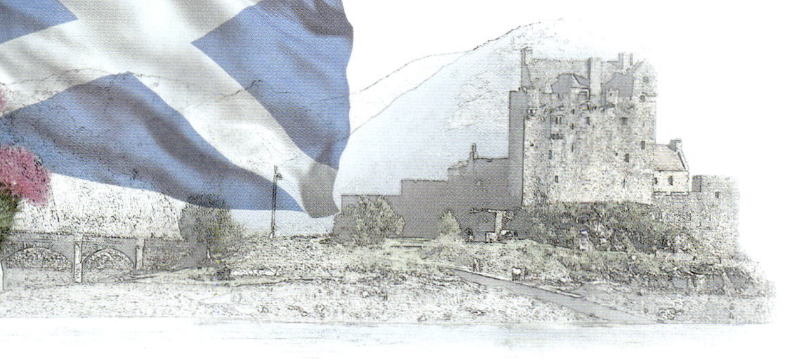

Tolquhon Castle

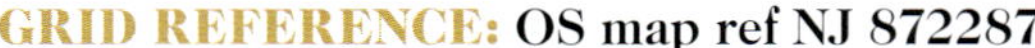

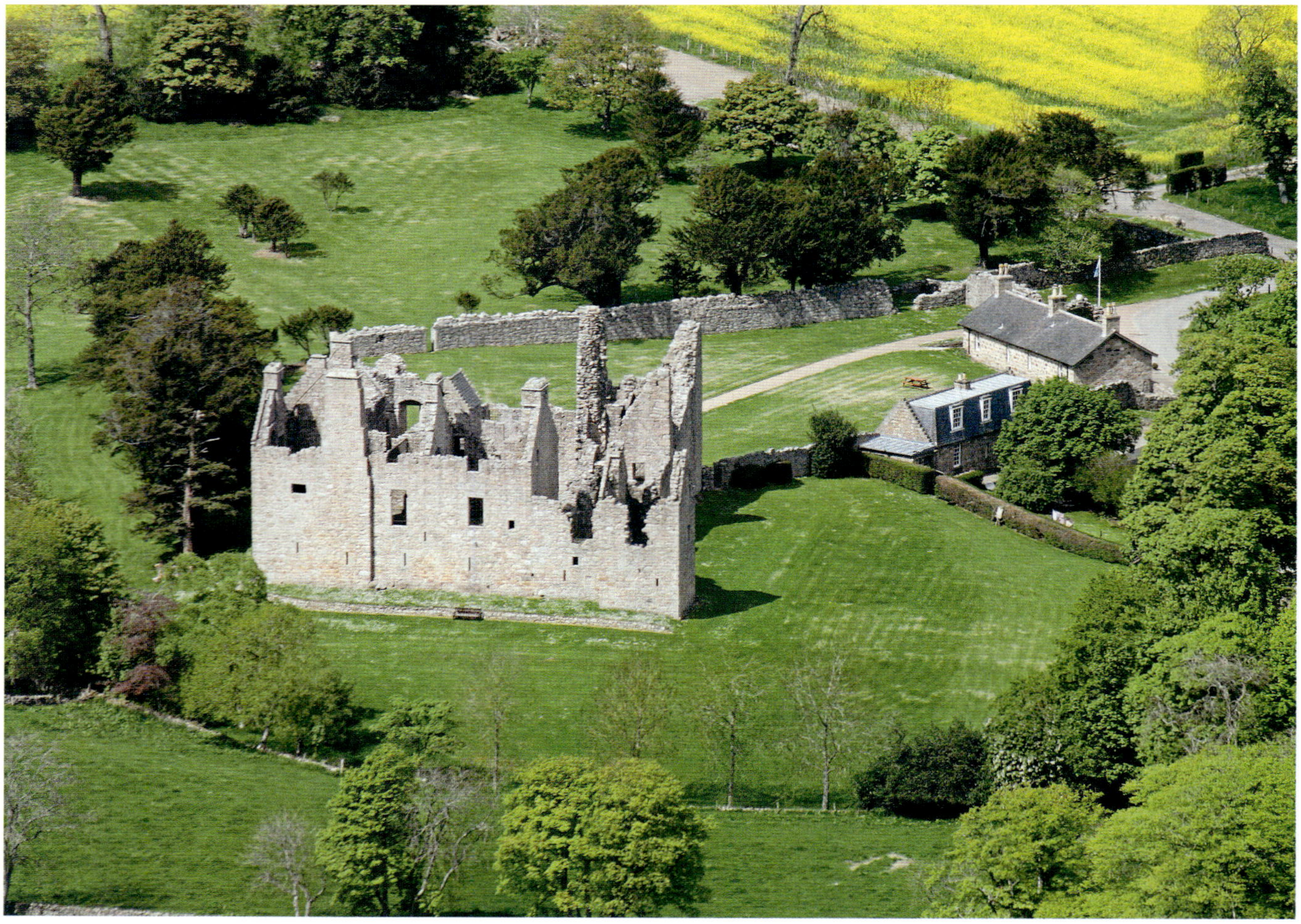

Apart from a tongue twisting name this castle proved an obstacle to potential invaders. It was actually easy to gain entry if you were a merchantman looking to establish trade deals however. That is how the Forbes clan based here made their fortune. They would eventually come undone as a result of an adventure abroad which went disastrously wrong.

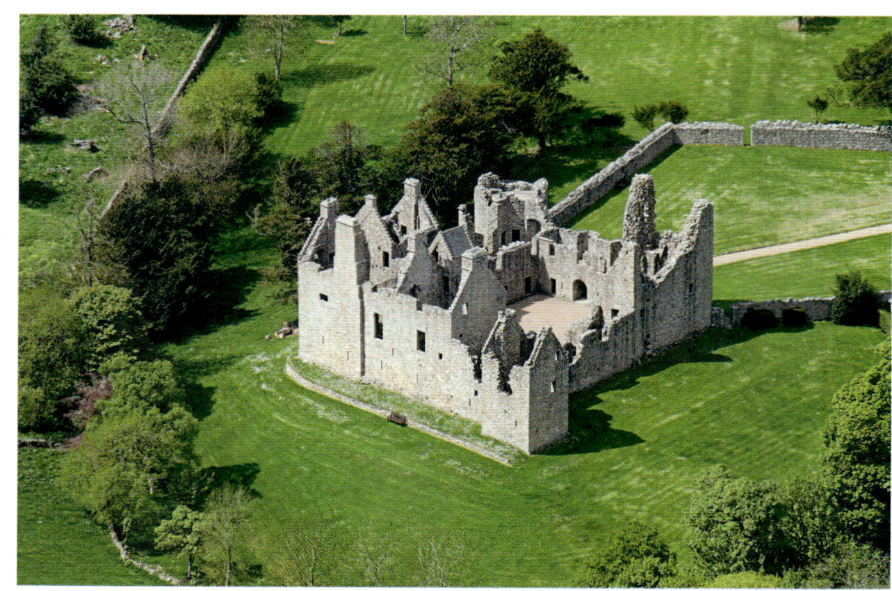

◼ ABOUT THE CASTLE

Visitor Details

www.historicenvironment.scot/visit-a-place/places/tolquhon-castle/

01651 851286

Open Daily April to September except Thursdays.

Ruin.

On site shop with refreshments.

Access on level paths but steep steps to higher viewpoints.

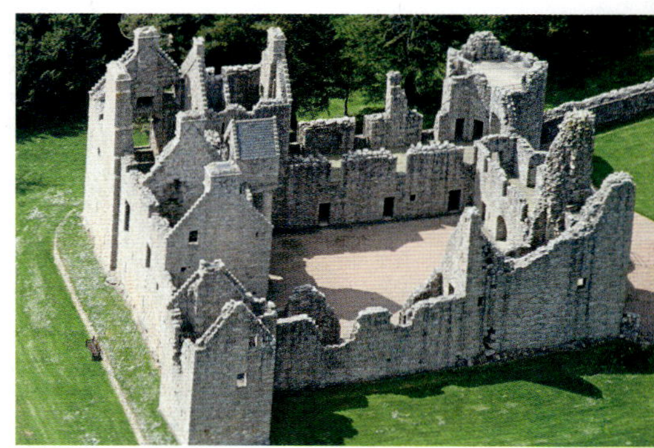

Location: Tolquhon Castle can be found in Aberdeenshire, four miles east of Oldmeldrum and two miles south of Tarves.

The first structure on this site was Sir Henry Preston's Tower, built around 1400. The Forbes Clan became owners via marriage and William Forbes decided he needed a showpiece castle and estate. So in 1584, he employed master mason Thomas Leiper who took just six years to complete everything. Unusually, we know this because of an inscription visible on the elaborate gatehouse. The aerial views show the many ranges added which included a brewery, bakery, and kitchen with a grand wide fireplace for roasting pigs and more on spits. Above the kitchens was the hall and below a pit prison and a separate wine cellar. Many of the different rooms and levels can still be explored which makes this site a great place for children to enjoy. The hall on the first floor has a large decorated fire place with a geometric-patterned paved floor. Nearby is a secret room reached by a trap door from above.

King James VI was hosted by the Forbes in 1589. His host was happy to keep away from political ambition. In preference, he sought to improve his castle mansion and estate living as a laird rather than a warrior. No one came to attack his castle and he was well regarded locally. Later lairds included Alexander who saved Charles II at the Battle of Worcester in 1651 and was knighted as a reward.

In 1700, the Scots tried to rival the Spanish, Dutch and English by financing a scheme to create a trading company and colony in the Darien area of Panama. Money was raised by loans from Scottish banks and wealthy families such as the Forbes of Tolquhon. This paid for a small fleet of merchant ships to convey supplies to be despatched accompanied by adventure seeking settlers.

A second expedition was financed the following year but it was discovered on arrival that the first colonists had landed and then almost all of them had died of disease and starvation. Everything that could go wrong did go wrong. This disaster ruined many investors and Scottish banks. The Forbes of Tolquhon had to leave the castle in 1718 after which it became roofless. It is now looked after by Historic Scotland.

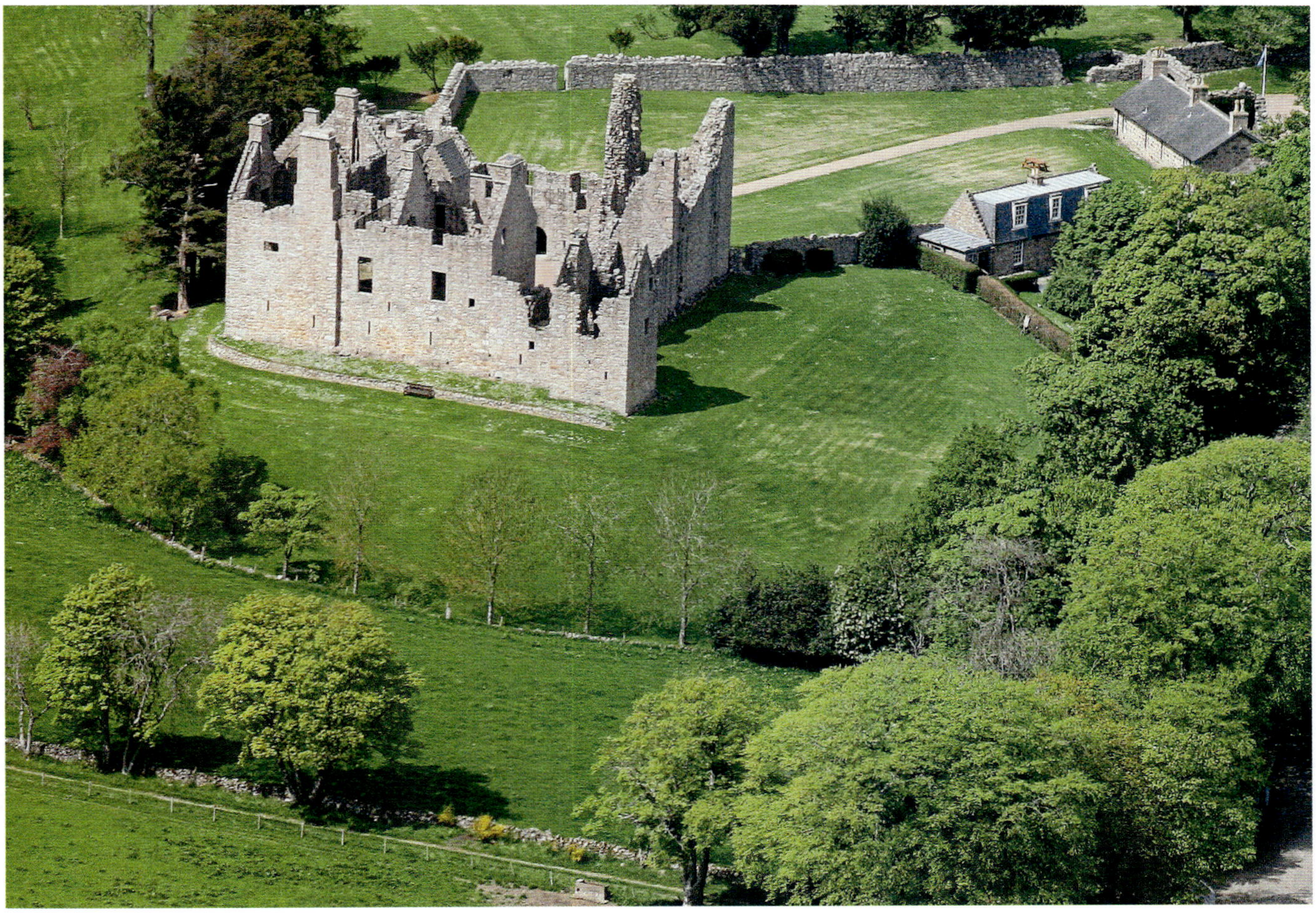

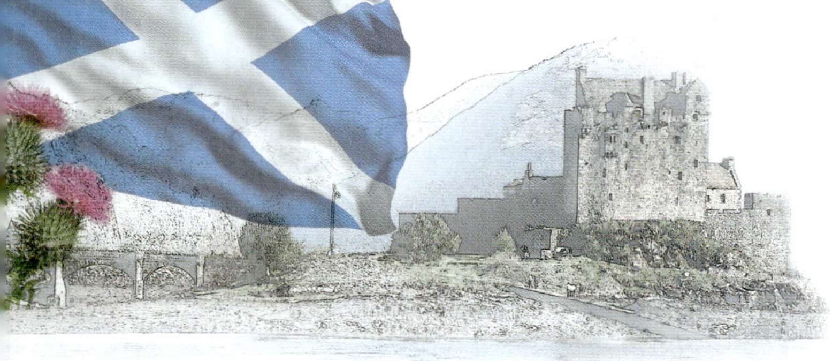

Urquhart Castle

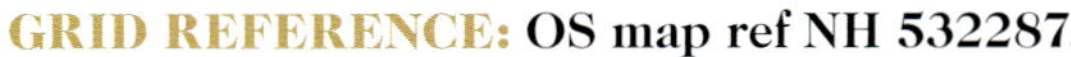

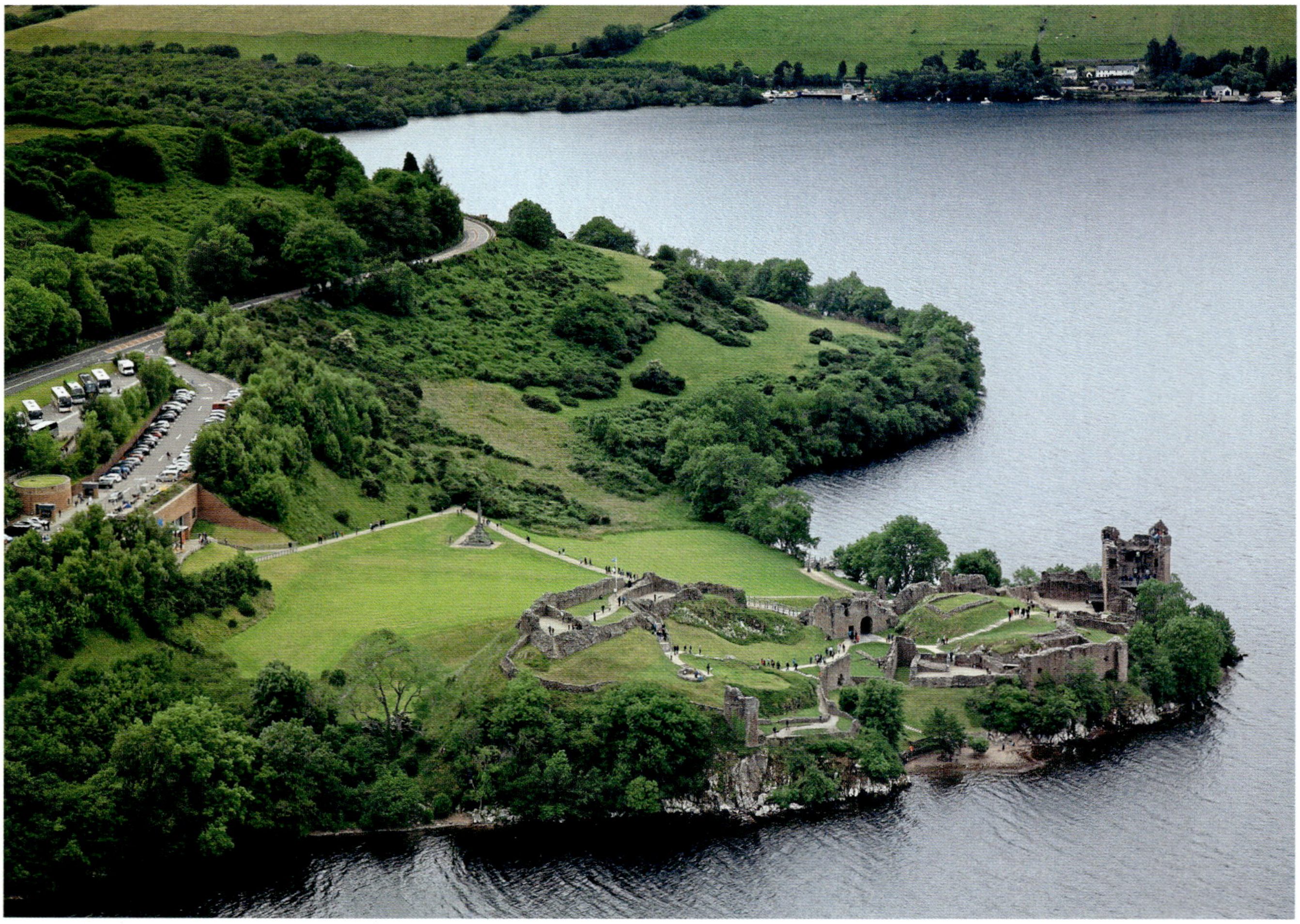

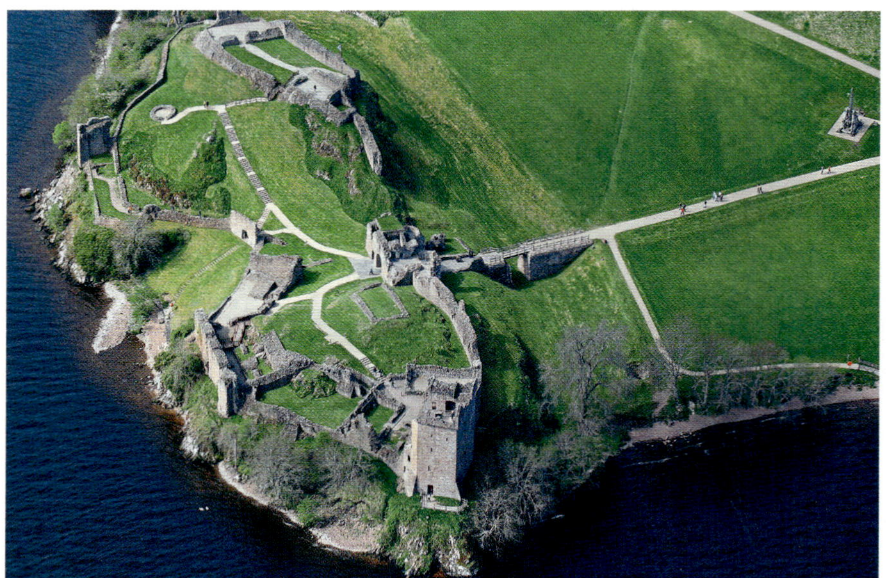

Visitor Details

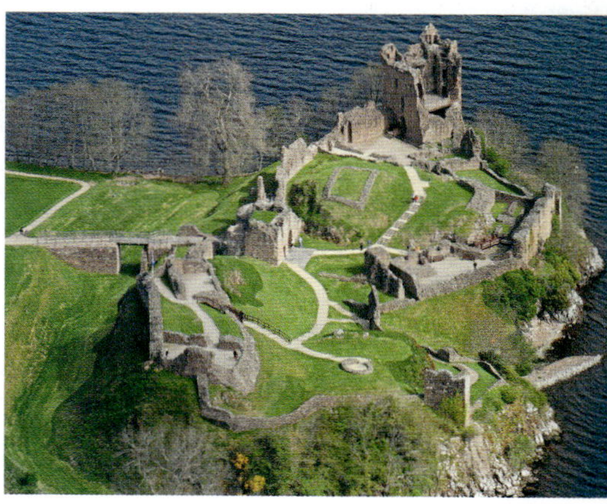

 www.historicenvironment.scot/visit-a-place/places/urquhart-castle

 01456 450551

 Open all year.

 A lift allows wheelchair access to the centre with onward passage to the open gravel castle approach path enabling a close view of the remains down a slope.

 The cafe is well stocked and the gift shop better than the average.

Admission includes an audio visual presentation in the modern visitor centre with a superb finale.

Location: 12 miles south west of Inverness on the northern bank of Loch Ness at Strone Point. Car and coach park adjacent to the A82. Can also be visited by boat excursion from Inverness.

The steep wooded slopes alongside Loch Ness offered few places suitable for a defensive position therefore it is not a surprise that evidence for a Celtic fortress has been unearthed at Strone Point. The Picts lived here, perhaps this is where they shared sightings of a giant waterborne beast with the visiting Saint Columba?

By the 13th century, rebellions in nearby Moray led to Alexander the Second expanding the redoubt by adding the masonry curtain wall surrounding the higher ground by the Loch. The lordship of Urquhart area and castle was awarded to his son in law Alan Durward in 1230 but the very powerful Comyns added the main courtyard after 1275. Sir Alexander Forbes had taken back the castle in 1297 from the English garrison who had occupied it during the Scottish war of Independence.

After a long siege, Edward's army took it back in 1303, killing all the occupants. When Robert the Bruce, now the King of Scotland, went on a rampage in the Great Glen around 1307 he included Urquhart in the castles taken from the English. Despite another siege by English forces in 1333 the castle occupants resisted and the Stewart kings invested time and money to add the keep, citadel, substantial gatehouse and deeper ditching. These are buildings and remains you see today. In 1342 King

David II stayed for a hunting trip this was likely the time when the castle was in its best condition.

The next wave of attacks came from the Lords of the Isles, the Macdonald Clan. From 1437 to 1452 they clashed until gaining entry but they only held the castle for four years. Surrounded by hostile clans the King's soldiers must not have relished the guarding of Urquhart.

Fortunately they could be resupplied by boat. During the time when Cromwell's men patrolled the Loch by ship they also used the castle as a convenient base. The Camerons and MacDonalds ransacked the castle around 1544 but departed afterwards. After almost two generations of relative peace the Covenanters also raided the castle .

The first Jacobite uprising in 1689 brought an attempt on the fortress which was then partly demolished in a massive series of explosions by the government garrision after which they abandoned the ruins. You can see the tumbled gate house when you visit. That marked the end of occupations.

The site is now owned by the National Trust for Scotland and managed by Historic Scotland. It has the finest views, lots of nooks and crannies to explore, castle keep to climb and plenty of information boards with illustrations.

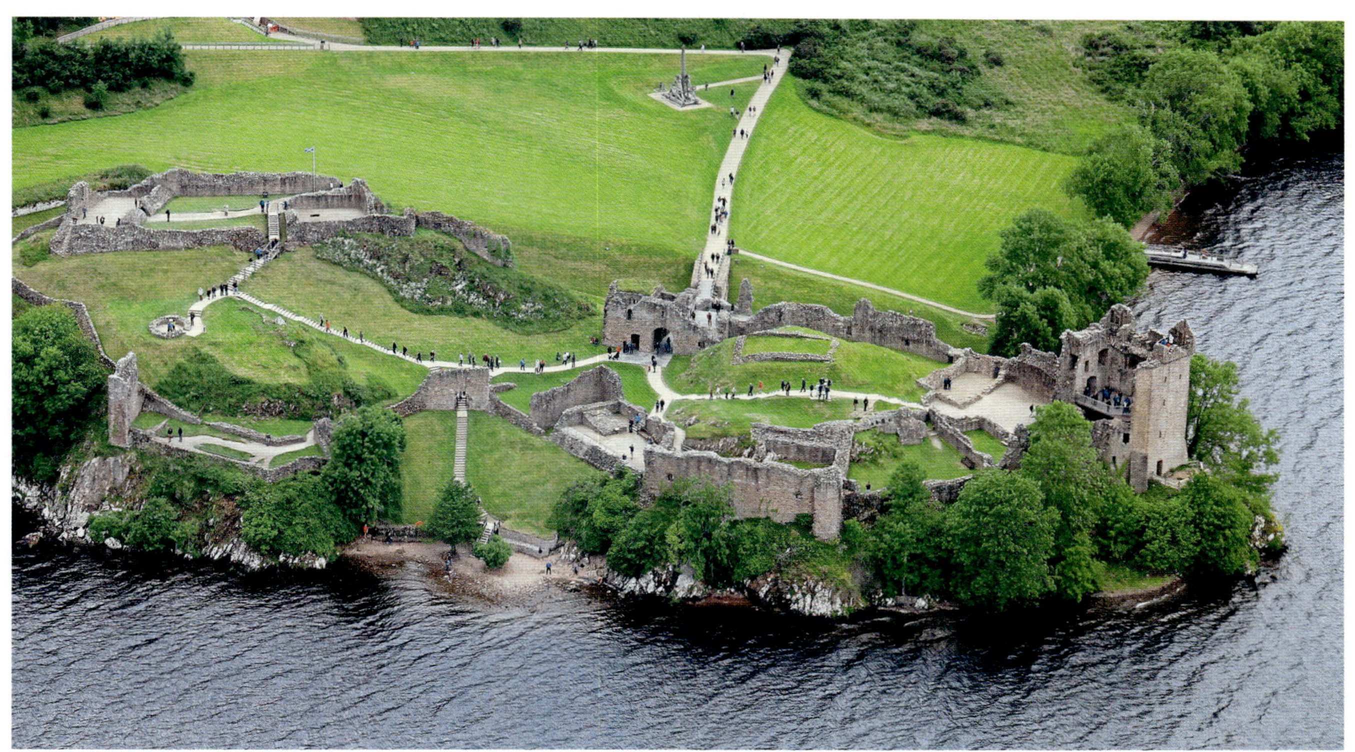

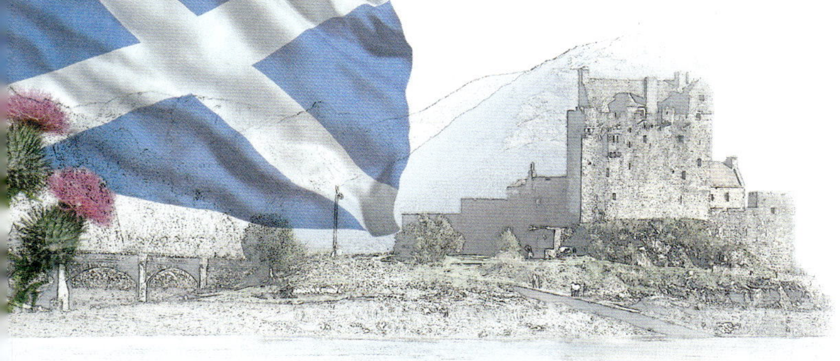
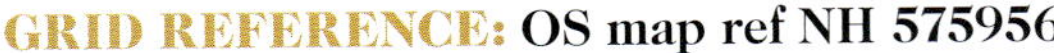

Last built Carbisdale Castle

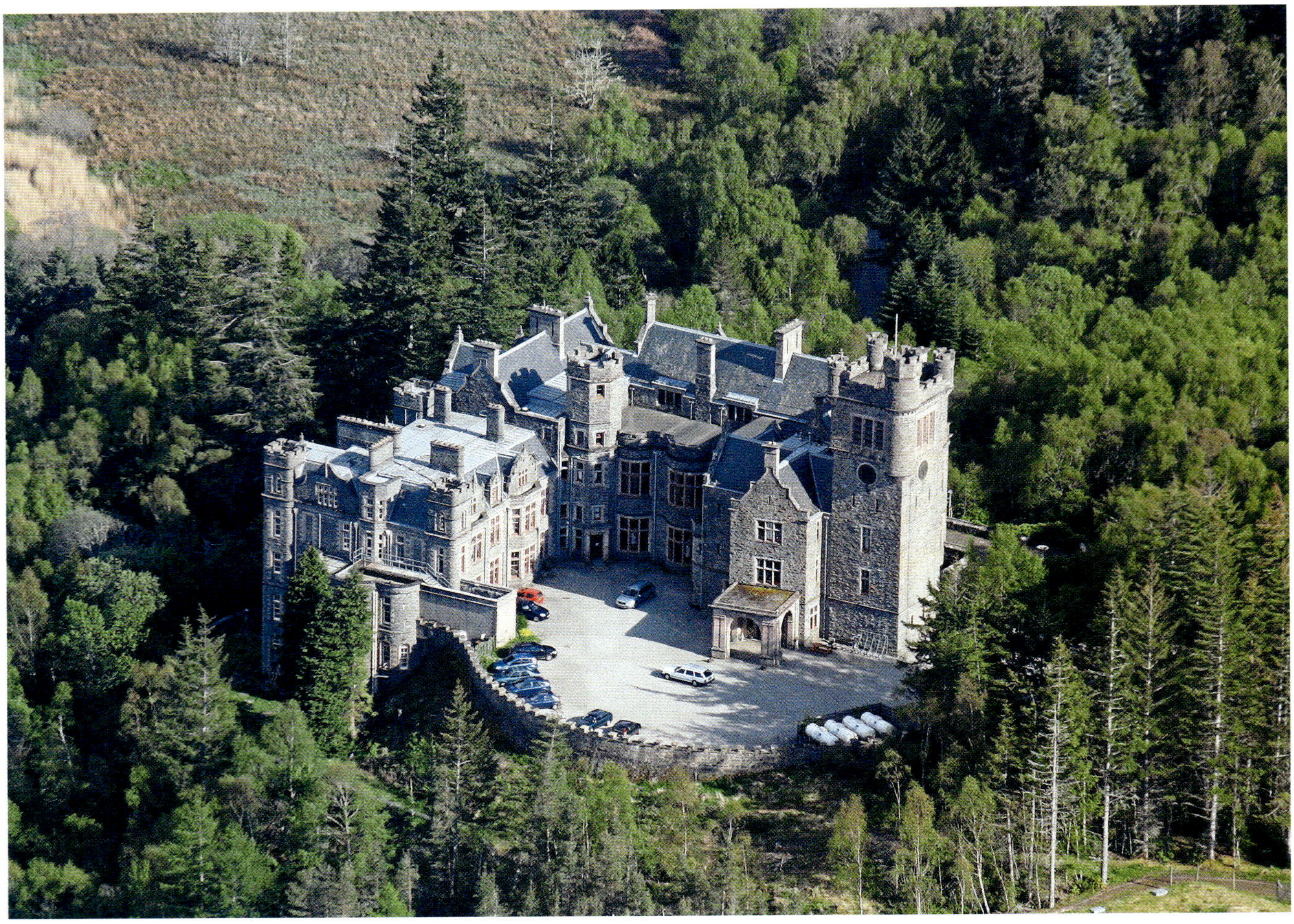

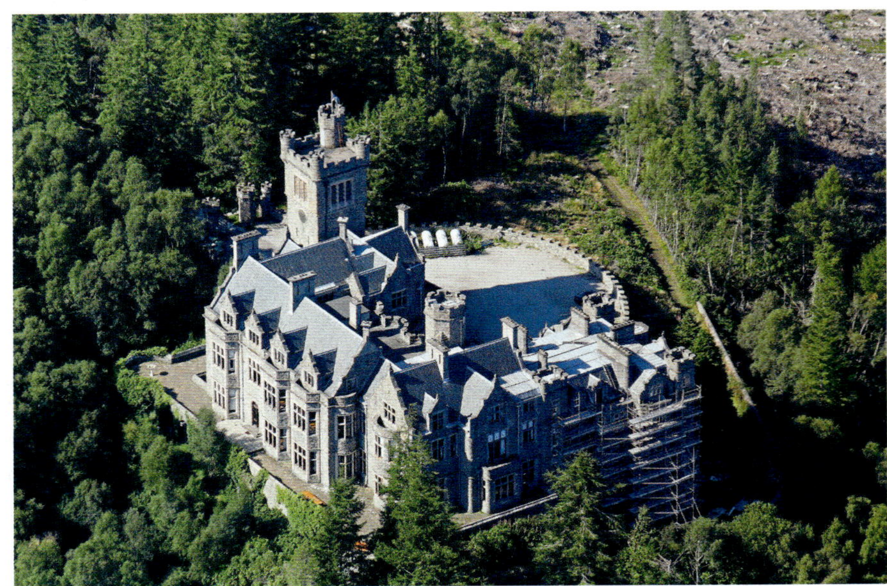

A lavish home for a Sutherland Duchess built in a romantic gothic style, the beautiful 'Castle of Spite' was the last of its type to be finished in Scotland. At a later point in its history it would become the residence of the Salveson whalers. The castle is due to be reborn soon as a luxurious new five-star hotel with bothy lodges in the grounds.

■ ABOUT THE CASTLE

Visitor Details

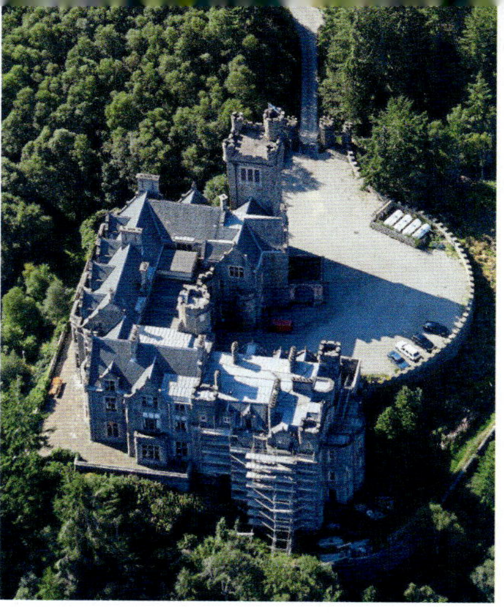

No website.

No telephone.

Currently no access but a new visitor centre is planned.

Location: Carbisdale Castle is in Sutherland district, three miles north-west of Bonar Bridge.

Carbisdale was the last castle to be constructed in Scotland. It was started in 1905 and finished in 1917 on the site of a former lodge. The 40-bedroom castle was styled in the Scots' baronial manner and has become a B-listed building. The first owner was Mary Caroline, the Duchess of Sutherland (although she preferred the title Duchess Blair after her first husband). Her second husband was the 3rd Duke of Sutherland. After his death in 1892, his will was contested by the Duke's son. After the prolonged court cases were resolved, she was able to inherit substantial funds. The cost of building Carbisdale Castle was also met but it had to be built outside Sutherland lands. She choose a hilltop clearly visible to the main road and railway to ensure that the Sutherland Clan would be reminded of her presence as they travelled to their estate. The so-called 'Castle of Spite' had no clock face visible from the railway as it was said she objected to giving the Dunrobin Sutherlands the time of day.

The castle owners from 1933 were the Salveson family who became operators of the largest whaling fleet in the world. They stopped hunting whales in 1963 from their base in South Georgia which they named Leith Harbour after the Edinburgh home port. They also built up a large international transport and logistics company. During the Second World War, the castle was used as a residence for the exiled Norwegian royal family. After the war, Captain Harold Salveson gave the castle and the contents of the art collection to the Scottish Youth Hostel Association. This was a typical gesture from the family who were noted for philanthropy which included bringing the first penguins to Edinburgh zoo.

Over one million hostellers enjoyed staying in this castle location although some said it could be scary with all the marble statues looking ghostly at night. The Association decided to sell the property in 2014 to recover some of the large repair costs due to structural damage. This is yet another example of the large costs involved in maintaining such large buildings. It is now undergoing upgrading by a property development group. The upgrading includes permits to install an indoor swimming pool. Public access is planned for the estate with a campsite, bothy-style accommodation and a visitor centre highlighting the Battle of Carbisdale in 1650. Carbisdale is significant as it was the last battle of James Graham, the 1st Marquis of Montrose. His forces lost and he was captured and later imprisoned in Ardvreck Castle.

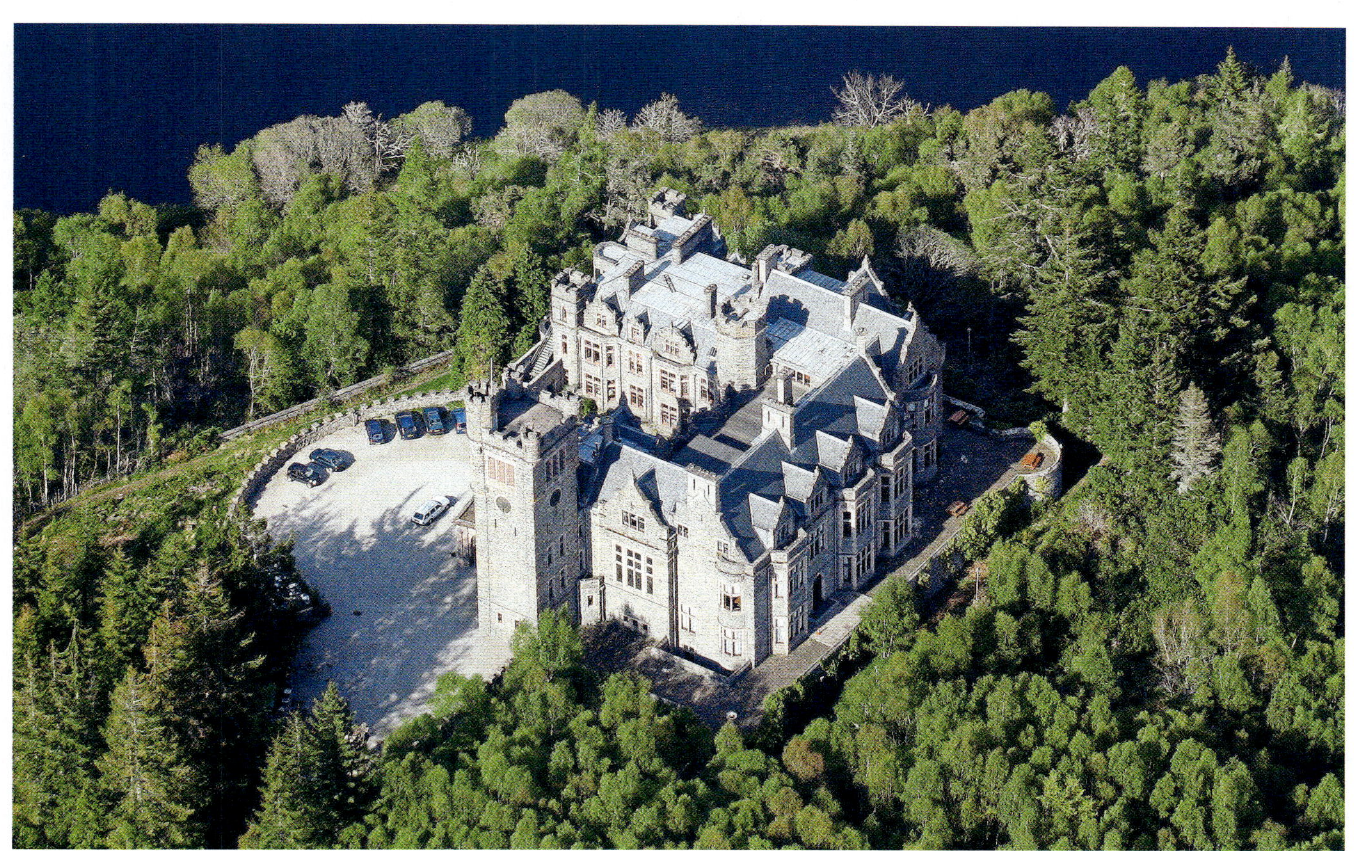